PRIMITIVE CHRISTIAN ESCHATOLOGY

PRIMITIVE CHRISTIAN ESCHATOLOGY

THE HULSEAN PRIZE ESSAY FOR 1908

BY

E. C. DEWICK, M.A.

TUTOR AND DEAN OF ST. AIDAN'S COLLEGE, BIRKENHEAD
AND TEACHER IN ECCLESIASTICAL HISTORY IN THE UNIVERSITY OF LIVERPOOL

ΟΥ̓Κ ἮΛΘΟΝ ΚΑΤΑΛΥ͂ΣΑΙ, ἈΛΛᾺ ΠΛΗΡΩ͂ΣΑΙ

WIPF & STOCK · Eugene Oregon

Wipf and Stock Publishers
199 W 8th Ave, Suite 3
Eugene, OR 97401

Primitive Christian Eschatology
The Hulsean Prize Essay for 1908
By Dewick, E. C.
ISBN 13: 978-1-60608-246-1
Publication date 11/17/2008
Previously published by Cambridge University Press, 1912

TO

THE RIGHT REVEREND

THOMAS WORTLEY DRURY, D.D.

LORD BISHOP OF RIPON

WHOSE GUIDANCE AND ENCOURAGEMENT

FIRST LED THE WRITER OF THIS ESSAY

TO UNDERTAKE THE STUDY

OF PRIMITIVE CHRISTIAN ESCHATOLOGY

PREFACE

THIS essay in its original form obtained the Cambridge University Hulsean Prize for the year 1908. Since then, with the sanction of the University authorities, I have revised it throughout, and have made a few brief additions. The process of revision, which of necessity has been carried out in the midst of the activities of a large suburban parish, has tended at times to encroach somewhat seriously upon the claims of pastoral duties; and I am deeply grateful to the Rev. H. A. Wilson, Vicar of Norbiton, for the generosity with which he arranged that I might devote a considerable amount of time to this extra-parochial work.

It is a pleasant duty to acknowledge the debt which I owe to the many friends who have helped me with counsel and criticism. Among these I would specially mention the Rev. Dr. J. B. Mayor, who most kindly read through the whole essay as originally written, and by his careful criticisms enabled me to remove many blemishes. To Professor Burkitt I am indebted for much valuable advice, which more than once has opened up new and fruitful lines of thought.

In revising the Old Testament section, I have received no little help from my friend Mr. R. S. Cripps, formerly of St. John's College, Cambridge. To another old friend of Cambridge days, Mr. C. W. Previté-Orton, Fellow of St. John's College, I owe a very special debt of gratitude. During the past four years his wide knowledge and critical ability have been constantly brought to my assistance, both during the time when this essay was first being written at Cambridge, and also during the subsequent period of revision. I am also grateful to my father, for much helpful advice, and especially for reading the proofs. And lastly, I wish to express my appreciation of the valuable suggestions and the invariable courtesy which I have received from the authorities of the University Press.

The contents of the present volume are somewhat wider in their scope than might be inferred from the title; but I have thought it best not to alter the title, which was assigned as the subject for the Hulsean Essay in 1908, nor yet to delete or abridge the earlier sections in order to produce a closer agreement between the title and the contents.

That there are many faults in the following pages I do not for a moment doubt; I would only venture to hope that there may also be some thoughts which will contribute towards a clearer understanding of the truth.

E. C. D.

St. Aidan's College, Birkenhead,
December 1911.

CONTENTS

INTRODUCTION 1

PART I.—OLD TESTAMENT ESCHATOLOGY

CHAPTER I

PRIMITIVE BELIEFS 7

    Lack of direct evidence—Animism—Ancestor-worship—Nature-worship.

CHAPTER II

EARLY HEBREW ESCHATOLOGY 11

    Traces of primitive beliefs—The Babylonian background of ideas—Egyptian influence—The rise of Jewish 'Nationalism'—Its hostility to animistic ideas—But as yet no eschatology of its own.

CHAPTER III

THE DOCTRINE OF THE PROPHETS. (*a*) *The Future of the Individual* 16

    Fundamental ideas of the Hebrew prophets—Their doctrine of retribution—Their confidence in the fulfilment of the Covenant-Promises—Effect of these upon the doctrine of personal immortality—Individualism—The doctrine of the Resurrection.

CHAPTER IV

THE DOCTRINE OF THE PROPHETS (*Continued*). (*b*) *The Future of the World* 26

    The same fundamental ideas at work—The birth of 'cosmic eschatology'—The 'Last Judgment'—The 'Kingdom of God'—

x   PRIMITIVE CHRISTIAN ESCHATOLOGY

PAGE

The Messianic King—The City of God—How could these things be ?—The doctrine of the Remnant—The New Covenant—The 'Two Worlds'—Universalism—Summary of prophetic eschatology.

CHAPTER V

THE ESCHATOLOGY OF THE POST-EXILIC JEWS . . . 40

After-effects of the doctrines of the prophets—Increasing reverence for the past—Cessation of prophecy—Predestination—Sense of the transcendental character of God—Zoroastrian and later Egyptian influence—Job—The Psalms—Ecclesiastes—Summary of Old Testament eschatology.

PART II.—THE APOCALYPTIC LITERATURE OF LATER JUDAISM

CHAPTER VI

THE CHARACTERISTICS OF THE APOCALYPTIC LITERATURE . 50

The importance of the apocalyptic books—Their resemblance to the prophetic books—The contrast between the two—The literary form of the apocalypses—The historical circumstances which helped to produce them—The threefold classification of the Jewish apocalyptic books.

CHAPTER VII

THE APOCALYPSES OF THE MACCABEES 58

The history of the Maccabean revolt, and the rule of the priest-kings—The five apocalypses written in this period, and the internal evidence of their dates: Daniel; Enoch lxxxiii.-xc.; Enoch i.-xxxvi.; Jubilees; The Testaments of the XII. Patriarchs (parts of)—The eschatology of these books :—(a) The Intermediate State and Prayers for the Dead—(b) The Resurrection—(c) The Last Judgment—(d) The Messianic Hope (the 'Son of Man' in Daniel)—(e) Final Destinies—(f) The Doctrine of Angels.

CHAPTER VIII

THE APOCALYPSES OF THE PHARISEES 80

The course of Jewish history from 135 B.C. to the Christian Era —The Pharisees an oppressed minority—Characteristics of the writings of this period: Enoch xci.-civ.; Enoch xxxvii.-lxxi.; parts of the

CONTENTS

Testaments of the XII. Patriarchs ; Psalms of Solomon ; Assumption of Moses—Eschatology of these books :—(a) The Intermediate State—(b) The Resurrection—(c) The Last Judgment—(d) The Messianic Hope (the 'Son of Man' in Enoch, and the Messiah in the Psalms of Solomon)—(e) Final Destinies—(f) Foreign Influence—Importance of these apocalypses, which were popular among the Jews in the time of our Lord.

CHAPTER IX

THE APOCALYPSES OF THE FALL OF JERUSALEM . . 95

Two Jewish apocalypses written after A.D. 70: 4 Ezra and the Apocalypse of Baruch—Their relation to apostolic Christianity—Their gloomy outlook—Stern exclusiveness—Doctrine of a temporary Messianic Kingdom on earth—The resurrection-doctrine in Baruch—Salvation by works—Contrast with Christ's teaching.

CHAPTER X

THE ESCHATOLOGY OF THE JEWS OF 'THE DISPERSION'. . 100

The apocalypses discussed above, all Palestinian—Characteristics of Greek eschatology—The apocalyptic writings produced among the 'Diaspora'—Sibylline Oracles (part of)—Their wide outlook, and doctrine of the Messiah—Slavonic Enoch (the Seven Heavens and the Millennium)—Wisdom of Solomon—Its strongly-marked Hellenism—Philo—Summary.

PART III.—CHRIST'S ESCHATOLOGY

CHAPTER XI

INTRODUCTORY 110

Οὐ καταλῦσαι, ἀλλὰ πληρῶσαι—The significance of the claim—Supreme importance of this part of our subject—Special interest in it at the present time—The 'eschatological school'—Difficulties of the subject—Mystery of Christ's Person—'Prophetic' character of His teaching—The Synoptic Problem—Problem of the Fourth Gospel—Standpoint of the present essay.

CHAPTER XII

THE PEOPLE TO WHOM CHRIST PREACHED . . . 119

The form of Christ's teaching influenced by the attitude of His hearers—The 'Pharisaic standpoint' of the apocalypses—The Sadducees—The Herodians—The Essenes—The Roman authorities—All inclined to be hostile to a new teacher—Yet true religion doubtless was to be found in quiet places.

CHAPTER XIII

OUR LORD'S PREPARATION FOR HIS MINISTRY . . . 125

The 'growth in grace'—Coming of the Forerunner—Significance of our Lord's Baptism—The beginning of the Messianic Consciousness.

CHAPTER XIV

THE PREACHING OF 'THE KINGDOM OF GOD' . . . 128

Christ's opening message: 'The Kingdom of God is at hand'— Was this 'Kingdom' eschatological?—The eschatological element certainly present — But was it exclusively eschatological?— Schweitzer's view—Objections to this form: (a) Current Jewish beliefs; (b) certain sayings of our Lord; (c) the 'mystery' of the Kingdom; (d) the emphasis on the human factor in the advent of the Kingdom—The solution of the problem—Christ recognises value of partial realisations of His ideal—His preaching was dependent on moral conditions—'The offer of a great opportunity'— "'Η βασιλεία τοῦ Θεοῦ ἐντὸς ὑμῶν ἐστιν"—Summary.

CHAPTER XV

THE MESSIANIC CONSCIOUSNESS OF OUR LORD . . . 147

Christ's eschatology centres round His claim to Messiahship— Did He claim to be Messiah on earth, or only in the future?—When did He first possess the Messianic Consciousness?—How far was His Messiahship recognised by His contemporaries?—The two landmarks in the unveiling of His Messiahship: (a) Peter's confession; (b) Christ's answer to the High Priest—The phrase 'Son of Man'— Its past history—Its occurrences in the Gospels—Used to guide the thoughts of the disciples to a right conclusion.

CHAPTER XVI

THE GREAT REFUSAL 164

The popularity of Christ's earliest preaching short-lived—He foresaw the end from the beginning—Growth of Pharisaic hostility, culminating in the Crucifixion—Effects of this upon Christ's eschatology: (a) 'the Kingdom of God' becomes the antithesis of 'the World'; (b) the Messiah must suffer; (c) for His disciples, too, suffering will be the gateway to eternal life—The above change in Christ's teaching is apparent rather than real, and due to changed circumstances.

CONTENTS

CHAPTER XVII

THE ESCHATOLOGICAL DISCOURSE, ETC. 173

    The great sermon on the Last Things—Its main outlines—Very similar to many of the apocalypses—The difficulty: Did our Lord foretell His immediate return?—The gravity of the issue—The theory of the 'Little Apocalypse' unsatisfactory—The keynote of the Discourse is the call to watchfulness—The 'logia' may have been 'interpreted,' or moved from their original context—The predictions may have been qualified by conditions now obscured—But the Discourse contains several unmistakable points of positive teaching.

    Other eschatological sayings of our Lord: The Parable of Dives and Lazarus; the Parable of the Ten Virgins; the Parable of the Pounds; the description of the Last Judgment—The problem of Eternal Punishment.

CHAPTER XVIII

THE EVENTS OF PASSION WEEK AND THE POST-RESURRECTION TEACHING 190

    The Triumphal Entry into Jerusalem—The answer to the Sadducees' question regarding the Resurrection—The Last Supper—Our Lord's answer to the High Priest's question, 'Art thou the Messiah?'—The promise to the dying thief—'Through failure to victory.'

    The influence of Christ's Resurrection upon Christian eschatology: a type of our resurrection; a pledge of Christ's authority—The post-Resurrection teaching of our Lord—Striking absence of eschatology therein—The significance of this.

CHAPTER XIX

THE ESCHATOLOGY OF OUR LORD IN THE FOURTH GOSPEL . 203

    The need for supplementing the Synoptists with the Fourth Gospel—The Christology of St. John: 'Son of Man' and 'Son of God'—Both Messianic titles—Apparent contrast with the Synoptists—Yet striking incidental resemblances—The paradoxical sayings in the Fourth Gospel—Designed to reveal the spiritual meaning of eschatology—'Judgment' and 'eternal life' are present as well as future—The value of St. John's Gospel for the student of eschatology.

CHAPTER XX

Christ's Eschatology—General Conclusions . . . 215

Christ's eschatology of the World: faith in the final victory of God's will—The method of this victory, catastrophic or evolutionary?—Christ's teaching generally points to the former—Yet need for caution—The uncertainty of the future, due to human free-will—The centrality of Christ's Person in His eschatology—The charge against Him of erroneous prediction not proven.

Christ's eschatology of the individual: the human soul is immortal—The resurrection affirmed, but not defined—The Last Judgment—Its clear moral significance—Rewards and punishments objective or subjective?—Final destinies and eternal punishment.

The general impression produced by Christ's life—The principle 'Through death to life'—Christ's resurrection as a sure historical basis for Christian doctrine.

Christ's eschatology compared with current ideas—Omission of details, national prejudices, and politics—Additional emphasis on practical morality, and on the Person of Christ—No sign of borrowing from non-Jewish eschatological ideas.

The Eschatological Theory—Irreconcilable with the evidence of the New Testament—But has done a useful work—Its failure due to over-consistency—Conclusion.

PART IV.—THE ESCHATOLOGY OF THE APOSTLES

CHAPTER XXI

The Most Primitive Christian Eschatology (The Acts of the Apostles) 232

The Primitive Church as the standard of true Christianity—Contrast between the last words of Christ and the first preaching of the apostles—Christ's promise of the gift of the Spirit the authoritative source of the early Christian eschatological expectation—The apostolic preaching recorded in Acts—The Messiahship of Jesus—His imminent return in glory—The urgent call to repentance—Why were the Christians persecuted?—Their preaching was calculated to produce excitement and unrest—Eschatology formed the background of the practical morality—A true echo of Christ's teaching—The eschatology of Acts essentially Judaeo-Christian—Its simplicity—Its motives pure and unselfish—Its enthusiasm and inspired conviction.

CONTENTS

CHAPTER XXII

THE ESCHATOLOGY OF THE NON-PAULINE EPISTLES . . 244

Classification of the New Testament Epistles—The non-Pauline letters designed for Jewish converts only—James and Hebrews—Their Jewish Christology — Doctrine of Christ's priesthood in Hebrews—The problem of suffering—The problem of Christian sinfulness—Its relation to the idea of Heaven and Hell.

The non-Pauline letters addressed mainly to Gentiles—1 Peter, 2 Peter, and Jude—1 Peter's emphasis on predestination—'Preaching to the dead' in 1 Peter—The apocalyptic 'tone' of 2 Peter and Jude.

The Epistles of St. John—The most spiritual example of primitive Judaeo-Christian eschatology.

CHAPTER XXIII

THE ESCHATOLOGY OF ST. PAUL. 261

The four groups of St. Paul's letters—1. The Judaeo-Christian Epistles—(*a*) 1 Thessalonians (the nature of Christ's Second Coming)—(*b*) 2 Thessalonians (the delay of the Coming, and the 'Man of Sin').

2. The Epistles of the Third Missionary Journey (1 and 2 Corinthians, Galatians, and Romans)—Signs of Gentile influence—The position of the Gentiles in the Church—The Doctrine of the Resurrection—The Final Consummation ('that God may be all in all')—The relation of 'Justification' to eschatology.

3. The Epistles of the Imprisonment (Ephesians, Philippians, Colossians, and Philemon)—Salvation present as well as future—Christ the goal of humanity.

4. The Pastoral Epistles—Eschatological heresies—Apostasy a sign of the imminence of the end—The Prayer for Onesiphorus—The value of St. Paul's eschatology.

CHAPTER XXIV

THE APOCALYPSE OF ST. JOHN 292

Date, character, and plan of the book :—(*a*) The Prologue—(*b*) The Letters to the Seven Churches—(*c*) The Vision of the Opening of the Sealed Book — Apocalyptic evidence of date — The 'Two Witnesses'—(*d*) The Vision of the Fall of Rome—(*e*) The Vision of the Last Judgment—(*f*) The Vision of the City of God—The significance of St. John's Apocalypse—Summary of apostolic eschatology.

PART V.—ESCHATOLOGY IN THE SUB-APOSTOLIC CHURCH

CHAPTER XXV

The Decline of Primitive Judaeo-Christian Eschatology . 306

Effects of international intercourse under the Roman Empire—Spread of Eastern cults—Jewish Christianity strongest in Palestine, Syria, and Asia Minor—The extant literature of this type :—1. The Didache (its eschatology thoroughly Jewish, yet Catholic) ; 2. The Epistle of Polycarp ; 3. Papias—The reasons for the decline of this type of Christianity. [Note on the Odes of Solomon.]

CHAPTER XXVI

The Apocalyptic Literature of Early Christianity . 318

The Christian apocalypses adopt many foreign ideas—Mostly written in Egypt or Alexandria—The Epistle of Barnabas—The Ascension of Isaiah — The Sibylline Oracles — The Apocalypse of Peter—The Testament of Abraham—The Testament of Isaac—The Vision of Paul—Other Christian apocalypses—Gnostic eschatology.

CHAPTER XXVII

The Influence of Greek Thought upon Primitive Christian Eschatology 335

Greek influence specially felt in European Christianity—The contrast between Greek and Jewish eschatology—Christian writers influenced by, or wishing to influence, Greek thought :—1. Clement of Rome—The phoenix legend ; 2. Ignatius—His non-Jewish exegesis—Decline of expectation of immediate return of Christ—His exaltation of Church authority ; 3. 2 Clement—Peculiar doctrine of the Church and of immortality ; 4. Shepherd of Hermas—Penance and purgatory.

The Apologists :—1. Aristides ; 2. The writer to Diognetus—Clear signs of Greek thought ; 3. Justin Martyr—The Second Coming indefinitely postponed—Doctrine of Intermediate State—Anti-Christ and the Millennium — The First and the Second Parousia — The Resurrection ; 4. Athenagoras—Material idea of the Resurrection ; 5. Irenaeus—His systematic eschatology, based on Scripture—His resemblance to normal teaching of later Church—But survival of

CONTENTS xvii

some primitive features — His Chiliasm — His sobriety — Greek influence affects his methods rather than his doctrines.

The School of Alexandria—Their appeal to Reason and Conscience—Clement— His use of allegory, and its effect upon Primitive Christian Eschatology—His view of history—Doctrine of Purgatory—Ideas learnt from Eastern philosophies—Influence of the Greek Mysteries—Origen.

CHAPTER XXVIII

THE CHARACTERISTICS OF SUB-APOSTOLIC ESCHATOLOGY . 370

General features — The decline of the hope of an immediate return of Christ—Interests of the Christians become more diffused—Multiplication of detailed beliefs—Use of proof-texts from Scripture—The Alexandrian methods of exegesis—Influence of foreign beliefs, and especially of Greek thought — Yet some primitive features retained—The decline of Chiliasm—Beginnings of later Catholic doctrines—Purgatory and Prayers for the Dead—Repentance after death—The essentials of Christian eschatology never lost.

PART VI.—THE EVIDENTIAL VALUE OF PRIMITIVE CHRISTIAN ESCHATOLOGY

CHAPTER XXIX

GENERAL CONCLUSIONS 376

Does the history of early Christian eschatology support the claims of Christianity ?—The centre of Christianity is the Person of Christ—Christ's eschatology, therefore, the vital point.

Summary of Christ's eschatology : His faith in the final victory of the good is of self-evident value—A catastrophic consummation contrary to science ? The alternative more unthinkable — The centrality of Christ's doctrine of Himself forbids a half-acceptance of His claims—No proof that His view of the future was erroneous—The immortality of the soul ; Essential to faith in God—The Resurrection of the Dead :—Current objections based on crude misrepresentations—The Last Judgment :—Beneficent practical effect of the doctrine ; the motive not merely selfish—Eternal punishment : an insoluble problem, owing to the mystery of free-will—A comparison of Christ's eschatology with Jewish, wholly favourable to the former — Christ's doctrine of human responsibility — His eschatology consistent with the highest ideal.

The evidential significance of the 'Eschatological Problem'—Schweitzer's Theory would undermine Christianity—The eschatological Christ merely a Jew—[Note on Tyrell's *Christianity at the Cross-Roads*].

Does the history of early Christian eschatology show signs of

xviii PRIMITIVE CHRISTIAN ESCHATOLOGY

PAGE

Divine guidance? — Not a 'golden age' — But moral influence of primitive Christian eschatology always for good—Development and corruption side by side — The apostolic writings contain really valuable contributions to eschatology—The sub-apostolic writers mostly commonplace and degenerate—Yet Christ's spirit present—Results of Greek influence a sign of Divine Purpose.

Conclusion : two practical considerations :—(1) The value of parabolic teaching rather than abstract doctrine ; (2) Eschatology never to be separated from practical morality.

APPENDICES ON THE ESCHATOLOGY OF THE RELIGIONS OF BABYLONIA, EGYPT, AND PERSIA

APPENDIX A

BABYLONIAN ESCHATOLOGY 401

APPENDIX B

EGYPTIAN ESCHATOLOGY 403

APPENDIX C

ZOROASTRIAN ESCHATOLOGY 406

INDEX 409

AUTHORITIES

THE following are the chief authorities consulted in the preparation of this essay. Books referred to only for the elucidation of special points will be found mentioned in the notes *ad loc.*

PART I.—OLD TESTAMENT

R. H. Charles, *A Critical History of the Doctrine of a Future Life in Judaism* (London, 1899).
S. R. Driver, *An Introduction to the Literature of the Old Testament* (7th edition, Edinburgh, 1905).
S. D. F. Salmond, *The Christian Doctrine of Immortality* (4th edition, Edinburgh, 1901).

PART II.—THE JEWISH APOCALYPSES

For editions and translations of the apocalyptic books, see below, p. 50, note (1). The works of Charles and Salmond cited above also deal with this subject.

PART III.—CHRIST'S ESCHATOLOGY

Burkitt, *The Gospel History and its Transmission* (Edinburgh, 1907).
Muirhead, *The Eschatology of Jesus* (London, 1904).
Sanday, *The Life of Christ in Recent Research* (London, 1907).
Schweitzer, *Von Reimarus zu Wrede* (Tübingen, 1906), (now published also in an English translation by W. Montgomery, under the title, *The Quest of the Historical Jesus*, London, 1910).
Stanton, *The Jewish and Christian Messiah* (Edinburgh, 1886).
J. Weiss, *Die Predigt Jesu vom Reiche Gottes* (Göttingen, 1882).

PART IV.—THE APOSTOLIC CHURCH

Many of the above-mentioned authorities deal also with this period. Others are referred to in the foot-notes.

PART V.—THE SUB-APOSTOLIC CHURCH

The quotations have been taken from the following texts and translations :—

Clement of Rome
Ignatius
Polycarp
Didache
Epistle of Barnabas
Shepherd of Hermas
Epistle to Diognetus
Papias
  Texts and translations in Lightfoot's *Apostolic Fathers* (one-volume edition, ed. Harmer, London, 1898).

Justin Martyr
Athenagoras
Irenaeus
Clement of Alexandria
  Texts in Migne's *Patrologia* ; Translations in the Ante-Nicene Christian Library.

Ascension of Isaiah .   R. H. Charles's edition (text and translation, London, 1900).

Apocalypse of Peter .   Robinson and James, *The Gospel and Apocalypse of Peter* (London, 1892).

Testament of Abraham
Testament of Isaac
Vision of Paul .
  M. R. James's edition of the texts, in *Texts and Studies*, vols. ii. and iii.

Apology of Aristides .   J. Rendel Harris's edition, in *Texts and Studies*, vol. i.

Sibylline Oracles . .   Alexandre, *Oracula Sibyllina* (Paris, 1869).

For the period in general :—

Bigg, *The Church's Task under the Roman Empire* (Oxford, 1905).
Bigg, *The Christian Platonists of Alexandria* (Oxford, 1886).
Cruttwell, *A Literary History of Early Christianity* (London, 1893).
Hatch, *Influence of Greek Ideas upon the Church* (London, 1890).
Robertson, *Regnum Dei* (London, 1901).

INTRODUCTION

It would scarcely be possible to name any theme more vast or complex than that which is covered by the term 'Eschatology,' or 'the Doctrine of the Last Things.' The term is generally used to include two subjects, closely allied to one another, yet always distinct: first, the destiny of the individual human soul after death; and secondly, the destiny of the world at large. It is often convenient to speak of these two branches of our subject as 'Individual Eschatology' and 'Cosmic Eschatology' respectively.

Eschatology, dealing as it does with the unknown future, possesses at all times a peculiar fascination for the human mind; and at the present moment there are special circumstances which make the eschatology of the primitive Christian Church a subject of more than ordinary interest and importance.

It is indeed true that during the latter part of the nineteenth century, the Doctrine of the Last Things seemed to be receding into the background of Christian teaching. Nor is the reason for this far to seek; for this doctrine, more than any other part of Christianity, is strange and foreign to modern ideas. Even the brief articles of eschatological belief contained in the Creeds of the Church offer difficulties to many minds. And the difficulty is only increased if we go back to the still earlier forms of Christian belief. When the man who stumbles at the brief statements in the Apostles' Creed turns back to the New Testament, he will find that, while the eschatological phrases doubtless have a familiar sound, their original vivid significance remains no longer altogether the same. For instance, the hope of the Second Coming of our Lord, with its attendant features of resurrection and judgment, was in the very forefront of primitive Christian teaching. But to-day, while the Life of Jesus is still the greatest power in the world, the expectation of the Son of Man coming on the clouds of heaven has receded to a comparatively subordinate place. And further, the scientific research of the past century has been ever bringing to light new laws of nature which work on and on without variation; while the idea of evolution has helped to bridge over many apparent gaps in the natural order of the world. All this means that it is increasingly difficult for the modern man to appreciate the expectation of a catastrophic end to this world, which, as we shall see later, was an essential feature of Primitive Christian Eschatology, and offered no difficulty to the men of old time.

Now it was because many Christian teachers of modern times themselves felt these difficulties keenly that it became customary to leave the Doctrine of the Last Things somewhat on one side, as a troublesome and not very vital part of the Christian Religion. But in the last few years this very doctrine has been thrust forward into great prominence by the efforts of a certain school of thought in Germany, who maintain that the very core and essence of Christianity, as taught by Jesus Christ, lay in His eschatological teaching. The views of this school have aroused widespread interest in England; and the whole question of the Christian

Doctrine of the Last Things stands in the forefront of modern theological problems.

The subject of this essay is thus one of exceptional importance at the present time; but it is a very large and difficult subject, interwoven on many sides with other subjects of great complexity; and from what has been said it will be evident that it is not an easy matter to write an essay upon Primitive Christian Eschatology which shall fulfil the purpose of the founder of the Hulsean Prize, and 'evince the truth and excellence of the Christian religion.'

A few words are now desirable with regard to the proposed scope of the present essay. It would, no doubt, be deeply interesting to discuss the permanent value of the doctrines which will come under our notice, from the standpoint of the moralist or the philosopher. But this would require a knowledge to which the present writer can make no claim. Therefore this aspect of the subject has only been referred to very briefly in the following pages, and mainly from the point of view of untrained 'common-sense.' But even if the last word of apologetics lies in the appeal to Reason and Conscience, there is at least a preliminary task to be done first in the field of historical inquiry. The historian must determine what was really taught, before the philosopher or the moralist can discuss whether the teaching was of permanent value. Such a preliminary historical investigation, in the subject of Primitive Christian Eschatology, will be the aim of this essay. But, even within this field of study, there is no thought of claiming completeness of treatment. Many side-issues, intimately connected with the main subject, have been deliberately passed by, for reasons of time and space. And doubtless in many other cases there are unintentional omissions, due to the large field which has to be covered in gleaning information with regard to our subject.

The method which has been pursued is as follows.— The first two Parts of the essay form an introductory section of considerable length, dealing with the eschatological beliefs which preceded and surrounded those of the early Christian Church. In Jewish history, the link which binds together the beliefs of earlier and later generations is peculiarly close, owing perhaps to the continuous and diligent study of the same Old Testament Scriptures by each successive age; and therefore, in dealing with primitive Christian teaching, cradled as it was in Jewish surroundings, it seems desirable to devote more time than might at first sight appear necessary to the introductory study of pre-Christian beliefs, especially among the Jews.

In Part I. the main features of Old Testament eschatology are discussed. The Jews in our Lord's day were steeped in the language and thought of their Sacred Books, and many features of Primitive Christian Eschatology may be traced back with very little change to the Old Testament.

In Part II. we have dealt with the writings of later Judaism, and especially the apocalyptic literature. The importance of these books, as illustrating a peculiar type of thought which was prevalent among the Jews to whom our Lord preached, and also forming a link between the eschatology of the Old and New Testaments, is now generally recognised. As this type of literature is very singular and not widely read, we have treated at some length of its literary characteristics, and the methods by which the apocalyptic books may often be dated.

Part III. deals with the most important section of our subject — the eschatology of our Lord. Here special attention has been given to the views of the recent 'eschatological school' of German critics, of which mention has already been made.

In Part IV. we have considered the eschatology of the apostles, as depicted in the Acts of the Apostles and in the Epistles of the New Testament.

Part V. treats of Christian eschatology in the first and second centuries, when the peculiar characteristics of Primitive Christianity were gradually sinking into the background. There does not appear to be any date generally recognised as marking the close of the 'primitive' age of the Christian Church. But so far as eschatology is concerned, the *distinctively* primitive features come to an end (with a very few exceptions) before the close of the second century; and in this essay we have taken Irenaeus and Clement of Alexandria—two contemporary writers representing divergent tendencies of Christian thought—to provide us with a convenient *terminus ad quem* for our present investigation.

In Part VI. we have endeavoured to indicate the evidential value of Primitive Christian Eschatology, and to point out some of the ways in which it confirms the claims of Christ's Religion.

The Doctrine of the Last Things is full of unusual difficulty and complexity, and it is also a great and sacred subject which ought to be studied with reverence and awe. May these pages partake, at least in some small measure, of the spirit which inspired St. Augustine's oft-quoted prayer:—

'Domine Deus, quaecumque dixi de tuo, agnoscant et tui; si qua de meo, et tu ignosce et tui.'

PART I

OLD TESTAMENT ESCHATOLOGY

CHAPTER I

PRIMITIVE BELIEFS

WHEN we begin the study of eschatology by endeavouring to trace its origin in the thoughts and ideas of primitive man, we are met on the threshold by this difficulty, that there is little or no direct evidence available. Here and there we may find some indications of the beliefs of our early forefathers with regard to their own destiny after death; but these indications are by no means clear, and are capable of more than one interpretation. The beliefs, too, are always confined to the destiny of the individual; there is no sign that primitive man held any definite views concerning the destiny of the world at large. And indeed, it would appear improbable, on *a priori* grounds, that early man would be disposed to forecast the end of the external world, which had outlived so many generations of its inhabitants, and which the human mind instinctively regards (even in our own day) as the very symbol of stability and permanence, 'made so sure that it cannot be moved.' Another cause, too, would cooperate to check speculation on the wider issues of the future.—'The idea of a final condition of the world could not arise apart from a general conception of the meaning of human life and history.'[1] But there is no evidence that any such conception had a place in the mind of primitive man; and therefore the time was not ripe for a 'cosmic eschatology.'

With regard, however, to his own personal destiny after death, man was hardly likely to remain long indifferent or without some kind of a theory; and there is not wanting evidence that certain ideas on this point did take shape at a very primitive period, though the exact form of these earliest beliefs is a matter on which the highest authorities, even in our own times, have not come to universal agreement.

The majority of students of Comparative Religion hold that the most primitive religious beliefs were of the kind that we now call 'animistic.' Briefly stated, man supposed that above and within the visible world, and dwelling in the various objects which it contains, were countless 'spirits'—thin, shadowy beings, which he regarded with awe, an awe mingled, perhaps, with the vague dislike which is naturally inspired by the unknown. To some of these spirits—and especially to those which were believed to inhabit human bodies—a human form, and a more or less human character, were attributed. From this it was but a short step to identify the spirits with the invisible 'something' which appears to leave the human body at the moment of death; and the spirits would come to be regarded as the 'wraiths' of men and women who had died. Then the feelings of awe which always enshroud such occult matters would grow into a definite reverence for the spirits of the departed; and thus animism would readily develop into ancestor-worship. Now ancestor-

[1] A. B. Davidson, *Theology of the Old Testament* (Edinburgh, 1904), p. 400.

ANIMISM

worship implies some kind of belief in the survival of individuals after death ;—scarcely an eschatological belief in the full sense, for it contained no idea of purpose or final destiny; but still, a belief which must always remain an integral element in all eschatology.[1]

The theory outlined above is now generally regarded as containing the most probable explanation of the beginnings of eschatology. Yet it is well to remember that it rests on a somewhat precarious foundation of speculation. There are not wanting scholars of the front rank who doubt whether animism was, after all, the most primitive form of religious belief, and would regard it rather as a corruption of earlier and purer ideas. Take, for instance, the following words of Professor Ramsay :—

> 'Wherever evidence exists, with the rarest exceptions, the history of religion among men is a history of degeneration. . . . Whether there lies behind this historical period a primitive savage period, I am not bold enough or skilful enough to judge.'[2]

So, again, Dr. Inge :—

> 'I am convinced that those who have traced the beginnings of religion to a single source are mistaken. Neither the dream hypothesis, nor "animism," nor (with Statius and Petronius) the simple feeling of vague fear, will account for the birth of religion.'[3]

Under the circumstances, the student who has not made a special study of the subject of 'animism' and its relation to the origin of religion will feel constrained to suspend judgment for the present.

---

[1] For animism and ancestor-worship, see (*e.g.*) Tylor's *Primitive Culture* (London, 2nd ed., 1873), and cf. Salmond's *Christian Doctrine of Immortality* (4th ed., Edinburgh, 1901), pp. 8-20.
[2] Ramsay, *The Cities of St. Paul* (London, 1907), pp. 17, 23.
[3] Inge, *Truth and Falsehood in Religion* (London, 1906), p. 7.

Besides 'animism,' it is possible that some early forms of Nature-worship may have influenced the growth of eschatology—not only of the individual, but also of the world. In particular, the cults of the Sun-god and of the Earth-god would constantly remind their devotees of phenomena akin to death and resurrection. The return of the light, morning by morning, after the darkness, brings with it the hope of a dawn beyond the grave. The green blade of spring naturally suggests the thought: 'So also is the resurrection of the dead.'[1]

These early beliefs may seem to have but little bearing on Primitive Christian Eschatology. Yet the connection between the two is perhaps closer than we think; for simple ideas akin to those of primitive man probably underlie much of our own more developed language. The Spirit of God has taught men to reject much that was crude in their beliefs, and to add much that was new and good; but there appears to have been no break in the continuity of thought, and the great problems of life have remained the same.

[1] For Nature-worship, see (*e.g.*) Frazer, *Adonis, Attis, and Osiris* (London, 1907).

CHAPTER II

EARLY HEBREW ESCHATOLOGY

IF we now turn from primitive times to the later ages when historical evidence becomes available, we shall naturally give our chief attention to the eschatology of Israel. It was in Jewish soil that the Church of Christ was first planted; and the terms in which Christian eschatology expresses itself bear to this day the marks of their Hebrew ancestry. Most of the great religions of the ancient world have indeed contributed something to Christianity; but their influence has generally been indirect, and in many cases has affected Christianity only through the medium of the religion of Israel.

There are various passages in the Old Testament which suggest that animism and ancestor-worship were not unknown among the Hebrews. But whether or not these indicate a survival from primitive beliefs is a question on which there are wide divergences of opinion. Ancestor-worship was certainly regarded with stern displeasure by the strict worshippers of Jahveh. The Israelite whose produce was being tithed had to confess before his God :—' I have not eaten thereof in my mourning . . . nor given thereof for the dead.' [1]

Nevertheless, the beliefs and practices of ancestor-worship were very persistent, at any rate among the lower classes. Even in the Book of Wisdom there is

[1] Deut. xxvi. 14. For animistic beliefs, see (*e.g.*) 1 Sam. xxviii. (the story of Saul and the Witch of Endor), especially vv. 11-15. (The quotations from the English Bible throughout these pages are from the *Revised Version*, except in a few cases, where the original Hebrew or Greek is given for comparison.)

an apparent reference to them.¹ But in our Lord's time they had probably lost their vitality in Judaea, and had little direct influence on Primitive Christian Eschatology.²

Indications of the influence of primitive Nature-worship in the Old Testament are still less evident.³ It is probable that in later times Nature-myths may be discovered in some features of the apocalyptic literature; but these reached the Jews through foreign religions, such as those of Egypt and Greece, and are not relics of a primitive stage of Hebrew religion.

Passing now from these general considerations to the Old Testament itself, we find that the early chapters of Genesis give us no help in tracing the origins of Hebrew eschatology. Except for one brief passage which may hint at the final victory of good over evil,⁴ the problem of the Last Things is not touched upon.

The same silence on this subject is maintained throughout the narratives of the patriarchs. But we have every reason to suppose that when Abraham came forth from Ur of the Chaldees, he would bring with him the outlines of his ancestral faith, the religion of Babylonia,⁵ as yet but little modified by the beginnings of a higher faith in his own heart. The very silence of the narratives of Genesis concerning eschatology implies that before the descent into Egypt, no important change, such as required to be specially recorded, took place in the beliefs of the Hebrews on this subject. The promises to Abraham⁶ do indeed suggest a bright earthly future for his race, but there is nothing eschatological in the words used.

[1] Wisd. xiv. 15, etc. But perhaps this indicates rather the influence of Classical 'Euhemerism.'
[2] Augustine, however, tells us that in the fourth century their influence was felt in the Catholic Church in Africa (Aug. *Conf.* vi. 2).
[3] Tylor, however, finds some traces in Joel (*Primitive Culture*, vol. i. p. 330).
[4] Gen. iii. 15.
[5] For outline of Babylonian religion, with references, see below, Appendix A.
[6] Gen. xii. 2, 3, etc.

Of cosmic eschatology there appears to be no trace in the Babylonian religion. With regard to the future life of the individual, the outlook of the Babylonians seems to have been peculiarly gloomy. The abode of the dead was an underground pit, dark and filthy; and all men, good and bad alike, were fated to dwell there for ever, unless delivered by the arbitrary caprice of the gods. A joyless immortality was the curse of the many; a joyful resurrection was the good luck of a few. Ideas of this type doubtless formed the background of early Hebrew religion, just as Judaism later on provided the background of primitive Christianity.

The sojourn of the Children of Israel in Egypt brought them into contact with an entirely fresh set of beliefs, forming one of the greatest religious systems of the ancient world,—a system, moreover, already closely associated with eschatological doctrines. Each generation of the Egyptians, as it passed away, added to the strange medley of beliefs with regard to the future life.[1] For several centuries the Hebrews lived surrounded by these complex and varied ideas of the Egyptians; and we should expect to find that after the Exodus Hebrew eschatology would show distinct traces of Egyptian influence. But in fact there is hardly a feature in the Biblical narratives of the period which can be traced with certainty to Egyptian (rather than Babylonian) eschatology. Perhaps some of the varying doctrines of 'soul' and 'spirit' in the Old Testament may have been influenced by the complicated Egyptian ideas of man's nature; but even these features are capable of other explanations.[2] Due allowance should

[1] In Egypt, as in Babylonia, there appears to be no evidence of any belief in a series of events closing the present World-Era. See also below, Appendix B, on Egyptian Eschatology.

[2] See Charles, *A Critical History of the Doctrine of a Future Life in Judaism* (London, 1899), pp. 36-49; cf. Warburton's *Divine Legation of Moses* (London, 1738-41).

also be made for the possibility that the Biblical history of the period may have been coloured by later views; but even so, the independence of the Hebrew tradition remains very striking.

The explanation of this may be found, partly at any rate, in the rise of a 'nationalist' spirit among the Children of Israel. A period of oppression and trouble is naturally favourable for the initiation of a new national or religious movement. The Egyptian oppression had united the Children of Israel in a common hatred and a common desire for deliverance; and after the Exodus, they were united in a common gratitude to the God who had delivered them. Henceforth the Hebrews were proud to feel that they were the Kingdom of Jahveh, bound to Him by the sacred ties of the Covenant; and they watched eagerly to see how He would lead on His people from victory to victory. The national hopes were all-important; the future of the individual seemed of little moment. So Egyptian eschatology was not only distasteful to the Israelites because of its associations with racial hatred, but it was also of little interest to them, because it lay outside the sphere of practical national politics.

The absence of eschatology in the Mosaic Code may thus be due partly to this indifference of the people with regard to the future life; but it still more reflects the attitude of the religious leaders of Israel. Now their attitude was determined by the following facts:—

So far as the Israelites at the time of the Exodus believed at all in the survival of the individual after death, their belief was completely dissociated from any sound moral principles. It was a vague tradition handed down from their Babylonian forefathers, retaining a background of animistic ideas, and bound up with the practice of magical arts. The story of Saul and the

ABSENCE OF POSITIVE TEACHING

Witch of Endor indicates how strong a hold such beliefs and practices might have upon the Hebrew mind.

But the writers of the Old Testament consistently maintain that the worship of Jahveh the God of righteousness is irreconcilable with the practice of sorcery, witchcraft, and magic;[1] and this teaching no doubt reflects the attitude of the leaders of Hebrew religion from the Exodus onwards. Now it is more than probable that their efforts to suppress these practices led them to look with disfavour on the allied belief in survival after death, which was then the only form of eschatology prevalent among the Hebrews. So for many generations the religious teachers of Israel continued to withhold their sanction from any doctrine of the future life.

It is true that the Old Testament nowhere affirms that man is annihilated at his physical death; but the same might be said of the Babylonian religion, and even of animism. When primitive man said that 'the dead live no more,' he did not mean that they were annihilated, but only that they no longer had a share in this life.[2] So the early Hebrews believed that the individual did indeed survive death, and went to join his ancestors; but he lived on only in the shadowy pit of Sheol,[3] where the life was no true life.

In short, it would appear from the evidence at our disposal that *cosmic* eschatology was entirely absent from Hebrew thought from the time of the Exodus till the seventh or eighth century B.C.; and that even the hope of *personal* immortality played no important part in Israel's religious aspirations.[4] The Old Covenant destroyed before it began to fulfil.

[1] Exod. xxii. 18; Deut. xviii. 10, 11; 2 Chron. xxxiii. 6; Mic. v. 12, etc.
[2] See Tylor's *Primitive Culture*, vol. ii. p. 20.
[3] Cf. the Babylonian 'Aralu' (see below, Appendix A).
[4] Possible exceptions are, some of the Psalms (see p. 46), and the obscure passages Hosea vi. 2 and xiii. 14 (see p. 23).

CHAPTER III

THE DOCTRINE OF THE PROPHETS

(a) *The Future of the Individual*

THAT the mission of the Hebrew prophets was not only to predict the future, but also broadly to interpret the character and will of God to His people, is a principle of Old Testament scholarship which few to-day are likely to dispute. The influence of prophetic teaching on the Doctrine of the Last Things was profound and far-reaching, though scarcely direct or immediate.

In the first place, the great principles which the prophets taught threw fresh light upon every aspect of life, and not least upon the problem of the future. And secondly, the vivid illustrations by means of which the prophets brought home to the people the practical bearing of their teaching—for instance, the descriptions of the Last Judgment and the Kingdom of God—have come to be a permanent 'dramatic setting' to the eschatology of later ages.

Two great fundamentals of early prophetic teaching were, first, the doctrine of retribution on a moral basis; and secondly, faith in the ultimate fulfilment of the Covenant-Promises to Israel.

1. The law of retribution needed much to be emphasised in the days of the prophets. True, there was no lack of outward devotion to the Name of

Jahveh; indeed Israel was proud to be 'a people dwelling alone, and not reckoned among the nations.'[1] But this very spirit of national pride, while in a measure necessary for the fulfilment of Israel's special vocation, brought with it grave dangers. On the one hand, there was the inclination to think that the 'peculiar people' would be treated by God with peculiar favour, and might safely ignore the responsibilities of their position, while claiming its privileges to the full. And on the other hand, there was the tendency to disregard the requirements of justice, mercy, and truth, and to rest content with the performance of the ritual and ceremonial features of religion, which were less arduous to fulfil, and more attractive, by reason of their resemblance to the cults of the neighbouring peoples.

In sharp opposition to these tendencies, the prophets placed in the very forefront of their teaching the doctrine of retribution on a moral basis. That sin will assuredly be punished, and righteousness rewarded, is the very essence of their message. And by 'righteousness' they meant, not the correct observance of rites and ceremonies, but what we call 'practical morality.'—

> 'I desire mercy, and not sacrifice; and the knowledge of God more than burnt offerings.'[2]
> 'Cease to do evil: learn to do well; seek judgment, relieve the oppressed, judge the fatherless, plead for the widow.'[3]

It is such a conception of 'righteousness' as this which underlies the prophets' doctrine of retribution. Again and again they insist upon the great law, that

---

[1] Num. xxiii. 9.—Even when foreign customs were adopted (Hosea v. 13, vii. 8, viii. 11, etc.); they were probably introduced into the worship of Jahveh, not substituted in its place.
[2] Hosea vi. 6.   [3] Isa. i. 16, 17.

wrong-doing is invariably followed by punishment, and that the performance of 'righteousness' is met without fail by reward.

As this doctrine went home to the hearts of men, it was felt that this all-important law of righteousness, which is the only true test of conduct in this life, must also determine the doctrine of the future. To us it may seem obvious that a true Doctrine of the Last Things must rest upon a moral basis. It was not obvious to the men of old time,[1] until the Spirit of Jahveh had proclaimed it by the mouth of His prophets.

2. Side by side with the prophetic doctrine of retribution, we must place the prophetic hope in the ultimate fulfilment of the Covenant-Promises to Israel. It is possible to hold a belief in a universal law of justice in a spirit of deep-rooted pessimism; and it would not have been surprising to find this spirit among the Hebrew prophets. For Israel had obviously failed to realise the obligations of the Covenant; and there was no visible sign that the ideal of the Covenant was ever likely to be fulfilled.

But the prophets are perfectly confident that the Covenant *will* be fulfilled sooner or later, and that the last end will be light, and not dark :—

> 'Thou wilt perform the truth to Jacob, the mercy to Abraham, which thou hast sworn unto our fathers from the days of old.'[2]

Yet how could these things be? To a superficial observer, the two great fundamentals of prophetic

---

[1] 'The grounds of future reward and punishment are so far from uniform among the religions of the world, that they differ widely within what is considered one and the same creed' (Tylor, *Primitive Culture*, vol. ii. pp. 83, 84).

[2] Micah vii. 20.

teaching might well seem to be mutually irreconcilable. For the law of retribution required that the Covenant-Promises to Israel should be fulfilled only as the reward of national righteousness; and the utter lack of this national righteousness was unveiled in scathing language by the prophets. Yet these same prophets, who maintained so vehemently the law of retribution, loved also to paint bright pictures of the fulfilment of the Covenant. From one point of view, they *were* inconsistent; yet behind the inconsistency lay their sublime faith in God's justice on the one hand, and in His beneficent and sovereign power on the other hand; and this faith supplied an answer to all apparent impossibilities.—

> 'For why? the Lord our God is good,
> His mercy is for ever sure;
> His truth at all times firmly stood,
> And shall from age to age endure.'

We shall find that from this seeming inconsistency between the law of retribution and the fulfilment of the Covenant there sprang several important developments of the prophetic teaching, which profoundly influenced the history of Hebrew eschatology. It will be convenient first to consider the extent of this influence upon the doctrine of *personal immortality*.

As we have seen, the national religion of the Hebrews was not, in its earlier stages, favourable to the growth, or even the continuance, of this belief. The Israelites, in common with most ancient peoples, appear to have retained a vague belief that the soul survived after death, but only in a colourless and joyless existence which could arouse but little interest, and inspire no living hope :—

'The land of darkness and of the shadow of death;
A land of thick darkness, as darkness itself;
A land of the shadow of death, without any order;
And where the light is as darkness.'[1]

The main doctrines of the prophets were not directly concerned with this belief, such as it was; but indirectly, by inspiring the Israelites with new ideas, the way was prepared for a nobler doctrine of human immortality.

One new line of thought suggested by the prophets was that which we now commonly designate by the term 'individualism.' In olden times, while the general principle of retribution was recognised, it was not held that the punishment in every case fell upon the wrongdoer himself. The responsibility of the individual was in a measure shared by his fellow-tribesmen during his lifetime, and by his descendants after his death. His guilt—or at least so much of it as had not been atoned for by retribution coming upon himself in his lifetime—was left behind him as a legacy to his heirs, and the sins of the fathers were thus literally visited on the children.[2]

Dissatisfaction with this conception of the law of retribution is first expressed by Jeremiah:—

'In those days they shall say no more, "The fathers have eaten sour grapes, and the children's teeth are set on edge." But every one shall die for his own iniquity: every man that eateth the sour grapes, his teeth shall be set on edge.'[3]

And Ezekiel, writing when the national life of the Hebrews was virtually suppressed, asserts the principle of individual retribution yet more strongly:—

---

[1] Job x. 21, 22.
[2] See Davidson, *Theology of the Old Testament*, pp. 406-7.
[3] Jer. xxxi. 29, 30.

' The soul that sinneth, it shall die: the son shall not bear the iniquity of the father, neither shall the father bear the iniquity of the son; the righteousness of the righteous shall be upon him, and the wickedness of the wicked shall be upon him.'[1]

We are naturally inclined to interpret such language as this by the standard of our own ideas, and to suppose that the prophets were thinking of retribution beyond the grave. But if we compare the later writings on this same question of retribution,[2] there can be little doubt that Jeremiah and Ezekiel believed that every man did, in fact, receive his due reward within the span of this life.[3]

We shall see, further on, how later ages felt the difficulty of reconciling this teaching of Jeremiah and Ezekiel with the facts of human experience. Yet this early 'individualism' was unquestionably right in affirming that a true doctrine of retribution must render justice not only to nations but to individual men. Jeremiah and Ezekiel were among the first men of the Old Dispensation to perceive, even dimly, the value of each single human soul; and this feature of their teaching has become a permanent element in later eschatology.

Another far-reaching development of Jewish thought which may be traced indirectly to the doctrine of the prophets was the belief in the resurrection of the individual. The beginnings of this great eschatological doctrine may be found in the pre-exilic prophets; but it played no important part in the religious ideas of the Jews until after the Exile.

[1] Ezek. xviii. 20.
[2] *e.g.* Job, Ecclesiastes, Ps. xxxvii., etc.
[3] See A. B. Davidson's 'Ezekiel' (*Camb. Bible for Schools*), p. 126 (notes on Ezek. xviii. 4).

In order to understand clearly the history of the doctrine of the resurrection among the Jews, it is needful to bear in mind the earlier beliefs with regard to the fate of the individual after death. It used to be supposed that every man, however great his devotion to Jahveh in this life, disappeared at death into the gloomy pit of Sheol, which was outside the dominion of the God of Israel :—

'Sheol cannot praise thee;
Death cannot celebrate thee;
They that go down into the pit cannot hope for thy truth.'[1]

These, we read, are the words of one 'who trusted in Jahveh, the God of Israel, so that after him was none like him among all the Kings of Judah, nor among them that were before him.'[2]

It was no wonder that in face of this teaching, the captive Israelites in Babylon complained that 'the way of Jahveh was not equal.' Ezekiel's 'individualism' did not afford them a satisfactory solution; for it seemed to be irreconcilable with their own experience. Many of them knew that their own loyalty to Jahveh was sincere; and yet they were personally involved in the general doom of the nation, and could see no prospect of a brighter future. The problem was especially puzzling to those who inherited the ancient hope of a great national future for Israel; for they felt that their forefathers, who had been made sharers in the Covenant by circumcision, ought to share also in the fulfilment of the Covenant-Promises. But how could this become possible? One answer, and only one, appeared to meet the difficulty. Jahveh would rescue the generations of the faithful dead out of the hand of

---

[1] Isa. xxxviii. 18. A different thought, however, is found in Deut. xxxii. 22, where God's *wrath*, at any rate, is described as reaching to Sheol.
[2] 2 Kings xviii. 5.

THE RESURRECTION 23

Sheol, and bring them up to the Jerusalem of the future.

It is not easy to determine when the doctrine of the resurrection of *individuals* first came to be taught by the Hebrew prophets. The thought of a *national* 'resurrection,' in the sense of a restoration from captivity, is frequently met with; and the Vision of the Dry Bones in Ezekiel xxxvii. shows how this would lead on naturally to the belief in the deliverance of individuals from the realms of Sheol. Perhaps the earliest expression of this latter belief is found in Hosea, as early as the seventh century B.C. After describing the doom coming upon Ephraim, the prophet continues : ' I will ransom them from the hand of Sheol ; I will redeem them from death.' [1] The passage is singular, and without a parallel in contemporary writings. It *may* imply that Jahveh has power to raise men from the 'living death' of Sheol, and to restore them once more to true life ; but it *need* not mean more than that they will be saved from being *overtaken* by death.[2]

The 26th chapter of Isaiah contains one of the most famous of the Old Testament passages dealing with the resurrection.[3] In verse 14 the prophet describes the doom of the enemies of Israel :—

' They are dead, they shall not live ;
They are shades, they shall not rise ;
Therefore hast thou visited and destroyed them,
And made all their memory to perish.' [4]

---

[1] Hosea xiii. 14. In Hosea vi. 2 ('After two days will he revive us . . .,' etc.) the reference is primarily to the restoration of *national* life, but the resurrection of individuals seems also to be implied.

[2] Cf. Ps. xxxiv. 22, and the quotation from Dr. Kirkpatrick, below, p. 46.

[3] Isa. xxiv.-xxvii. are generally considered to be post-exilic ; but see W. E. Barnes, *An Examination of the Objections brought against the Genuineness of Isa.* xxiv.-xxvii. (Cambridge, 1901.)

[4] Isa. xxvi. 14 : מֵתִים בַּל־יִחְיוּ רְפָאִים בַּל־יָקֻמוּ לָכֵן פָּקַדְתָּ וַתַּשְׁמִידֵם וַתְּאַבֵּד כָּל־זֵכֶר לָמוֹ

Next the prophet speaks, in contrast, of the dealings of Jahveh with His people:—

> 'Thou hast increased the Nation, Jahveh, thou hast increased the Nation.'

And then, after a reference to the repentance of the people, he explains in verse 19 the means by which Jahveh will 'increase the nation':—

> 'Thy dead ones shall live; my dead bodies shall arise[1]; awake and sing, ye that dwell in the dust! for thy dew is as the dew of herbs, and the earth shall cast forth the shades.'

In these stirring, if somewhat obscure, words, the prophet seems to feel that the doctrine of the resurrection of individuals is needed to satisfy his highest hopes and beliefs. It satisfies his highest hopes of a national future, because it enables the whole nation, past, present, and future, to share in the coming Kingdom of God; it satisfies his belief in the law of retribution, because it offers another opportunity when the injustice of this world may be perfectly remedied. But it is important to notice how strictly the resurrection is limited to the *faithful* dead; it is a privilege for God's people, and explicitly contrasted with the fate of the world at large.

This passage in Isaiah is the most notable in the prophetical books for the doctrine of the resurrection. There are indeed many passages in the Psalms and in Job which at first sight seem to suggest that the resurrection was in the writers' minds. But there is always some uncertainty about the original meaning of these passages. We have to wait till we come to the apocalypses before we find, in Daniel and many of

[1] יִחְיוּ מֵתֶיךָ נְבֵלָתִי יְקוּמוּן

his successors, the new doctrine of the *general* resurrection, both of the just and unjust.

These two lines of thought which we have been considering—the value of the individual soul, and the consequent need for a doctrine of the resurrection—indicate the two main channels by which the Hebrew prophets influenced the later Jewish and Christian eschatology of the individual. In the next chapter we shall endeavour to trace the effects of their teaching upon the doctrine of the last events in the world's history.

CHAPTER IV

THE DOCTRINE OF THE PROPHETS (*Continued*)

(b) *The Future of the World*

In pre-prophetic times, Hebrew eschatology, as we have seen,[1] was silent concerning the ultimate destiny of the world at large. But under the influence of the prophets, there appears for the first time in Hebrew history a belief that this present world-era will at some time come to a definite end, and that its close will be marked by a certain series of unique events. It is this belief which constitutes in the strict sense 'the Doctrine of the Last Things,' and may be conveniently defined as 'Cosmic Eschatology.'

The chief factors in the development of this doctrine in the prophetic writings are the same as those which influenced the eschatology of the individual;—namely, belief in the law of retribution on a moral basis, and faith in the ultimate fulfilment of the Covenant-Promises to Israel. And it is well to remember that this faith in the fulfilment of the Covenant meant to an Israelite very much what 'faith in the final victory of Good over Evil' means to us in modern times. Both alike imply a spirit of fundamental optimism founded upon religious faith.

Perhaps the most important feature of the cosmic

[1] Above, pp. 13-15.

eschatology of the prophets was their doctrine of the 'Last Judgment.' A vivid description of a judgment-scene is singularly well fitted to teach what the law of retribution means on its practical side; and we find that there are frequent references to a judgment in the prophetic writings. But the prophets imply further, that there will be one great Judgment, when Jahveh 'shall make an end, yea, a terrible end, of all them that dwell in the land.'[1] The descriptions of this Last Judgment vary considerably. It seems probable, however, that the general form of the picture was first suggested by the current popular expectation of 'the Day of Jahveh.' The people were hoping for a day when Jahveh should visibly appear as their leader in battle, and utterly destroy all the foes of Israel. This was apparently the origin of the phrase 'the Day of Jahveh'; but its significance soon came to be much greater than that of any normal 'battle-day.' We learn from Amos that as early as the eighth century B.C. the phrase was a familiar one in Israel; and he uses the phrase to denote no ordinary incident in the course of Israel's history, but a supernatural event of supreme moment, bringing to pass the close of the present conditions of life on earth, and introducing a new era of ideal happiness.[2]

Such a conception of the 'Last Judgment' was in harmony alike with the law of retribution and with the final fulfilment of the Covenant-Promises. No judgments of the past or present seemed completely to satisfy the requirements of perfect justice; there was yet need of another and final Judgment, which should

---

[1] Zeph. i. 18; cf. Joel iii., Amos ix., Isa. ii. 12-21, xxiv. 21 ff., etc.
[2] Amos v. 18, ix. 1-15. Some critics consider that the concluding vision of restoration in Amos is a later addition. Even if so, it would reflect the afterthoughts suggested by the original prophetic teaching, and, thus throw light upon the development of eschatology.

leave no wickedness unpunished, and no righteousness unrewarded. And further, the doctrine of a Last Judgment seemed just what was wanted to fill the gap between the present evil world and the bright future foretold by most of the prophets.[1] The Last Judgment would mark the end of the injustice of this world, and the beginning of the era of righteousness, when the Covenant-Promises would be perfectly fulfilled.

The value of this doctrine as a simple and forcible illustration of the law of retribution and the final victory of the Good is nowhere more clearly seen than in the Book of Joel.[2] In chapter ii. the 'Day of Jahveh' is the day when He visits His people for their sins, in the terror and darkness of the locust-cloud. The thought of the 'coming of Jahveh' for judgment and retribution fills the hearts of a sinful people with dread.[3] But the prophet goes on to tell us of Israel's repentance; and then, in chapter iii., follows another picture of the 'Day of Jahveh.' As before, it is a visitation for judgment and retribution on the sinners; and Jahveh takes His seat as judge in the Valley of Jehoshaphat. But this time it is the Gentile enemies of Israel, whose 'wickedness is great,' that are punished; while Israel, being repentant, is delivered, and receives a special gift of the spirit of prophecy.[4] Thus the twofold application of the law of retribution is vividly illustrated; and it is further clear that this Last Judgment is regarded by the prophet as final and unique. Henceforward the Covenant receives its perfect fulfilment, and the forces of evil are completely vanquished. Jerusalem

---

[1] See below, pp. 31 ff.
[2] Cameron, in Hastings' *Dictionary of the Bible* (vol. ii. pp. 673-674, Art. 'Joel'), favours an early date for the Book (eighth century), but Driver and many others prefer a post-exilic date. The eschatology seems suitable to an early date.
[3] Joel ii. 1-11.   [4] Joel iii. 11-17; cf. ii. 15-18, 28-29.

will be cleansed from the profane presence of the
Gentiles, and will enjoy an unending (and apparently,
material) prosperity, which is thrown into strong relief
by the desolation of the nations around:—

> 'Egypt shall be a desolation, and Edom shall be a
> desolate wilderness; . . . but Judah shall abide for ever,
> and Jerusalem from generation to generation; . . . for
> Jahveh dwelleth in Zion.'[1]

In Amos, the 'Day of Jahveh' is the day when He
judges *Israel* rather than the world at large; and since
Israel is corrupt, it will be a day of punishment and not
of deliverance:—

> 'Woe unto you that desire the "Day of Jahveh"!
> Wherefore would ye have the "Day of Jahveh"? it is
> darkness, and not light; . . . even very dark, and no
> brightness in it.'[2]

In his concluding chapters, Amos describes one
vision after another, all foretelling a coming judgment,
till they culminate in the vision of Jahveh Himself
standing upon the altar, and commanding that His
Temple is to be shattered in pieces. Not till after this
last and most fearful judgment does Amos turn to
describe the bright 'remoter future.'[3]

In Isaiah the judgment associated with the Day of
Jahveh seems to be *universal*:—

> 'There shall be a Day of Jahveh Sabaoth upon all
> that is proud and haughty, and upon all that is lifted up,
> and it shall be brought low; . . . and Jahveh alone
> shall be exalted in that Day. . . . Jahveh standeth up to
> plead, and standeth to judge the peoples; Jahveh will
> enter into judgment with the elders of his people, and
> the princes thereof.'[4]

---

[1] Joel iii. 19-21.   [2] Amos v. 18, 19.   [3] Amos vii.-ix.
[4] Isa. ii. 12, 17, iii. 13-14.

As time went on, the prophetic pictures of the Last Judgment were further elaborated by later writers. Ezekiel describes the great final assault of the nations under Gog and Magog;[1] and in the later chapters of Zechariah, the last days before the New Era are marked by all kinds of wars and tumults and strange portents,[2] forming a dramatic contrast to the peace and happiness of the Kingdom of God, which follows immediately after the Last Days have culminated in the Last Judgment. Here we have the source of two important features of the apocalyptic books. The portents of the last days develop into the 'birth-pangs of the Messianic Kingdom'; and the last assault of the nations gives rise to the legend of Anti-Christ and his hosts of evil, which we shall meet with in the apocalyptic literature.[3]

To us the Last Judgment is liable to seem a vague far-off event; to the prophets it was very real and near at hand. 'The great Day of Jahveh is near,' cries Zephaniah; 'it is near, and hasteth greatly.'[4] So also the language of Joel and Amos implies that the Day of Jahveh might be expected in their own time; while Hosea, Micah, Isaiah, and Jeremiah, see the signs of the Last Judgment upon Israel in the political movements around them.

> 'Whenever a man earnestly, and out of the depths of his own heart, points others to God, . . . whether it be deliverance or judgment that he preaches, it has always, so far as history tells us, taken the form of announcing that the end is at hand.'[5]

[1] Ezek. xxxviii., xxxix.
[2] Zech. ix.-xiv., especially chapter xiv.; cf. Haggai ii. 6, etc.
[3] For the doctrine of Anti-Christ, see below, on 2 Thessalonians, Part IV. Chapter III.
[4] Zeph. i. 14.
[5] Harnack, *What is Christianity?* (English translation, London, 1901, p. 41); cf. Davidson, *Theology of the Old Testament*, pp. 379-381.

So it was with the prophets; as they looked out into the future with hearts full of enthusiasm for the law of righteousness, it seemed to them impossible that this world of injustice could last much longer. The Day *must* be at hand.

Just as the pictures of judgment were well fitted to teach the meaning of the law of retribution, so the descriptions of the restoration of Israel to ideal national life brought home to the people the unchanged promises of the Covenant. The ideal national life is depicted by the prophets in many ways, but there is always one central thought, that then Israel will truly be 'the Kingdom of God.' For though the phrase belongs to the New Testament, the idea of the sovereignty of Jahveh is one of the keynotes of the Hebrew prophets.

There are two features in the descriptions of the Kingdom of God which require at least a passing reference. The first is the figure of the Messianic King. Jahveh had not only made a Covenant with His people, but also a special Covenant with the House of David.[1] At the restoration of Israel, when the national Covenant is fulfilled, the Davidic Covenant will also receive its perfect fulfilment in the person of the anointed Messiah. His rule will show the great principles of justice for which the prophets had contended :—

> 'His delight shall be in the fear of Jahveh; and he shall not judge after the sight of his eyes, neither reprove after the hearing of his ears; but with righteousness shall he judge the poor, and reprove with equity for the meek of the earth.'[2]

The Messianic King will also be 'The Prince of

---

[1] 2 Sam. vii. 12-16 ; cf. 1 Kings xi. 36, Ps. lxxxix. 3, 4, etc.
[2] Isa. xi. 3, 4 ; cf. ix. 6, 7, and Micah v. 2-5, and Jer. xxx. 21.

Peace.'¹ This would surely not have been part of the ideal of the Hebrews when the national life was yet young. Victory, not peace, was then their desire; but now the prophet has learnt the lesson of suffering, and longs for the day when 'nation shall not lift up sword against nation, neither shall they learn war any more.'² There is another feature of the Messianic reign :—

> 'Of the increase of his government and of peace there shall be *no end,* upon the throne of David, and upon his Kingdom, to establish it, and to uphold it with judgment and with righteousness *from henceforth even for ever.*'³

The Messianic Kingdom is thus to be everlasting; and the language suggests that the Messiah himself will also live for ever. Nothing is said about the subjects of the Kingdom; but we are evidently not far from the doctrine that all the faithful who see the beginning of the Kingdom of the Messiah will live to enjoy it for ever. The belief in the everlasting Kingdom would thus lead very naturally to the belief in individual immortality.

A very different Messianic ideal is set before us in the prophecies of the 'Suffering Servant of Jahveh' in the latter part of Isaiah. The thought of 'perfection through suffering' which pervades these passages is in complete accord with the distinctive note of Christian eschatology; and the Christian Church has always recognised in them the most striking of all the Old Testament prophecies of Jesus the Messiah. Yet the picture of the 'Suffering Servant' does not appear to have influenced the later Messianic ideals of the Jews. 'It is doubtful,' says Dr. A. B. Davidson,⁴ 'if the

---

[1] Isa. ix. 6.   [2] Isa. ii. 4.
[3] Isa. ix. 7. The phrase עַד־עוֹלָם ('for ever') is a little indefinite, but is generally used to signify an infinitely long time.
[4] *Theology of the Old Testament,* p. 373.

prophets identified in their own minds the Servant of Jehovah and the King Messiah,' although 'later revelation showed them to be one.'

The relation of the Messiah to God is more than once expressed in the Old Testament by the term 'sonship.' In the original Covenant, as made with David ('I will be his father, and he shall be my son'[1]), the word 'son' can hardly be said to imply a super-human relationship. But it was a term pregnant with deeper meaning, and we can trace here and there signs of the gradual enrichment of its significance. Such passages as Psalm lxxxix. 27, 'I will make him my firstborn, higher than the kings of the earth'; or Psalm ii. 7, 'Thou art my son, this day have I begotten thee,' prepare the way for the idea of a super-human sonship, such as is implied in some of the apocalyptic writings, where 'God's Son' is almost, if not quite, divine. It is scarcely necessary to point out that the history of the term 'Son of God' is of the deepest significance for the understanding of the New Testament.

The other important feature of the 'restoration' in the prophetic writings is the idea of the perfect 'City of God.' Jerusalem is always thought of as the abode of the restored people. The tabernacle of David is to be rebuilt as in the days of old,[2] and the Holy City will no more be profaned by unhallowed feet.[3] The Gentiles will indeed flock to the House of Jahveh, but it will be in a spirit of conversion, to worship, not to profane.[4] Ezekiel dwells at length on the features of the New Jerusalem, and though at times the details may seem to us somewhat wearisome, the closing thought is a noble one:—

'The name of the City from that day shall be, Jahveh is there.'[5]

[1] 2 Sam. vii. 14.   [2] Amos ix. 11.   [3] Joel iii. 17.
[4] Isa. ii. 2 ff.; cf. Micah iv. 1 ff.   [5] Ezek. xlviii. 35.

In connection with the prophetic eschatology of the individual, we noticed how hard it was to reconcile the two great principles of the prophetic teaching—the law of justice and the final victory of the good—with each other and with experience. The same difficulty was met with in the history of the eschatology of Israel and of the world at large. How could a people steeped in sin ever enjoy the full blessings of the holy Covenant?

One of the answers to these doubts was given by the doctrine of 'the Remnant,' which we find especially in Isaiah and Zephaniah. The full breadth of the older national hopes are abandoned, and the doom of the nation as a whole is admitted to be fixed beyond recovery; but yet there is hope:—

> 'I will take away out of the midst of thee thy proudly exalting ones, and thou shalt no more be haughty in my holy mountain; but I will leave in the midst of thee an afflicted and poor people, and they shall trust in the Name of Jahveh.'[1]

And Isaiah tells how, after the great fire of judgment, 'the remnant of the trees of the forest shall be few, so that a child may write them.'[2] It is the doctrine of a Church in contrast to the world; and in matters eschatological it is more closely allied to the Puritan desire for an elect few than to the hope of a world-wide Kingdom of God. It is the affirmative answer to the question: 'Are there few that be saved?'

Jeremiah meets the spirit of pessimism with a bolder answer than that of Zephaniah. He fully recognises that the Covenant has been broken by God's people, and that repentance on their part is the only remedy. Nor has he much hope of that repentance in the near future. Yet he will not surrender any part of the national hope:—

[1] Zeph. iii. 11, 12.   [2] Isa. x. 19.

THE NEW COVENANT

> 'Behold, the days come, saith Jahveh, that I will make a New Covenant with the house of Israel and with the house of Judah; . . . I will put my law in their inward parts, and in their heart will I write it.'[1]

Under the New Covenant, the people will not be subjected to outward ordinances, but will be animated by the Spirit of Jahveh within. Israel will be a nation of prophets.[2]

This doctrine of the New Covenant shows deep spiritual insight; it is also of interest because the writer evidently believed that the New Era to come must be something more than a mere replica of this present world. One aspect of this thought may be found in Isaiah, in the passages where he describes the transformation of Nature into harmony with the perfect conditions of the future national life.[3] The same idea is again, and yet more clearly, expressed in the 65th chapter of Isaiah :—

> 'Behold, I create New Heavens and a New Earth; and the former things shall not be remembered, nor come into mind.'[4]

In the non-canonical book '4 Ezra,'[5] we find this thought in an extreme form; the future will be the antithesis of the present, and this world must end before the next begins :—

> 'Jacob's hand held the heel of Esau from the beginning; for Esau is the end of this world, and Jacob is the beginning of that which followeth.'[6]

---

[1] Jer. xxxi. 31, 33.
[2] Cf. Joel ii. 28 ('I will pour out my Spirit on all flesh, and your sons and your daughters shall prophesy'). Cf. also Isa. xxxii. 15, Ezek. xxxix. 29.
[3] Isa. xi. 6-8, xxx. 26. For questions of date, see Skinner's *Isaiah*, notes *ad loc.*
[4] Isa. lxv. 17. For questions of date, see (*e.g.*) Driver, *Literature of the Old Testament* (7th edition, Edinburgh, 1905), pp. 245-6, or Skinner, *ad loc.*
[5] Called 'II Esdras' in our English A.V. and R.V., but the title '4 Ezra' is less liable to confusion.
[6] 4 Ezra vi. 8, 9.

This doctrine of the 'Two Worlds' forms an important element in the history of eschatological thought. For there are three main conceptions of the other world: on the one hand there is the idea of a world which will be but an improved copy of that which now is; on the other hand there is the philosophical conception of a transcendental existence which cannot be adequately described in human language, and is independent of limitations of time or space; and between these two is the doctrine of the 'Two Worlds,' the world to come beginning, in point of time, immediately upon the close of this present world-era, and differing diametrically from it in character, while yet remaining more or less material in general idea.[1]

Yet one more line of development in Hebrew eschatology remains to be mentioned. Those who were zealous to proclaim the universal supremacy of the law of retribution, found that the thoroughly 'nationalist' conception of the restoration of Israel was somewhat modified thereby. This tendency took the form now known as 'universalism,' in which the normal Jewish antipathy towards the Gentiles is softened, and morality, rather than nationality, is held to be the supreme test in the sight of God.[2]

The greatest prophet of universalism was Amos of Tekoa. He cannot conceive of any exceptions to the law of retribution, nor of any limits to the dominion of Jahveh :—

'Are ye not as the children of the Ethiopians unto me, O Children of Israel? saith Jahveh.—Have not I

[1] 'A transcendental sphere of existence, such as we conceive of heaven, could not occur to the Israelite' (Davidson, *Theology of the Old Testament*, p. 414).

[2] For a fuller treatment of the 'universalist' teaching of the prophets, the reader is referred to A. J. Tait, *Christ and the Nations* (London, 1910), Part I. chaps. iv. and v.

brought up Israel out of the land of Egypt, and the Philistines from Caphtor, and the Syrians from Kir?'[1]

This teaching did not at once become part of the national creed; indeed it never found entire favour with the 'peculiar people.' But the wide outlook of Amos was not without its effect on later eschatology. It is true that many of the Old Testament writers continued to regard the Gentiles as the natural enemies of Israel, doomed to utter destruction. But it was generally felt that the Doctrine of the Last Things cannot simply *ignore* the Gentiles, as the Hebrews of earlier times had done. And side by side with Jewish exclusiveness, a wider hope now and again manifested itself, and found expression among the leaders of Jewish thought :—

> 'Many peoples shall come and say, Come ye, and let us go up to the mountain of Jahveh, to the house of the God of Jacob; and he will teach us of his ways, and we will walk in his paths.'[2]

And again :—

> 'In that day shall Israel be the third with Egypt and with Assyria, a blessing in the midst of the earth, for that Jahveh Sabaoth hath blessed them, saying, Blessed be Egypt my people, and Assyria the work of my hands, and Israel mine inheritance.'[3]

But though Isaiah was willing that the Gentiles should obtain a share in the Kingdom of God, he claimed for Israel an everlasting supremacy :—

> 'The house of Israel shall possess them [the peoples] in the land of Jahveh for servants and for handmaids; and they shall take them captive, whose captives they were; and they shall rule over their oppressors.'[4]

---

[1] Amos ix. 7.   [2] Isa. ii. 3 ; Micah iv. 2.
[3] Isa. xix. 24, 25. For questions of date, see Skinner, *ad loc.*
[4] Isa. xiv. 2.

In the later prophets, we can often trace a spirit nearly akin to universalism,[1] but there are few parallels to the uncompromising language of Amos. We read much of the restoration of the scattered Israelites from among the nations, but little of the restoration of the nations themselves.

The return from the Captivity revived the national hopes, and something of the old national exclusiveness and aggressiveness. But the universalist spirit of Amos lives again in those passages where the writers look forward to a catholic Church of Judaism. The Gentiles are not to be crushed by political aggression, but won over by the attracting power of the pure worship of Jahveh.[2]

In the above pages, we have only been able to indicate the most essential features of Hebrew prophecy. We have seen how the teaching of the prophets was founded on two great principles :—the law of retribution on a moral basis, and the ultimate fulfilment of the Covenant-Promises. And partly through the desire to reconcile these two principles with one another in the light of experience, there arose the first Hebrew 'Doctrine of the Last Things.' In pre-prophetic times there had been no sign that men troubled themselves about the final destiny of the world. But the prophets taught that this world will end in a great Day of Judgment, after which a New Era will begin. The prophets were thus the first true eschatologists in the history of Israel.

We have also glanced at other doctrines of the prophets, which, although subordinate to the two great foundation principles, are yet of much importance to later eschatology :—the international sympathies of

---

[1] *e.g.* in Jeremiah's description of the New Covenant ; see above, pp. 34, 35.
[2] Cf. Zech. viii. 22, 23, Malachi i. 11, etc.

SUMMARY OF PROPHETIC TEACHING

Amos, the individualism of Jeremiah and Ezekiel, the doctrines of the Remnant and of the New Covenant, and the splendid pictures of the Messianic King and of His Kingdom.

Our consideration of the teaching of the prophets has necessarily been incomplete; but such as it is, it may help us to obtain a clearer idea of the subsequent history of Jewish thought; for the language and ideas of the prophets, and above all their sublime faith in the fulfilment of the Divine purpose, has become the permanent heritage of both Jewish and Christian eschatology. The voice of the Spirit who spake by the prophets may still be heard in these latter days. Some well-known words, which we owe to an essentially modern poet, might nevertheless have been the epitaph of one of the prophets of ancient Israel :—

'One who never turned his back but marched breast forward,
  Never doubted clouds would break,
 Never dreamed, though right were worsted, wrong would triumph,
 Held we fall to rise, are baffled to fight better,
  Sleep to wake.'

CHAPTER V

THE ESCHATOLOGY OF THE POST-EXILIC JEWS

WE have seen that although the great principles proclaimed by the Hebrew prophets were not primarily eschatological in character, they exercised a deep, albeit indirect, influence upon the subsequent history of eschatology. Many new thoughts were suggested by their teaching; and while these explained some problems which had before seemed inexplicable, they also brought to light new difficulties hitherto unnoticed. So the prophetic 'word of Jahveh' is questioned and defended and examined again and again, and each fresh controversy led on to further doctrinal development. This might be called the intellectual influence of the doctrine of the prophets.

There was also another line of influence, springing from the growing spirit of reverence for all that was ancient in Israel's history and religion. The pictures of judgment and restoration, which seem originally to have been intended to illustrate and explain the great underlying principles, were valued in later times for their own sake, and came to be a fixed part of the traditional Jewish Doctrine of the Last Things. This feeling of reverence for the past was specially fostered by the teaching of the scribes, whose influence in post-exilic times became a factor of considerable importance.

For one thing, their teaching was closely associated with the cessation of prophecy. Their extreme veneration for the past went hand in hand with a corresponding depreciation of the present ; and they would have held it presumptuous to make the old claim of the prophets : 'The word of Jahveh came to *me*.' So in the teaching of the scribes we miss the spiritual conviction of the prophets, and in its place we find the constant appeal to authority. This led on the one hand to Pharisaic legalism, which tended to obscure the moral element in eschatology ; and it also helped to produce the pseudonymous apocalyptic literature, which shelters itself under the authority of the great names of old time. In the apocalypses we still find faith in a bright future, but that faith is not based solely on the personal conviction of the writers, but rather on the authority of the prophets of earlier times.

The teaching of the scribes was also favourable to the doctrine of predestination, which looms so large in later Judaism. We have seen how the prophets were confident that the great principles of the Covenant would be fulfilled in time to come. Later on, under the guidance of the scribes, the Jews came to believe that every detail in the Sacred Writings must similarly be fulfilled. So we find the Pharisees in our Lord's time watching every little event in the hope that it would prove to be a fulfilment of some ancient 'word of God.' The same idea of predestination runs through all the apocalypses ; they assume that the details of the Last Things are already determined, and revealed in Holy Scripture ; and the writers seek, not to preach a new 'message of God,' but to discover and explain what has been already revealed. This led to a certain artificiality in later Jewish eschatology ; for on the one hand, the thoughts of the writers are no longer allowed to find free and natural expression,[1] but are shaped and fashioned till they agree with the traditional doctrine; and on the other hand there is a tendency to adopt a forced exegesis of the older Scriptures, in order that they may harmonise with later ideas. On the whole, the teaching of the scribes did not help to produce a noble Doctrine of the Last Things; but at least, by encouraging the study of the prophets, it kept alive a spirit of reverent hopefulness for the future. There may be some traces of the tendencies of which we have been speaking in some of the later prophets,[2] but only with the rise of the apocalyptic literature do we see the full effect of this teaching of the scribes.

Another characteristic of post-exilic Judaism was an increased sense of the transcendence of God. The Exile had not only suppressed the national life of the Jews for a time, but it had also cut them off from the old *local* associations of their religion. So the pious Israelites who continued loyal to Jahveh in Babylon were thrown, as it were, upon their own resources of worship. They were obliged by force of circumstances to worship in the spirit alone, without the help of the ancient rites and ceremonies, and humbled by the feeling that the Exile was the punishment for national sin. And as they sang the songs of Jahveh in a strange land they realised, as they had never realised before, the awful mystery of a God who is everywhere :—

> 'Whither shall I go from thy spirit,
> Or whither shall I flee from thy presence?'[3]

The thought of the great gulf between God and man is continually present to the post-exilic Jew, and it may be seen in much of the later eschatology. Men were beginning to shrink from the thought that God would

---

[1] The daring scepticism of Ecclesiastes is an exception.
[2] *e.g.* Zechariah 9 ff., and Malachi.   [3] Ps. cxxxix. 7.

deal in person with themselves, and rather pictured Him as surrounded by the pomp and splendour of an Oriental despot, executing His pleasure by means of secondary agents. In Malachi, for instance, we find that the Almighty is to send 'Elijah' as a herald before Him to announce His own coming to judgment. And the growth of the belief in angels, perhaps due partly to the influence of Zoroastrianism, is also an expression of the increasing reverence for an Almighty God, the Lord of heaven and earth.

In tracing the history of post-exilic eschatology, some allowance should be made for the possibility of influence from Zoroastrian and Egyptian doctrines. After the decline and fall of Babylon, the Hebrews were surrounded on all sides by Zoroastrianism;[1] and since there was little ill-will between the Hebrews and Persians,[2] it is not surprising to find many important resemblances between the religions of the two peoples.[3] And yet modern scholars do not seem disposed to estimate the direct influence very high. Some of the resemblances may be explained by a parallel development of thought along natural lines, and in other cases it is difficult to determine which of the two religions has been the borrower.[4]

There was also constant intercourse between Judaea and Egypt from the ninth to the seventh centuries B.C.;

[1] For outline of Zoroastrianism, with references, see below, Appendix C.
[2] e.g. in Isa. xlv. 1, Cyrus is called 'the Anointed of Jahveh.'
[3] These resemblances are specially striking in the following doctrines:—
    (a) The conflict between good and evil (cf. the Jewish legend of Anti-Christ).
    (b) The doctrine of retribution and resurrection on a moral basis.
    (c) The doctrine of angels and spirits, and especially of 'Fravashis' (cf. the late Jewish idea of the 'heavenly copies' of things on earth).
    (d) The legend of Saoshyant the Zoroastrian Messiah. For further details, see below, Appendix C.
[4] See Moulton's article in Hastings' *Dictionary of the Bible*, vol. iv. p. 993b.

and later on, under the Ptolemies, the Hebrew colonies at Alexandria and elsewhere were little Jewish islands amid a sea of Egyptian life and thought. The discoveries at Elephantiné in 1907 suggest that the Jewish settlements in Egypt were earlier and more important than had previously been supposed, and we shall find evidence, especially in the apocalypses, that post-exilic Judaism was influenced by Egyptian ideas.[1]

Those features of post-exilic Judaism which we have so far been considering have contributed little that is of permanent value to eschatology. But in some of the post-exilic literature, we are conscious of a new and deep spiritual 'tone,' which is an unmistakable sign that in the writers' hearts there is the deep quiet mysticism and communion with God, which passeth all understanding. We find the most notable expressions of this spirit in the Book of Job and in the Psalter.

Whatever be the exact date of the Book of Job,[2] the groundwork might be described as a criticism of the individualistic theory of retribution. That theory is amply set forth by Job's companions, whose irritating but unanswerable platitudes provoke the patriarch to impotent wrath. Although he knows from his own experience that suffering is not always the punishment for sin, yet his intellect is unable to discover an effectual reply. In deep gloom he looks forward into a hopeless future :—

> 'Man dieth, and wasteth away;
> Yea, man giveth up the ghost, and where is he?
> The waters fail from the sea,

---

[1] See below, Appendix B, for outline of Egyptian doctrines; and especially Erman, *Handbook of Egyptian Religion*, pp. 194-219. For the Elephantiné papyri, see Driver's article in *The Guardian* for Nov. 6, 1907.

[2] Driver (*Literature of the Old Testament*, 7th edition, p. 432) says: 'Most probably it was written either during or shortly after the Babylonian captivity.'

And the river decayeth, and drieth up;
So man lieth down, and riseth not;
Till the heavens be no more, they shall not awake,
Nor be roused out of their sleep.'[1]

And yet his faith at once prompts a cry of anguish to the God in whom he had trusted:—

'Oh that thou wouldest hide me in Sheol,
That thou wouldest keep me secret, till thy wrath be past,
That thou wouldest appoint me a set time, and remember me!'[2]

And once more, in chapter xix., after further sententious remarks from his pious friends, the hope of justice in the end breaks out strong and clear:—

'But I know that my redeemer liveth,
And that he shall stand up at the last upon the earth;
And after my skin hath been thus destroyed,
Yet from [or, "without"] my flesh I shall see God.
Whom I shall see for myself, and mine eyes behold, and not another.'[3]

For the moment, the irresistible conviction of the mystic breaks through where cold reason had stood baffled. The translation and interpretation of the passage are alike difficult, but it seems probable that what Job hoped for was that in the pit of Sheol a vision of Jahveh would be granted to him. He does not seem to have any thought of deliverance from Sheol, or of a resurrection-life,[4] but he does hope that the gloom

---

[1] Job xiv. 10-12.
[2] Job xiv. 13.
[3] Job xix. 25-27; the Hebrew runs thus:—

וַאֲנִי יָדַעְתִּי גֹּאֲלִי חָי וְאַחֲרוֹן עַל־עָפָר יָקוּם:
וְאַחַר עוֹרִי נִקְּפוּ־זֹאת וּמִבְּשָׂרִי אֶחֱזֶה אֱלוֹהַּ:
אֲשֶׁר אֲנִי אֶחֱזֶה־לִּי וְעֵינַי רָאוּ וְלֹא־זָר . . . :

[4] And yet the phrase, 'He shall stand up at the last upon the earth,' suggests the Last Crisis.

of the Pit may be illuminated by the presence of the God who had been his comfort in this life.

The Hebrew Psalter, even more than the Book of Job, contains many expressions of a deep sense of communion with God, which clearly influenced the writers' outlook on the future. We have not hitherto referred to the eschatology of the Psalms, partly because there is often much uncertainty as to their date, and also because the language of the Psalmists is frequently capable of more than one interpretation. In particular, those Psalms which are generally assigned to a *pre-exilic* date contain few, if any references to eschatology which are free from ambiguity.

> 'Some of the expressions which appear at first sight to imply a sure hope of deliverance from Sheol and of reception into the more immediate presence of God are used elsewhere of temporal deliverance from death or protection from danger, and may mean no more than this.'[1]

But there can be little doubt that the mystical feeling of personal communion with God, which is the very keynote of many of the Psalms, prepared the way for a doctrine of personal immortality :—

> 'I am continually with thee;
> Thou hast holden my right hand;
> Thou shalt guide me with thy counsel;
> And afterward receive me to glory.'[2]

It is possible that the writer of these words had never consciously adopted a doctrine of personal immortality; but if so, this was 'not from lack of religion, but from excess of religion'; because 'the future life was overshadowed by the [present] consciousness of the presence

---

[1] Kirkpatrick, *Psalms* (Cambridge, 1906), Introduction, p. xcv.
[2] Ps. lxxiii. 23, 24; cf. Ps. xvii. 15.

of God Himself.'[1] This sense of God's presence was not physical, but spiritual, and a spiritual bond need not be broken by physical death. The communion between God and the individual human soul, which was so real to the Hebrew Psalmists, is the surest pledge of the soul's personal immortality; and hence a doctrine of personal immortality is more truly implied in the mysticism of Job and the Psalmists than in any other writers of the Old Testament.

One Old Testament writer stands out in striking contrast to the general trend of Hebrew religion, with its firm faith in the ultimate triumph of goodness. This was the writer of Ecclesiastes. His date is generally assigned to the fourth or third centuries B.C.,[2] and his book shows us that the doctrines of the prophets were not accepted by all who believed in the God of Israel. He sees that Ezekiel's doctrine of retribution within the span of this life is hard to reconcile with the facts of experience, but he does not attempt to justify God's dealings by holding out hopes of an unknown beyond :—

> 'All things come alike to all; there is one event to the righteous and to the wicked. . . . A living dog is better than a dead lion; for the living know that they shall die; but the dead know not anything, neither have they any more a reward.'[3]

Nor was the Preacher cheered by the consciousness of the nearness of God's presence within himself; he had as little sympathy with the mystic as with the prophetic enthusiast :—

---

[1] Stanley, *History of the Jewish Church* (2nd ed., London, 1873), vol. i. p. 157.
[2] See (*e.g.*) A. S. Peake in Hastings' *Dictionary of the Bible*, vol. i. pp. 637 f.
[3] Eccles. ix. 2-5.

> 'God is in heaven, and thou upon earth; therefore let thy words be few.'[1]

And yet, if the closing verses be authentic,[2] he still believes that somehow and at some time

> 'God shall bring every work into judgment, and every secret thing, whether it be good, or whether it be evil.'

We may now gather up as shortly as possible the results of our study of Old Testament eschatology.[3] Broadly speaking, two lines of development have been distinguishable. One of these, starting from the early hopes of tribal success, culminates in the prophetic doctrine of the world-wide Kingdom of God. The end of this world is to be catastrophic;[4] for the Last Judgment, with all its attendant turmoil, is to precede the commencement of the New Era. From first to last this national and world-wide eschatology is inspired by a confident faith in the Covenant-Promises.

The eschatology of the individual has developed less uniformly and less consistently. In the early stages of Hebrew history, we found the belief in personal survival after death on the wane, and lacking any sanction from the religious leaders of Israel. And the teaching of the prophets seems to have had at the first no primary reference to the fate of the individual after death, though in course of time the question was, so to speak, forced upon their notice by their zeal for the law of retribution.

---

[1] Eccles. v. 2.

[2] See Driver, *Literature of the Old Testament*, 7th edition, pp. 477-478.

[3] The consideration of one Old Testament book, the Book of Daniel, of great interest to the student of eschatology, has been deferred to a later stage. The reasons for this will appear below, p. 62.

[4] In a very few passages (*e.g.* Zech. xii. and xiii.) there appears to be an expectation that the Chosen People will be *gradually* purified, till they are made fit for the Messianic Era.

The doctrine of the resurrection of the righteous has indeed been proclaimed once and again, but it has not won its way to general acceptance. This doctrine, as we find it, for instance, in Isaiah xxvi., does indeed imply that the rule of Jahveh extends to Sheol. But as yet we have found no clear belief that Sheol is either a place of rewards and punishments, or an intermediate state between death and resurrection for mankind in general.

Another line of eschatological thought has been suggested by Job and the psalmists. The mystical sense of communion with God refuses to be limited by the things of this world. In contrast to the doctrine of the prophets, this mystical eschatology contains no thought of impending catastrophe. It is a doctrine of immortality, not a doctrine of the Last Things.

But side by side with the hopes of the prophets and the quiet faith of the psalmists we have had to place the scepticism of Ecclesiastes. And indeed, throughout the Old Testament, while the brightness of the *national* hopes have been marred by no shadow of doubt, the doctrine of *personal* immortality has generally suggested something of the plaintive note of Tennyson :—

> ' Thou wilt not leave us in the dust:
> Thou madest man, he knows not why;
> He thinks he was not made to die;
> And thou hast made him: thou art just.'

PART II

THE APOCALYPTIC LITERATURE OF LATER JUDAISM

CHAPTER VI

THE CHARACTERISTICS OF THE APOCALYPTIC LITERATURE

BEFORE we pass from our study of the eschatology of the Old Testament to that of the New, it will be necessary to speak at some length of the Jewish apocalyptic literature, which was produced in the two centuries preceding the Christian Era. It is true that the chief source of Primitive Christian Eschatology is the Old Testament itself; but the background of contemporary ideas, which helps us to realise the historical setting of the earliest Christian teaching, is nowhere so vividly portrayed as in the Jewish apocalyptic books. And as these books are still comparatively little known, a few introductory remarks concerning their general characteristics may not be superfluous.[1]

---

[1] Also, as the titles of the non-canonical apocalypses are somewhat unfamiliar, it may be well to give here the abbreviations used in the footnotes to this section, and the editions and translations from which the quotations have been taken:—

Ethiopic Enoch (often called simply 'The Book of Enoch')   Eth. En. (trans. R. H. Charles, Oxford, 1893).
Jubilees . . . . . .   Jub. (trans. Charles, London, 1902).

(*Continued on next page.*)

APOCALYPTIC AND PROPHECY

Recent research in the field of Old Testament study suggests that the interval of time which separates the prophetical books from the apocalypses may not be so great as was formerly imagined. But however this may be, and in spite of many features common to both, there remains a marked cleavage between the two groups of literature.

Before we consider the contrast between them, it will be well to glance at the features which are found in both alike. Apocalyptic was the child of prophecy, and it retains not a little of its parent's character—generally in an accentuated form. One feature in common is that both groups of writings are the literature of a minority. However great their popularity with subsequent generations, they were for the most part written not to express public opinion but in order to influence or alter it. The prophets were disliked by the religious officialdom of their day;[1] and the apocalyptic literature in like manner was regarded by the Rabbis with grave displeasure.[2] Neither prophecy nor apocalyptic were congenial to a period of peace and prosperity; but they sprang up afresh at each crisis of Jewish history, and grew strong in face of persecution and apparent failure. And further, the apocalyptist

---

Testaments of the Twelve Patriarchs.	Test. XII. Patr. (ed. Charles, London, 1908; trans. Charles, London, 1908).
Assumption of Moses . . .	Ass. Moys. (trans. Charles, London, 1897).
Apocalypse of Baruch . . .	Ap. Bar. (trans. Charles, London, 1896).
Slavonic Enoch	Slav. En. (ed. and trans. Charles and Morfill, Oxford, 1896).
Psalms of Solomon . . .	Pss. Sol. (ed. and trans. Ryle and James, Cambridge, 1891).
Sibylline Oracles	Sib. Or. (ed. Alexandre, Paris, 1869).

These books, together with Daniel and 4 Ezra, will be frequently denoted by the convenient general term 'apocalyptic.'

[1] See Amos vii. 10-17; Jer. xx. 1-6, etc.

[2] 'Orthodox Rabbinic Judaism,' says Dr. Oesterley, 'practically banned the entire apocalyptic literature' (*The Doctrine of the Last Things*, p. 66).

resembles the prophet in his firm faith in the Divine purpose. The visions of the prophets remained still unfulfilled, but the apocalyptic writers take up the pen to justify God's ways, and to show how His promises will yet be accomplished. This is the great redeeming feature of the apocalypses; and amid wearisome details and extravagant imagery it is a genuine bond uniting them with the greater men who went before them and who followed after.

But although the prophets and apocalyptists are thus far alike each other, the differences between them are by no means slight.[1] In the first place, the religion of prophet and psalmist was a religion of the Spirit; they spake things which they knew for themselves, and testified of what they had seen in their own spiritual life. But the religion of the Jewish apocalyptist is a religion of authority; he speaks of things which other men had seen. He searches the Scriptures diligently, and interprets the old message anew; but he states explicitly that it is not a fresh message. Apocalyptic is the literature of an age which had lost faith in its own inspiration; which reverenced the past, and had hope for the future, but held the present in low esteem.

And there is another point of contrast. The enthusiasm of the prophets was an enthusiasm for great moral principles; in their writings the preaching of *righteousness* is never absent,—indeed, it is the dominant keynote, to which everything else is subordinated. But in the apocalyptic books, 'righteousness' tends to become merely one among the many features of the traditional religion, all of which are regarded as equally authoritative. Hence we find that the little details, which the prophet freely employed, simply in order to

---

[1] The remarks which follow apply only to the Jewish apocalypses, not to the Christian Apocalypse of St. John, and not in all cases to the Book of Daniel.

illustrate his main contention, are regarded by the apocalyptist as possessing great importance in themselves; so that he studies them with the painstaking diligence of the antiquary, and discovers a hidden meaning in them with the ingenuity of the learned specialist. In his eyes, every sentence of the prophetic writings is a prediction of some event which is predestined to happen, in order 'that it may be fulfilled which was spoken by the prophets.' We find, for instance, in many of the apocalypses, elaborate calculations as to the number of days destined to elapse before the final Consummation. These calculations sometimes take the form of a new interpretation of an old prophecy. Thus the prophecy of Jeremiah, which foretold that seventy years would elapse before the New Era would begin,[1] is interpreted afresh by Daniel to mean seventy *weeks of years* (*i.e.* seventy periods of seven years each),[2] in order that the prophecy may apply to the present distresses under Antiochus.

And because the majority of the apocalyptists lacked the prophetic sense of the supreme importance of moral teaching, their attitude towards the Last Things, while similar in form to that of the prophets, is in spirit considerably different. The prophets look for a catastrophic end of this world on moral grounds, because human sin must bring down a terrible judgment. Most of the apocalyptists, on the other hand, believe that the Last Things are at hand chiefly because the times are too evil to last any longer, and because the predestined signs are already fulfilled. The prophets speak of the future judgment mainly as an incentive to well-doing in the present; the apocalyptists seem to delight to dwell on the Last Things rather because they will afford a relief from the miseries of this present world. That

---

[1] Jer. xxv. 12.   [2] The phrase used is שָׁבֻעִים שִׁבְעִים, Dan. ix. 24, etc.

'prophecy sought to make men better; apocalyptic sought to make men better off,'[1] may be an exaggerated statement; but it draws attention to a difference which really exists.

But it is above all in their *literary form* that the apocalypses display their most distinctive feature, as compared with the prophetical books. For one thing, all the Jewish apocalypses are pseudonymous. Whether this was originally intended to deceive, or whether it was at the first a recognised conventional form, may be open to doubt; but it is certain that in later times Jews and Christians alike believed that the apocalypses were genuine writings by the Fathers of the Jewish Church. Enoch, Abraham, the Twelve Patriarchs, Isaiah, Baruch, Ezra,—these and many other famous names were adopted to give a semblance of authority to the aspirations of unknown Jews who lived in the closing years of Israel's national existence.

The assumption of a spurious authorship also involved the assumption of spurious dates; and so we are dependent upon the internal evidence alone for determining the real dates of the books. Fortunately the peculiar structure of the apocalypses renders the determination of their dates easier than might be expected. They generally begin by describing how a revelation was given long ago to the supposed author of the book, and sometimes there is a further explanation of the way in which this revelation had been lost to mankind and only recently discovered. Then follows an account of the revelation itself, which in most cases takes the form of a 'prediction' of the history of Israel from the times of the supposed author till the Last Things. Generally, the first part of this 'revelation' is easily interpreted; if once we can get the clue to the

[1] C. W. Votaw, in the *Biblical World* (Chicago), April 1908.

VALUE OF THE APOCALYPSES

writer's symbolism, we find no difficulty in following his descriptions of past history, which are for the most part obvious enough, though given in the form of predictions of the future. But just before the 'revelation' comes to deal with the Last Things, we always find a sudden change. The symbolical description ceases to agree in detail with any known historical events, and often becomes simply an enlarged reproduction of the eschatological imagery of the prophets. This gives the clue to the date of the book. The point where the symbolism ceases to correspond with earthly history, and shoots up (as it were) into the realms of visionary expectations, is the point in history at which the writers themselves were living, and up to which they were able to describe the events that lay behind them, with elaborate, and sometimes picturesque, symbolism; but after that point, when they come to the evil times which lay before them, they all repeat with varying language and imagery the same message: 'The end is at hand.'[1]

Perhaps some may feel inclined to ask if there can be any value in a literature founded on a pious fraud and ending in an irresponsible fancy. We would answer that an acquaintance with this literature is not only valuable, but essential, to the student of primitive Christianity. The apocalypses, because they were popular rather than official, give us a unique picture of the hopes and thoughts of the masses to whom our Lord preached; they help to bridge the gulf between the Old Testament and the New; and they throw perhaps more light on Primitive Christian Eschatology than does even the Old Testament itself. Every part

[1] It is interesting to note that, as far back as 1840, Dr. Arnold of Rugby clearly perceived this characteristic in the Book of Daniel. 'You can trace distinctly,' he says, 'the date when it was written, because the events up to that date are given with historical minuteness, totally unlike the character of real prophecy; and beyond that date all is imaginary' (Stanley, *Life of Dr. Arnold*, London, 1845, vol. ii. p. 195).

of eschatological doctrine is discussed by the apocalyptic writers; not only the Last Judgment and the Kingdom of God, but also such matters as the intermediate state, prayers for the dead, the nature of the resurrection-body, the number of the elect, and many other like questions. The difficulty for the student of eschatology is to select out of the perplexing mass of details those features which are of real importance.

From what has been said above, it will be evident that if we would appreciate the teaching of apocalyptic literature aright, it will be necessary for us first to consider the historical circumstances under which it came into being.

For some centuries after the return from the Captivity, Jewish history, under the rule of the Persians and the Ptolemies, was on the whole uneventful. Later ages looked back on this period as a time of trouble and oppression,[1] but there was no great outstanding crisis. This absence of stirring events tended to foster that extreme reverence for the past, to which reference has already been made in connection with the teaching of the scribes.[2] For there was no special call rousing men to vigorous action, nothing to draw out striking traits of character; and so the contrast between the commonplace present and the romantic past was brought home to the people, and increased their reverence for the days of old. In moderation, this reverence was right and good; but it soon began to degenerate into Pharisaic legalism, and sapped the vigour of all wholesome self-confidence in the present.

In this period, there was one very far-reaching movement, resulting from the settlements of Jews in Egypt and Alexandria. These colonial Jews soon began to

---

[1] Eth. En. lxxxix. 73-77. See below, and Charles's *Enoch*, notes *ad loc.*
[2] See above, p. 40 ff.

CLASSIFICATION OF THE APOCALYPSES 57

adopt broader views than their brethren of the mother country, and the rise of the Hellenising party at Jerusalem—that is to say, the party which favoured the adoption of Greek customs and ideas among the Jews—may be traced mainly to the spread of their opinions. The conflict between the Hellenising Jews and their stricter brethren forms an important element in the background of the apocalyptic literature, from its rise in the second century B.C., onwards till the Christian Era.

The course of Jewish history during this period suggests a convenient classification of the apocalyptic books :—

1. The apocalypses of the Maccabean period.
2. The apocalypses of the Pharisees.
3. The apocalypses of the fall of Jerusalem.

Under these three headings the apocalyptic writings will be considered in the chapters that follow.

CHAPTER VII

THE APOCALYPSES OF THE MACCABEES

THERE is now a general agreement among scholars that the age which gave birth to the earliest Jewish apocalypses that have come down to us was the age of the Maccabees (*circa* 170-100 B.C.). In order to understand the evidence upon which this conclusion is based, it may be well to recall briefly the circumstances of the Maccabean revolt.

Under the favour of the Seleucid dynasty the Hellenising Jews flourished exceedingly; and as they grew stronger, the rigid Jews, for their part, grew more and more exclusive. In the Books of the Maccabees, we find the pious 'Chasidim' or Puritan Jews gazing horror-struck at the half-naked athletes who disported themselves in the Greek gymnasium under the very shadow of the House of the Lord.[1] The enthusiasm for sport infected every class; the very priests abandoned the performance of their sacred duties and rushed away to the palaestra as soon as they heard the signal for the games to begin.[2] It was no wonder that the indignation of the devout Jews became uncontrollable, and that the city was in a state of perpetual riot.[3] At length the King (Antiochus Epiphanes) determined to tolerate it no longer; and in 170 B.C. he entered Jerusalem on his

---
[1] 1 Macc. i. 14; 2 Macc. iv. 12, 13.
[2] 2 Macc. iv. 13-15. [3] 2 Macc. v. 1-10.

return from Egypt, pillaged and profaned the Temple, and massacred many Jews.[1]

But even this was not the end. The next year he was bitterly enraged at the failure of his third Egyptian campaign through Roman interference, and apparently determined to vent his wrath on the unhappy Jews. He appears in the rôle of the champion of the gods of Greece, determined at all costs to convert the Jews from their narrow superstition, and bring them into an enlightened and world-wide church of paganism. The Jews were forbidden on pain of death to perform the rites of their national religion. Swine's flesh was forced into their mouths, and those who persisted in the practices of their faith were subjected to terrible tortures. Worst of all, the Temple at Jerusalem was filled with the immoral orgies of the Syrian cults; and on the 15th of Chisleu, B.C. 168, the tide of profanity reached its height, when upon the sacred altar of Jahveh was placed 'the abomination of desolation'—a little idol altar of Zeus Olympius.[2]

An impartial observer would have said that the Jewish religion must be doomed to annihilation before the forces of the Syrian Empire. But it was not so. A mere handful of Jewish fanatics rose in revolt, thrust back the forces of pagan civilisation, and saved the Chosen People of God. And the leader of the insurgents was Judas the Maccabee.

This organised attempt by the Syrian king to crush out the very existence of Judaism was the greatest crisis which had come upon the religion of Israel since the days of the Exile,—if not since the days of Elijah; and it was this crisis which first gave birth to the Jewish apocalypses. From this time onwards they continued

---

[1] 1 Macc. i. 20-28 ; 2 Macc. v. 11-23.
[2] 1 Macc. i. 41-64 ; 2 Macc. vi. 1-vii. 42.

to appear at intervals till the end of the first century A.D., when the Jews ceased to exist as a nation.

The Maccabean revolt was followed by the rule of the Maccabean priest-kings and their Hasmonean successors. For the moment, the complete success of the revolt disarmed all hostile criticism, and the rule of the first priest-kings seems to have given general satisfaction. Indeed, it appears that some enthusiasts held that the Messianic Era was actually being fulfilled through the rule of the Levitical Maccabees; and even the puritan Chasidim, now generally known as the 'Pharisees,' gave their support to the movement, and sought to justify by spurious prophecies this novel supremacy of the tribe of Levi.[1]

But the Hasmoneans did not long retain the primitive zeal of their Maccabean forefathers. Prosperity made them worldly and secular; and they allied themselves with the Sadducees or 'latitudinarian' party, who used every opportunity of oppressing the strict Pharisees. So ill-will grew up between the Pharisees and the Hasmonean dynasty, and under Hyrcanus (B.C. 135-106) it culminated in an open breach between the Pharisees and the allied forces of Hasmoneans and Sadducees. But in the 'Maccabean period' this party-feeling, although steadily growing in intensity, had not yet become the all-absorbing topic of national interest, as it did become in the following century.

There are five apocalypses generally assigned to the Maccabean age—three of them apparently written about the time of the revolt, and two under the priest-kings :—

[1] See Charles's *Test. XII. Patriarchs* (Eng. transl.), Introduction, pp. xv f.

A. {
 1. Daniel
 2. Ethiopic Enoch, 83-90
 3. Ethiopic Enoch, 1-36
} Time of the revolt.

B. {
 4. Book of Jubilees
 5. Testaments of the XII. Patriarchs (groundwork of)
} Period of the priest-kings.

Several of these writings are of the very first importance to the student of Christian eschatology; and our estimate of their character and place in the history of doctrine, will depend in great measure upon the historical period to which we are led to assign them. And since the question of their dates has been the subject of much controversy—particularly in the case of Daniel and Enoch [1]—it seems desirable at this point to indicate the reasons why they are assigned in these pages to the period of the Maccabees.[2]

---

[1] The Ethiopic 'Book of Enoch' is admitted on all hands to be a collection of various apocalypses, all written under the same pseudonym, but of different dates; nor does the present order of the component parts appear to be in chronological succession. It is not always easy to determine with certainty the dates of the various sections; but on the whole, Dr. Charles's conclusions appear to be the most probable, and have been followed in these pages, the references being in all cases to his chapter-divisions:—

Chapters i.-xxxvi.   Circ. 170 B.C.
,,   xxxvii.-lxx.   First half of first century B.C. ('The Similitudes.')
,,   lxxii.-lxxviii. etc.   Date uncertain. ('The Book of Celestial Physics.')
,,   lxxxiii.-xc.   Circ. 166 B.C. ('The Dream-Visions.')
,,   xci.-civ.   Last quarter of second century B.C.

The chapters not included in the above, together with many short sections, are pronounced by Charles to be interpolations.

[2] The following table gives the chief dates in the Maccabean period:—

A. *The revolt*—
 B.C. 170 (or 169).   Antiochus Epiphanes pollutes the Temple.
 B.C. 168.   Daily sacrifice interrupted, and the 'abomination of desolation' set up, on the 15th of Chisleu.
 B.C. 167.   Beginning of the Maccabean revolt.
 B.C. 166.   Battle of Emmaus.—Success of the insurgents.

B. *The period of the priest-kings*—
 B.C. 165.   The Temple again dedicated to the God of Israel.
 B.C. 156-135.   Jonathan and Simon High-priests.—Growth of Secularisation.

(*Continued on next page.*)

The most famous of all Jewish apocalypses is the Book of Daniel. The recent discoveries of hitherto unknown examples of the apocalyptic books have shown how closely Daniel is allied with these. Yet in some respects the tone of the book reminds us of the prophets; for Daniel was one of the pioneers of the new type of literature,[1] and so we find a freshness and vigour which is characteristic of prophecy rather than of apocalyptic. It is the one representative of the apocalypses in the Canon of the Old Testament, and it is worthy of this distinction.

The first six chapters of Daniel are narrative, and the date of their composition is by no means certain. But the later chapters are thoroughly in the style of the apocalypses generally. If we interpret the visions in these latter chapters by the method which we should unhesitatingly apply to the non-canonical apocalypses, we find that the visions cease to correspond with history when they reach the account of the persecution of Antiochus Epiphanes. At this point the writer always begins to describe the portents of the Last Days, which he depicts with intense longing and immediate expectation. Three times the visions unmistakably end with this same historical crisis.

For instance, in chap. vii. we first read of the beasts which symbolise the Kingdoms of the world, and then of the little horn,[2] the meaning of which is thus interpreted:—

'Another King shall arise . . . and he shall speak words against the Most High, and shall wear out the

---

B.C. 135-106.   John Hyrcanus.—Zenith of the worldly prosperity of the Priest-Kings.—Open breach with the Pharisees.
B.C. 106-69.   Decline of the Hasmonean dynasty.

[1] With the possible exception of Eth. En. i.-xxxvi. (see below, p. 66), Daniel is the earliest of the Jewish apocalyptic books.
[2] Dan. vii. 8.

saints of the Most High, and he shall think to change the times and the Law; and they shall be given into his hand until a time and times and half a time.'[1]

The description applies perfectly to Antiochus Epiphanes. Immediately after this vision of the 'little horn,' comes the famous picture of the Last Judgment by the 'Ancient of Days.'

Similarly, the Vision of the Ram and the He-goat in chap. viii. culminates with a 'little horn' which takes away the continual burnt offering and casts down the place of the sanctuary. But in the end he will be destroyed by Divine power.[2]

The interpretation of the third vision (chap. ix.) is so obscure[3] that it can scarcely be used as evidence of date; but in the fourth vision (chaps. x. and xi.) there is a full account of the history of Antiochus Epiphanes, and his Egyptian campaigns:—

'Ships of Kittim [the Romans] shall come against him; therefore he shall be grieved, and shall return, and have indignation against the Holy Covenant, and shall do his pleasure; he shall even return, and have regard unto them that forsake the Holy Covenant. And arms shall stand on his part; and they shall profane the sanctuary, even the fortress, and shall take away the continual burnt offering, and they shall set up the abomination that maketh desolate. And such as do wickedly against the Covenant shall he pervert by flatteries; but the people that know their God shall be strong, and do exploits. . . . And he [the King] shall prosper till the indignation be accomplished; for that which is determined shall be done.'[4]

Further accounts of political events follow, closing

---

[1] Dan. vii. 24, 25.   [2] Dan. viii. 11-25.
[3] See Driver, *Literature of the Old Testament*, 7th edition, pp. 495-496, and Bevan's *Daniel, ad loc.*
[4] Dan. xi. 30-32, 36.

with the death of Antiochus. Then immediately the Messianic Woes, the Resurrection, and the heavenly Kingdom are to take place.

The quotations given above are sufficient to show that the detailed historical references in these visions are of a kind entirely different from the predictions of the prophets. And unless they are unique examples of miraculous prediction, to which we have no parallel elsewhere, the evidence clearly points to a date soon after 168 B.C.[1] Persecution was then pressing heavily on the people, and the success of the Maccabean revolt was not yet assured. The purpose of the book was to strengthen the hands of the Maccabees, and to cheer the hearts of those who were despondent. Under the dramatic form of a revelation to one of the Hebrew saints, the writer proclaims his faith in a miraculous salvation near at hand.

We have considered the evidence for the date of Daniel at some length, because the eschatology of the book is exceedingly important, and our whole view of the development of Jewish eschatology would be changed if we held that it was really written in the Babylonian Captivity.

In the 'Dream-Visions' of Enoch (Eth. En. lxxxiii.-xc.) we have another very interesting apocalypse of the time of the Maccabean revolt. Enoch relates to his son Methuselah two visions which he has seen. The first is a short vision of the destruction of the earth,

---

[1] Some put the date as late as 164 B.C.; but the language suggests that the anticipated repulse of the persecutor had not yet been fully accomplished; and the vague prediction in viii. 14 (וְנִצְדַּק קֹדֶשׁ) suggests that the manner in which the Holy Place was to be 'justified' was not yet known—in other words, that the Temple had not yet been cleansed. If so, the date will be before 165 B.C. In any case, it is clear that the death of Antiochus, 164 B.C., was still in the future, for it is described as contemporaneous with the advent of Michael the archangel.

THE 'DREAM-VISIONS' OF ENOCH

and the second (chaps. lxxxiv.-xc.) is a detailed apocalypse of the history of Israel. At first sight the imagery seems hopelessly confusing; we read of horses and bulls and goats and wolves and lambs and rams and shepherds, till all seems chaos; but when once certain historical events are recognised, the surrounding symbolism begins to become clear. Throughout the vision, 'the sheep' denote Israel. For the determination of the date, only the concluding portion is important. In chap. lxxxix. 72 ff., we read an unmistakable picture of the return from Babylon, the rebuilding of the Temple, and the dispersion among the Gentiles. Then, in chap. xc., we are brought down to the period of the Ptolemies; after which we are told that lambs are born by the sheep, and begin to open their eyes and cry. But the sheep do not cry to them nor hear them.[1] This, as Charles suggests, is doubtless a reference to the rise of the strict 'Chasidim,' who lifted up their voices unsuccessfully against the growing popularity of Hellenism. Then comes the persecution under Antiochus: 'the ravens flew upon those lambs and took one of those lambs, and dashed the sheep in pieces and devoured them.'[2] But the sheep and the rams band themselves together under 'a great horn of one of the sheep' (*i.e.* Judas the Maccabee), and against them are gathered 'all the eagles and vultures and ravens and kites' (*i.e.* the Gentile oppressors), together with 'the sheep of the field' (*i.e.* the apostate Jews who had submitted to the pagan rites).[3]

At this point the vision ceases to correspond with history, and begins to describe a Divine intervention and the great Last Judgment. This defines the date with unusual sharpness; and there can be little doubt that

[1] Eth. En. xc. 6, 7.   [2] Eth. En. xc. 8.   [3] Eth. En. xc. 9-16.

the vision was written just before the Battle of Emmaus, 166 B.C., when Judas routed the Syrian army under Gorgias.[1] In the view of the seer, the preparations for this battle (one of the most momentous in Jewish history) are the fulfilment of the last 'gathering of the nations' foretold by the prophets, which was to be one of the signs of the Last Things.

In Ethiopic Enoch i.-xxxvi. there are scarcely any direct references to contemporary historical events. We find mention of 'oppression and unrighteousness,'[2] but the speculative tone of the book suggests that the writer did not live in the midst of a great crisis.

Dr. Charles considers that this section of Enoch is the earliest of all the apocalypses, written *circa* 170 B.C., before the days of the great persecution.[3] This conclusion is based mainly on the study of the literary relations between this section of Enoch and chapters lxxxiii.-xc., which clearly date from the age of the Maccabees. Apart from the evidence of the relation between these two sections of Enoch, there seems very little to indicate whether the book was written (as Charles holds) before 170 B.C., or some thirty years later, when the first enthusiasm for the Maccabees had departed, but before the open breach between them and the Pharisees. The elaborate character of the eschatology seems in favour of the later date. But in either case, we shall not be far wrong in considering this section among the apocalypses of the Maccabees.

The Book of Jubilees was clearly written by a Pharisee of the Pharisees. Nowhere do we find the teaching of the scribes in its extreme form more clearly

---

[1] 1 Macc. iv. 1-25.   [2] Eth. En. x. 20.
[3] Charles's *Enoch*, pp. 56, 220-221.

reflected. The author provides us with a 'revised edition' of the Mosaic Books, in which everything that could shock the feelings of the most fastidious Pharisee is carefully removed or altered. He deplores the guilt and profanity of Israel,[1] but does not blame the rulers or the priesthood. On the contrary, he assigns the highest honours to Levi as well as to Judah.[2] Hence it seems reasonable to infer that 'Jubilees' was written by a Pharisee who adhered to the Hasmonean dynasty. Dr. Charles considers that the date falls between 135 and 105 B.C.[3]

In the case of the Testaments of the Twelve Patriarchs,[4] the determination of the date is peculiarly complicated, owing to the numerous interpolations which appear to have been made at various periods of history. It was formerly regarded as a Christian apocalypse,[5] and there are numerous passages obviously from Christian hands. But the Christian tone is limited to these sections, and there can be little doubt that Dr. Charles is right in concluding that these are interpolations, and that the groundwork is Jewish. But then comes a further difficulty. In parts of the Testaments we find, as in Jubilees, that the glorification of Levi is specially prominent,[6] while in other sections the priesthood is denounced with relentless severity.[7] Dr. Charles explains this by a theory that the original parts of the book were written circa 109-107 B.C., by a Pharisee who was favourably disposed towards the powers that be; but that Jewish interpolations were

---
[1] Jub. iv. 1-26, xxiii. 16-19.
[2] Jub. xxxi. 13-17.   [3] Charles's *Jubilees*, Introduction, p. xiii.
[4] The references below, where not otherwise specified, are to Dr. Charles's *English translation*, not to his *Greek Versions*.
[5] *e.g.*, see Sinker, *Testaments of the Twelve Patriarchs*, 1869.
[6] Test. Levi viii., Test. Judah xxi., Test. Issachar v., etc.
[7] Test. Levi xiv.-xvi., Test. Dan. v., etc.

made by another Pharisee, after the breach with the Hasmonean High Priests. Granting that Dr. Charles is probably right in his main contentions, it remains necessary to use the evidence of the 'Testaments' with caution, because it is exceedingly difficult to determine the exact points where the interpolations begin and end.

Having thus indicated the character of the evidence for the Maccabean date of this group of apocalypses, we are now in a position to consider the Doctrine of the Last Things as taught in their pages. The outlines of the eschatology of the prophets are retained by these early apocalyptic writers. The Last Judgment and the coming of the New Era continue to be the supreme events of the future. The doctrine of the resurrection receives new importance; on the other hand the hope of a Davidic Messiah all but disappears. We find new speculations about the intermediate state of departed souls, and an elaborate doctrine of angels. In the days of the prosperous Maccabean High-Priests, the hope of a Messianic Priest from the tribe of Levi comes much to the fore. And for the study of the New Testament, perhaps the most important feature of all is the figure of the 'son of man' in Daniel vii.

It will be convenient to consider the apocalyptic doctrines of the Last Things in what we may roughly call their chronological order:—

(a) The Intermediate State.
(b) The Resurrection.
(c) The Last Judgment.
(d) The Messianic Hope.
(e) Final Destinies.
(f) The Doctrine of Angels.

THE INTERMEDIATE STATE

(a) *The Intermediate State of Departed Souls*

In the Old Testament we found no details of the condition of souls after death; all alike shared in the colourless fate of Sheol. Nor is this theme dealt with in Daniel, nor in Ethiopic Enoch lxxxiii.-xc. But in Ethiopic Enoch i.-xxxvi. we find a highly elaborate and detailed description of the intermediate state. As the belief in a future resurrection of individual souls became more and more definite, it was natural that men should desire to know something about the 'waiting-time.'

In Ethiopic Enoch xxii. the patriarch goes to a mountain in the west, and sees there four deep hollows in the mountain, smooth and black. The archangel Rufael tells him that these are the abodes of dead souls until the Judgment. Unlike the Sheol of the ancient Hebrews, there are here divisions between the righteous and the wicked, and there is also a division between the wicked who escaped the hand of justice on earth and those sinners who met their deserts and are 'complete in their crimes.' These last will not have to undergo the judgment; but the other two classes of souls are even now experiencing a foretaste of their final destinies; the righteous are happy, the sinners are 'in great pain.' Thus the moral law, the sign of the rule of Jahveh, is now regarded as supreme even in the abodes of the dead.

In Jubilees, 'Sheol' denotes the final place of punishment for 'the profane.' The moral law reigns in Sheol, but apparently only in its sterner aspect, as the law of punishment :—

> 'There will be no hope for them [the profane] in the land of the living; for they will descend into Sheol, and into the place of condemnation will they go.'[1]

[1] Jub. xxii. 22.

From the Second Book of Maccabees, an historical work written about 160 B.C.,[1] we gather some interesting sidelights on the current idea of the intermediate state. We are there told that prayers and sacrifices offered by the living can help to remit the guilt of those among God's people who have fallen into sin. The circumstances are as follows: Judas the Maccabee and his adherents, in bringing back the bodies of some of their comrades who had fallen in battle, find under the clothes of the latter some idolatrous images.[2] This discovery naturally causes dismay to the orthodox Jews :—

> 'All therefore . . . betook themselves unto supplication, beseeching that the sin committed might be wholly blotted out. And the noble Judas . . . sent unto Jerusalem to offer a sacrifice for sin, doing therein right well and honourably, in that he took thought for a resurrection. For if he were not expecting that they who had fallen would rise again, it were superfluous and idle to pray for the dead. . . . Wherefore he made the propitiation for them that had died, that they might be released from their sin.'[3]

This passage is of unusual interest, expressing as it does a clear belief in the value of prayers and sacrifices for the dead, of which we find no trace in earlier Jewish thought, and which never seems to have secured a recognised place in Judaism.

(b) *The Resurrection*

In the Old Testament, the resurrection was always regarded as a special privilege for the righteous Jews. But when we come to the apocalypses, we find a new doctrine; not only will the righteous be raised unto life,

---

[1] See (*e.g.*) Fairweather in Hastings' *Dictionary of the Bible*, vol. iii. p. 191.
[2] 2 Macc. xii. 38-40.   [3] 2 Macc. xii. 41-45.

but the sinners will be raised for judgment. So in the famous passage of Daniel :—

'Many of them that sleep in the dust of the earth shall awake, some to everlasting life, and some to shame and everlasting contempt.'[1]

Again, in Enoch i.-xxxvi., we are told that sinners who have met their deserts in this world will not be raised for the judgment;[2] but it is implied that all other Israelites will share in the resurrection, both the righteous, and also the sinners who have escaped unpunished in this life. In neither case is there any thought of a 'general' resurrection, in the sense which would include the Gentiles; but the resurrection of the *sinners* among the Israelites is certainly found in these Maccabean apocalypses, and found there for the first time in Jewish history.[3]

In one passage of the Book of Jubilees, we find mention of a purely spiritual resurrection of the righteous, or rather of immortality without a resurrection of the flesh :—

'Their bones will rest in the earth; and their spirits will have much joy.'[4]

The earlier Jews never seemed to think of the spirit apart from the body; and this passage suggests that Greek thought is here making itself felt.

In Enoch lxxxiii.-xc. there is no clear reference to the resurrection. But after the judgment-scene there is a strange account of the birth of a white bull, to which all beasts and birds do reverence; and this is followed by a transformation of 'all their kinds' into white oxen;

---

[1] Dan. xii. 2.   [2] Eth. En. xxii. 13.
[3] The older prophetic idea, of a resurrection restricted to the just, still continued; see Test. XII. Patr., Judah xxv.
[4] Jub. xxiii. 30.

and the first among them (*i.e.* the white bull) becomes a 'great animal,' and the Lord of the sheep rejoices over them all.[1] It is not easy to gather exactly what the writer intended to symbolise; but apparently he hoped for a general 'transformation' of all men who survived after the Last Judgment. This idea of 'transformation' is very nearly akin to that of the spiritual resurrection in Jubilees; but in this section of Enoch there is nothing corresponding to the wide resurrection-doctrine of Daniel; for the 'transformation' is a privilege granted to the righteous only, and it follows after the Judgment instead of preceding it.

It is interesting to compare with these apocalypses a passage from the account of the Maccabean revolt in the Second Book of Maccabees. The narrative tells of seven brothers who were tortured to death by having their tongues and hands cut off and their bodies burnt because they would not conform to the demands of Antiochus. Of the third brother we read:—

> 'He quickly put out his tongue, and stretched forth his hands courageously, and nobly said: From heaven I possess these; and for his laws' sake I contemn these; and from him I hope to receive these back again.'[2]

And the fourth brother tells his executioner:—

> 'We shall be raised up again by God; as for thee, thou shalt have no resurrection unto life.'[3]

The doctrine implied by these two passages, taken in conjunction with one another, is that there will be a bodily resurrection, and that the righteous only will share this privilege.

(c) *The Last Judgment*

Probably few passages in the Old Testament have exercised so great an influence upon Christian eschatology

---
[1] Eth. En. xc. 37, 38.   [2] 2 Macc. vii. 10, 11.   [3] 2 Macc. vii. 14.

as the picture of the Last Judgment in Daniel vii. 9-14. After the vision of the little horn (Epiphanes), the seer perceives the Almighty in the form of a patriarch ('an ancient of days')[1] taking His seat on a throne, surrounded with fire and ministering spirits; 'the judgment was set, and the books were opened.'[2] Throughout the visions of Daniel, the empires of the world are frequently depicted under the symbols of great beasts. But in this vision there enters a new figure; not this time in the form of a beast, but in human form,—'one like unto a son of man.'[3]

> 'I saw in the night visions, and, behold, there came with the clouds of heaven one like unto a son of man, and he came even to the ancient of days, and they brought him near before him. And there was given him dominion, and glory, and a kingdom, that all the peoples, nations, and languages should serve him; his dominion is an everlasting dominion, which shall not pass away, and his kingdom that which shall not be destroyed' (verse 14).

In verse 27 the interpretation of this vision of 'a son of man' is given :—

> 'The kingdom and the dominion, and the greatness of the kingdoms under the whole heavens, shall be given to the people of the saints of the Most High; his kingdom is an everlasting kingdom, and all dominions shall serve and obey him.'

Comparing this language of the interpretation with the language of the vision in verse 14, there can be little question that the 'son of man' symbolises 'the people of the saints of the Most High.' Just as the savage kingdoms of this world were seen in the forms of fearsome beasts, so the Kingdom of God, the Israel

---

[1] See Rev. i. 14.
[2] For the 'Divine register,' in which the names of the elect are enrolled, cf. Ezek. xiii. 9, etc.
[3] כְּבַר אֱנָשׁ

of the future, appears under the nobler form of a human figure, and its Divine origin is symbolised by the descent from heaven. In some of the later apocalypses[1] we find a 'revised edition' of this vision, in which the 'son of man' is explained to be the Messiah of Israel. But there is little or nothing in the original narrative in Daniel to imply this identification of the 'son of man' with the Messiah;[2] though it is easy to see how it might naturally be suggested by the fact that the purified Israel of the future (symbolised by the 'son of man') and the Messiah are both alike in being God's agents to execute His judgment on the earth.

In Ethiopic Enoch lxxxiii.-xc., the description of the Last Judgment begins at xc. 18: 'I saw till the Lord of the sheep came unto them, and took the staff of His wrath into His hand, and smote the earth so that it was rent asunder.' The judgment-scene is similar to that in Daniel vii. First the fallen angels and apostate Jews are judged and cast into the abyss of fire on the South of the Temple, where the faithful watch them burning.[3] The old Temple is 'folded up,' and 'laid in a place in the south of the land'; and the Lord of the sheep brings a new and greater Temple, and sets it up on the site of the old one.[4] Before the New Temple are gathered the pure white sheep (the strict Chasidim), and all the sheep who had been dispersed. They are so many that the Temple will not hold them, and all the beasts of the earth do obeisance to them.[5] We are reminded of the great white-robed multitude, 'which no

[1] *e.g.* the Similitudes of Enoch. See below, p. 86.
[2] See, however, p. 88, note 1.
[3] Eth. En. xc. 26, 27; 'a mark of the savage feelings excited by the persecution.'
[4] Eth. En. xc. 29; based on the prophetic promises of the 'New Jerusalem.' See above, p. 33.
[5] Eth. En. xc. 30.

man could number,' in the 7th chapter of the Apocalypse of St. John.

There is more originality in the idea of the Judgment in the Book of Jubilees. The writer places his 'golden age' in the days of Abraham; the times since then have been a period of corruption, which will culminate in the Messianic Woes. 'Calamity follows on calamity'— illness, snow, famine, sword, captivity, etc.[1] But as the Woes increase, the profanity of Israel will grow worse, till God raises up against them 'the sinners of the Gentiles.' Then will come a change :—

> 'The children will begin to study the Laws, . . . and to return to the path of righteousness; and the days will begin to grow many amongst those children of men, till their days draw nigh to a thousand years . . . and the righteous will see all their judgments and all their curses on their enemies.'[2]

This picture differs in several respects from the earlier descriptions of judgment. Instead of the Messianic Woes being the *immediate* prelude to the Judgment, they are here a kind of chastisement upon Israel in order to produce a spirit of repentance; and not till then, after Israel has repented, is there a judgment of condemnation, on the Gentiles alone. The era of perfection is not to be inaugurated by a catastrophic miracle of Divine power, in accordance with the normal teaching both of the Old Testament and of the apocalypses; but it is to be brought about (at any rate in part) by a gradual evolutionary and purgatorial process.[3] And closely allied with this idea of the 'upward trend' of this world's history we find the belief that the goal of history is to be, not the destruction of this world, but the establishment of the Kingdom

---

[1] Jub. xxiii. 16-19.   [2] Jub. xxiii. 26-30.
[3] Cf. Test. XII. Patr., Dan. vi. 6.

of God on earth, when God will 'descend and dwell with Israel throughout eternity.'[1] But these ideas—in some ways anticipating a point of view which has become prevalent in modern times—do not seem to have gained any general acceptance among the Jews, and scarcely a trace of them is found in later Jewish literature.

In the original parts of the Testaments of the Twelve Patriarchs, the Judgment is to follow the resurrection, and apparently there is to be a double judgment, first on Israel, and then on the Gentiles.[2] There is one remarkable passage, in which we read how the individual soul meets with retribution at once after death :—

> 'The latter ends of men do show their righteousness or unrighteousness, when they meet the angels of the Lord and of Satan. For when the soul departs troubled, it is tormented by the evil spirit which also it served in lusts and evil works. But if it is peaceful with joy, it meeteth the angel of peace, and he leadeth it into eternal life.'[3]

The language is strongly reminiscent of the Zoroastrian Avesta.[4]

One other passage in this group of apocalypses, dealing with the Last Judgment, is of interest, because it is quoted in Jude 14, 15 :—

> 'And lo! He comes with ten thousands of Holy Ones, to execute judgment upon them, and He will destroy the ungodly, and will convict all flesh of all that the sinners and ungodly have wrought and ungodly committed against him.'[5]

---

[1] Jub. i. 26.
[2] Test. Benjamin x. Perhaps the whole passage (and not merely part of it, as Charles thinks) is a Christian interpretation.
[3] Test. Asher vi. 4.
[4] See below, Appendix C. [5] Eth. En. i. 9.

THE MESSIAH

Except for this New Testament quotation, the judgment-scene in this section of Enoch does not call for special comment.

(d) *The Messianic Hope*

In most of the Maccabean apocalypses, the hope of a personal Messiah is not prominent. As long as the Maccabees prospered under able leadership, the expectation of a Davidic King seemed scarcely necessary.[1] A few passages, though, may be noticed in this connection.

In Enoch xc. 37 ff. the 'white bull'[2] is evidently a chief man among the people, and Dr. Charles thinks that it is a 'literary reminiscence' of the Messiah of prophecy. But it is a lifeless figure, and plays no essential part in the vision.

In Jubilees there is one passing reference to a coming Prince of the tribe of Judah,[3] but the Messianic Hope is not prominent.

In the Testaments of the Twelve Patriarchs, however, there is a very keen expectation of a great Messianic Priest-King, of the tribe of Levi, side by side with the traditional hope of a Davidic Prince of Judah.[4] The writer links his admiration for the existing dynasty of the Levitical Maccabees with the time-honoured hopes of the prophets—

> 'Levi and Judah were glorified by the Lord even among the sons of Jacob; for the Lord gave them an inheritance; and to Levi He gave the priesthood, and to Judah the Kingdom; and do ye therefore obey them.'[5]

---

[1] The words of Dan. ix. 26, 'the Anointed One shall be cut off,' which suggest a prophecy of the death of the Messiah, are now generally taken to refer to the anointed High-Priest, Onias III., assassinated in 172 B.C. The verses that follow seem to refer to Antiochus Epiphanes.

[2] See above, p. 71. [3] Jub. xxxi. 18.

[4] Test. Levi viii. and xviii., Test. Judah xxi. ; cf. Ps. cx. 4.

[5] Test. Issachar v. 17.

In the 'Testaments' we also find the spirit 'Beliar' referred to as the great opponent of the Messiah; in other words, Beliar is Antichrist.[1]

(e) *Final Destinies*

In the apocalypses of the Maccabean revolt, the Gentiles are viewed simply as instruments in God's hand, by which He carries out His purpose for Israel. As soon as they have performed their appointed work, they are to be destroyed. This exclusive spirit is even more marked in Jubilees.[2] But the author of the Testaments of the Twelve Patriarchs takes a more sympathetic attitude, and hopes for a Messiah who will 'save the race of Israel, and gather together the righteous from amongst the Gentiles.'[3]

In reading of the final destinies of the wicked in these apocalypses, it is well to remember that the distinction which is generally made nowadays between 'destruction' and 'everlasting punishment' was not a distinction recognised by the Jews. They found it very difficult to conceive of utter annihilation; and when they spoke of 'destruction,' they were thinking of the taking away of all that makes life worth living, rather than of 'annihilation' as we understand it. It did not seem to them inconsistent to say: 'The years of your destruction shall be multiplied.'[4]

The descriptions of the final destinies of the righteous call for little comment; they are for the most part repetitions of the prophetic pictures of the Kingdom of God at Jerusalem. Too often we meet with the fierce longing to behold the sufferings of the enemies of Israel.

---

[1] Cf. 2 Cor. vi. 15 (R.V. marg.).
[2] Jub. xxii. 21 ff., etc.; cf. Dan. vii. 11, Eth. En. xc.
[3] Test. Naphthali viii. 3; cf. Test. Levi xviii.; Test. Judah xxiv.; Test. Benjamin x.; but some of these seem very much like Christian interpolations.
[4] Eth. En. v. 5.

ANGELS

The thought of 'spiritual immortality' in Jubilees xxiii., to which we have already referred, is the most important development in this group of apocalypses.

(f) *The Doctrine of Angels*

Angels play such an important part in later eschatology that it seems well to note the extraordinary advance in angelology which is manifest in the Maccabean apocalypses. The names of many of the angels are given,[1] and the fate of fallen angels excites as much interest as the fate of human souls.[2] Michael is the national guardian-angel of Israel,[3] and it is the duty of the angels to intercede for men.[4] This last belief, doubtless, prepared the way for the Christian 'Ora pro nobis.' These beliefs concerning angels and spirits became a special characteristic of the Pharisaic party.[5] Probably they might be traced, at least in part, to Zoroastrian influence.[6]

In conclusion, if we were asked to name the dominant characteristic of the eschatology of the Maccabean period, we might say, that it is inspired by the hope of deliverance from external danger, rather than by the desire for purification from profanity within the nation. In this it differs from the apocalypses of the Pharisees, which we shall consider in the next chapter.

---

[1] *e.g.* Eth. En. xx. and xl.
[2] Eth. En. vi.-x., etc.   [3] Dan. xii. 1, Jub. xv. 31.
[4] Eth. En. xv. 2; cf. Test. Levi v.   [5] Ac. xxiii. 8.
[6] See below, Appendix C. There seem to be traces of Zoroastrianism also in the 'heavenly copies' referred to in Jubilees xv. 27.

CHAPTER VIII

THE APOCALYPSES OF THE PHARISEES

UNDER the head of 'Apocalypses of the Maccabees' we dealt with those 'revelations' which supported the early Maccabean leaders and their successors, the Hasmonean priest-kings. These apocalypses always emanated from the party of the stricter Jews. Soon after the time when the men of this party began to be commonly called 'The Pharisees,' a formal breach took place between them and the powerful State-party, composed of the Hasmoneans and Sadducees. So in this chapter on 'the Apocalypses of the Pharisees,' we shall consider the apocalyptic literature produced by the Pharisees during the period when they were in the minority, and subject to frequent persecution.

After the open rupture with the Hasmoneans in the reign of Hyrcanus, the lot of the Pharisees went from bad to worse. Aristobulus, 'King of the Jews,' was in close league with the Sadducees; and the reign of Alexander Jannaeus (105-78 B.C.) was a time of anarchy, when the Pharisees were ruthlessly massacred. Then followed nine years during which the tables were turned, and a Pharisaic government under Queen Alexandra ruled the Jews. But after Alexandra's death in 69 B.C., another period of Sadducaic oppression and incessant civil wars set in, until order was partially restored by the intervention of Pompey. Thenceforward until the

HISTORY OF THE PHARISEES

Fall of Jerusalem the threatening figure of Rome always forms a dark background to Jewish life. The Romans disliked the Pharisees, who were the most exclusive section of the Jews; but under Roman rule there was less fear of open persecution, and the Pharisees gradually gained the admiration of the people at large, till in the time of our Lord we find that they were the most influential school of thought in the internal politics of Judaea. After that, the Pharisees themselves began to be divided into two sections; the one desiring to transform their aspirations into action in the sphere of practical politics, and the other deprecating any attempt to interfere with the plans of Providence by mingling in secular matters.

The above brief outline of the history may serve to explain why the strong 'party-character' of the apocalypses of the Pharisees begins with the reign of Hyrcanus, and ceases soon after the capture of Jerusalem by Pompey.[1] Thenceforward the all-absorbing topic is the power of Rome.

The chief apocalypses which express the hopes of the oppressed Pharisees are:—

(1) Ethiopic Enoch xci.-civ.
(2) The Similitudes of Enoch (Eth. En. xxxvii.-lxxi.).
(3) Parts of the Testaments of the Twelve Patriarchs.
(4) Psalms of Solomon.
(5) Assumption of Moses.

The evidence for the dates of most of these books depends, not so much on the determination of the exact

---

[1] The chief dates for this period are:—

B.C. 135-106.	John Hyrcanus.—Breach with the Pharisees.
B.C. 106-78.	Alexander Jannaeus.—Severe persecution.
B.C. 78-69.	Pharisaic ascendancy under Alexandra.
B.C. 69-64.	Sadducees again in power.—Incessant wars.
B.C. 63.	Pompey takes Jerusalem.
B.C. 63-A.D. 6.	Judaea more or less subject to Rome; but nominal authority granted to the Herodian dynasty.
A.D. 6.	Judaea annexed to the Roman Province of Syria.

point where the writer ceases to review past history, as on the general tone of the books, which express the feelings of an oppressed and somewhat puritanical minority.

Ethiopic Enoch xci.-civ., for instance, is one long cry for vengeance against the party of the 'unrighteous,' who are rich and powerful,[1] and are aided and abetted by the authorities of law and order.[2] The writer hopes for a great judgment, but there are no clear references to a Messiah. Dr. Charles prefers a date between 104 and 95 B.C., but admits the possibility of a later date (95-79 or 70-64 B.C.). A similar general situation is implied throughout the 'Similitudes' of Enoch (chaps. xxxvii.-lxxi.). 'The sinners' are constantly described as 'the kings and the mighty,' a phrase which suggests the later years of the Hasmonean rulers when they were styled 'Kings of the Jews,' and were in open alliance with the Sadducaic party. The 'Similitudes' may reasonably be assigned to the early years of the first century B.C.[3]

Similarly, certain sections of the Testaments of the Twelve Patriarchs are full of the denunciation of an apostate priesthood. Dr. Charles considers these to be interpolations by a Pharisee after the breach with the Hasmoneans.

In the Psalms of Solomon, we again meet with an incessant outcry against the sinners and ungodly, who are profaning the holy priesthood. But the clear references to the capture of Jerusalem by Pompey and to the death of the great general show that this book is to be placed after 48 B.C.[4]

---

[1] Eth. En. xciv. 6-9, etc.   [2] Eth. En. ciii. 15.

[3] See Charles's *Enoch*, pp. 107-108. Schürer, however, assigns them to the times of Herod (*Jewish People in the time of our Lord*, Eng. trans. Div. II. vol. iii. p. 68).

[4] It is possible that some of the Psalms may be a little earlier. Ryle and James in their edition of the Psalms consider 70-40 B.C. the extreme limits (Introduction, p. xliv).

In the Assumption of Moses, the general tone is considerably different; the denunciation of the Sadducees is not so incessant, and the evidence for date depends rather on the historical allusions. The first six chapters contain a review of Jewish history from the death of Moses down to the reign and death of Herod. After that, the sons of Herod will reign for short periods; and *then* the narrative begins to deal with supernatural portents. It appears from this that the book was written in the early years of the first century A.D. The writer protests against 'the scornful and impious' rule of the Sadducees,[1] but he gives no countenance to the political schemes of the new school of Pharisaic Zealots. Hence Dr. Charles considers that he was an old-fashioned 'Pharisaic Quietist.' It is probable that the Assumption of Moses is the only extant Palestinian apocalypse contemporary with our Lord's life.

We shall now consider the various features of the eschatology of this Pharisaic group of apocalypses in the same order as in the previous chapter.

(a) *The Intermediate State*

We noticed that the Maccabean apocalypses described the abode of the dead as a place of retribution for the deeds done on earth; and the same view is repeated in the apocalypses of the Pharisees, without any developments of special interest. 'Sheol' is generally the place of punishment for the wicked,[2] while the righteous dwell together with the angels in resting-places in heaven, where the Messiah is waiting to be revealed in the Last Days.[3]

---

[1] Ass. Moys. vii.   [2] Eth. En. ciii. 7, etc.
[3] Eth. En. xxxix. 4, 5.

(b) *The Resurrection*

In the earlier apocalypses we found two different expectations of the resurrection; the one, a resurrection of the righteous and the wicked, apparently with their bodies, before the Last Judgment;[1] the other, a spiritual resurrection or 'transformation' of the righteous only, which was to take place after the Judgment, at the beginning of the New Era.[2]

Both these ideas are found again in the apocalypses of the Pharisees. A spiritual resurrection may perhaps be indicated in Ethiopic Enoch xci.-civ.,[3] and possibly also in the Psalms of Solomon;[4] while in Ethiopic Enoch li. the more familiar idea of restoration from the abodes of the dead with a view to the Judgment is clearly expressed.

> 'In those days will the earth also give back those who are treasured up in it, and Sheol also will give back that which it has received, and Hell will give back that which it owes.'[5]

(c) *The Last Judgment*

In the Testament of Benjamin,[6] we noticed an apparent reference to *two* judgments in the Last Days, first upon Israel, then upon the Gentiles. Again, in the Pharisaic apocalypse, Enoch xci., more than one Last Judgment seems to be implied; but the text appears to be confused. As the text stands, the Last Things are described in the following order:—

(i.) In the eighth 'week' of the world's history, the 'righteous' (the Pharisees) will gain the upper hand; they will execute a 'judgment of righteousness' on the

---

[1] Dan. xii. 2; Test. Judah 25, etc.
[2] Eth. En. xc.; Jub. xxiii. 30.
[3] Eth. En. xci. 10, xcii. 3, ciii. 4.
[4] Pss. Sol. iii. 16, xiii. 9, etc.
[5] Eth. En. li. i.
[6] Test. Benj. 10.

THE LAST JUDGMENT

'sinners' (the Sadducees); they will acquire houses for themselves and rebuild the House of God.[1]

(ii.) In the ninth 'world-week,' 'the righteous judgment will be revealed to the whole world,' and 'the world will be written down for destruction.'[2]

(iii.) In the tenth 'world-week' there will be 'the great eternal judgment' on the angels, and the New Heaven (*not* a New Earth) will be created, and 'there will be many weeks without number in goodness and righteousness.'[3]

It seems, then, that Enoch xci. describes three Last Judgments; the first on the apostate Jews, the second on the Gentiles, and the third on the fallen angels. The New Era will begin with the first judgment, but will not be fully realised till after the third.[4]

In the 'Similitudes' of Enoch, the Last Judgment is to follow the resurrection and precede the New Era, as in the prophets and most of the earlier apocalypses. The importance of this section consists in the rôle played by the 'Son of Man' (described below, under the heading of 'the Messianic Hope'). Apart from this, the description follows the normal lines of the apocalyptic books.

(d) *The Messianic Hope*

We have seen that under the prosperous rule of the Maccabees, the old prophetic hope of a Messiah-King of David's line either lay dormant, or else became transformed into the expectation of a great Maccabean Priest-King of the House of Levi.[5] But when the Pharisees found themselves oppressed by the existing

---

[1] Eth. En. xci. 12-13.   [2] Eth. En. xci. 14.
[3] Eth. En. xci. 15-17.
[4] Charles (p. 261) says that the Last Judgment in xci. 15 'marks the close of the Messianic Kingdom.' But does the text warrant this statement?
[5] See above, p. 77.

Kings of the Jews, the Messianic Hope revived. Of this revival there are two notable examples in the extant apocalypses of the Pharisees. The first of these is in the 'Similitudes' of Enoch (*circa* 100 B.C.), the second in the Psalms of Solomon (*circa* 48 B.C.). These two doctrines of the Messiah are very different from each other; but both are of great interest, because they throw much light on the Messianic Hope in the years immediately preceding the birth of our Lord.

We will first consider the picture of the Messiah in the 'Similitudes' of Enoch. There we find a 'revised edition' of Daniel's famous vision of the 'son of man.' It will be remembered that in Daniel this figure symbolised the Israel of the future;[1] but in Enoch it is interpreted to be the Messiah himself. The vision is thus described :—

> 'I saw One who had a head of days, and His head was like white wool; and with Him was another being, whose countenance had the appearance of a man, and his face was full of graciousness, like one of the holy angels. And I asked the angel who went with me and showed me all the hidden things, concerning that Son of Man, who he was, and whence he was, and why he went with the Head of Days. And he answered and said unto me, "This is the Son of Man, who hath righteousness, . . . who reveals all the treasures of that which is hidden."'[2]

In chapter xlviii. we learn that this 'Son of Man' is the Saviour of the righteous from their enemies, and the appointed Judge of all the world; and that he was pre-existent with God 'before all worlds.' The ideas cannot fail to suggest to us the Johannine Christology :—

> 'Before the suns were created, before the stars of the

---

[1] See above, p. 73.
[2] Eth. En. xlvi. 1-3. The Ethiopic text contains several different phrases, all rendered 'Son of Man' by Charles; see his notes *ad loc.*

THE 'SON OF MAN' IN ENOCH

heaven were made, his Name was named before the Lord of Spirits. . . . He has been chosen and hidden before Him, before the creation of the world, and for evermore. And the wisdom of the Lord of Spirits hath revealed him to the holy and righteous ; . . . for they are saved in his Name, and he is the avenger of their life.'[1] . . .

'He will judge the secret things, and no one will be able to utter a lying word before him ; for he is the Elect one before the Lord of Spirits according to His good pleasure.'[2]

And in chapter lxix. the language is even more suggestive of the New Testament doctrine of Christ's judicial authority :—

'He sat on the throne of his glory, and the sum of judgment was committed to him, the Son of Man, and he caused the sinners and those who have led the world astray to pass away and be destroyed from off the face of the earth. With chains shall they be bound, and in their assemblage-place of destruction shall they be imprisoned, and all their works shall vanish from off the face of the earth. And from henceforth there will be nothing that is corruptible ; for the Son of Man has appeared, and sits on the throne of his glory ; and all evil will pass away before his face and depart ; but the word of the Son of Man will be strong before the Lord of Spirits.'[3] . . .

'The righteous and elect will be saved in that day ; and will never again from thenceforth see the face of the sinners and unrighteous. And the Lord of Spirits will abide over them, and with that Son of Man will they eat, and lie down, and rise up, for ever and ever.'[4]

There are many important points to be noted in connection with this description of the 'Son of Man' in Enoch.

---

[1] Eth. En. xlviii. 3, 6, 7. In lxx. 1 the 'Son of Man' is described as being with the Lord of Spirits at the time when Enoch was translated.
[2] Eth. En. xlix. 4.   [3] Eth. En. lxix. 28, 29.
[4] Eth. En. lxii. 13, 14 ; cf. xlv. 4, 'I will cause Mine Elect One to dwell among them [the righteous].'

In the first place, it suggests that the vision of Daniel vii. was well known among the Jews *circa* 100 B.C.; and it also shows how it was interpreted at that time. The Danielic 'son of man' affords the writer of the 'Similitudes' a title and a popular figure, to which he attaches an elaborate and remarkable doctrine of the Messiah.[1] Regarding the present Sadducean regime as a profane mockery of the theocratic ideal, he turns in despair, not to the thought of a Davidic Prince, but to the conception of a Messiah who is to come down from heaven. The prophets had spoken of the Divinity of the Messiah; but the Son of Man in Enoch belongs to another line of thought, and to an age when the rigid monotheism of the Hebrews had been modified by contact with the spirit-doctrine of Persia and by the polytheism of Greece. For this Messianic 'Son of Man' is a Divine or semi-Divine Being, pre-existent with God before all worlds, taking His seat on the throne of God, and performing the office of Divine Judge. As we read of 'the Son of Man' in Enoch, we feel that we are nearer than anywhere else in Jewish literature to the Christian conception of 'the Son of God.' Indeed, in Ethiopic Enoch cv. 2 (a passage, however, of doubtful date), the Divine Messiah is explicitly called 'My Son' by the Almighty: 'I and My Son will unite with them [the righteous] for ever.' And yet there is one great fundamental difference; 'the Son of Man' in Enoch may be Divine, but he is clearly not human; and by this he is sundered by an impassable gulf from the Religion of the Incarnation. But wherever the 'Similitudes' of Enoch were read and accepted, there the claim to be

[1] G. P. Gould, in Hastings' *Dictionary of Christ*, vol. ii. p. 660 (art. 'Son of Man'), thinks that the Enochic interpretation was also the original meaning of Daniel. But surely there is plenty of evidence that the apocalyptists often gave a new meaning to old prophecies. Cf. Jer. xxv. 12 with Dan. ix. 24.

THE MESSIAH IN PSALMS OF SOLOMON 89

Messiah on the part of any man would be equivalent to making himself virtually equal with God. And this is of great moment in studying the history of our Lord.[1]

Another and very different phase of the Messianic Hope is found in the Psalms of Solomon. Like the writer of the 'Similitudes' of Enoch, the psalmist has no hope in the existing rulers of the Jews. 'The holy things of God they took for spoil; and there was no inheritor ($\kappa\lambda\eta\rho o\nu\acute{o}\mu o\varsigma$) to deliver out of their hand.'[2] But yet the Psalmist is strengthened by the hope of the 'Inheritor' who shall come in God's good time, even the Messiah foretold by the prophets of old; and under the inspiration of this hope comes forth the stately prayer of Psalm xvii. :—

> 'Behold, O LORD, and raise up unto them [the people] their King, the Son of David, in the time which thou, O God, knowest, that he may reign over Israel thy servant; and gird him with strength, that he may break in pieces them that rule unjustly. . . . He shall thrust out the sinners from the inheritance; . . . he shall destroy the ungodly nations with the word of his mouth. . . . And he shall gather together a holy people, whom he shall lead in righteousness; and shall judge the tribes of the people that hath been sanctified by the Lord his God. And he shall not suffer iniquity to lodge in their midst; and none that knoweth wickedness shall dwell with them. . . .
>
> 'And a righteous king, and taught of God, is he that reigneth over them; and there shall be no iniquity in his days in their midst; for all shall be holy, and their King is the Lord Messiah.[3] For he shall not put his trust in horse and rider and bow, nor shall he multiply unto him-

---

[1] See especially Mark xiv. 61, 62. See also above, p. 33, for the Messianic significance of 'Son of God' in the Old Testament.

[2] Pss. Sol. viii. 12.

[3] "$X\rho\iota\sigma\tau\grave{o}\varsigma$ $K\acute{\upsilon}\rho\iota o\varsigma$." Ryle and James conjecture that this is a textual corruption from "$X\rho\iota\sigma\tau\grave{o}\varsigma$ $K\upsilon\rho\acute{\iota}o\upsilon$," 'the Lord's Anointed.'

self gold and silver for war, nor by ships[1] shall he gather confidence for the day of battle. In holiness shall he lead them all, and there shall no pride be among them, that any should be oppressed.

'This is the majesty of the King of Israel, which God hath appointed[2] to raise him up over the house of Israel, to instruct him. . . . Blessed are they that shall be born in those days, to behold the blessing of Israel, which God shall bring to pass in the gathering-together of the tribes. May God hasten his mercy toward Israel!'[3]

This passage is of great interest, as showing us a type of Messianic Hope fundamentally different from that in the 'Similitudes' of Enoch. The Messiah here is much more 'in line' with the Messiah of the older prophets; he is to be a son of David, not a supernatural being descending from heaven, but a human king 'raised up' from among God's people. Although not trusting in the force of arms, his mission nevertheless will be so far political as to include the expulsion of the 'sinners' (a title which in these Psalms regularly denotes the Sadducees[4]) from their present position of authority. The sphere of his activity, unlike that of Enoch's 'Son of Man,' lies in this world alone. Above all, his reign will be crowned with those moral qualities so dear to the ancient prophets—righteousness, justice, and holiness.

These two writings,—the 'Similitudes' of Enoch and the Psalms of Solomon—show that in the same school of thought, and approximately about the same time, there were two forms of the Messianic Hope among the devout Jews. Some, like the author of these Psalms, retained the ancient prophetic expectation of a Christ

---

[1] "$\pi\lambda o$ίοις." So Ryle and James conjecture; but the MSS. have "$\pi o\lambda\lambda o$ῖς," which, if rendered 'multitudes,' gives good sense.

[2] Literally 'foreknown' (ἔγνω).

[3] Pss. Sol. xvii. 23-29, 35-37, 48, 50-51.

[4] See Ryle and James's note on Pss. Sol. i. 1.

of David's line,—a human king who should rule God's people on earth in fulfilment of the highest ideal of the Covenant. In this type of Messianic Hope there is little that is eschatological, and nothing that is apocalyptic in character. But others among the Pharisees of this period, such as the writer of the 'Similitudes,' turned their hopes from earth to heaven, and watched for a supernatural being, coming on the clouds from the Divine presence to rescue the faithful and judge the sinners with more than human authority and might.

But although these two Pharisaic writings both contain such clear and remarkable expressions of the Messianic Hope, yet it would seem that this Hope never obtained universal acceptance even among the Pharisees; or else, that in later times it was dropped by certain adherents of the party, perhaps because it was being degraded by association with political schemes of which they disapproved. For instance, in the Assumption of Moses, the latest of the Pharisaic apocalypses, we find no reference to a Messiah.—'The eternal God *alone* will appear to punish the Gentiles.'[1]

It is clear then that in the times of our Lord, we need not expect to find one stereotyped form of Messianic Hope. It was a pious belief of certain individuals, not a recognised article of the Pharisaic creed; and where the belief was held, its expression varied very considerably.

(e) *Final Destinies*

The bitter feelings which prompted the oppressed Pharisees to write their apocalypses are reflected in the references to the final fate of 'the sinners.' For 'the sinners,' as we have seen, were the apostate but prosperous Sadducees; and the Pharisees describe their

[1] Ass. Moys. x.

future destiny not merely with the traditional antipathy which the Jews have always felt towards 'the uncircumcised Gentiles,' but with the keener hatred which springs from the sense of personal injury.[1] It is with evident satisfaction that the writer of the 'Similitudes' describes the instruments of torture prepared for the souls of the sinners and for the fallen angels.[2] And in the Assumption of Moses, we read :—

> 'Thou, O Israel, wilt be happy, . . . and God will exalt thee;
> And He will cause thee to approach the heaven of stars,
> And He will establish thy habitation among them;
> And thou wilt look from on high, and wilt see thine enemies in Gehenna,
> And thou wilt recognise them, and rejoice.'[3]

In the descriptions of the final destinies of the righteous, the chief point to notice is the prominence given to the thought of *companionship* with the angels,[4] with the Messiah, and with God Himself.[5] It is not really new; for it is the old idea underlying the narratives of the Assumptions of Enoch and Elijah, and is a concrete expression of the deep faith of the mystic. In one passage, the writer apparently expects that the righteous will themselves become 'angels in heaven.'[6]

(f) Foreign Influence

In these apocalypses of the Pharisees we continue to notice many features which are probably borrowed from non-Jewish religious systems. Angels figure largely,

---

[1] In Eth. En. xcv.-civ., the coming miseries of 'the sinners' form the chief topic.
[2] Eth. En. liv. 4-6, lvi. 1-3.   [3] Ass. Moys. x.
[4] Eth. En. civ. 6.   [5] Eth. En. xlv. 4, lxxi. 16, 17.
[6] Eth. En. li. 4; cf. Mark xii. 25.

and the value of their intercessions is frequently mentioned.¹ One might almost say that the 'Son of Man' in the 'Similitudes' is a deified angel. Angels, of course, are mentioned in the early Hebrew literature, but after the contact with Zoroastrianism, the references are far more frequent.

In the 'Similitudes' we find mention of the weighing of men's deeds.² This is a special characteristic of Egyptian eschatology, though there are a few Old Testament references to the 'weighing of spirits' by God.³

Another feature which does not seem to be part of the normal development of Hebrew thought is the description of the spirits of the sea, of the thunder, of the mist, of the rain, and of the other phenomena of nature.⁴ These might probably be traced to the Nature-worship of Egypt or Greece.

These apocalypses of the Pharisees are probably the latest extant examples of Palestinian Jewish literature before the time of our Lord. There are, indeed, as we shall see in a later chapter, some apocalypses which may well have been written by *Alexandrian* Jews in the latter part of the first century B.C., but the Assumption of Moses appears to be the only extant product of the later Pharisaism in Palestine. The apocalypses written during the last years of Jerusalem, which will form the subject of the next chapter, are of great interest because they are contemporary with the beginnings of Christianity, and may have been known to the apostles of our Lord. But no less interest attaches to the apocalypses of the Pharisees; for the doctrines contained in them had had time to become widely spread among the people before the times of Jesus Christ. So far as our

---

¹ Eth. En. xl. 6, civ. 1; cf. c. 5.   ² Eth. En. xli. 1.
³ Prov. xvi. 2, xxi. 2, xxiv. 12, Ps. lxii. 9.   ⁴ Eth. En. lx. 15-21.

knowledge goes, at the end of the first century B.C., the apocalypses of the Pharisees represented the most recent phase of popular religion; and it is by no means unlikely that their teaching formed part of the religious atmosphere in which our Lord Himself was brought up.

The leading characteristics of these apocalypses have been dealt with above. How shall we best gather up a general impression? In the first place, there is a notable absence of fixed dogma concerning the Last Things. The Law and the prophets remained immutable; but the speculations with regard to the resurrection, the Messiah, and kindred subjects varied with each successive writer. Public opinion on these matters was as yet unformed, and ready to hear any new thing. Another feature that strikes us as we study these apocalypses is the rarity of the precepts of practical well-doing. The 'righteous' and the 'sinners' are indeed incessantly contrasted with one another; but the contrast is not so much one of moral qualities as of ceremonial observances or semi-political parties.

In each of the great Jewish schools of thought there were doubtless not a few saintly men (though their names may be now forgotten) with whom righteousness was more than ritual, and who went about doing good. But a study of the apocalypses indicates that generally speaking Sadducaic indifference and Pharisaic legalism were alike in sharp contrast to the life and teaching of Jesus of Nazareth.

CHAPTER IX

THE APOCALYPSES OF THE FALL OF JERUSALEM

ONE other little group of Palestinian apocalypses requires a brief consideration. It consists of two books: the *Apocalypse of Baruch*, and the *Apocalypse of Ezra* which is contained in our English Bible under the title of II Esdras.[1] Both of these were probably written after the Fall of Jerusalem had taken place, when the outlook for the Jews was very gloomy. Thus they help us to understand the ideas of the Jews in the apostolic age.

It is necessary, however, to remember that where there are resemblances between these apocalypses and contemporary Christian doctrine, the borrowing need not have been entirely on the Christian side. For although these writings mainly represent an essentially Jewish type of eschatology, which helps to throw into relief the distinctive features of Christ's teaching, yet there are hints that the Jewish apocalyptists were on their side acquainted with some parts of the teaching of the primitive Christian Church.

It is also well to bear in mind that by this time the earlier apocalyptic books had obtained a high reputation for sanctity among the people, and it is likely enough that portions of earlier 'visions' may be incorporated in these later Jewish apocalypses.

[1] Referred to in these pages as '4 Ezra.' The Latin text is published in *Texts and Studies*, vol. iii. No. 2.

Everything in these books, especially in 4 Ezra, is coloured by the writers' depression of mind. It was the last despairing attempt of Jewish faith to explain why God had thus forsaken His people; and we find a reckless pessimism which will stop short at no doctrine, however harsh and repellent, which seems to offer a chance of solving the problem. The two books alike maintain that the times are too evil to last any longer, yet the confident assurance of immediate deliverance is less buoyant than in the earlier apocalypses;[1] and their ideas of the future life are more exclusive than in any of their predecessors. In Baruch we read:—

'There is no numbering of those whom the fire devours.'[2]

And in 4 Ezra, words of terrible callousness are attributed to God Himself:—

'I will rejoice over the few that shall be saved, inasmuch as these are they that have made my glory now to prevail, and of whom my name is now named. And I will not grieve over the multitude of them that perish; for these are they that are now like unto vapour, and are become as flame and smoke; they are set on fire and burn hotly, and are quenched. . . . The Most High hath made this world for many, but the world to come for few.'[3]

The Messianic Woes are described at length in both these apocalypses. Baruch holds that they will not affect the Holy Land.[4] In 4 Ezra, the last of the 'birth pangs' of the New Era will be seven days of primeval silence.[5]

The Messianic Hope is found in these two books; but it is not very inspiring. In Baruch, the Messiah will 'begin to be revealed' in the midst of the Messianic

---

[1] 4 Ezra iv. 51, 52.   [2] Ap. Bar. xlviii. 43.
[3] 4 Ezra vii. 60a, 61a, viii. 1.   [4] Ap. Bar. xxix. 2.
[5] 4 Ezra vii. 30.

Woes, and after a temporary reign on earth will return in glory to heaven.[1] In 4 Ezra, the Messiah will reign on earth four hundred years, and will then die, together with every living thing. Thereupon, after seven days' silence, the New Era will begin.[2] These are among the earliest clear instances of the idea of a *temporary* Messianic Kingdom, which developed later on into the Christian expectation of a 'Millennium.'[3] It is interesting to notice that the New City where the Messiah is to reign is called 'the bride.'[4] At present this city is existing in the heavens, but 'withdrawn from the earth.' In 4 Ezra also, the term 'My Son' is frequently used to designate the Messiah. In some of these passages the text has apparently been altered by Christian interpolations;[5] but in other cases there appears no good reason to doubt its genuineness.[6] In an apocalypse so nearly contemporary with our Lord, this usage is of great interest and significance.

In the Apocalypse of Baruch, there is a peculiar doctrine of the resurrection. Baruch asks, 'In what shape will those live who live on Thy Day? . . . Will they resume the form of the present, . . . or wilt Thou perchance change the things which have been in the world, as also the world?' In reply, he is told that all men will first be raised in their bodies, in order that they may be recognised for the purposes of judgment.[7]

---

[1] Ap. Bar. 29 and 30, and 69-73. The well-known fragment of Papias's writings, which describes the millennial Kingdom of Christ on earth (Iren. *Adv. Haer.* v. 33. 3 f.), is in part a verbal quotation from Ap. Bar. xxix. 5. See below, Part V. Chap. I.   [2] 4 Ezra vii. 28-31.

[3] But see p. 85, note 4.   [4] 4 Ezra vii. 26; cf. Rev. xxi. 2.

[5] 4 Ezra vii. 28, xiii. 32.—In the former of these two passages, the name 'Jesus' occurs only in the Latin version, not in the Oriental versions.

[6] 4 Ezra vii. 29, xiv. 9, etc.

[7] Ap. Bar. 50. A similar thought is found at times in modern writers;— for instance, in *In Memoriam*, § xlvii. :—

> 'Eternal form shall still divide
> The eternal soul from all beside;
> And I shall know him when we meet.'

After that, the outward appearance of those raised will become a revelation of their inward character; that of the wicked will become loathsome, but the righteous will be transformed and will surpass the angels in glory.[1] In 4 Ezra the doctrine of the resurrection is quite normal.[2]

In Baruch, salvation at the Last Judgment will be strictly in accordance with men's works; the treasuries will be opened to see what stores of merit they have laid up for themselves in heaven.[3] The doctrine of original sin is expressly repudiated.[4] Dr. Charles thinks that on these points there may be an intentional reference to the teaching of St. Paul.

If we place the eschatology of these late Jewish apocalypses side by side with the teaching of our Lord and His apostles, we find that while the general ideas of the Last Things, and the peculiar eschatological terms in use, are the same in both cases, there is little real community of spirit. The contrast will be discussed at greater length at the close of our study of Christ's eschatology in Part III. of this essay. It will suffice here to mention two typical and significant instances.

In times of trial the Jewish apocalyptist declared that it would have been better had he never lived;[5] but our Lord in the hour of deepest agony prays: 'Father, not my will, but thine, be done.'—The apocalyptist tells us that God cares nothing for the destruction of all men, if only a handful of the elect are saved;[6] but Christ has taught us to think of a Heavenly Father who is 'not willing that any should perish, but that all should come to repentance.'

---

[1] Ap. Bar. 51. [2] 4 Ezra vii. 32. [3] Ap. Bar. 14 and 24.
[4] Ap. Bar. liv. 15. [5] 4 Ezra iv. 12.
[6] 4 Ezra vii. 61a (quoted above, p. 96).

Yet we shall do well not to judge these later Jewish apocalyptists with rigour. They were men upon whom the hand of trouble had been very heavily laid, and there was much excuse for their repellent harshness. At least they had not lost faith in God, and they still believed that things would come right in the end. And that needed no little courage in those dark days when they took up the pen to try to explain the ways of the Most High.

CHAPTER X

THE ESCHATOLOGY OF THE JEWS OF 'THE DISPERSION'

ALL the literature which we have lately been considering bears indications of Palestinian origin. The writers were no doubt men who had rarely, if ever, been outside the boundaries of Judaea, and their interests are strictly limited to their own people.

But even among the 'Jews of the Dispersion' the peculiar features of apocalyptic found a certain amount of favour. There are at least two extant apocalypses which are considered by the best authorities to be of Alexandrian or Egyptian origin; and various other writers of the 'Diaspora' use language which reminds us of the apocalyptists. Greek and Jewish features are curiously mingled in these Alexandrian books. At times the traditional Jewish phrases are re-presented, only in a more liberal spirit; at other times we find unmistakable Hellenic doctrines, interpreted in a Jewish manner.

The Palestinian Jews were probably not influenced by the doctrines of these Hellenistic writings as much as by the literature which originated in their own land. Still, there was frequent intercourse between the 'Diaspora-Jews' and the mother-country, and in later times the School of Alexandria handed on the teaching of the Hellenist Jews to the Christian Church. For these reasons the eschatology of these books requires a brief consideration.

But before discussing these 'Apocalypses of the Diaspora,' it may be well to recall briefly some of the chief features of Greek eschatology. Greek influence came to bear upon the Jews from the fourth century B.C. onwards, and naturally the Diaspora-Jews living in Hellenic surroundings were specially inclined to adopt Greek ideas.

In the eschatology of the early Greeks, the moral element had been almost absent. Homer had regarded death as the greatest of all evils, and had taught that the abode of the dead is colourless and gloomy. There is little fundamental difference between such ideas and those of the early Babylonians or Egyptians.

But before the time when the Greeks came into contact with the Hebrews, a great change had taken place. Thoughtful men had come to realise the sense of their own imperfection, and to desire purity of life; and they expressed their feelings by the symbolism of the Mysteries, which were designed to suggest not only the prospect of happiness in the life beyond the grave, but also the thought of future retribution.[1] With some of the Greek thinkers, the immortality of the soul was proclaimed with a clearness and conviction that has rarely been surpassed; but generally this is closely linked with a doctrine of Pre-existence and (sometimes) of Transmigration. Our present bodily existence is but a phase in the course of the life of the soul; physical birth and death do not mark the beginning nor the ending of the soul's true life :—

---

[1] See (*e.g.*) Salmond's *Christian Doctrine of Immortality*, 4th edition, p. 110. For Greek Religion, cf. chap. iii. in Charles's *Critical History of the Doctrine of a Future Life of Judaism*, and Ramsay's article, 'Religion of Greece,' in Hastings' *Dictionary of the Bible*, extra vol. pp. 109-156.

> 'Our birth is but a sleep and a forgetting:
> The Soul that rises with us, our life's Star,
>   Hath had elsewhere its setting,
>   And cometh from afar:
>   Not in entire forgetfulness,
>   And not in utter nakedness,
> But trailing clouds of glory do we come
>   From God, who is our home.'

Such ideas lead naturally to a disparagement of the body as 'the prison-house of the soul,' in contrast to the Hebrew conception of the body as an essential part of the man; and in Jewish writings a contempt for things material is one of the most obvious signs of Greek influence.

Another characteristic of Greek eschatology was that its highest aspirations for the future were dominated, not so much by the prospect of happiness, or of rest, but, above all, to the desire for purity: 'They did not so much seek purity that they might become divinely immortal; they needed immortality that they might become divinely pure.'[1] And what the Greek meant by 'purity' is clearly shown us in Plato's *Phaedo*:—

> 'Does not purification seem to be this—the separation, as far as possible, of the soul from the body, and the accustoming it to dwell, as far as possible, both in the present and in the future, alone by itself, freed from the body as though from bonds?'[2]

Such aspirations led naturally to a doctrine of retribution beyond the grave. For the devout Greek would be conscious that he needed further purification after death; and the extent of these purifications would

---

[1] J. E. Harrison, *Prolegomena to the Study of Greek Religion* (London, 1903), p. 478.

[2] Plato, *Phaedo*, § 12 (Blagrave's translation).

depend on the state of his soul at the close of this life. Hence a moral connection was established between this world and the world to come; but the character of the retribution tends to be subjective rather than objective, and, unlike that in Hebrew religion, is not essentially bound up with the conception of a dramatic Judgment Day. And the idea of national or corporate resurrection appears to be rarely present to the mind of the Greek thinker.

On the other hand, in some of the Greek or Roman authors, we meet with ideas which are thoroughly dramatic, and much more akin to those of the Hebrews. Familiar instances occur in Virgil's description of the rewards and punishments in the under-world in the *Aeneid*,[1] and in the same poet's 'Messianic Eclogue.'[2] In such cases the influence may have been mutual.

The following writings illustrate the eschatology of the 'Diaspora-Jews':—

1. Sibylline Oracles, iii. 97-825.
2. Slavonic Enoch.
3. Wisdom of Solomon.
4. Philo.

In *Sibylline Oracles*, iii. 97-825, the historical references indicate that the date of writing was in the second century B.C.[3] The outlines of the Jewish doctrine of the Last Things are maintained, but there are several peculiar features which indicate that the writer was a Jew of the Dispersion, probably living at Alexandria.

Two points are worthy of notice. First, the author

[1] Virg. *Aen.* vi. 548-627.
[2] See Mayor, Fowler, and Conway, *Virgil's Messianic Eclogue* (London, 1907), especially pp. 31-32.
[3] See Alexandre, *Oracula Sibyllina* (Paris, 1869), Introduction, p. xxi.

is keenly interested in the conversion of the Gentiles to the worship of the God of Israel.[1] Probably he chose to write under the pseudonym of the Gentile Sibyl in order to appeal to a non-Jewish circle of readers. And secondly, the doctrine of the Messiah is that of a Divine Messenger from God, rather than of a human king of David's line, and the Messiah's office will be to inaugurate the New Era of peace :—

> 'And then from the sun [or perhaps, "from the East"] God
>   shall send a King,
> Who shall cause all the world to cease from wicked war;
> Some men indeed he shall slay; with others he will make
>   a sure treaty.'[2]

Another apocalypse, which Dr. Charles considers to have sprung from Egyptian Judaism, is the *Slavonic 'Book of the Secrets of Enoch.'* The date assigned is the first half of the first century A.D., but parts of the book are earlier.[3]

The plan of the book is that Enoch visits the Seven Heavens, and inspects their contents. The idea of the Seven Heavens, each above the other, is probably of Babylonian origin. It was accepted by some of the early Christians,[4] and is very prominent in the 'Ascension of Isaiah' and other Christian apocalypses. The Hellenic influence is indicated by the doctrine that 'every soul was created eternally before the world.'[5]

On one point the writer's beliefs are distinctly

---

[1] Sib. Or. iii. 624-632, 702-731, etc.
[2] Sib. Or. iii. 652-655 :—

καὶ τότ' ἀπ' ἠελίοιο θεὸς πέμψει βασιλῆα
ὃς πᾶσαν γαῖαν παύσει πολέμοιο κακοῖο
οὓς μὲν ἄρα κτείνας, οἷς δ' ὅρκια πιστὰ τελέσσας.

Cf. also iii. 766-772.

[3] See Charles, *The Book of the Secrets of Enoch*, Introduction, pp. xvii-xxvi.
[4] Cf. 2 Cor. xii. 2, and the 'Ascension of Isaiah' (below, Part V. Chap. II.).
[5] Slav. En. xxiii. 5.

unusual, for he affirms the immortality of the souls of the beasts, who will have their special place in the world to come.¹

Another interesting feature is the well-defined expectation of a 'Millennium' at the end of the world. This idea is derived from the Creation narrative in Genesis, which is treated as an 'apocalypse' of the world's history. The six days of the creation symbolise six periods of a thousand years each; for is it not written that 'a thousand years in God's sight are but as yesterday'? The seventh day, on which God rested, is symbolical of the last thousand years of this world's existence, which will be a period of blessing and peace. After this, the Kingdom of God will begin, and will be the 'eighth eternal week.'² There is no mention of a Messiah.

'*The Wisdom of Solomon*' is perhaps the most typical of all the writings of Hellenistic Judaism. 'The most recent attempts to fix the date vary between 150 B.C. and A.D. 40.'³ Nowhere in Jewish literature are the Greek ideas of the pre-existence and immortality of the soul and of the essential baseness of material things so clearly visible :—

'God created man for incorruption;'⁴

but

'A corruptible body weigheth down the soul,
And the earthy frame lieth heavy on a mind that is full of cares.'⁵

The writer believes that his soul is both pre-existent

¹ Slav. En. lviii.
² Slav. En. xxxiii. 2. Cf. below, Part V. Chap. II. on *The Christian Apocalypses*.
³ Siegfried, in Hastings' *Dictionary of the Bible*, vol. iv. p. 931a.
⁴ Wisd. ii. 23.   ⁵ Wisd. ix. 15.

and immortal, and that the character of a man's earthly body depends on the merits of his soul before it has become incarnated:—

> 'A good soul fell to my lot;—nay rather, being good, I came into a body undefiled.'[1]

And yet the Hellenism of the Book of Wisdom is strongly coloured by Jewish modes of thought. The writer never swerves from his loyalty to the God of Israel. The immortality that he believes in is not the natural lot of all mankind, but the privilege of the faithful worshipper of God.—'To know Thy dominion is the root of immortality.'[2]

Few writings of this period are so refined and attractive as the 'Wisdom of Solomon.' After our study of the harsh and artificial doctrines of the later apocalypses it is a genuine pleasure to meet with a simple and devout belief in a future life, expressed in language that is not unworthy of the Christian Hope itself:—

> 'The souls of the righteous are in the hand of God,
> And no torment shall touch them.
> In the eyes of the foolish they seemed to have died,
> And their departure was accounted to be their hurt,
> And their journeying away from us to be their ruin;
> But they are in peace.
> For even if in the sight of men they be punished,
> Their hope is full of immortality;
> And having borne a little chastening, they shall receive
>   great good;
> Because God made trial of them, and found them worthy
>   of Himself.'[3]

In *the writings of Philo* the cast of thought is still more Hellenic. The Alexandrian philosopher regarded

---

[1] Wisd. viii. 19, 20.   [2] Wisd. xv. 3.   [3] Wisd. iii. 1-5.

matter as essentially evil, and our existence on earth as a living death :—

> 'When we are alive, we are so though our soul is dead and buried in our body, as if in a tomb. But if it were to die, then our soul would live according to its proper life, being released from the evil and dead body to which it is bound.'[1]

He believes in the immortality of the soul, but there appears to be no connection between this belief and his expectation of a good time coming for Israel on earth.[2] Indeed this hope for a future Kingdom of God in this world agrees but awkwardly with the general trend of Philo's teaching; but it was part of the recognised tradition of his people, and he did not like to ignore it.

The influence of Philo upon the writers of the New Testament is a disputed question; but it is beyond all doubt that in later times the great Christian doctors of Alexandria were deeply imbued with his teaching. It has been said that Philo 'prepared a sort of philosophical mould in which the fluid doctrines of Christianity could acquire consistency and shape.'[3] Perhaps, too, Philo indirectly influenced the history of eschatology by inculcating among the Jews a philosophical attitude of mind, which instinctively disliked the pseudonymous and realistic methods of the apocalyptists, and thus hastened the decline of the apocalyptic literature.[4]

Our brief review of these writings of the 'colonial' Jews will have indicated their strength and weakness

[1] *De Sacr. Leg. Alleg.* i. 33.   [2] *De Execrat.* ix.
[3] James Drummond, in Hastings' *Dictionary of the Bible*, art. 'Philo,' extra vol. p. 208b.
[4] See Hassé, *Apocalyptic Schools of Judaism* (Manchester Theological Lectures, 1905), pp. 158 ff., where it is suggested that Josephus also, by his historical methods, helped to diminish the popularity of the apocalypses.

compared with the contemporary Palestinian apocalypses. They were more tolerant, more enlightened, more philosophical; but they lack the nervous enthusiasm which characterises most of the Palestinian books, and which accounts in great measure for the widespread popularity of the latter. The Jews of the mother-country were face to face with the great crises which threatened their nation; the Jews of the Dispersion viewed the course of events from a more dispassionate standpoint. The latter may have seen things in a truer perspective; but it is the Palestinian apocalypses which did most to form the thoughts of the people among whom the seed of the Gospel was first sown.

It is not easy to gather up the general characteristics of Jewish apocalyptic eschatology. The age of the apocalyptists, like many another age which has lost confidence in its own inspiration, exhibits the strange combination of a strict profession of deference to ancient tradition, side by side with a somewhat irresponsible tendency to multiply new details of doctrine, till the general impression becomes somewhat confused. When we endeavour to probe below the bewildering mass of apocalyptic details, we find that the really fundamental ideas common to all these writers are very simple, and very few in number. All the apocalyptists, without exception, looked forward to a future 'Kingdom of God' in which the faithful are to participate. Nearly all of them believed that the beginning of this Kingdom was very near, that it would be ushered in by violent and miraculous means, and that its inauguration would be associated with the resurrection of the dead and the Last Judgment. These are, so to speak, 'fixed points' in the apocalyptic eschatology; on other matters, such as the intermediate state of the departed, the final destinies of the wicked, or the advent of the Messiah, there appears to have been an almost unlimited variety of speculation. The class of readers for whom the apocalypses were intended—in other words, the less-educated section of the Jewish populace—were evidently not disposed to resent apparent discrepancies, so long as the teaching was definite and the 'revelations' sufficiently minute to be interesting. A 'new teaching' would always be welcome, so long as its general scheme was not aggressively unconventional.

One warning should perhaps be added. We have dwelt so much upon the apocalyptic literature that there is a danger of forgetting that it represents the beliefs and aspirations of only one section of the Jewish people. All through the years when these apocalypses were being written and circulated, there was doubtless a large body of educated opinion of a Sadducaic type among the Jews, worldly, cultured, and rationalistic, neither sharing in nor sympathising with visions and hopes of the kind which have engaged our attention in the above pages.

The eschatology of our Lord now claims our attention. Our study of the apocalyptic literature has been somewhat lengthy; but if we would rightly appraise the value of our Lord's teaching, it is essential to be well acquainted with the circle of ideas in which He lived. The significance of His message lies not only in what He taught, but also in what He *omitted* to teach; and this can be realised only when we are able to compare His doctrine with the doctrines of the apocalyptic writers.[1]

[1] See the 'General Conclusions' at the end of Part III.

PART III

CHRIST'S ESCHATOLOGY

CHAPTER XI

INTRODUCTORY

οὐκ ἦλθον καταλῦσαι, ἀλλὰ πληρῶσαι — 'I came, not to undo, but to fulfil.'—Such was our Lord's own estimate of His mission, and of the place which He holds in the history of the world. The words imply a stupendous claim; that all the past history of the Chosen People, all their wealth of law and prophecy and psalmody, was but the preparation for Him who came in the fulness of time as a humble prophet of Nazareth. The claim must have seemed amazing at the time; and yet it has commended itself to the conscience of a large part of the civilised world.

Herein lies the supreme importance of this part of our study. If Jesus of Nazareth be indeed the fulfilment of the Old Dispensation, then His teaching is both the touchstone by which the truth or falsehood of earlier beliefs may be tested, and also the true foundation of the subsequent eschatology of the Christian Church. Nor is the teaching of Jesus Christ a matter of merely historical interest, but also of far-reaching practical importance. For if it were possible to determine with certainty what was the true 'mind of Christ' with regard to the life beyond the grave and the final destiny of this world, by far the largest part of Christendom would accept that teaching, and believe in it as an authoritative revelation, beyond which no appeal is admissible. And there can be little doubt that the effects of such a belief would be seen in the everyday life of our times.

During the last few years, the eschatology of Jesus has come into special prominence in consequence of the writings of the so-called 'Eschatological School' on the Continent. It is contended that the eschatological element in the teaching of Jesus was far greater than has generally been supposed, and that the real 'centre of gravity' of His message is to be found, not in His moral teaching, nor in His life or death, but in His eschatology. A number of new problems have been raised, and many fresh lines of thought suggested.[1]

[1] The 'Eschatological Theory' of our Lord's life and teaching was foreshadowed, as far ago as 1768, by Reimarus; but it is only recently that it has begun to attract general interest. The pioneers of the theory in the last few years have been Johannes Weiss and Albert Schweitzer. In 1882 the former wrote *Die Predigt Jesu vom Reiche Gottes*, in which he maintained that the teaching of Jesus was far more impregnated with eschatology than was commonly supposed. His views, however, did not find much favour till, in 1906, Albert Schweitzer developed the same ideas in greater detail and with relentless consistency, in his now well-known book, *Von Reimarus zu Wrede*. This book was first brought to the notice of English readers in 1907 by Dr. Sanday's *Life of Christ in Recent Research*; and since the present essay was written, Father Tyrell's *Christianity at the Cross Roads* has introduced Schweitzer's views to an even wider circle, while Schweitzer's book itself is now accessible in an English translation by W. Montgomery, under the title of *The Quest of the Historical Jesus*. Still more recently, a careful review and criticism of Schweitzer's theory has appeared in Dr. von Dobschutz's *Eschatology of the Gospels* (London, 1910), written from a standpoint which may be broadly described as that of the Liberal Protestant.

The interest aroused throughout this country may be gauged from the Cambridge Church Congress of 1910, when a number of leading English theologians—including Bishop Gore, Dean Bernard, Dr. Charles, and Professor Stanton—read papers before the Congress on the subject of Schweitzer and his Theory. Under the circumstances, it seems needless to apologise for the large amount of space which has been devoted to the consideration of the 'Eschatological Theory' in the following pages.

All these have increased the importance of the study of Christ's Doctrine of the Last Things.

But while the eschatology of our Lord is thus at the present time a subject of unusual interest, it also presents peculiar difficulties to the student. Indeed, the endeavour to surmount these difficulties constitutes no small part of the interest aroused.

To begin with, it will be admitted on all hands that we are here face to face with a unique Personality. Even the non-Christian generally admits that in the words of Jesus there is a depth of insight and a width of outlook which cause him to hesitate before he ventures to define or to limit their precise significance. And those who have been admitted into the fellowship of Christ's religion must feel that they are here treading upon holy ground. The servant who would seek to discover the mind of a Master whom he believes to be one with the Maker of all, cannot but realise his own weakness and the awful greatness of the task before him :—

> 'Hardly do we divine the things that are on earth,
> And the things that are close at hand we find with labour;
> But the things that are in the heavens who ever yet traced out?
> And who ever gained knowledge of thy counsel, except thou gavest wisdom,
> And sentest thy holy spirit from on high?'[1]

Some of the gravest difficulties are connected with the problem of the 'Kenosis,' or the limitations of our Lord's human knowledge. This question comes specially to the fore in the study of His eschatology; for much of His teaching suggests at first sight that He held expectations of the future which were not in fact fulfilled. These are among the most perplexing passages that

[1] Wisd. ix. 16, 17.

confront the student of the Gospels. To those who hold 'extreme' views on either side the difficulty is not very great. On the one hand, the advanced critic claims these sayings as proofs of the fallibility of Jesus. They show, we are told, that He was sometimes mistaken; and, if so, the difficulty is largely solved. On the other side, some, desiring at all costs to maintain the inerrancy of our Lord's own vision of the future, have insisted that the natural and obvious meaning of the passages is not the true one; He was speaking in parables, and His words are to be interpreted mystically, not literally. Here, again, the difficulty is partly solved; but while the former solution ignores the uniqueness of Christ, the latter obscures 'the human reality of His message to His hearers.

Another difficulty, closely connected with the problem of the Kenosis, is to determine how far our Lord shared the peculiar national ideas of His fellow-countrymen. In other words, To what extent was Jesus a Jew? Were His thoughts from the very first free from all Jewish peculiarities, or did the 'increase in wisdom,' of which St. Luke speaks, involve a gradual widening of His outlook, until He came to the fulness of the knowledge of the Perfect Man?

Those who are willing to concentrate their attention on one aspect alone of the Person of Jesus will find little difficulty in supplying an answer to questions such as these; but a satisfactory solution of the problem of our Lord's human limitations is one of the tasks which still lies before the Church of the future. In the meantime, it behoves the Christian scholar to remember the limitations of his own knowledge, and to abstain from hasty dogmatism on such matters.

Another difficulty which confronts the student of Christ's eschatology springs from what we may call the 'prophetic' character of His teaching. The reader will remember that, in studying the eschatology of the Hebrew prophets, we noticed that their real message consisted of a few great principles, and that the details were valued chiefly because they helped to illustrate the main issues. This is even more true of the teaching of our Lord. He did not come primarily to reveal details of the unknown future, but to teach men the will of the Father. And herein lies this difficulty, that there is nothing in His teaching to compare with the minute 'revelations' of the future which we find in the apocalyptic literature. The eschatology of the Gospels is to be found rather in the parabolic pictures of the Last Things and of the Kingdom of God, together with a few incidental allusions to the future life of the individual. Consequently it often needs no little care, first to read aright the principle hidden under the veil of parabolic teaching, and then to apply that principle to the problems of eschatology.

The prophetic character of our Lord's teaching is also marked by the note of conviction: 'He taught them as one having authority, and not as the scribes.' He knew that He possessed the authority within Himself, and so He did not merely repeat the traditions of His earthly forefathers. He does indeed appeal at times to the witness of the Old Testament, where this confirms His own message; but He never suggests that His own authority is dependent on the authority of the Hebrew Bible. Nay, rather: 'We speak that we do know, and testify of that we have seen.'

This same note of prophetic conviction suggests the reason why our Lord never appeals to the authority of the apocalyptic books, although He often adopts their language to enforce His teaching. The apocalypses, as we have seen, were full of details, but great moral principles were often sadly wanting. Our Lord was willing to use the familiar language of apocalyptic, when that language served to make His own meaning plainer to His hearers. But the parallels between His words and those of the apocalyptists are always incidental, and essentially different from the direct quotations which He often draws from the Old Testament prophets, by whom the same Spirit had spoken who now was speaking by Himself, the Prophet of Nazareth.

But the difficulties of our study do not lie only in the uniqueness of Christ's Person and teaching. The sources also, from which we derive our information, present problems of unusual complexity. The Synoptic Problem, and the Problem of the Fourth Gospel, are interwoven with our subject at every point. We are constantly tempted to diverge from the study of eschatology and enter the devious paths of literary criticism. It is evident that in the present essay it would be out of place to attempt any full discussion of these vast problems. But as they are so intimately connected with the subject of our Lord's eschatology, it will be well to indicate as briefly as possible the standpoint which is assumed in the following pages. The reader will then be better able to make due allowance for the existence of opinions and presuppositions with which he may be unable to agree.

Of all these problems, the most vital of all is that which concerns the Person of Jesus Christ; and the attitude taken up with regard to this question will inevitably modify the whole method of studying a subject such as Christian eschatology. Any attempt at precise definition in this matter is liable to lapse either into shallow irreverence or meaningless obscurity; but perhaps the standpoint of the present essay with regard to this fundamental question will be sufficiently indicated by two quotations. The first is from the definition of Christ's Person in an ancient Confession of Catholic Christendom :—

> 'Perfect God, and perfect Man: of a reasonable soul and human flesh subsisting:
> Equal to the Father, as touching his Godhead: and inferior to the Father, as touching his Manhood.'

The second quotation is from Dr. Moberly :—

> 'In [our Lord's] human life on earth, as Incarnate, He is not sometimes, but consistently, always, in every act and every detail, Human. The Incarnate never leaves His Incarnation. . . . Whatever the reverence of their motive may be, men do harm to consistency and to truth by keeping open, as it were, a sort of non-human sphere, or aspect, of the Incarnation. . . . By looking for the Divine side by side with the human, instead of discerning the Divine within the human, we miss the significance of them both.'[1]

These two quotations briefly express the conception of our Lord's Person which has been continually present to the writer of these pages. It is only too probable that in discussing a question of such magnitude some things will be said which may seem to be inconsistent with the position indicated above. If so, it is the writer's hope that these will be attributed to an error of judgment, not to any intentional disloyalty to the faith of Christendom.

In those places where the Synoptic Problem underlies our subject, the reader of this essay will find that the general lines of modern English scholarship are followed. St. Mark's Gospel, and the non-Marcan sections common to St. Matthew and St. Luke,[2] are accepted as the two earliest witnesses, preserved with little or no change from the dates when they were originally committed to

---

[1] R. C. Moberly, *Atonement and Personality* (London, 1904), p. 97.
[2] Generally referred to as 'Q' (*i.e.* 'Quelle').

writing, *circa* A.D. 60-70; and the remaining portions of St. Matthew and St. Luke are regarded as preserving the tradition of the Church shortly before or shortly after the Fall of Jerusalem, and showing at times a 'reflection' of that tradition in their presentment of the life of our Lord. The order of events as recorded in St. Mark is taken as the best general basis for enabling us to grasp the main course of events during Christ's ministry.

With regard to the Fourth Gospel, the traditional Johannine authorship is not called in question. In the following pages it is assumed that if the author was not St. John himself, he was at any rate one who was in personal touch with Jesus during His earthly life. Nevertheless, it is well to remember the explicit statement of the Fourth Evangelist that he wrote with a definite purpose: 'that ye may believe that Jesus is the Messiah, the Son of God, and that believing ye may have life in his name.'[1] It was not, then, the author's first object to record a series of historical incidents; for the outlines of the events of the Lord's life were already well known to his readers. His aim was rather to interpret these events, and to explain their inner meaning. 'The author of the Fourth Gospel did not look so much without as within; he sank into his own consciousness, and at last brought out what he found there. He dwelt upon the past till it became luminous to him; and then he took up his pen.'[2] We may recall in this connection the well-known saying which Clement of Alexandria is said to have learnt from the early presbyters: 'John, perceiving that what had reference to the body in the Gospel of our Saviour was sufficiently detailed, . . . wrote a spiritual Gospel.'[3]

[1] John xx. 31.
[2] Sanday, *Criticism of the Fourth Gospel* (Oxford, 1905), p. 189.
[3] Eusebius, *Ecclesiastical History*, vi. 14.

This being so, we shall not turn to the Fourth Gospel primarily to learn the course of history as it appeared to the outside world; but we shall recognise that the Johannine picture of Christ does show us what manner of Person He seemed to be in the eyes of those who were nearest to Him in His life on earth. We shall not be dismayed by the possibility that the speeches of Christ in St. John's Gospel may not in all cases be verbal reports of the words which He actually spoke; on the other hand, we shall feel confident that they truly represent the substance of His teaching as it was understood by His most intimate disciples.

Approaching the Fourth Gospel from this standpoint, how shall we best deal with the Johannine eschatology? If we are right in holding that St. John meant his Gospel to be 'the interpretation of a life already known from other sources,'[1] we shall be adhering most closely to the design of its author if we first study the Synoptic Gospels, in order to learn what was the outward form of our Lord's eschatological teaching; and then turn to the Fourth Gospel to understand at least one of the ways in which it was interpreted by the early Church.

The above brief summary will, it is hoped, be sufficient to indicate the general lines on which the Gospel narratives will be studied in the present essay, with special reference to our Lord's eschatology.

[1] Drummond, *The Fourth Gospel* (London, 1903), p. 65.

CHAPTER XII

THE PEOPLE TO WHOM CHRIST PREACHED

It may be well, before turning to the heart of our subject—the New Testament narratives—to review briefly the chief features of Jewish life in the time of our Lord, in order to realise better the attitude taken up towards Him by the various sections of the Jewish People, and the effects of this upon His teaching and eschatology. We have already gained some idea, from our study of the apocalypses, of the various types of contemporary eschatological beliefs. But it must be remembered that the apocalypses reflect mainly, if not entirely, the Pharisaic standpoint, and give us no idea of the views of the Sadducees.

Even the 'Pharisaic standpoint' is not altogether easy to define with precision. For though we are accustomed to speak of the 'party of the Pharisees' as if it were a compact and united body, the phrase is in reality little more than a convenient term for a certain type of Judaism, which contained within itself various classes of people—on the one hand some of the best-educated Jews of the day, such as the scribes and lawyers, and on the other hand a large body of adherents from the illiterate masses of the population. It is clearly improbable that such heterogeneous elements of the 'Pharisaic party' would all take up the same attitude on important questions. True, there are one or two characteristics which we are accustomed—no doubt rightly—to associate universally with the name of 'Pharisee.' First among these was a zeal for the ancient Faith of Israel, its laws and ceremonies and traditions—a zeal which tended to degenerate into a rigid and barren legalism, because it lacked the living certainty of personal inspiration, which alone can give that 'sense of proportion' that enables men to discern between the essential and the secondary elements in religion. And there is another equally familiar feature of Pharisaism,—the exclusive spirit which bitterly disliked everything Gentile (particularly the Roman protectorate over Judaea), and refused to compromise religious principles for the advantage of maintaining friendly relations between Church and State. These two characteristics—which may seem, to English minds, to blend somewhat strangely, the former being suggestive of 'strict Churchmanship,' and the latter more akin to Puritanism—appear to have been generally recognised as of the essence of Pharisaism; but in connection with such matters as eschatology and the Messianic hope, the adherents of the 'Party' differed widely among themselves. The best type of educated Pharisee did not, so far as we know, associate his religious hopes with political schemes; he was willing to wait quietly for the moment when the Lord should intervene, as in the days of old, to deliver His people. If he hoped for a Messiah, it would be for a Divine Being, such as we found described in the 'Similitudes' of Enoch; and the Kingdom which he longed for was to be a spiritual 'Kingdom of the Heavens.' But among the masses of the people these hopes would naturally take a cruder form. The expectation of an earthly Prince of David's line, and of a Kingdom of Israel on earth, would be more intelligible and congenial to them than the refined ideas of their religious leaders. The spirit of the later Zealots was already stirring among the populace; and many were anxious to force on the coming of 'the Kingdom' by political agitation.

But while on these and many other matters the party of the Pharisees was by no means unanimous, it is probable that some idea of retribution beyond the grave was a recognised part of Pharisaic belief; and they trusted that the souls of their fathers who had passed away from earth before the advent of the Kingdom were yet safe in the hands of God.

We see, then, that among the Pharisees there were eager hopes ready to welcome eschatological teaching; but only if it was of the conventional type. The Pharisaic leaders, while theoretically expecting a Messiah, were not prepared to accept as such one who had sprung from a peasant home, and who showed but little respect for *their* authority. And, similarly, the popular adherents of Pharisaism, while even more ready than their teachers to hail the Messiah and enter the Kingdom, were determined to insist that the Messiah should act in accordance with their own expectations—which in this case were political—and should found the kind of kingdom which they desired,—that is to say, a kingdom of material prosperity.

Of almost equal importance with the Pharisees, though less prominent in the New Testament, were the Sadducees, composed mainly of the priests and the aristocracy. They were, for the most part, able men of the world, priding themselves on their sober and well-balanced reasonableness. They upheld the 'ancient and laudable customs' of the national religion, as conducive to sober conduct and morality; but they deprecated an excess of enthusiasm, and were sceptical of new-fangled doctrines of the future life, which offended their staid common-sense. They were particularly anxious to maintain friendly relations with the Roman power, and to check internal disorders and the spirit of 'nationalist' disaffection. They were sufficiently statesmanlike to see that, from a worldly point of view, the wisest course for the Jews was that of submission to the sovereignty of Caesar; and their desire to maintain the political *status quo* was fostered, no doubt, by the pleasant prospect of maintaining at the same time their own position of social dignity and comfort.

Hence we can see why the Sadducees looked upon eschatological speculations, not only with contempt, but with definite hostility. Had the apocalypses been always free from political intent, the enthusiastic visions of their writers would have drawn from the Sadducees only a smile of enlightened superiority. But many of the apocalypses, as we have seen, were definitely anti-Roman and anti-Sadducean in tone; and consequently they were regarded by the Sadducees as the pernicious products of a dangerous fanaticism which was anxious to undermine the political stability (such as it was) of Judaea. So their hand would be set against all who seemed disposed to kindle any unwonted enthusiasm among the 'common people,' and they would be certain to regard with grave suspicion all public teachers and preachers;—and not least, the 'Prophet of Nazareth.'

In so far as the party of the Herodians, whose interest was centred in maintaining the influence of the Jewish King, are to be accounted as a separate force in the Jewish life of the day, their distinctive characteristics would produce a dislike of popular Messianic expectation, very similar to that of the Sadducees. The influence of a prophet, such as Jesus of Nazareth, was not likely to strengthen the position of the Herodian dynasty; and so it is not surprising to find the Herodians allied with the Pharisees[1] in the endeavour to procure our Lord's downfall.

The ascetic sect of the Essenes, with their strange mixture of Hebrew, Persian, and Pythagorean beliefs, do not come into prominence in the Gospels. The attempts to prove that our Lord was connected with this sect[2] are now admitted on all hands to be mere flights of imagination. In apostolic or sub-apostolic times Essenic influence may perhaps be traced; but not in the Gospels.

As for the Roman military authorities in Palestine, their attitude towards our Lord was one of complete indifference, so far as the religious elements in His teaching were concerned; but their indifference was distinctly tinged with suspicion, lest He should fan the smouldering embers of popular 'Messianism' into a raging fire of revolt and anarchy. The sooner His preaching could be decently suppressed the better for the maintenance of Imperial law and order.

This brief review of the various parties in Judaea will enable us to perceive that from almost every quarter our Lord's teaching would be viewed with unfriendly eyes, and in particular, that part of it which referred to the Last Things and the coming of the Messiah. Sadducee, Herodian, and Roman would dislike it on political grounds, as a new and unsettling form of fanaticism; while the scribes and Pharisees, interested primarily in the religious aspect of the matter, would refuse to recognise the authority of an independent preacher who had sprung from the common people. And the common people themselves,

[1] Mark iii. 6.
[2] See (*e.g.*) Von der Alm's *Theological Letters* (1863), referred to in Schweitzer's *Von Reimarus zu Wrede*, pp. 160-178; cf. pp. 38-47 and 323-326. (The paging in the English translation of Schweitzer's book varies only very slightly from the German.)

though ready to welcome the 'new teaching,' were but a broken reed to lean upon; for when once it became clear that the Prophet of Nazareth was not going to be a political reformer or a nationalist leader, their enthusiasm was changed to bitter disappointment and resentment.

In the chapters that follow we shall see how the varying forms of opposition to our Lord played an important part in determining the form (though not the substance) of His eschatological teaching.

None of the leading parties among the Jews of our Lord's time commend themselves much to our sympathies to-day. But there were doubtless not a few pious and godly souls in whom the spirit of the Old Testament still lived on. They were zealous for a righteousness which was something more than conformity to the Law, and the Messiah whom they expected was above all one who should 'save his people from their sins.'[1] This is the atmosphere which pervades the early chapters of St. Matthew and St. Luke, and especially the Lucan canticles. The faith of Simeon has become the faith of the Church of Christ :—

'Mine eyes have seen thy salvation,
Which thou hast prepared before the face of all peoples;
A light for revelation to the Gentiles (ϵἰς ἀποκάλυψιν ἐθνῶν),
And the glory of thy people Israel.'[2]

[1] Matt. i. 21.   [2] Luke ii. 30-32.

CHAPTER XIII

OUR LORD'S PREPARATION FOR HIS MINISTRY

WE need not dwell long upon the life of our Lord before He began His public ministry. We read that 'the grace of God was upon him,' and the consciousness of His Divine mission was ever growing stronger, and, upon one occasion at least, found clear expression, in the memorable words: 'Knew ye not that for me it is necessary to be ἐν τοῖς τοῦ πατρός μου?'[1]

At length the years of silent growth are fulfilled, and their close is signalised by the trumpet-note of the Forerunner. The coming of John the Baptist seems like a revival of the ancient days of Old Testament prophecy. Here at last, after so many centuries, is a man who has the courage to deliver a message straight from God. He does not shelter himself under the great names of the past, but speaks out with boldness, conscious of his own inspiration. The great Messianic crisis is coming upon the nation—so runs the refrain of John's message; and like Amos of old, he summons the Chosen People to repent, in order that they may be prepared to meet their God in the impending Day of Judgment. But the Baptist explicitly rejects any office beyond that of the Lord's Messenger; it was his to sound the warning, not actually to bring about the crisis. He that is coming after John will inaugurate the Messianic Era

[1] Luke ii. 49.

by pouring out the gift of the Holy Spirit, as foretold by the prophets.[1] So much is recorded by St. Mark;[2] from St. Matthew we learn that John described the New Era as 'the kingdom of the heavens' ($\dot{\eta}$ βασιλεία τῶν οὐρανῶν);[3] and St. Luke mentions the popular expectation that John might be the Messiah.[4] All three evangelists emphasise the strong practical advice which accompanies the eschatological preaching of the Baptist. He took up the message of the apocalyptic writers, not as an end in itself, but as a means to lead men to repentance and righteousness.

It is not infrequently assumed that because our Lord submitted to be baptized by John, the Gospel of Jesus must have been at the outset only a subordinate branch of the movement inaugurated by the Baptist. But the explanation of the action which is given by our Lord is characteristic of His attitude towards the Old Covenant in this early period :—' Suffer it now ; for thus it becometh us to fulfil every righteous requirement (πᾶσαν δικαιοσύνην).'[5] The Baptism was no confession of inferiority, but rather one of the first signs that Jesus had come 'not to undo, but to fulfil.'

All the Synoptists record that at the Baptism our Lord received a special revelation of His Divine Sonship. We may recall that in the Jewish apocalypses the Messiah is referred to by the Almighty as 'My Son';[6] so that the voice, 'Thou art my beloved Son,' might be understood to be a proclamation of the Messiahship of

---

[1] Joel ii. 28 ; Isa. xxxii. 15 ; Ezek. xxxix. 29 ; Zech. xii; 10.

[2] Mark i. 2-8. The additional details in Matthew and Luke (probably from the 'Q' document) are in complete accord with the brief Marcan account.

[3] Matt. iii. 2.   [4] Luke iii. 15.

[5] Matt. iii. 15 ; for δικαιοσύνη = 'whatever is right,' see Grimm and Thayer's *Lexicon of the New Testament* (4th edition, 1901), p. 149.

[6] Eth. En. cv. 2 ; 4 Ezra xiii. 32, 37, 52, xiv. 9, etc.; cf. Ps. ii. 7, lxxxix. 27.

THE TEMPTATION

Jesus, though apparently it was not a very common Messianic title.[1]

The presumption that our Lord's Messianic Consciousness dates in its fulness from His Baptism is strengthened by the narratives of the Temptation in St. Matthew and St. Luke.[2] The suggestions of Satan are intended to persuade our Lord to misuse His Messianic Sonship. He is tempted to give way to carnal desires, to make a display of His miraculous powers, and to found an empire of this world. Each temptation is firmly withstood; and there seems little doubt that our Lord's attitude in face of these great issues was determined once and for all before He entered on His public ministry.

[1] See Dalman, *Words of Jesus*, pp. 268-273.
[2] Matt. iv. 1-11; Luke iv. 1-12.

CHAPTER XIV

THE PREACHING OF 'THE KINGDOM OF GOD'

JOHN'S call to repentance, and his announcement that the Kingdom of God was at hand, were still ringing in the ears of the people of Judaea, when Jesus came into Galilee with the same solemn message upon His lips:—

> 'The time is fulfilled, and the Kingdom of God is at hand; repent ye, and believe the good tidings.'

Was this 'Kingdom of God' which our Lord proclaimed 'eschatological,' or was it not? This is one of the most momentous questions in the study of Christian eschatology.

To avoid misconceptions, it may be well to define at the outset what we mean by an 'eschatological kingdom.' We have seen that the 'Kingdom of God' in Jewish eschatology might be either on earth or in heaven, material or spiritual. But there have been two essential characteristics always associated with the idea of an 'eschatological kingdom'; it must be in the future, separated from the present conditions of this world by a definite historical crisis (the Last Judgment), and it must be an era of perfection, when the sovereignty of God holds absolute sway. So, when we ask whether 'the Kingdom of God' as preached by our Lord was 'eschatological,' we are asking whether He meant to preach the coming of a kingdom which would begin

THE ESCHATOLOGICAL ELEMENT 129

after a great catastrophe, and which would then satisfy every religious ideal.

A very little reflection will suffice to show that when our Lord spoke of 'the Kingdom of God,' He must have wished to retain an element of eschatology in His teaching. For the study of contemporary Jewish literature has made it clear beyond doubt that His message, 'The Kingdom of God is at hand,' would be understood by Jewish hearers in an eschatological sense. This being so, we cannot doubt that this meaning of the term was agreeable to our Lord's teaching; otherwise we should accuse Him of deliberately creating an impression which He believed to be untrue. At the same time, it does not follow that this was the only aspect of 'the Kingdom' which was present to His mind.

Besides this *a priori* argument, there are certain sayings of our Lord which speak of 'the Kingdom' in a sense which can only be eschatological.[1] One or two examples will suffice. In St. Matthew vii. 21, 22 we read:—

> 'Not every one that saith unto me, Lord, Lord, shall enter into the Kingdom of Heaven; but he that doeth the will of my Father which is in Heaven. Many will say to me in that day, Lord, Lord, . . .' etc.

Now in this passage, the phrase 'that day' unmistakably refers to the last Day of Judgment;[2] and the close association implied between 'that day' and 'entering the Kingdom of Heaven' leaves no room for doubt as to the eschatological significance of the latter phrase.[3]

---

[1] It is noteworthy, however, that in St. Mark's account of the Galilean ministry, these sayings are almost, if not entirely, absent; and in other cases it is difficult to be sure of the original context of the 'logia.'

[2] Cf. Matt. vii. 22, 23 with Matt. xxv. 44-46.

[3] See, however, Von Dobschutz, *Eschatology of the Gospels*, p. 81, where it is contended that the eschatological 'tone' of this passage is due to the Evangelist.

K

Another passage which clearly looks forward to the Last Crisis is the following:—

> 'Many shall come from the East and the West, and shall sit down . . . in the Kingdom of Heaven.'[1]

And once more, in the Parable of the Tares, 'the Kingdom of the Father'[2] can only refer to the Final Consummation. These 'logia' confirm the very strong probability that our Lord did not wish to exclude the eschatological element in the idea of 'the Kingdom.'

But in recent years, certain Continental writers of the 'Eschatological School,'[3] not satisfied with the admission that there undoubtedly was an element of eschatology in our Lord's preaching of the Kingdom, have affirmed that this was His sole and exclusive meaning. He expected—so we are told—that in the immediate future a transcendental Kingdom of God would be inaugurated by a special Divine intervention. The coming of this kingdom was to be quite independent of the actions of men in general or of Jesus in particular; it was to be a pure miracle, the time and manner of its advent being predestined in God's purpose, and revealed in the Scriptures and in the apocalyptic literature. Johannes Weiss, for instance, writes thus:—

> 'The disciples are to pray that the Kingdom may come, but, generally speaking, no human being can re-establish it. Even Jesus cannot bring to pass the Kingdom of God, or found it, or set it up; God alone can do that.'[4]

Schweitzer, in his book *Von Reimarus zu Wrede*, is even more thorough-going in his eschatological conception of the Kingdom. It is to be so transcendental

---

[1] Matt. viii. 11. In Luke xiii. 29 this saying is placed in the later ministry.
[2] Matt. xiii. 43.   [3] See above, p. 111, note (1).
[4] Joh. Weiss, *Die Predigt Jesu vom Reiche Gottes*, p. 62.

WAS IT PURELY TRANSCENDENTAL? 131

that nothing positive can be predicated of it, not even the great principles of right and wrong :—

> 'For Jesus, there can be no morality (*Sittlichkeit*) of the Kingdom of God; since in the Kingdom of God all the conditions of this world, even the distinctions of sex (St. Mark xii. 25) are suspended; temptation and sin exist no more.'[1]

Schweitzer apparently thinks that this extremely 'other-worldly' idea of the Kingdom was universal among the Jews; at least he is very severe on those who suggest that Christ may have wished to transform or ennoble the general expectations of the people.[2] Schweitzer and Johannes Weiss certainly possess the virtue of consistency; but it remains to be seen whether the facts bear them out.[3]

In the first place, is their contention, that Christ's idea of a purely transcendental kingdom was simply the generally-accepted belief of His contemporaries, supported by the study of the apocalyptic literature? It is true that the 'Similitudes' of Enoch, about a century before Christ, afford an example of such a belief.[4] But in the Psalms of Solomon—a book which is more nearly contemporary with our Lord—the expectation of the Kingdom is distinctly mundane and political.[5] The internal evidence of the Gospels themselves is even more convincing, as showing that the idea of a political Messiah was by no means inconceivable to the Jews of that era. Those who brought the tribute-money to Jesus evidently thought that they might persuade Him

---

[1] Schweitzer, *op. cit.* p. 362 (Eng. trans. p. 364).

[2] See especially chaps. xvi. and xviii., and his review of Johannes Weiss's work in pp. 235-238 (Eng. trans. pp. 237-240).

[3] For the practical importance of the 'Eschatological Controversy,' see below, Part VI.

[4] Even here the political element is not entirely absent; see above, p. 87.

[5] Pss. Sol. xvii. 23-57. See above, pp. 89, 90.

to declare Himself a political anti-Roman Messiah.¹ And the question of the primitive Church to the Lord after His resurrection, 'Dost thou at this time restore the Kingdom to Israel?'² surely reflects an expectation of the Kingdom which was by no means purely transcendental. It is wholly inconsistent with the general tenor of the Gospel narratives to suppose that Christ's teaching and the popular eschatology were at one in implying that 'the Kingdom of God' was an altogether other-worldly state of existence.

We read, moreover, that 'the Kingdom,' as first preached by our Lord, was a 'mystery,' revealed to the disciples, but deliberately hidden from the people. Before explaining the Parable of the Sower, He tells them: 'Unto you is given the mystery (τὸ μυστήριον) of the Kingdom of God; but unto them that are without, all things are done in parables.'³ Now these words certainly imply that Christ was not merely accepting the current view of 'the Kingdom'; for in that case there would have been no mystery about it, either to the disciples, or to 'those that were without,' the common people. Schweitzer's attempts to reconcile 'the mystery of the Kingdom' with his theory are most unconvincing. He tells us that 'the mystery' or 'secret' was the esoteric teaching by which Christ revealed to the disciples the reasons for the *nearness* of the Kingdom.⁴ But why should He have wished to conceal *this* from the populace? Indeed, had He not already divulged it in His own preaching, 'The Kingdom of God *is at hand*'? And when we are told that the central purpose of the Parables of the Sower and

---
¹ Mark xii. 13-27, etc.   ² Acts i. 6.
³ Mark iv. 11; cf. Matt. xiii. 11, Luke viii. 10. Matt. and Luke have "τὰ μυστήρια."
⁴ 'The secret must therefore explain why the Kingdom must now come, and how men are to perceive how near it is.'—Schweitzer, p. 352 (Eng. trans. p. 354).

THE 'MYSTERY OF THE KINGDOM' 133

the Mustard-seed was to contrast the feebleness of the human 'sowing' with the magnitude of the supernatural advent of the Kingdom, and thus to emphasise the omnipotence of predestination,[1] we are inclined to wonder whether any impartial reader, not already prepossessed with a clear-cut theory, would gather this lesson at first sight from the parables in question; so forced is the interpretation needed to reconcile them with the 'Eschatological Theory.'

But if our Lord, instead of indiscriminately adopting the popular idea of the Kingdom, was in reality desirous of transforming it and freeing it from its political associations, then it becomes easier to understand why the preaching of the Kingdom was kept a 'mystery' outside the circle of His disciples. For it would then be necessary to teach the people by veiled metaphors, lest the repeated announcement of the nearness of the kingdom should arouse a popular tumult. The utmost that could be attempted at first would be to guide the thoughts of the people in a right direction. To the disciples it was given to know more of 'the mystery,' because the inner meaning of the parables was explained to them by the Master. And this inner meaning was something new; no one before Jesus had thought of likening the homely events of country life to the eschatological Kingdom of God. So this saying about 'the mystery of the Kingdom,' occurring, as it does in all three Synoptists, in the midst of the Galilean parables, affords strong evidence that our Lord's idea of the Kingdom was not limited by the old ideas of Jewish eschatology, but was, in part at least, unfamiliar and mysterious to His hearers.

Another grave objection to the purely eschatological view of Christ's preaching occurs in certain of the sayings

---

[1] Schweitzer, *op. cit.* p. 353 (Eng. trans. p. 355).

of Jesus which imply that the Kingdom is present here in this world. One instance may be cited, which evidently belongs to the period of the Galilean ministry :—

> 'If I by the finger of God cast out devils, then is the Kingdom of God come upon you (ἔφθασεν ἐφ' ὑμᾶς).'[1]

This was our Lord's reply when He was accused of using the power of the arch-devil. The phrase "ἔφθασεν ἐφ' ὑμᾶς" seems most naturally to mean that the Kingdom had actually come.[2] Or take St. Matthew xi. 12 :—

> 'From the days of John the Baptist until now the Kingdom of Heaven suffereth violence, and the violent take it by force.'

Now whatever be the exact meaning of this difficult saying, it certainly implies that the Kingdom of Heaven *has been* in existence 'from the days of John the Baptist' until the time when the words were spoken. The parallel passage in St. Luke xvi. 16 is equally clear on this point :—

> 'The law and the prophets were until John; from that time the Gospel of the Kingdom of God is preached, and every man entereth violently into it.'

The same impression is even more clearly conveyed by the Parables of the Kingdom. Many of these do not naturally suggest anything like the eschatology of the Jewish apocalypses.[3] If we read through the Parables of the Sower, or the Mustard-seed, or the Leaven, or the Draw-net, with a mind freed as far as possible from preconceptions, can we fairly say that

---

[1] Matt. xii. 28 (=Luke xi. 20); generally assigned to the 'Q' document.

[2] In 1 Thess. ii. 16, if "ἡ ὀργὴ" be the Last (eschatological) Crisis, then "ἔφθασεν" must be 'is on the point of coming.' But "ἡ ὀργὴ" there may well be some punishment which *had* actually come upon the offenders.

[3] See Temple, *The Faith and Modern Thought* (London, 1910), p. 93.

they suggest a supernatural Kingdom in the heavens, which has no connection with the things of earth? It is, as we have said, of the very essence of an eschatological kingdom that it should be the *perfect* realisation of every hope and desire. But the Galilean parables speak of growth from small things to great; and the Parables of the Draw-net and the Tares assume that there will be evil in the Kingdom as well as good. Is this conceivable in an eschatological kingdom? Nor is even more direct evidence lacking. What could be plainer than the language of the Parable of the Tares?—'The Kingdom of Heaven is like unto a man that sowed good seed in his field. . . . The field is the world (ὁ κόσμος).'[1] And again, we are reminded that the Kingdom is associated with earth as well as with heaven, by the two phrases which we meet with in our Lord's explanation of this same parable: 'The Kingdom of the Son of Man' and 'The Kingdom of the Father.'[2] The former, we read, will continue till 'the end of the world.' To rule out this aspect of the Kingdom, as is done by the 'consistent eschatologists,' involves a forced and unnatural interpretation of one of the most distinctive and unique features of Christ's teaching—His Galilean parables.

Once more, the evidence of the Synoptic Gospels cannot be reconciled with the contention of Weiss and Schweitzer, that in the founding of the Kingdom there is no place for human agency.[3] This contention unquestionably includes an element of truth. We all admit that the final destinies of this world and all other

---

[1] Matt. xiii. 24, 38. The Parable of the Tares, like the other Galilean parables, depicts events of agricultural life; but the general tone suggests that it belongs to a late period in the Galilean ministry, when the opposition of the Pharisees had become very strongly marked.

The genuineness of the explanation in Matt. xiii. 37-43 is sometimes questioned, but on somewhat arbitrary grounds.

[2] Matt. xiii. 41-43.   [3] See above, p. 130.

worlds must lie ultimately in the hands of the Almighty. But the Kingdom of God which Christ proclaimed was to be a kingdom for men. And Christ teaches that where man's destiny is concerned, man's will and conduct is always one of the factors which determine that destiny.[1] We may well ask, If the coming of the Kingdom was to be wholly independent of the conduct of mankind, why does the Herald of the Kingdom devote so much of His teaching to practical morality? And, above all, why does He, in His later ministry, denounce the Jews again and again for their rejection of the Divine offer? For the Parables of the Great Supper and of the Husbandmen (to name only two examples) clearly teach that the advent of the Kingdom was, for all practical and human purposes, dependent on the attitude of the Jews; otherwise Christ would be blaming the Jews for rejecting that which they had not the power to choose.

Or, if we turn again to the Galilean 'parables of the field,' we find here, too, that earthly agencies play a part in the advent of the Kingdom. We read of growth in the Kingdom, and growth by natural law. The Sower sows the seed, but only that which falls on good ground bears fruit. And in the Parable of the Seed Sown we even read that the growth is unknown to the Sower.[2] Can this be reconciled with Schweitzer's ideas of rigid predestination? So, in the Parables of the Treasure and the Pearl, the Kingdom has to be discovered by man, as well as given by God. It seems impossible to reconcile these parables with the purely eschatological Kingdom described by the 'consistent eschatologists.' For if they were right in holding that our Lord's first purpose was to proclaim an unconditional coming of the Kingdom, then His moral teaching ought

---

[1] Cf. Mark vi. 5, 6, John v. 40.   [2] Mark iv. 27.

to have occupied a secondary place.¹ But this does not seem to have been the view of the writers of our Gospels. If they believed that the essential part of Christ's teaching was His proclamation of the New Era, why is it that in the Gospels His moral teaching, with its vital relation to the present life, is recorded at much greater length than His eschatological sayings?² If all moral distinctions were to be swept away by the coming of the Kingdom, which might be expected any hour, we should be driven to ask whether the teaching of the Sermon on the Mount was not, after all, somewhat irrelevant. Our Lord Himself did not consider that His moral teaching was only destined to last for a few days: 'Heaven and earth shall pass away; but my words shall not pass away.'³ But those who adopt the 'consistent eschatological' position ask us to believe that men who wrote when eschatological hopes were at their height deliberately shifted the centre of gravity of the message of Jesus from His eschatology (its true position) to His moral teaching. In other words, it is assumed that there is a 'tendency' in the Gospels, which runs directly contrary to the tendencies of contemporary Jewish thought. Is this sound historical criticism?

We conclude, then, that in our Lord's preaching of the Kingdom there was some other element besides eschatology—something which was a 'mystery' to the Jewish people; which might rightly be spoken of in terms of this present world; and which allows us to attribute to our Lord's moral teaching that supreme importance which is given to it in the Gospels. And on the other hand, we cannot doubt that, whatever new meaning our Lord wished to put into the conception of 'the Kingdom,' He must have intended to include the

---
¹ See below, p. 391, note (1).
² Cf. Harnack, *Sayings of Jesus*, pp. 250, 251.   ³ Matt. xxiv. 35.

current eschatological ideas, which would naturally be suggested to His hearers by the language He chose to adopt.

From what has been said above, it will be evident that it is not easy to define how far our Lord's preaching of the Kingdom might fairly be called 'eschatological.' Indeed we cannot expect to realise completely what was in His mind. But a few considerations may help us to reconcile some of the apparent inconsistencies in His language.

The first is this: that Christ recognises the value of partial realisations of the highest ideal, even in this present life. It is characteristic of the greatest men to be sympathetic towards the failings of others, whilst themselves refusing to be content with anything short of the very highest ideal. So with our Lord; His eyes are fixed on the ideal Kingdom to come, but He does not despise the imperfect efforts of men to realise it here in this world.

As an example of this, we may refer to our Lord's attitude towards the Old Testament. He does not scruple to alter its teaching where necessary, and yet He affirms its value and authority.[1] Very similar was His teaching with regard to the peculiar claims of the Jewish people. Although Israel had palpably failed to realise the ideal of the Kingdom of God on earth, our Lord still recognises their unique position. It was no sign of exclusiveness, but simply the outcome of His general attitude to the Old Testament revelation, when He commanded His disciples: 'Go not into any way of the Gentiles, and enter not into any city of the Samaritans; but go rather to the lost sheep of the house of Israel.'[2] For we must remember that the message

---

[1] Matt. v. 17-48.   [2] Matt. x. 5, 6.

could not be preached all over the world at once by the small handful of Christ's followers. Their efforts must be concentrated in order to be effective. And where could the good news of the Kingdom be more fitly inaugurated than among the people who had ever cherished the hope of the Kingdom? But our Lord's outlook was by no means limited to Israel. In the synagogue at Nazareth, standing on the threshold of His ministry, and as if striking the keynote of His life's aim, He points to the widow of Zarephath and to Naaman the Syrian as signs of the future extension of the Gospel to the Gentiles.[1] But He was sent first to the ancient people of God,[2] in order that through them all the nations of the earth might be blessed. Though they had only realised their ideal in part, that partial realisation of theirs was not without its value.

So again, when our Lord cast out the devils, He felt that in Himself the Kingdom of God had already come among the Jews.[3] It was but a partial advent, for it was complete in Him alone; but it was a real advent. And when the Seventy returned and reported that the evil spirits were obedient to their command, He tells them that this is a sign that the reign of Satan is potentially overthrown.[4] Similarly we understand those parables where a present kingdom seems to be implied. In the Parables of the Sower and the Seed Sown, only the beginnings of the Kingdom are described; but the little seed is truly 'seed of the Kingdom,' and it is recognised as such by the Master, in every age.

This may help us to understand the Parables of the Tares and of the Draw-net. Here our Lord not only speaks of the Kingdom as present, but tells us that evil

---

[1] Luke iv. 24, 25.
[2] Cf. Mark vii. 27.
[3] Matt. xii. 28.
[4] Luke x. 17, 18.

will exist in it by the side of the good. Probably the description of the Tares was suggested by the old Hebrew idea that Israel as a nation was the Vineyard of Jehovah. Jesus recognised that claim when He describes the Jews as God's 'husbandmen';[1] and yet Israel's national life had been far from faultless. So, in the Parable of the Tares, He describes this present world as 'His Kingdom,' although there are weeds in it as well as wheat. But He clearly distinguishes between *this* kingdom of mingled good and evil and the eschatological 'Kingdom of the Father' which will follow the Last Judgment :—

> 'In the end of the world, the Son of Man shall send forth his angels, and they shall gather out of his Kingdom all things that cause stumbling; . . . then shall the righteous shine forth as the sun in the Kingdom of their Father.'[2]

And similarly in the Parable of the Draw-net, the good and bad are present in the Kingdom till the end of the world.[3]

It seems, then, that our Lord recognised a non-eschatological, earthly, and imperfect aspect of the Kingdom of God; and His words justify us in speaking of the Church of Christ as the Kingdom of God on earth. Only we shall do well to remember that in His teaching the value of the present imperfect Kingdom lies not in what it is, but in what it is to be. It is the eschatological kingdom that gives to the imperfect kingdom of to-day whatever value it may possess. But the two are essentially the same kingdom, only in different stages of development.

---

[1] Mark xii. 1-9, etc.

[2] Matt. xiii. 41, 43. Some critics assume that Matt. xiii. 36-43 (the explanation of 'the Tares') is a later 'reflection' of early Church teaching. But Mark iv. 11 suggests that Christ did give esoteric instruction.

[3] Matt. xiii. 48, 49.

THE CONDITIONS OF ITS ADVENT

Another important consideration to bear in mind is, that Christ's preaching of the Kingdom was dependent on moral conditions. In an earlier section of this chapter we came to the conclusion that man, as well as God, had his part to play in bringing in the Kingdom. Unless man fulfils certain conditions, the Kingdom will not come. Nor have we far to seek for the conditions. In St. Matthew and St. Mark the first recorded preaching of our Lord is summed up in two sayings: 'The Kingdom is at hand' and 'Repent ye.' The connection between the two is most intimate; indeed we might almost say that they express the human and Divine aspects of the same thing. Human repentance is a necessary prelude to the coming of God's Kingdom; God's Kingdom is the certain sequel to human repentance. Or from another point of view, they are expressions of the two great Divine attributes, Love and Righteousness. 'The Kingdom is at hand'—there is God's love, ever wishing to pour upon man the highest blessings. 'Repent ye'—there is God's righteousness, refusing to award the blessing unless the recipient strive to be worthy of it.

It follows that Christ's preaching of the Kingdom was from the first essentially on a moral basis. It was not so much the prediction of a coming event, but rather the proclamation of a great opportunity, and the good news of God's *willingness* to inaugurate the Kingdom. Christ's moral teaching is no mere ornamental appendage to His eschatology, but is inseparably bound up with it. The eschatology of our Lord shows us the goal of His moral teaching; but without the moral teaching the eschatology has little real value.

It is often said that Christ's teaching sets forth an impossible standard of morality; and this is partly true, for in His moral teaching there is always an eschatological element. The moral standard of which He speaks is not the standard of the past or present, but of the future Kingdom of God. That is why the world does not outgrow the moral teaching of Jesus Christ. To each generation His message comes : ' Be ye therefore perfect, as your heavenly Father is perfect.'[1]

If we are right in concluding that our Lord's announcement of the Kingdom was really the offer of a great opportunity, then the moral conditions attached to His preaching can never be ignored, even where they are not explicitly mentioned. A case in point is the 'hard saying' in St. Matthew x. 23 : 'Ye shall not have gone through the cities of Israel, till the Son of Man be come.' There can be no doubt that to the mind of the Evangelist the coming of the Son of Man was synonymous with the coming of the eschatological Kingdom.[2] But, in fact, the disciples made their round of the cities, and returned to Jesus, and the eschatological Son of Man did not come. The reason may have been that the disciples were sent to go through the cities *in order that men might repent*; this purpose was not fully realised, and so the moral conditions essential to the coming of the Kingdom were not fulfilled. The 'logion,' as recorded in St. Matthew, appears to be an unqualified prediction, without any moral conditions attached; but in face of the general tenor of our Lord's preaching, it is at least probable that some such conditions were present to His mind, if not expressed by His lips. There is, however, another possible explanation : that the evangelist reported what seemed to him to be our Lord's general meaning, but did not adhere to His exact words. In this way 'the coming of the Son of Man' might be substituted for 'the coming of the Kingdom,'

---

[1] Matt. v. 48.
[2] See below, on the 'Son of Man Problem,' pp. 153 ff.

by which our Lord might have meant one of the partial 'advents' which He certainly seems to have recognised. There seems to be an instance of this in the parallel passages, St. Mark ix. 1, St. Matthew xvi. 28, St. Luke ix. 22. In St. Mark we read: 'There be some standing here, which shall in no wise taste of death, till they see the Kingdom of God come with power.' St. Luke's version is substantially the same; but in St. Matthew the last clause runs, 'till they see *the Son of Man coming in His Kingdom.*' Now while the words of St. Mark, the earlier evangelist, are at least capable of a non-eschatological interpretation, St. Matthew's phraseology can only refer to the Last Crisis. The passage is very interesting, as illustrating a tendency on the part of (at any rate the later) evangelists to 'read into' our Lord's words an eschatological significance which may not have been originally contained in them.[1]

Before we conclude our study of 'the Kingdom of God' in our Lord's preaching, one notable passage claims our attention—St. Luke xvii. 21 : " Ἡ βασιλεία τοῦ θεοῦ ἐντὸς ὑμῶν ἐστιν " (R.V. 'The Kingdom of God is within you;' R.V. margin, 'in the midst of you'). The Pharisees had come to ask *when* the Kingdom was to come. Jesus answers : 'The Kingdom of God cometh not with observation (παρατήρησις); neither shall they say, Lo here! or, There! for lo! the Kingdom of God is ἐντὸς ὑμῶν.'[2] Many commentators, rendering " ἐντὸς ὑμῶν " by 'within you,' see in this passage a parallel to the 'spiritual' doctrine of the Fourth Gospel, which regards 'the Kingdom' primarily as a state of mind.[3]

[1] See also below, on the Eschatological Discourse, pp. 178, 179.

[2] Luke xvii. 20, 21.

[3] This interpretation is also found in one of the Oxyrhynchus Logia : "Ἡ βασ[ιλεία τῶν οὐρανῶν] ἐντὸς ὑμῶν [ἐ]στι[ν, καὶ ὅστις ἂν ἑαυτὸν] γνῷ ταύτην εὑρή[σει· καὶ εὑρόντες] ἑαυτοὺς γνώσεσθε [ὅτι υἱοὶ καὶ θυγατέρες] ἐστὲ ὑμεῖς τοῦ πατρὸς τοῦ π[αντοκράτορος, καὶ] γνώσεσθε ἑαυτοὺς [ἐν τῇ πτόλει ὄντας]· καὶ ὑμεῖς ἐστε ἡ πτ[όλις]."

(*Continued on next page.*)

But this exegesis ignores the fact that the saying was addressed to the Pharisees, who were at that time rejecting the offer of the Kingdom of God. How could it possibly be said that the Kingdom was within their hearts? Hence to obtain a reasonable meaning, it seems best to follow the margin of the Revised Version, and translate "ἐντὸς ὑμῶν" by 'in your midst.'[1]

Then a second question arises: Does the saying mean that the Kingdom is *now* in the midst of the Jews, or is the verb (ἐστιν) in the 'prophetic present' tense, so that it refers to a *future* coming? The first meaning is not inconsistent with our Lord's teaching, which recognises the imperfect realisations of 'the Kingdom' here in this world. But the second interpretation is the more forcible; in that case the meaning will be, that when the Kingdom has come, it will be universally recognised. It will not come because men watch for it (μετὰ παρατηρήσεως); but when it does come, it will not be a petty insurrection under some fanatical pseudo-Messiah, so that men can cry, 'Here it is!' or 'There it is!' but it will be known by all men to be 'in their midst.'

This interpretation possesses the additional advantage that it is in exact agreement with the 'Logia' which follow :—

> 'They shall say to you, Lo there! Lo here! Go not away, nor follow after them; for as the lightning when it lighteneth out of the one part under the heaven shineth unto the other part under heaven; so shall the Son of Man be in his day.'[2]

The bracketed portions are Dr. Swete's conjectural restorations. For further particulars, see Grenfell and Hunt's *Sayings of Jesus* (Oxford, 1897), part i. pp. 3 ff.

[1] So Grimm and Thayer's *Lexicon of the New Testament*, p. 218. Von Dobschutz, however (*Eschatology of the Gospels*, pp. 129-131), advocates the rendering 'within you.'

[2] Luke xvii. 23, 24.

Suddenness and universality are to be characteristics of the coming of the Kingdom of God and of the Son of Man. This is the lesson taught by the words: "Ἡ βασιλεία τοῦ θεοῦ ἐντὸς ὑμῶν ἐστιν."

Our brief examination of Christ's preaching of the Kingdom in His Galilean ministry has shown us how very wide was the meaning of the phrase in His teaching; so wide that it is hard to describe it concisely. Perhaps we may say (though the definition has a somewhat modern sound) that by 'the Kingdom of God' our Lord meant 'the ideal life for the nation and for the individual.' The eschatological usage of the phrase also expresses a faith in the ultimate triumph of good over evil, and in the final fulfilment of the Divine purpose. The consistent pessimist cannot hope for a future Kingdom of God.

The phrase was one which was full of venerable memories for the men of our Lord's time; and, apart from its associations, it suggests an essential element in the ideal life—harmony with the Sovereign Will that rules the world. To the Jews, the mention of 'the Kingdom' would bring with it many eschatological thoughts of the Messianic Crisis, the Resurrection, and the Last Judgment. Our Lord nowhere contradicts these current ideas; indeed, in the Parables of the Tares and the Draw-net He seems distinctly to sanction them. But in the records of the Galilean ministry, and especially in St. Mark's account, eschatology forms only a small part of Christ's teaching. He does not dwell upon eschatological details, as the apocalyptists had done; and the more savage features of the apocalypses—such as the exulting descriptions of the fate of the wicked—find no echo in His teaching. The Kingdom that He preached was transcendental rather than political; but the all-pervading moral tone redeems it from 'otherworldliness.' In the apocalypses the great dividing-line was between this world and the next; in Christ's teaching the division is rather between those who accept and those who reject the great moral principles upon which the Kingdom of God is founded.

But even to our day, the Kingdom remains in part 'a mystery,' as it was to the first disciples. Each age learns fresh truths of the Kingdom, but the depth of the Divine purpose remains unfathomable as ever. It may be well for us to remember that to unlearned and ignorant men the mysteries of the Kingdom were first revealed.—

> 'I thank thee, O Father, Lord of heaven and earth, that thou didst hide these things from the wise and prudent, and didst reveal them unto babes. Even so, Father, for so it seemed good in thy sight.'

CHAPTER XV

THE MESSIANIC CONSCIOUSNESS OF OUR LORD

CHRIST'S eschatology is so indissolubly linked with His own Person as the central Figure in the Drama of the Last Things, that a careful study of His own claims to be the Messianic Judge is essential for our purpose. Very few scholars of note have denied that our Lord, at least in the later years of His ministry, believed Himself to be the Messiah of Israel. Doubts on this point are possible only for the most thorough-going sceptic. But granting that the existence of Christ's Messianic Consciousness is beyond reasonable question, there are further questions to be asked, concerning the time when He first possessed it, the extent to which He publicly proclaimed it, and the conception of Messiahship implied in it.

The last-named point may conveniently be considered first. The 'Eschatological School' on the Continent, while emphasising the Messianic Consciousness of Jesus, maintain that it was the consciousness of *future* Messiahship only. In other words, Christ believed that He was *going to be* the Messianic 'Son of Man,' who was to inaugurate the New Era, and assume the rule of the eschatological Kingdom of God; but during His earthly life He had no thought of claiming Messianic authority.[1]

[1] Schweitzer, *op. cit.* chap. xix.; see especially pp. 369 ff. (Eng. trans. pp. 370 ff.).

But can this theory be reconciled with the evidence of the Gospels? Could a higher assertion of present authority be found than in the Sermon on the Mount: 'Ye have heard that it was said . . ., but *I* say unto you'? What but the Messianic Consciousness could have given the courage thus to alter the Divine 'Torah'? Or who but a claimant to the Messiahship would have dared to say that a Mosaic ordinance was merely a temporary and regrettable necessity?[1] And further, the Lord's assertion that He had authority to forgive sins in this present world cannot reasonably be understood except as an assertion of present Messiahship. For the Messiah, as Judge at the Last Day, was then to have the power to remit or enforce the penalty for sin; and Christ's 'authority to forgive sins' on earth is simply this same Messianic and judicial power, exercised by Him during His earthly life.[2] If He believed Himself to be already the Messiah, the claim to forgive sins was a natural part of His Messianic office; if otherwise, the claim would have been strangely premature. Or once more, if we turn to St. Luke's narrative of the visit to the Synagogue at Nazareth, the Messianic claim is not for the future, but for the present:—

> 'The Spirit of the Lord *is* upon me; because he hath anointed me to preach good tidings. . . . To-day *hath* this scripture *been fulfilled* in your ears.'[3]

[1] Mark x. 5.

[2] Dalman, *Words of Jesus* (Eng. trans., Edinburgh, 1902), p. 262, states that Judaism never asserted that the Messiah had power to forgive sins. But even if it is not explicitly asserted, it is surely implied in the doctrine of the supreme judicial functions of the Messianic 'Son of Man,' as we find Him described (*e.g.*) in the Book of Enoch. For although 'forgiveness' is something *more* than simply the cancelling of punishment, the two are closely akin to one another.

[3] Luke iv. 18, 21. It appears from verse 23 ('what we have heard done at Capernaum') that the incident occurred later than might be gathered from its position in St. Luke; but, still, it must belong to the early ministry.

ITS EARLIEST MANIFESTATIONS   149

In face of this and other similar evidence, the assertion of Schweitzer, that Jesus did not recognise Himself as the present Messiah, involves a purely arbitrary excision of numerous passages from every one of the four Gospels.

The next problem before us is, When did our Lord begin to possess the Messianic Consciousness? In the first place, we note that from the beginning of the ministry He accepts the title 'Son of God,' both at His Baptism and when hailed by the 'unclean spirits.'[1] Now the term 'Son of God,' though apparently not a frequent term for the Messiah, was distinctly associated with Messianic prophecy and expectation,[2] and it seems unlikely that Jesus would have accepted it without demur thus early in His ministry, unless He were already fully convinced of His Messiahship. Again, the Messianic claim to forgive sins, to which we have just referred, is one of the earliest recorded incidents of the ministry in Galilee. And at a somewhat later period, but still in the Galilean ministry, we read of our Lord's answer to John the Baptist. It is true that He does not directly reply to the Baptist's question, 'Art thou the Coming One?' but the significant saying, 'Blessed is he who shall not find occasion of stumbling in me,'[3] leaves little room for doubt as to what was in His mind. If at this time our Lord believed Himself to be Messiah and was only restraining for a time the public avowal, these words are natural and impressive. If He did not as yet possess the Messianic Consciousness, they are unintelligible or even misleading.

Thus the Synoptic Gospels, including St. Mark, distinctly imply that, at any rate from the outset of the Galilean ministry, and probably from the time of His

[1] Mark i. 11, iii. 11, etc.   [2] See above, pp. 33, 97, 127.
[3] Matt. xi. 6 = Luke vii. 23, generally assigned to the 'Q' document. Cf. Matt. xiii. 16.

Baptism, Jesus believed that He was the Messiah, and was invested with full Messianic authority.

This view of our Lord's Messianic Consciousness does not appear to be in vogue among the 'orthodox Liberal' school of German criticism. 'We must assert,' says Harnack,[1] 'that the consciousness of Divine Sonship and of Messiahship could not have existed together from the beginning; for the consciousness of Messiahship never meant anything else for our Lord than a consciousness of what *He was about to become.* In His soul the consciousness of what He *was* must have come first.' No doubt it would come first; but we have just referred to certain passages which show that Christ's Messianic Consciousness did not refer only to what He was about to become, but also to what He *was*; so that the Messianic Consciousness may also have been among the things which 'came first' in our Lord's experience. And further, is not Harnack's argument based on an artificial distinction between 'Divine Sonship' and 'Messiahship'? It is of course true that 'the Son of God' in Christian dogma means something very different from the 'Messiah' of the Hebrews; but this is due in great part to the influence of Greek ideas upon the Jewish theology of the primitive Church. Unless we have greatly erred in our study of the Old Testament and of Jewish apocalyptic literature, it will be evident that it was by no means impossible that the consciousness of Divine Sonship and of Messiahship should have existed together from the first; for in Jewish thought they might be almost synonymous expressions.[2] Harnack's contention would be weighty if Jesus had lived in the Germany of to-day; it does not apply to the conditions of life among the Jews twenty centuries ago.

[1] *Sayings of Jesus* (Eng. trans., London, 1908), p. 242. [2] See above, pp. 97, etc.

Another question now confronts us: How far was Christ's Messiahship recognised by His contemporaries? It is evident that there was great need for caution in proclaiming the fact. The preaching of a coming Kingdom of God would be sure to suggest thoughts of its King. These might be political or spiritual; or (more probably) both elements would be unconsciously blended. Among the uneducated classes, to whom our Lord chiefly preached, the coarser features would naturally predominate. From the general tenor of our Lord's teaching we can infer with confidence that He would not wish to be recognised as Messiah by the people until He had effected a considerable change in the tone of their Messianic Hope. But this was no easy matter. The popular fanaticism was ready to blaze up if the slightest inducement were offered; and the Jewish officials were on the look-out for any pretext which would justify an immediate arrest of the would-be Messiah. It was inevitable, then, that our Lord, though He Himself realised His Messiahship from the outset of the ministry, should use the utmost caution in communicating this knowledge to the people, and even to His disciples. To make an open proclamation of His Messiahship at the first would have been (humanly speaking) to court disaster, and to ruin His Divine mission.

In the Synoptic narratives we find two great turning-points in the history of the gradual unveiling of the Messiahship of Jesus. The first is the 'Great Confession' of St. Peter at Caesarea Philippi:—'Thou art the Messiah (ὁ Χριστός).'[1] The whole incident is intelligible only if it was the *first* explicit avowal by the disciples that they recognised the Messiahship of their Lord. It is likely enough that glimmerings of

[1] Mark viii. 29; cf. Matt. xvi. 16 and Luke ix. 20.

the truth may have flashed upon them before; and doubtless the Master had been guiding their thoughts in the right direction. But as we read the Synoptic narratives, and especially St. Mark, we notice that, after the 'Great Confession' of St. Peter, the attitude of the disciples towards the Lord has changed. They are now incessantly plying Him with questions about the Kingdom,[1] and underneath these questions is the belief that they are asking One who knows. We do not find questions of this kind in the earlier period. Thus the 'Great Confession' at Caesarea marks the end of the first stage in the revelation of Christ's 'Messianic Secret.' But as yet it was known only to the faithful few: 'He charged the disciples that they should tell no man that he was the Messiah.'[2]

The second great landmark is our Lord's answer to the question of the High Priest, 'Art thou the Messiah, the Son of the Blessed?'—'*I am*.'[3] On hearing this answer the Jews promptly pronounce that Jesus is guilty of death:—'What further need have we of witness? Ye have heard the blasphemy.' Jesus had indeed seemed to accept Messianic honours on Palm Sunday;[4] but that was not enough to prove the charge of blasphemy. They needed to hear it from His own mouth; and up till then He had never openly claimed to be the Messianic 'Son of God.' So this answer of Jesus to the High Priest marks His first *public* avowal of His Messiahship; and it was this which gave the Jewish authorities a pretext for putting Him to death.

These two landmarks help us to fix the outlines of Christ's method of revealing His Messiahship to the world. Further light is thrown upon this question by

---

[1] *e.g.* Mark x. 35-45 and xiii. 3-37. [2] Matt. xvi. 20.
[3] Mark xiv. 61, 62; cf. Matt. xxvi. 64, Luke xxii. 70.
[4] See below, pp. 190-192.

His use of the term 'the Son of Man,' which we must now consider.

"Ὁ υἱὸς τοῦ ἀνθρώπου."

The first question raised by this term, which has occasioned some of the most complicated controversies of New Testament study, is concerned with the original Aramaic phrase which our Lord actually used. On this point there are wide divergences of opinion. Dalman considers that "ὁ υἱὸς τοῦ ἀνθρώπου" was chosen by the Evangelists to represent the general sense of בַּר אֱנָשָׁא or בַּר אֱנָשׁ and is a 'literary reminiscence' of the בַּר אֱנָשׁ ('Son of Man') of Daniel vii.[1] He holds, further, that although this Aramaic term 'Bar-enasha' was somewhat antique, and therefore obscure, it was yet 'perfectly suitable as the special name of a definite personality.'[2] On the other hand, Wellhausen[3] maintains that 'Bar-enash' could only have meant 'Somebody'; "ὁ υἱὸς τοῦ ἀνθρώπου" being a misrendering prompted by the eschatological views of the Evangelists.

When the greatest authorities thus differ, what is the layman to say? Dalman, on his part, seems to have made it clear that where the term is naturally interpreted in a personal sense, as 'the Son of Man,' we need have no hesitation in so doing. But Wellhausen's position warns us that it is probable that the phrase was not free from ambiguity.

Bearing these considerations in mind, we may now ask what manner of person would be intended in those New Testament passages where "ὁ υἱὸς τοῦ ἀνθρώπου" seems naturally to refer to an individual? Let us first recall the past history of the phrase :—

[1] Dalman, *Words of Jesus*, pp. 234-267.
[2] Dalman, *op. cit.* p. 240.
[3] Wellhausen, *Israelitische und judische Geschichte* (Berlin, 1894) ; see Schweitzer's *Von Reimarus zu Wrede*, chap. xvii.

(a) In Psalm viii. 4 (5), בֶּן־אָדָם is a synonym for 'mankind,' here described in his weakness, and yet possessing delegated authority from God: 'What is man that thou art mindful of him; or *the son of man*, that thou visitest him?'

(β) In Ezekiel, the writer is repeatedly addressed by Jahveh as בֶּן־אָדָם ('son of man').

(γ) In Daniel vii. we have the famous vision of the figure 'like a son of man' (כְּבַר אֱנָשׁ), which symbolises 'the people of the saints of the Most High.'

(δ) In the 'Similitudes' of Enoch, the 'Son of Man'[1] is a supernatural Messiah, pre-existent with God, and entrusted with authority to preside over the Last Judgment, and to rule over the Kingdom of God.

In our Lord's time the phrases בַּר אֱנָשָׁא or בַּר אֱנָשׁ might have suggested any of the above passages, for the Hebrew בֶּן־אָדָם was generally rendered into the Aramaic of our Lord's time by בַּר־אֱנָשׁ.[2] The most recent usage of the term was that in Enoch; but there is very little evidence as to the extent of the popularity of that book besides what we may glean from the New Testament itself. Probably the impression conveyed by this phrase 'Bar-enash' would depend largely on the context in which it occurred. It might be taken to mean 'mankind,' or 'a human being,' or 'the [Danielic] Son of Man.' But it is important to notice that in no case was the phrase associated with the political expectation of a Davidic Prince.

[1] There are three forms of the Ethiopic phrase; but Dr. Charles considers that the original Aramaic may have been בר אנש in each case. See his note on Eth. En. xlvi. 2.

[2] See Dalman, *op. cit.* p. 237. In the Targum of Jonathan, however, the בן אדם of Ezekiel is rendered בר אדם (E. A. Abbott, *The Message of the Son of Man*, Introduction, p. xvii).

A study of the passages in the Synoptic Gospels where the phrase "ὁ υἱὸς τοῦ ἀνθρώπου" is found shows that these fall into two well-marked divisions—those which are connected with eschatology, and those which are not. In St. Mark the former class are found only after the 'Great Confession' of St. Peter. Now by the time that the Synoptic Gospels were composed, the phrase "ὁ υἱὸς τοῦ ἀνθρώπου" was simply a title for our Lord, which was becoming obsolete and was not of any doctrinal significance. It is thus exceedingly unlikely that the division between these two classes of passages where the phrase occurs is due to any artificial 'tendency' of the Evangelist,[1] or indeed to anything other than a genuine historical basis. In St. Mark's record of the Galilean ministry the phrase only occurs twice:—

(α) 'The Son of Man hath power on earth to forgive sins' (Mark ii. 10).
(β) 'The Son of Man is lord also of the sabbath' (Mark ii. 28).

Now the early Christians, when they read these passages, would no doubt feel that they could substitute 'Jesus' for 'the Son of Man' without making any change in the sense. But it does not follow that this interpretation of the phrase 'Bar-enash' was self-evident to our Lord's hearers at the time He spoke. Let us look at the contexts more closely.

In the first of the two instances the scribes had protested against the boldness of our Lord's words, 'Thy sins are forgiven thee.' 'Who can forgive sins,' they said, 'except one, even God?' To them Christ's reply might mean no more than, ' In order that ye may

---

[1] Dr. E. A. Abbott, indeed, accuses St. Mark of 'a non-spiritual bias' (*op. cit.* p. 116). But while this no doubt indicates a divergence between St. Mark and Dr. Abbott's theory, it is perhaps pardonable to question whether the 'bias' is on the side of the Evangelist.

know that *a son of man* (Bar-enash) hath authority to forgive sins on earth, . . . etc.'¹ The words would seem to bring out the contrast between the action of God in heaven and that of a human being (or 'son of man') on earth, and it is not certain that at the time any further meaning would be suggested to the hearers; though there is good reason (as we shall shortly see) to suppose that some further meaning was present to the mind of our Lord Himself.

The saying concerning the Sabbath is a yet better example. To the people the answer would seem to be as follows: 'The sabbath was made for man's sake, and not man for the sake of the sabbath; therefore *mankind* (Bar-enash) is lord even of the sabbath.'² For since בַּר אֱנָשׁ is the Aramaic for בֶּן־אָדָם, a reference to Psalm viii. will show that it might well denote 'mankind'; and even though it was apparently an obsolete and poetical phrase,³ it would seem suitable enough in the mouth of a prophetic teacher.

There is no valid reason for doubting that St. Mark is right in placing these two sayings in the early days of our Lord's ministry, when He was first proclaiming the offer of the Kingdom, and before the official opposition had begun to manifest itself seriously. We may also note that the sayings occurred in public preaching, not in the private instruction of the disciples.

In the parallel versions of the saying regarding the Sabbath in St. Matthew and St. Luke,⁴ we notice that the wording is slightly different, so that the term 'the Son of Man' more clearly refers to our Lord. But the version of St. Mark is probably the earlier, and the more accurate record of the actual words used.

It would not be wise to trust too much to the

---

[1] Mark ii. 10; cf. Matt. ix. 6, Luke v. 24.
[2] Mark ii. 28; cf. Matt. xii. 8, Luke vi. 5.
[3] Dalman, *op. cit.* p. 237.   [4] Matt. xii. 8; Luke vi. 5.

evidence of these two Marcan passages by themselves; but, so far as they go, they suggest that in the early days of the Galilean ministry our Lord did not use the term 'the Son of Man' (Bar-enash) in such a way as to make it plain to the people at once that He was referring either to Himself or to the eschatological 'Bar-enash' of Daniel and Enoch. The use of the phrase was antique and unusual, and would be likely to attract some attention. More than this could not be attempted at first, for fear of arousing the popular fanaticism.

In St. Mark the phrase "ὁ υἱὸς τοῦ ἀνθρώπου" does not occur again till the 'Great Confession' of St. Peter. If we turn to the other Synoptists, our attention is first claimed by the report of Christ's public use of the term in answer to the question of the Baptist: 'Art thou the Coming One (ὁ ἐρχόμενος), or are we to expect another?'[1] From the position of this section in St. Luke it appears probable that the incident occurred in the Galilean ministry, not very long after the open breach with the Pharisees, when the withered hand was healed on the Sabbath. The passage is full of importance for our present study.

In the first place, John's question implies that as yet Jesus had made no public claim to Messiahship. The result was that John felt anxious and perplexed. Our Lord replies in language which is at once guarded and yet significant of His own consciousness of Messiahship.[2] He then turns to the people, and after speaking of John's unique position in history, denounces the inconsistent attitude of the Jews:—

'John came neither eating nor drinking, and ye say, He hath a devil. 'Bar-enash' (ὁ υἱὸς τοῦ ἀνθρώπου) came eating and drinking, and ye say, Behold a man who

[1] Matt. xi. 2, Luke vii. 18; probably from the 'Q' document.
[2] See above, p. 149.

is a glutton and a toper, a friend of tax-gatherers and disreputable people.'[1]

Comparing this with our Lord's reply to John, 'Blessed is he who shall not find occasion of stumbling in me,' we cannot doubt that *for Him* the phrase 'Bar-enash' bore substantially the same meaning as for ourselves to-day. He identified Himself with 'the Son of Man,' and He interpreted the phrase in a Messianic sense. But yet the words could hardly have appeared *to the people* to be an avowal of Messiahship. The whole context spoke of mundane matters, eating and drinking; and it would seem profanity to connect these with the Messianic 'Son of Man' who was to come from Heaven. On the other hand, it is clear from the context that the people would not here have understood 'Bar-enash' to be 'a human being,' or 'mankind.' These interpretations would have given no sense. Probably in this case Wellhausen's translation 'Somebody' would not be far from giving the impression which the phrase 'Bar-enash' produced on the people. It was a mysterious saying of the great Teacher's; and it was well calculated to rouse further thoughts, 'Who is this "Bar-enash"? Can he be Jesus of Nazareth?'[2]

Another occurrence of the phrase is in St. Matthew x. 23, when, after sending forth the disciples, Christ tells them:—

> 'Ye shall not have gone through the cities of Israel, till the Son of Man be come.'[3]

Here the context is unmistakably eschatological, and the coming of the Son of Man would remind His hearers of the Last Crisis in Daniel and Enoch. But unless the disciples already knew that Jesus was 'the

---
[1] Matt. xi. 18, 19; cf. Luke vii. 33, 34.   [2] Cf. John xii. 34.
[3] Matt. x. 23. For the exegesis of the passage, see above, p. 142.

PARABLE OF THE TARES

Son of Man,' there was nothing in this saying to suggest 'the identification' of the two.

In St. Luke vi. 22 we read of persecutions 'for the Son of Man's sake.' Here the reference can only be to Jesus Himself. But this 'logion' occurs in a group of sayings, and we cannot feel here that it was originally spoken before the 'Great Confession' of St. Peter. Also in St. Matthew v. 12, which is nearly parallel, there is no reference to 'the Son of Man.' Too much uncertainty attaches to the original form and context of this and several other sayings [1] where 'the Son of Man' is mentioned for any sure conclusions to be based upon them.

More important for our purpose is the explanation of the Parable of the Tares :—

> 'He that soweth the good seed is the Son of Man. ... In the end of the world, the Son of Man shall send forth his angels, and they shall gather out of his Kingdom all things that cause stumbling, and do iniquity.' [2]

If we compare this Parable of the Tares with the Parable of the Sower, and our Lord's explanation of the latter,[3] it seems beyond doubt that by 'the Sower' our Lord meant to designate Himself. He alone at that time was 'sowing the seed of the Kingdom.' There is no reason to doubt that the disciples quite understood this cardinal point in the meaning of the Parable of the Sower. So when in 'the Tares' He spoke again of a Sower, they would naturally infer that He again referred to Himself. And when he tells them, 'He

---

[1] *e.g.* Matt. viii. 20, cf. Luke ix. 58 ; Matt. xii. 32, cf. Mark iii. 28 and Luke xii. 10.

[2] Matt. xiii. 37, 41. For the circumstances of this parable, see p. 135, note (1).

[3] Matt. xiii. 19-23. We are assuming that the Parable of the Sower was first related at an earlier period than 'the Tares.' The relative positions of the two parables in the Gospel suggests this ; and it is confirmed by the note of struggle and conflict in the Tares, implying a more advanced stage of Pharisaic opposition.

that soweth the good seed is the Son of Man' (St. Matthew xiii. 37), He surely intended to reveal to His followers that He, Jesus of Nazareth, the 'Sower,' claimed to be 'the Son of Man.' But He did not stop here. After further details have been explained, He continues: 'So shall it be in the end of the world; the Son of Man shall send forth his angels, etc.' (verse 41). Now 'the Son of Man' in verses 37 and 41 must have been understood by the disciples to refer in each case to the same person. Hence they would perceive that Jesus not only identified Himself with the 'Bar-enash,' but also interpreted that phrase in an eschatological sense.[1] It is not likely that our Lord's meaning was fully grasped by the disciples all at once; but it gradually dawned upon them, till St. Peter's confession at Caesarea Philippi earned him the blessing of the Messiah whom he had been the first to recognise.

After the incident at Caesarea Philippi, there is no longer any veiling of the Messiahship in our Lord's words to His disciples. He has many new things to teach them about the character of 'the Son of Man,'[2] but He always assumes that His hearers are perfectly aware that 'the Son of Man' is none other than their Master Himself.

The later ministry was not primarily a period of public preaching, but the scanty records of our Lord's public use of the term 'the Son of Man' imply that to the people it was still a riddle, though a suggestive riddle. When, for instance, He compared Jonah, the preacher of repentance, with 'the Son of Man,'[3] the people could hardly fail to see that the resemblance extended also to the speaker. But still He made no

[1] It is to be noticed that the 'Kingdom of the Son of Man' is the period *before* the Last Crisis, which is unusual in the Jewish apocalypses.
[2] See below, pp. 169-170.
[3] Luke xi. 30.

open avowal. Even on Palm Sunday, when the vague questionings of the people crystallised into a momentary enthusiasm of conviction, Jesus makes no explicit statement of Messiahship. He accepts the popular acclamation; but He holds His peace.

Not till the very last crisis, when the great 'opportunity of the Kingdom' had been rejected by the Jews in the plainest possible terms, does Jesus openly proclaim that He is the true Messiah, the rejected Heir to the Vineyard of Israel. 'Art thou the Messiah, the Son of the Blessed?'—'I am; and ye shall see the Son of Man coming in the clouds of heaven.'[1] The parallel passage in St. Luke is specially interesting as showing that to Jewish minds the three terms 'the Christ,' 'the Son of Man,' and 'the Son of God' were so nearly synonymous as to be interchangeable in conversation. Our Lord is urged: 'If thou be *the Christ*, tell us.' He answers: 'From henceforth shall the *Son of Man* be seated at the right hand of God.' The Jews rejoin: 'Art thou *then* the *Son of God*?'[2] Evidently the three terms here expressed approximately the same idea in the minds of the speakers.

We may now gather up the conclusions we have drawn from our Lord's use of the term "ὁ υἱὸς τοῦ ἀνθρώπου."

(i.) *In public preaching,* His method appears to have been guarded and yet suggestive. At first, the phrase 'Bar-enash' was used in a way to attract attention, but without necessarily suggesting any thought of the Messiah. The later usage was calculated to arouse questionings in the minds of the people, whether the speaker might not be referring to Himself by this peculiar title. But only at the very last, when arrested before the High Priest, does Jesus use the phrase in public

---

[1] Mark xiv. 62.   [2] Luke xxii. 67-70.

in a way which leaves no doubt as to His claims to Messiahship.

(ii.) *In teaching the disciples.* On this point we have no recorded occurrences of the phrase which can with certainty be assigned to the early period of the ministry. But the evidence, so far as it goes, suggests that from the first our Lord began to reveal to His disciples (*a*) that by the phrase 'Bar-enash' He meant to indicate Himself; and (*b*) that He intended the phrase to be understood in a Messianic and eschatological sense. This does not, of course, exclude the possibility that our Lord selected the term partly to emphasise His humanity. But it must be confessed that a straightforward interpretation of the New Testament, viewed against the background of contemporary ideas, does not lend much support to this view. To us who are familiar with Christian theology and tradition, the phrase 'Son of Man' naturally suggests the idea of humanity; but to the Jews it would be associated far more with those Messianic ideas which (if our conclusions above be correct) it was designed by our Lord to awaken gradually in His hearers.

The objection may be made that it is inconceivable that our Lord should have thus used a phrase of doubtful interpretation. But, so far as we can judge, an open avowal of Messianic claims would have been premature, and would have led to grave misunderstanding of Christ's true meaning. 'One may hold that in using the title He purposely furnished them with a problem which stimulated reflection (*welches das Nachdenken herausforderte*) about His person, and gave such a tendency to this reflection that the solution of the problem fully revealed the mystery of the personality of Jesus.'[1] In the case of the disciples, these 'after-

[1] Dalman, *op. cit.* p. 259. Cf. Schweitzer, *op. cit.* p. 278.

thoughts' gradually developed, till they found expression in the Confession of St. Peter. But the Jewish people as a whole were yet slower of apprehension; they could not make up their minds as to the character of Jesus, and this indecision of theirs was responsible for the shame of a crucified Messiah.

It will be seen that these conclusions concerning our Lord's Messianic Consciousness are opposed to the views of Schweitzer and the new 'Eschatological School.' The latter assume that just as Christ accepted the current eschatological idea of the Kingdom, so He was content with the corresponding conception of the Messiah. Neither the Kingdom nor the Messiah were to have any connection with the things of earth, but were to be wholly miraculous, spiritual, transcendental.

But the Gospel narratives cannot be reconciled with this view. They show us that our Lord, so far from accepting the average Jewish ideal of Messiahship, spent His life, and at length laid down His life, for the sake of a higher ideal of authority and kingship—an ideal which He could best introduce to the Jews by means of a phrase which approximately suggested it.

> 'The Messianic consciousness was central. But to say that it was central is not the same thing as to say that it was adequate. The most we can say for it is that it was the nearest idea and the nearest expression that offered itself at the time.'[1]

Our Lord's ministry is only intelligible on the assumption that from first to last He believed Himself to possess full Messianic—indeed, more than Messianic—authority over the sons of men here on earth. 'Ye call me Master and Lord; and ye say well; for so I am.'[2]

[1] Sanday, *Christologies, Ancient and Modern* (Oxford, 1910), p. 175.
[2] John xiii. 13.

CHAPTER XVI

THE GREAT REFUSAL

THE early days of the Galilean ministry form a period of comparative prosperity in the story of our Lord's life—at least in contrast to the times which followed. The 'new teaching' at first attracted much interest, and even enthusiasm.[1] Our Lord's first summons to repentance seems to ring out confident of its own power to win obedience;[2] and in some of the Galilean parables the coming of the Kingdom is depicted as an unbroken progress culminating in complete victory.[3] But very soon it becomes clear that the leaders of the Jews will not accept Christ's offer. In St. Mark the conflict becomes clearly marked after the healing on the Sabbath day.[4] After this, it is only a question of time for the opposition to ripen into a crisis.

It would be a mistake, however, to assume that the apparent 'optimism' of our Lord's early preaching is a proof that He failed at first to foresee the true course of events. For side by side with sayings which imply the possibility that the offer of the Kingdom will be accepted, are other sayings which point to future conflict and earthly failure. And some of the latter are to be found among the earliest events of the ministry.

---

[1] Mark i. 28, 45, ii. 12, etc. [2] Mark i. 15.
[3] *e.g.* the Parables of the Leaven, the Mustard-seed, and the Seed Sown.
[4] Mark iii. 5 and 6.

THE REFUSAL FORESEEN

An instance is the reply of Christ to those who asked Him about fasting: 'The days will come, when the bridegroom shall be taken away from them, and then will they fast in that day.'[1] It is true that these words, read by themselves, might only imply that in course of time 'the bridegroom' would share the common fate of humanity, and be taken from this life. But since our Lord goes on at once to describe the conflict between His new teaching and the Old Dispensation,[2] it is not unreasonable to infer that when He spoke of 'the taking away of the bridegroom,' He already foresaw the fatal issue of that conflict.

So again in the Parable of the Sower, which is generally admitted to belong to the early Galilean ministry, our Lord expects a time of tribulation and persecution because of the message ($\tau \grave{o} \nu$ $\lambda \acute{o} \gamma o \nu$) which He is preaching.[3] And once more, in the incident at the Nazarene synagogue, recorded in St. Luke, the Great Refusal is undoubtedly in the Lord's mind: 'Verily I say unto you, No prophet is acceptable in his own country.'[4]

We conclude, then, that whilst our Lord offered to the Jews a genuine opportunity of repenting and thereby accepting the Divine offer of the Kingdom, yet from the beginning He foresaw the end. 'He knew what was in man.'

The first note of opposition to our Lord came (according to St. Mark) from the scribes, who were shocked at His claim to forgive sins.[5] It was the 'scribes of the Pharisees,' who exclaimed with pious horror: 'He eateth and drinketh with tax-gatherers and sinners.'[6] The popularity of the new Teacher among 'the masses'[7] only stiffened the resentment of the upper classes.

---

[1] Mark ii. 20. [2] Mark ii. 21, 22. [3] Mark iv. 17. [4] Luke iv. 24.
[5] Mark ii. 7.   [6] Mark ii. 16.   [7] Mark i. 45, ii. 12, v. 24, etc.

The Pharisees disliked unconventionality more even than secularism, and they joined hands with the supporters of the Herodian dynasty in the endeavour to suppress the new teaching.[1] It is evident that throughout the Galilean ministry the scribes and Pharisees were on the watch for every opportunity to thwart our Lord's plans. At last their hostility became too strong for Him to remain any longer in Galilee or in the territory of Herod Antipas;[2] and He started on the journeyings, first to the north, and later to Jerusalem, with His thoughts full of changed plans, to meet the changed circumstances. But the hostility of the Pharisees ever dogged His steps, and at the last, after He reached Jerusalem, they allied themselves with the Sadducean priests. 'The chief priests and the scribes . . . sought how they might destroy him; for they feared him, for all the multitude was astonished at his teaching.'[3] The balance of opinion thenceforward remained much the same—the populace friendly but fickle, ready to hail the Prophet as Messiah, but easily persuaded to clamour for His crucifixion; and on the other hand, the powerful alliance of Church and State, determined to suppress what they regarded as an unorthodox fanaticism.

This Great Refusal on the part of the Jews exercised an influence upon Christ's Doctrine of the Last Things which we must now consider. This influence is seen partly in the thought that the Kingdom of God is the antithesis of 'the World.' In the earlier Galilean preaching, we saw that the idea of the Kingdom of God, though partly eschatological, was not necessarily

[1] Mark iii. 6.
[2] See Burkitt, *The Gospel History*, pp. 91-93. Schweitzer (*op. cit.* pp. 349-350 and 360) thinks the journey to the north was prompted by the desire to be alone after the disappointment of the first hopes. Even if so, it was indirectly the result of Pharisaic opposition.
[3] Mark xi. 18.

opposed to the present world. It was not to destroy the imperfect attempts to realise the ideal of God's Kingdom on earth, but rather to fulfil them.

But as the attitude of the Pharisees towards Christ's preaching of the Kingdom became more and more hostile, so the preaching itself changed its character. It was no longer the glad tidings of a great opportunity, but a stern rebuke for an opportunity lost, and a warning of impending and retributive wrath. It was now clear that the moral standard of those who refused the call to repentance was fundamentally erroneous; and it was needful that they should learn that in the Kingdom of God their estimates of right and wrong will be reversed. This 'transvaluation of values' in the Kingdom of God will apply to every department of life.

It will apply to social life. The Pharisees were refusing the Kingdom; the populace were at least willing to hear about it. And so our Lord solemnly affirms that the tax-gatherers and harlots shall enter the Kingdom of God before the chief priests and elders.[1] 'I came,' He said in the early days of Pharisaic hostility, 'not to call the righteous, but sinners.'[2] The four great Lucan parables—the Great Supper, the Prodigal Son, Dives and Lazarus, and the Pharisee and the Publican—all point the same lesson: 'How hardly shall they that have riches enter into the Kingdom of God!'[3] The teaching of these parables, and the sweeping denunciation of the ruling classes in St. Matthew xxiii. and St. Luke xi., etc., can only be understood when we remember what was the crowning sin of the Pharisees. They had rejected Christ's call to repentance, and His offer of the Kingdom; they would not enter in themselves, and they hindered the people

---

[1] Matt. xxi. 31.   [2] Mark ii. 17.
[3] Luke xviii. 24 = Mark x. 24; cf. Matt. xix. 23.

who were willing to enter.¹ Only the most radical of remedies is now of any use ; they must unlearn all their massive Pharisaic erudition and be willing to be taught like little children ; for

> 'Whosoever shall not receive the Kingdom of God as a little child, he shall in no wise enter therein.'²

The same principle applies to politics. Although the Pharisees were the leaders of the Great Refusal, the Jewish people as a whole were not free from responsibility. They refused to co-operate with the Divine purpose that all the nations should be blessed through them; and so they are told that the nations will be blessed apart from them :—

> 'Many shall come from the east and the west, and shall sit down with Abraham, Isaac, and Jacob, in the Kingdom of Heaven; but the sons of the Kingdom shall be cast forth into the outer darkness.'³

. . . .

> 'The Kingdom of God shall be taken away from you, and given to a nation bringing forth the fruits thereof.'⁴

God's purpose will be fulfilled ; the good tidings of the Kingdom will be preached over all the world,⁵ but that share in the great work, which might have been the lot of the Jews, has been taken from them because of their hardness of heart. Thus in both social and political matters the standard of the Kingdom of God will reverse the standards of this world.

It was the Great Refusal, too, which similarly led to the emphasis placed upon the suffering of the Messiah in our Lord's later teaching. It is probable, as we have seen,⁶ that even at the beginning of His ministry Christ

---

[1] Matt. xxiii. 13.   [2] Mark x. 15.
[3] Matt. viii. 11, 12 ; cf. Luke xiii. 28, 29.
[4] Matt. xxi. 43 ; cf. Mark xii. 9.   [5] Mark xiv. 9.
[6] See above, p. 165.

foresaw that the Pharisees would not rest till they had compassed His death. But as long as He was proclaiming the great opportunity of the Kingdom, He seemed, as it were, to leave open the possibility that the Jews would avail themselves of this opportunity, and that He Himself would be accepted as the Ruler of God's People on earth. The Parable of the Vineyard, for instance, makes it clear that it was God's purpose that the Heir should be recognised by the husbandmen as their King; and if this was God's purpose, then it was not outside the range of possibility. In that event the Divine Mission of our Lord would have been accomplished (so far as our human minds can see) without the need for a suffering Messiah. But the growing opposition of the Pharisees soon showed that this was not to be. Just as the Pharisaic ideas of 'the Kingdom' are false, so is their Messianic Hope. The heavenly glory of the Messiah will be seen amongst them in the form of human suffering and shame.

Throughout the Galilean ministry, the future sufferings of the Messiah were not yet revealed to the disciples, for their faith was not strong enough to bear it. Only after they had hailed Him as the Messiah, at Caesarea, does He reveal to them that the future history of the Messiah was to be far other than they expected. At that moment the disciples would naturally be hoping that their faith in the Master, which had just reached its climax, was now to be rewarded by the revelation of a glorious future. Surely the time must now be at hand when He was about to reveal Himself to the world as the Messianic Son of Man, so that the present opposition of the Pharisees would be transformed into enthusiastic acclamation. But instead of this, they hear the solemn prediction :—

'The Son of Man *must suffer many things*, and be

rejected by the elders, and the chief priests, and scribes, and be killed.'[1]

It was no wonder that the closing words ('. . . and after three days rise again') were unheeded in the first rush of disappointed feelings, and that 'Peter took him, and began to rebuke him.'

It is hard for us to realise how startling the thought of a suffering Messiah must have been to the disciples. There is very little sign that Isaiah liii. was interpreted of the Messiah in contemporary writings,[2] for the Jews preferred to dwell on the more attractive side of the Messianic ideal. It is true that in some of the apocalypses (*e.g.* in 4 Ezra) the *death* of the Messiah is foretold; but this is to be simply a natural death, and there is no reference to suffering.

It would be foolish to pretend to explain completely the origin of this expectation of suffering on the part of our Lord; but there is no need to ignore the natural influence of Pharisaic opposition upon His outlook, or to maintain (as Schweitzer maintains) that Christ went to Calvary simply because He believed that His death was predestined.[3] It was not only the purpose of God, but also the sin of man, which led Christ to the Cross. But, on the other hand, a deep faith in God's purpose does undoubtedly run through all our Lord's predictions of His Passion; and it always leads Him on to speak of the Resurrection beyond. 'The Son of Man' may be destined to shame and death on earth, but He will assuredly come again on the clouds of heaven, and reign over the Kingdom of God. The Cross and its sequel form a sublime parable of the 'transvaluation of values' in the Kingdom of God.

[1] Mark viii. 31, 32.
[2] Cf. Stanton, *The Jewish and Christian Messiah* (Edinburgh, 1886), p. 122.
[3] Schweitzer, *op. cit.* p. 389; Eng. trans. p. 390.

And the same thought is present in our Lord's sayings which speak of the sufferings of the disciples. These, too, are the necessary prelude to the joy of the Kingdom. In the early Galilean preaching, the World and the Kingdom of God seem to be almost the same thing, only viewed from different aspects and in different stages of development. The Parables of the Sower and of the Tares are conspicuous instances of this. But after the Great Refusal it is different; Christ's followers, the inheritors of the Kingdom, are at war with the World. 'Ye shall be hated of all men for my name's sake.'[1]—'If they have called the master of the house Beelzebub, how much more, them of his household?'[2] For the disciple, as well as for the Master, trouble and suffering form the gateway to eternal life.

> 'O Cross, that liftest up my head,
>   I dare not ask to fly from thee:
> I lay in dust life's glory dead,
>   And from the ground there blossoms red
>   Life that shall endless be.'

There are some points where our Lord's doctrine of the contrast between the Kingdom and the World resembles the doctrine of the prophets in times of national apostasy; but the boldness of His teaching is without parallel in history. No one before Him had foretold that the Kingdom of God would be a Kingdom of converted malefactors; no prophet of the Old Covenant had predicted that the 'sinners of the Gentiles' would inherit the Kingdom *in place of* the Chosen People. But it is essential to remember that this apparent 'other-worldliness' of our Lord's later

---

[1] Mark xiii. 13.
[2] Matt. x. 25; cf. the request of James and John, and the answer, 'Ye know not what ye ask' (Mark x. 35-40).

teaching — His *Weltverneinung*, as the Germans call it—rested on a strictly moral basis. He shows no antagonism to the world as such, but only to the world which rejects the call to repentance. If the good tidings of the early ministry were conditional, so also are the stern predictions of the later teaching. In the face of new conditions, the message of our Lord is transformed outwardly from a gospel to a denunciation. But if we could see below the surface, we should realise that 'it was the attitude of the scribes and Pharisees that changed, not the teaching of Jesus Christ.'[1]

Our Lord's purpose never varied throughout His earthly life; but it was thwarted by human sin:—

> 'O Jerusalem, Jerusalem, which killeth the prophets, and stoneth them which are sent unto her; how often would I have gathered thy children together . . . and ye would not!'[2]

---

[1] Burkitt, *Gospel History*, p. 78.   [2] Matt. xxiii. 37; Luke xiii. 34.

CHAPTER XVII

THE ESCHATOLOGICAL DISCOURSE, ETC.

THE great sermon on the Last Things,[1] delivered by our Lord on the Mount of Olives shortly before His Passion, is of such importance that it seems to require a chapter to itself. The main features of this 'Eschatological Discourse,' common to the three Synoptists,[2] are as follows :— First, the disciples point out to the Lord the magnificence of the Temple, and receive the reply : 'There shall not be left here one stone upon another, which shall not be thrown down' (Mark xiii. 1, 2). Later on, four of the disciples ask for private information about the time when these things are to happen (xiii. 4). ('These things' must refer here to the destruction of the Temple.) Jesus answers : 'Take heed that no man lead you astray. Many shall come in my name, saying, "I am he" ("'Εγώ εἰμι"); and shall lead many astray' (xiii. 5, 6). Wars are to come first; these are the beginning of the Messianic Woes, the birth-pangs (ὠδῖνες) of the Kingdom (xiii. 7, 8). In the times of the Woes, the disciples will meet with persecution; 'but he that endureth to the end, the same shall be saved' (xiii. 9-13).

At length they will see the 'abomination of desolation' (τὸ βδέλυγμα τῆς ἐρημώσεως), and this will be a

[1] Mark xiii. = Matt. xxiv. = Luke xxi.; cf. Matt. x. 17-22 and Luke xvii. 22-37.
[2] The quotations below are from St. Mark, and also the references in brackets to chapter and verse.

warning to them to flee with the utmost haste out of Jerusalem (xiii. 14-20). In those days there will be many who claim to be the Messiah; but the disciples are not to heed them (xiii. 21-23). Then the portents in the natural world will become more and more fearsome :—

> 'The sun shall be darkened, and the moon shall not give her light, and the stars shall be falling from heaven, and the powers that are in the heavens shall be shaken. And then shall they see the Son of Man coming in clouds with great power and glory; and then he shall send forth the angels, and gather together his elect from the four winds, from the uttermost part of the earth to the uttermost part of heaven' (xiii. 24-27).

Then follows the Parable of the Fig-tree, and its lesson :—

> 'When ye see these things coming to pass, know that it is nigh, even at the doors. Verily I say unto you, This generation shall not pass, until all these things be accomplished. Heaven and earth shall pass away; but my words shall not pass away. But of that day or that hour knoweth no one, not even the angels in heaven, neither the Son, but the Father. Take ye heed, watch and pray; for ye know not when the time is. . . . What I say unto you, I say unto all, Watch' (xiii. 28-37).

Comparing the above outline with the general plan of the Jewish apocalypses, there can be little doubt as to the meaning which the Evangelists intended to convey to their readers. The Messianic Woes were at hand, in the course of which Jerusalem would be destroyed, and the Messianic Son of Man, whom the disciples had now learnt to identify with their Master Himself,[1] would come from heaven to inaugurate the eschatological Kingdom of God. And further, a

[1] See above, p. 160.

straightforward interpretation of the Synoptic narratives (at any rate, of St. Matthew and St. Mark) implies that the 'coming of the Son of Man' was to take place at the time of the Fall of Jerusalem. There is no necessary inconsistency between the two sayings: 'This generation shall not pass away, until all these things be accomplished,' and, 'Of that day or that hour knoweth no one;'[1] for the natural meaning might be simply this, that while our Lord foretold that 'all things' would certainly be accomplished *within a generation*, He did not know the *exact* date of the final crisis.

But if this be the true meaning of these two passages, we are led to a very momentous conclusion:—not merely that there were limits to our Lord's human knowledge, for that is affirmed plainly by the words of St. Mark, xiii. 32 ('of that day . . . *the Son* knoweth not'); but, if our Lord did actually use the words, 'This generation shall not pass, until all these things be accomplished,' with reference to the Last Crisis, it would follow that He believed Himself to know something which He did not really know. Many Christians will readily admit that God Incarnate might not be omniscient, and yet they would shrink from the thought that He could misjudge the limits of His own knowledge.

It is possible to soften the difficulty by pointing out that here there is no error of judgment with regard to *moral* values; or it may be inferred from the analogy of prophecy that our Lord would naturally see the future in a foreshortened perspective. But the hard fact still remains, that if Jesus spoke the sayings of St. Mark xiii. and St. Matthew xxiv. in the exact order and under the exact circumstances which the Evangelists

[1] Mark xiii. 30, 32.

relate, He misjudged the extent of His own knowledge, and uttered a definite prediction which was not fulfilled.

To the present writer it seems impossible to reconcile such a conclusion with the historic Faith of Christendom. But is there no alternative?

Some have taken refuge in the theory of the 'Little Apocalypse' of Jewish origin, inserted by fragments among genuine 'logia' of Jesus. This idea was started by Colani in 1864, and has found many adherents, including Wendt and Charles. It has been recently upheld in a learned exposition of this chapter by Fr. M. J. Lagrange,[1] who carefully analyses the 'Discourse,' and assigns the verses, one by one, to their 'original sources.' But these writers have failed to show any sufficient motive which would have induced the Evangelists to undertake this process of dissection and compilation. And further, it may be questioned whether a piece of literary patchwork by unlearned men would produce the coherent effect of our present text of the Gospels, in which the course of events develops along the normal lines of Jewish apocalyptic— first a time of war; then the persecution of the faithful; then the destruction of Jerusalem; then the pretenders to Messiahship; then the cosmic convulsions; and lastly the advent of the heavenly Messiah. If the discourse were not attributed to our Lord, the unity of authorship would probably never have been questioned. It is on doctrinal, not on critical, grounds that the theory of the interpolated 'Little Apocalypse' is really based.

Equally unsatisfactory are the attempts to make subtle distinctions between adjoining verses which naturally refer to the same thing. Lagrange, for

---

[1] 'L'Avènement du Fils de l'homme,' *Revue biblique internationale*, N.S. iii. (Paris, 1906).

THE CALL TO WATCHFULNESS

instance, discovers a 'rhythmic parallelism' in the discourse.[1] In this way he separates the references to the Fall of Jerusalem from the predictions of the end of the world in the alternate sections. This would be all very well if we were dealing with a Hebrew psalm; but where else do we find this 'rhythmic parallelism' in the Synoptic Gospels? We may well ask whether Lagrange's methods are not an example of learned but misplaced ingenuity. No solution can be satisfactory which attempts to distinguish between various elements in the Eschatological Discourse in this arbitrary and artificial manner.

We would now venture to suggest a few considerations which may help to remove some of the difficulties of the Eschatological Discourse.

In the first place, the keynote of the discourse is the call to watchfulness. The impressive closing words leave no doubt that our Lord's main purpose in delivering the discourse was to bring home the message: 'What I say unto you I say unto all, Watch.' It does not follow, however, that this point was the one which interested *the disciples* most. On the contrary, their question, 'When shall these things be?' indicates that the *time* of the end was uppermost in their minds. Hence they would be much more ready to note those parts of the discourse which dealt with their question, than to observe the general lesson which Christ desired to impress upon them.

And this brings us to our second consideration, that the original 'logia' may have been 'interpreted' by the disciples, and thereby made more definitely eschatological.[2] A comparison of the three accounts of this

---

[1] 'Une stance s'oppose à une stance, puis une troisième stance reprend la pensée de la première, tandis que la quatrième s'attache à la seconde.'—Lagrange, *op. cit.* p. 393. [2] See also p. 143, above.

discourse shows beyond doubt that St. Matthew and St. Luke tried to make the meaning clearer to their readers by expanding and interpreting the original 'logia.' We may take one or two instances: In St. Mark xiii. 4 we have, 'When shall these things be?' St. Matthew explains that 'these things' are the Parousia of Jesus and the consummation of the age (St. Matthew xxiv. 3). Again, in St. Matthew xxiv. 29 the writer adds to the Marcan record one significant word, telling us that the Fall of Jerusalem is to be *immediately* (εὐθέως) followed by the coming of the Son of Man. By these and other similar changes he endeavours to bring our Lord's words into more complete harmony with Jewish eschatological ideas. St. Luke's alterations are somewhat different in character. He interprets the 'logia' in the light of later history. For instance, he explains that the 'abomination of desolation' refers to the armies who will come to besiege Jerusalem.[1]

These 'tendencies' in the First and Third Gospels are too plain to be doubted; but is it not possible that even St. Mark may have 'interpreted' the original words of Christ to some extent? It is true that St. Mark generally gives us the impression of offering a simple record of facts without attempt at comment. But when our Lord spoke of the Fall of Jerusalem and of the end of the world, He was dealing with a subject on which His hearers already possessed very definite beliefs; and in such a case even the most accurate reporter is liable to read some of his own ideas into the words he hears. Only a short while before the Eschatological Discourse took place, the Parable of the Pounds had been spoken specially in order to show that the Kingdom was not so near as was commonly thought.[2] Now, if our Lord's main purpose in delivering the Eschatological Discourse

---

[1] Luke xxi. 20. [2] Luke xix. 11; and see below, p. 186.

WAS CHRIST MISUNDERSTOOD? 179

was to teach the need for watchfulness, it is quite possible that His hearers read into His words a meaning which was not precisely His own. It was no new thing for them to misunderstand the Master's meaning;[1] and it is probable that even the very earliest oral traditions, which must have been in existence for many years before the earliest written narratives, were slightly tinged with current Jewish ideas, which emphasised and defined the eschatological element in our Lord's discourse in a manner not strictly warranted by His own original words. But if this be so, it is useless for us to think that we can go behind St. Mark's text and discover the original teaching of Jesus by removing a verse here and there. The utmost that we can say is that the words actually used by our Lord were probably capable of a wider interpretation than is suggested by their present form. In particular, it is likely that the identification of the Fall of Jerusalem with the end of the world, which creates the greatest difficulty in the extant records of our Lord's words, may be traced to the mind of the evangelists rather than to the mind of Christ.[2]

It is also possible that some of the sayings in the Eschatological Discourse were originally spoken on other occasions. St. Mark xiii. 9-13 is placed by St. Matthew among the instructions at the Mission of the Twelve; and many of the sayings in St. Matthew xxiv. occur in St. Luke xvii., immediately after the question about the coming of the Kingdom of God. It seems, then, probable that each of the evangelists grouped certain eschatological sayings of our Lord round the historical occasion when He spoke to His disciples on the Mount of Olives concerning the Fall of Jerusalem. It would seem obvious to the followers of Jesus that the Fall of Jerusalem

---

[1] Mark ix. 32, etc.
[2] See also below, on the Parables of the Talents and the Pounds, pp. 185, 186.

would be coincident with the end of this world; and they would not be careful to distinguish between the two classes of our Lord's predictions, but would mingle them promiscuously together. It is well, though, for us to remember that our present knowledge is not sufficient to enable us to assign each 'logion' to its true context, nor even in every case to determine precisely its original significance.

One more consideration should be borne in mind. The conditions attached to the predictions may have been originally more prominent than they are now. The reader will remember that our Lord's proclamation of 'the Kingdom' was dependent upon the fulfilment of a moral condition—the repentance of the Jewish nation; and we pointed out that the presence of this conditional element helps to remove the difficulty of such passages as St. Matthew x. 23: 'Ye shall not have gone through the cities of Israel, till the Son of Man be come.'[1] This suggests that there may have been some similar condition attached to the promise of the return of the Son of Man in the eschatological discourse. And, in fact, we find this conditional element in all the Synoptists; for instance, in St. Mark xiii. 10: 'The good tidings must first be preached to all the nations.' It is only a passing reference; but so was the mention of repentance in connection with the Galilean preaching. And just as we saw that the later teaching of our Lord is unintelligible unless His first proclamation of 'the Kingdom' had really been a *conditional offer*, so the history of the Church can hardly be reconciled with our Lord's prediction of His Second Coming, unless we remember that here, too, there was a condition attached; —the world must first be evangelised.

In St. Matthew xxiv. 14 the necessity of this condi-

[1] See above, p. 142.

A CONDITIONAL PREDICTION?

tion is set forth with perhaps greater emphasis than in St. Mark:—

> 'These good tidings of the Kingdom shall be preached in the whole world for a testimony unto all the nations; and then shall the end come.'

In St. Luke there is no mention of preaching to the Gentiles, but the Fall of Jerusalem is to be separated from the Last Things by an interval, described as 'the times of the Gentiles.'[1] Perhaps this reflects the mind of the Church after the Fall of Jerusalem had taken place, and yet the Son of Man had not come. But even so, it is not impossible that when the first hopes remained unfulfilled, the disciples would remember that the Lord Himself had seemed to distinguish between the Fall of Jerusalem and the Last Crisis, though at the time they had hardly understood His meaning, because their minds were prepossessed with another belief. So the Lucan saying may well be a genuine echo of our Lord's own teaching.

The objection may be raised that these points which we have just considered are all on the negative side. We have suggested that the present form of the discourse may not be verbally identical with the original words spoken; that the historical context of some of the 'logia' is not certain; and that the predictions of the future are not so unconditional as they seem. What, it may be asked, is the use of these unsettling suggestions? We would reply, that the Eschatological Discourse in its present form offers a most promising field for attacks upon Christianity; critics of the type of Schweitzer point to it as a conclusive proof that Jesus shared the Jewish prejudices and limitations of His fellow-countrymen, and that

[1] Luke xxi. 24.

the mainspring of His life was a hope which history has shown to be unfounded. Under these circumstances, even if the possibilities indicated above do produce an atmosphere of uncertainty, the opponents of our religion will lose more than its defenders; for we can dismiss many of their arguments—such as the argument that our Lord's outlook upon the future was fundamentally erroneous—as 'not proven.'

But there are several points to be noted, on the positive side, which seem fairly independent of literary criticism :—

(i.) Our Lord predicts the Fall of Jerusalem and the destruction of the Temple, and is silent on the subject of a New Jerusalem to replace the old one.

(ii.) He definitely sanctions the preaching to the Gentiles (τὰ ἔθνη).

(iii.) He looks forward to a catastrophic end of this world and solemnly warns His followers to be always prepared for it.

These three points might be described as the completed results of the 'Great Refusal' of the Jews to accept the Kingdom of God. Because the Chosen People had rejected the supreme gift of Divine Love, they and their City were doomed to destruction. Because they had spurned the privileges given to them by God, those privileges were now to be offered to the Gentile nations. Because their rebellion had only become more bitter when brought face to face with Incarnate Goodness, and because Goodness conquered, not by a gradual process, but by the miracle of the Resurrection, they were to see in this a parable of the last and final conflict. From this point of view, the Eschatological Discourse may be regarded as a sermon explaining how the 'Great Refusal' would influence the course of the world's subsequent history until the close of this era.

From another point of view, the Discourse may be regarded as an exhortation to those who had accepted Jesus as their Messiah, reminding them that throughout the coming troubles their duty would be faithfully to work, and wait, and watch.

There are one or two of our Lord's later parables which throw further light upon His Doctrine of the Last Things. These may conveniently be considered in the present chapter.

The Parable of Dives and Lazarus at once attracts the notice of the student of eschatology, because it seems to partake, more than any other passage in the Gospels, of the character of a 'revelation' of the future life. In this, as in nearly all the later parables of Christ, the theme appears to have been suggested by the contrast between the rich men—the Pharisees—who rejected our Lord, and the poor men—the publicans and sinners—who were ready to welcome Him. It is well to bear this in mind, and also to remember the highly pictorial nature of the phraseology, ere we draw doctrinal conclusions from isolated expressions. But there are two or three eschatological ideas which undoubtedly receive support from this parable. The first is the thought of the *compensatory* value of the future life :—

> 'Son, remember that thou in thy lifetime receivedst thy good things, and Lazarus in like manner evil things; but now he is comforted, and thou art in anguish.'[1]

It is obvious that this idea might be (and in fact often is) pressed to unwarrantable lengths, and becomes tinged with a vindictive and unchristian spirit; and it should be noticed that our Lord does not in the parable

[1] Luke xvi. 25.

treat the case as an illustration of an universal law of cause and effect; for He does not say, '... *therefore* He is comforted ...' etc. But nevertheless His words do sanction the deep-rooted instinct of the human heart, which longs for a time when the seemingly unjust distribution of pains and pleasures in this world shall be readjusted so as to fulfil the laws of equity.

The Parable of Dives and Lazarus also teaches the *unchangeableness* of the future state of the soul:—

> 'Between us and you there is a great gulf fixed, that they which would pass from hence to you may not be able, and that none may cross over from thence to us.'[1]

The question of the possibility of repentance and the eternity of punishment is discussed more fully in the next two or three pages; but few sayings of our Lord are so difficult as the above to reconcile with the theory of universal salvation.

The words, 'Son, remember,' perhaps justify the conclusion that our Lord taught that some memory of this life will continue in the life to come.

The phrase 'Abraham's Bosom,' denoting the abode of the blessed, appears to be unusual;[2] and we should have expected the place of torment to be described as 'Gehenna' rather than as 'Hades.' Whether the scene of the parable is laid in the intermediate state before the Judgment, or after, is a question on which opinions differ.[3]

The Parable of the Ten Virgins,[4] which in St. Matthew immediately follows the Eschatological Discourse, resembles the latter in enforcing the call to

---

[1] Luke xvi. 26.
[2] See S. D. F. Salmond in Hastings' *Dictionary of the Bible*, vol. i. p. 18.
[3] See below, p. 188, on the idea of *time* in the world to come.
[4] Matt. xxv. 1-13.

watchfulness. The five virgins who are not ready when the bridegroom comes are excluded from the marriage-feast. If we compare the Parable of the Marriage of the King's Son,[1] it will be evident that the marriage-feast is a symbol for the perfected and eschatological Kingdom of God. Thus in the Parable of the Virgins our Lord clearly teaches that after His Second Coming our present opportunities for repentance will be closed. Are we then to say that there can be no hope of repentance beyond the grave? The answer will depend partly upon our interpretation of the 'Coming of the Bridegroom,' *i.e.* of the Last Judgment. If we are to think of each soul as judged immediately after death, the parable would imply that the opportunities for repentance are then closed for ever. But the parable does not preclude the idea of an intermediate state between death and judgment, either with or without opportunities for repentance. In any case, the message of the Parable of the Virgins is a practical one : 'Watch, for ye know not the day nor the hour.'

The Parable of the Talents,[2] and the description of the Last Judgment,[3] which follow the Parable of the Virgins, explain the reason why it is so necessary to watch, and show that true watchfulness involves work too. It is necessary to unite watchfulness with work, because as a man works here, so will he be rewarded when the Lord returns. He that has built up his character here will then receive yet more strength ; he that misuses his opportunities here will then find that his opportunities are more closely restricted. This

---

[1] Matt. xxii. 1-14.
[2] Matt. xxv. 14-30 ; cf. the Parable of the Pounds, Luke xix. 12-27.
[3] Matt. xxv. 31-46.

world and the next are united by the closest moral ties of cause and effect.—That is the lesson of the Parable of the Talents.

It is also worth noting that in this parable the lord of the servants does not return till 'after a long time' (μετὰ χρόνον πολύν).[1] And similarly, in the allied Parable of the Pounds—which (St. Luke tells us) was spoken 'because they supposed that the Kingdom of God was *immediately* to appear (παραχρῆμα ἀναφαίνεσθαι)'[2]—the master goes away 'into a far country'; and this too suggests considerable delay ere the return takes place. These passages warn us not hastily to assume that our Lord Himself expected that His Second Coming was to take place within a very short time. That the *disciples* did look for an immediate return of their Lord is beyond reasonable doubt; but there are various indications here and there in the Gospels which suggest that in our Lord's own vision the return may have appeared far more remote than a cursory perusal of the Gospels would lead us to suppose.

On the other hand, it might be maintained that the 'long time' dates from the first choice of Israel as God's people, when Jehovah appointed them His 'stewards,' and that the 'return of the lord of the servants' denotes the Incarnation of Jesus Christ *together with* the Last Crisis (the two events being regarded as synchronous). But this theory, if applied to the Parable of the Pounds, fails to explain how it would *correct* the belief 'that the Kingdom of God was immediately to appear.' And it is inconceivable that these last words are to be traced to any source other than our Lord's own authority; for they are in direct conflict (as we shall see later on) with the normal ideas of the primitive Christians.

---

[1] Matt. xxv. 19.   [2] Luke xix. 11.

THE LAST JUDGMENT

The vivid picture of the Last Judgment which follows the Parable of the Talents drives home with plainest language the kind of service which those who are watching for the Kingdom must render during the waiting-time on earth. They are to give food to the hungry and drink to the thirsty, to be hospitable to the stranger and to visit the sick. These are the conditions without which no man will inherit the Kingdom of God; these, rather than the observance of rites and ceremonies, are the only passwords to the Kingdom which the Messianic Judge will accept. And the reason assigned is one of the profoundest sayings which the world has ever heard :—

> 'Inasmuch as ye did it to one of these my brethren, even these least, ye did it unto me.'[1]

The service of man is the service of God.

This picture of the Last Judgment brings us near to the heart of our Lord's eschatology, and shows us how intimately it was connected with the call to practical morality. It helps us to understand why the primitive Christians, whose hopes were fixed on the world to come, yet drew from an unwilling world a tribute of admiration : 'See how these Christians love one another.'

In this narrative of St. Matthew xxv. we find some of the few recorded words of our Lord which bear upon the problem of eternal punishment. In verse 41 we read :—

> 'Depart from me, ye cursed, into the eternal fire (τὸ πῦρ τὸ αἰώνιον) which is prepared for the devil and his angels.'

And in verse 46 :—

[1] Matt. xxv. 40.

'These shall go away into eternal punishment (κόλασις αἰώνιος), but the righteous into eternal life (ζωὴ αἰώνιος).'

The *prima facie* meaning of such words undoubtedly suggests that after the Judgment souls enter upon a fixed and unending destiny. This impression is confirmed by the incidental references in our Lord's teaching to 'the Gehenna of fire,'[1] 'where their worm dieth not, and the fire is not quenched.'[2] The irrevocable nature of the doom seems to be further implied in the Parable of the Virgins, where we read that 'the door was shut.'[3]

On the other hand, there are considerations which warn us against hasty dogmatism on this point. In the first place, are we justified in applying the idea of *time* to the other world? True, we cannot divest our own minds of the idea, but neither can we divest our own minds of the idea of space; and yet few thoughtful Christians to-day would attempt to conceive of the Kingdom of Heaven in terms of feet and inches. We may have to use words which normally denote space in our descriptions of Heaven; but we are conscious that these descriptions are only relatively true. Ought we not to apply the same restraint in our discussions regarding *time* in the other world? In other words, when we are discussing our Lord's use of such terms as 'eternal' or 'never to be quenched,' may we not recognise the possibility that the *real* significance of these words is to express *intensity*, and that their association with the idea of time is due to the inadequacy of human language to express the whole of truth. It is generally agreed that "αἰώνιος" when applied to a sin[4] denotes intensity rather than duration of time; why not also when the same word is applied to 'punish-

---

[1] Matt. v. 22, etc. [2] Mark ix. 48. [3] Matt. xxv. 10.
[4] Mark iii. 29.

ment' or to 'life'? So long as we use the terms 'eternal fire,' 'eternal punishment,' to express the immeasurable gravity of the consequences of sin, and the urgency of the call to immediate repentance, we are true to our Lord's teaching; but if we allow our minds to dwell on the thought of an unending succession of ages of torture, we are introducing thoughts which the Gospels nowhere thrust into prominence.

> 'For spirits and men by different standards mete
> The less and greater in the flow of time.
> . . . . . .
> Precise and punctual, men divide the hours,
> Equal, continuous, for their common use.
> Not so with us in th' immaterial world;
> But intervals in their succession
> Are measured by the living thought alone,
> And grow or wane with its intensity;
> And time is not a common property.'

One other consideration should also be borne in mind. These sayings of our Lord concerning eternal punishment ought not to be isolated from the general tenor of His teaching. In that teaching great stress is laid upon the Infinite Love of our Heavenly Father; and the 'Universalist' who believes he can logically deduce from this a doctrine of the final salvation of all men is not hastily to be denounced as disloyal to Christ by those who, selecting another aspect of our Lord's teaching, deduce from that, with equal honesty and consistency, a doctrine of eternal punishment. In this, as in so many matters, the many aspects of truth refuse to be gathered together within the limits of a single system of consistent human logic; and the man who maintains that he has comprehended them all is in reality but proclaiming his own blindness.

CHAPTER XVIII

THE EVENTS OF PASSION WEEK AND THE POST-RESURRECTION TEACHING

MANY of the incidents which occurred during the last week of our Lord's earthly life throw much light on His eschatological teaching. This is especially the case with regard to Palm Sunday, and the question whether the Triumphal Entry was a claim to Messiahship or not. Now it is clear that the peculiar method of the entry was not due to force of circumstances, but was in accordance with our Lord's instructions to His disciples. And since in all His words and works at this period of the Ministry, His Messianic Consciousness is ever manifest, we can have little doubt that He designed this manner of entering the Holy City with a view to symbolise His Messianic claims. But it was only symbolical, and not an *explicit* claim to Messiahship;[1] otherwise it would certainly have been brought up at the trial as part of the charge against Him. And what did the Triumphal Entry mean in the eyes of the people of Jerusalem? Schweitzer holds that they thought that Jesus was the Elijah who was to precede the Messiah.[2] But none of the Synoptists give the slightest support to this view. The cries of the people, as

---
[1] Cf. the refusal to answer the question, 'By what authority doest thou these things?' unless the priestly party would acknowledge their error with regard to John.

[2] Schweitzer, *op. cit.* p. 391, Eng. trans. p. 392; and see Mal. iv. 5.

reported by the First and Second Evangelists, are perfectly applicable to the Messiah Himself, as He was conceived of by the populace, who looked for a Davidic Prince who should restore the political kingdom to Israel :—

'Hosanna! Blessed is he that cometh in the name of the Lord! Blessed is the kingdom that cometh, the kingdom of our father David; Hosanna in the highest.'[1]

And St. Luke is yet more explicit: 'Blessed is *the king* that cometh in the name of the Lord'[2]—words which are wholly inapplicable to Elijah. Schweitzer, however, urges that the words recorded in St. Matthew, 'This is Jesus the Prophet of Nazareth,' show that the people did not regard Him as Messiah. But it is highly probable that the less-educated Jews conceived of the Messiah very much as a glorified prophet; and there is nothing in these words to suggest Elijah, rather than the Messiah.

It may be asked, Why did our Lord thus encourage this popular form of the Messianic Hope, with which elsewhere He shows so little sympathy? But, in truth, He did *not* offer it any real encouragement. After entering Jerusalem He forms no political party, and assists in no political movement. The cleansing of the Temple is the only action which could possibly be construed as a public claim to Messiahship; and this was devoid of political significance. So the outburst of popular enthusiasm subsided as quickly as it arose, and, indeed, became changed into a feeling of disappointed resentment. What, then, was our Lord's purpose in thus entering the Holy City? Probably the symbolical action was intended to stimulate afterthoughts of the right kind. It was not without design

---

[1] Mark xi. 9, 10; cf. Matt. xxi. 9.   [2] Luke xix. 38.

that He chose to fulfil the vision of Zechariah : 'Behold, thy King cometh unto thee ; he is just, and having salvation ; lowly, and riding upon an ass.'[1] Justice, saving power, and human lowliness were an essential part of our Lord's ideal of Messiahship, and one which the Jewish people had yet to learn. We may fairly infer that this was what our Lord desired to suggest by His Triumphal Entry into Jerusalem ; and a reference to St. Matthew[2] shows us that His purpose was accomplished.

The Triumphal Entry is the most dramatic example of the unreality of the things of this world—a semblance of complete earthly success, followed in a few days by an appearance of utter failure. But Christ never wavered in His faith in the future Kingdom, where the true values of things will be manifest ; beyond the hollow pomp of Palm Sunday, and behind the bitter agony of the Cross, He sees the true glory of the Resurrection.

> 'Ride on ! Ride on in majesty !
> In lowly pomp ride on to die ;
> Bow Thy meek head to mortal pain,
> Then take, O God, Thy power, and reign !'

We may now pass on to an event which took place a day or two after the Triumphal Entry, and which was one of the very few occasions when our Lord spoke directly of the life after death. This was in answer to the question of the Sadducees[3] with reference to the Resurrection ; and His words in connection with this incident are of very special interest and importance. The following was our Lord's reply, as given by St. Mark :—

[1] Zech. ix. 9.   [2] Matt. xxi. 5.
[3] Mark xii. 18-23.

THE ANSWER TO THE SADDUCEES

'Is it not for this cause that ye err, that ye know not the Scriptures, nor the power of God? For when they shall rise from the dead, they neither marry, nor are given in marriage, but are as angels in heaven. But as touching the dead, that they are raised; have ye not read in the Book of Moses, in the place concerning the Bush, how God spake unto him, saying, I am the God of Abraham, and the God of Isaac, and the God of Jacob? He is not the God of the dead, but of the living: ye do greatly err.'[1]

There are three main points to be noted in these words of our Lord :—

(i.) He unhesitatingly affirms that 'the dead *are* raised.' On this point of fundamental importance, there is no room at all for doubt.

(ii.) He teaches that a belief in the resurrection is in accordance with — perhaps even a necessary deduction from—the Old Testament doctrine that there is a spiritual and living relationship between God and man ; and that those in living touch with God possess within themselves the beginnings of a life that is not merely physical, but spiritual and eternal. For 'He is not the God of the dead, but of the living.'

(iii.) The language here recorded by St. Mark does not necessarily imply a 'resurrection of the flesh'; it seems rather to suggest a spiritual revival, or perhaps a spiritual survival, after death.

St. Matthew's version of this incident displays no important variation.[2] St. Luke's version, however, introduces several new points.[3]

(i.) The resurrection is a privilege limited to those 'who are accounted worthy to attain to that world and the resurrection from the dead' (xx. 35).

---

[1] Mark xii. 24-27.   [2] Matt. xxii. 23-33.   [3] Luke xx. 27-38.

(ii.) The *unending* character of the resurrection-life is expressly affirmed: 'they cannot die any more' (xx. 36).

(iii.) The Marcan expression, 'as the angels' (ὡς ἄγγελοι) is made more definite: 'they are equal to the angels (ἰσάγγελοι), and are sons of God, being sons of the resurrection'[1] (xx. 36).

(iv.) The last words, 'not the God of the dead, but of the living,' are further explained by the addition: 'for all live unto Him' (xx. 38).

Whilst many of these variations are doubtless fully in accordance with the true meaning of our Lord, we can hardly doubt that St. Mark's version gives us the more accurate report of the actual words He used, and that St. Luke has 'interpreted' them to some extent. A comparison with other passages in St. Luke (*e.g.* xiv. 14, 'the resurrection *of the just*') confirms the impression that our Third Evangelist desired to emphasise the thought that the resurrection is a privilege reserved for the righteous.[2] But the essential point of this answer of our Lord's is the same in all three Gospels: He definitely proclaims the doctrine of individual resurrection and immortality, as a consequence of the Fatherhood of God.

Another event of eschatological significance was the Last Supper. Schweitzer considers that both the Feeding of the Five Thousand and the Last Supper were 'eschatological sacraments.'[3] By this he apparently means that Jesus instituted these two meals simply in order to fulfil the prophetic promises of a feast under the auspices of the Messiah, which was to

---

[1] Cf. Eth. En. li. 4: 'They [the righteous] will all become angels in heaven.'
[2] See also below, p. 221.
[3] *Op. cit.* pp. 373-378 (Eng. transl. pp. 371-376).

be one of the features of the New Era.¹ We may grant to Schweitzer the credit of originality in making this discovery; for neither previous commentators, nor the evangelists themselves, appear to have suspected that this was Christ's purpose on either occasion. With regard to the Feeding of the Five Thousand, Schweitzer's theory may help to explain some of the mystery which has always clung to this incident;² but as a sufficient explanation of the Last Supper it is absurd; at most it indicates an element of quite subsidiary importance.

One saying connected with the Last Supper is, however, distinctly eschatological: 'Verily, I say unto you, I will drink no more of the fruit of the vine, until that day when I drink it new in the Kingdom of God.'³ These words no doubt did suggest (and were intended to suggest) thoughts of the Messianic Feast in heaven; but if we recognise that the language is figurative, the meaning will simply be that our Lord foresaw that this would be His last meal on earth. In St. Matthew, however, we read: '. . . until I drink it new *with you.*'⁴ This would mean that before the next feast, the disciples, as well as our Lord, would be in the Kingdom; or, in other words, that the coming of the Kingdom (in the Jewish eschatological sense) was at the doors. Now in the times when our Gospels were compiled, while eschatological hopes ran high, the Matthaean addition would seem to be only a slight and very natural explanation, not involving any real alteration in the sense.⁵ And on the other hand it would be inconsistent with the general impression of 'straightforwardness' which we gain from St. Mark's Gospel, to suppose that the words 'with you' were deliberately omitted by St. Mark with

---

¹ See (*e.g.*) Ap. Bar. xxix. 3-8; Eth. En. lxii. 14; 4 Ezra vi. 49-52, etc.
² Mark viii. 21.   ³ Mark xiv. 25.   ⁴ Matt. xxvi. 29.
⁵ St. Luke's '*until the Kingdom of God come*' represents a slightly different form of the same tendency.

doctrinal intent. We conclude, then, that the Marcan form of the saying is the original, and that there is no evidence of any erroneous expectation on the part of our Lord. The passage is important, as showing the tendency of the first and third evangelists to read the ideas of Jewish eschatology into the sayings of Christ.

We may pass now to the Trial and Crucifixion. The significance of the high priest's question: 'Art thou the Messiah?' has already been discussed.[1] It is beyond doubt that previous to this our Lord had never made a claim to Messiahship which could be brought forward as legal evidence against Him. But now the answer is unmistakable :—

> 'I am: and ye shall see the Son of Man sitting at the right hand of power, and coming with the clouds of heaven.'[2]

This eschatological claim is at once pronounced to be a blasphemous pretension, which ought to be punished with death. Thus Calvary marks the completion of the 'Great Refusal.'

One incident of the Passion which claims a brief comment is our Lord's promise to the dying thief: 'To-day shalt thou be with me in Paradise.' This is one of those incidental sayings which ought not to be used without great caution for the establishment of accurate theological definitions. Dr. Salmond's admirable comment on this passage may well be applied to many similar cases :—

> '["Paradise"] was probably the word with which this rough criminal was most familiar, and which was most level to his understanding; and Christ adopts it as the one best fitted to give him the hope which he needed and could understand in his despair—the hope of rest, the

---

[1] See above, p. 161.   [2] Mark xiv. 62.

hope of a translation to a scene of life and peace like Eden. Whether Christ thought of it as the heavenly Paradise, or as the better side of Sheol, is beside the question here. It cannot be pressed beyond the large and general sense which His purpose then required, and which alone was appropriate to the occasion.'[1]

Among the many thoughts associated with the Cross of Christ, one bears closely upon our present subject. It is clear that among our Lord's keenest pangs was the sense that through the sin of the Chosen People the Divine purpose of His mission seemed to have been frustrated: 'My God, my God, why hast thou forsaken me?'[2] Yet He knew that the Cross itself was part of His Father's predestined purpose; it must come, in order 'that the Scriptures might be fulfilled.' So the conviction of His Messiahship remains firm up to the end. He does not refuse the homage of His fellow-sufferer; He never doubts the final fulfilment of the Divine purpose; and His dying words are the expression of perfect faith in the will of God: 'Father, into thy hands I commend my spirit.'[3]

It does not come within the scope of our present study to discuss in detail the nature and significance of our Lord's Resurrection. This is a great subject, the general consideration of which would lead us far beyond the field of Primitive Christian Eschatology. But it is of the first importance to remember that our Lord's Resurrection was in several ways an influential factor in the history of Christian eschatology.

In the first place, viewed from the Christian standpoint, it is naturally taken as the 'first-fruits' of the

[1] S. D. F. Salmond, *Christian Doctrine of Immortality* (4th edition, Edinburgh, 1901), p. 281.
[2] Mark xv. 24.   [3] Luke xxiii. 46.

general resurrection. So, in times when the interpretation of Christ's Resurrection has been materialistic, the belief in the resurrection of the dead has also been materialistic; when the former has been interpreted more or less spiritually, the latter has been interpreted spiritually too. It becomes therefore of interest briefly to recall the New Testament references to our Lord's Resurrection-body. In St. Mark, owing to the broken conclusion, there are none. From St. Matthew we learn that the women, on meeting our Lord after the Resurrection, 'took hold of his feet';[1] and St. Luke records His words to the disciples:—

> 'See my hands and my feet, that it is I myself: handle me, and see; for a spirit hath not flesh and bones, as ye behold me having.'[2]

These words, together with the comment that 'He did eat before them,'[3] emphasise strongly the *reality* of our Lord's Resurrection-body, as opposed to the phantom-body of a spirit. But we are warned against an over-crude material interpretation, by the story of the supper at Emmaus, a few verses earlier in the same Gospel, when after the breaking of bread 'He vanished out of their sight';[4] and also by the narratives of the Ascension.[5]

The impression produced by these brief references in the Synoptic Gospels is that our Lord's Resurrection-body was on the one hand real, and perceptible to our human organs of sense as having 'flesh and bones'; yet not a material body in any gross or carnal sense, which would imply that it was subject to the limitations of matter as we know it. It is interesting to notice that St. John, whom we might expect to concentrate

---

[1] Matt. xxviii. 9. [2] Luke xxiv. 39.
[3] Luke xxiv. 43. [4] Luke xxiv. 31.
[5] Luke xxiv. 51; Acts i. 9-11.

EFFECTS OF CHRIST'S RESURRECTION

attention upon the *spiritual* aspect, also emphasises the *reality*; especially in the command to Thomas :—

> 'Reach hither thy finger, and see my hands; and reach hither thy hand, and put it into my side: and be not faithless, but believing.'[1]

Yet the mysterious element is not forgotten in St. John; it is set before us in the appearances amongst the disciples when they met behind closed doors;[2] and in the warning to Mary Magdalene, 'Touch me not.'[3]

Our Lord's Resurrection also influenced Christian eschatology by confirming and establishing the authority of His teaching. If the earthly career of our Lord had ended on Calvary, His words would have seemed to lack the blessing of God upon them. But the Resurrection was the seal of God's approval upon the life and work of Jesus,[4] and the 'earnest' of the fulfilment, in God's good time, of all those things which He had promised. Especially was it the pledge of the resurrection of Christ's followers. The old objection, that a resurrection was contrary to experience, could now be confuted by the appeal to an historical fact; and strengthened by this new encouragement to faith, the instinctive but wavering belief in a future world grew into 'a sure and certain hope of the resurrection to eternal life.'[5]

There are many difficulties in connection with the Resurrection-narratives in the Gospels. It is impossible to discuss these here; but it may be well to state clearly that these pages are written from the standpoint of one who believes that the true history of Jesus of Nazareth is summed up in the words heard by St. John at Patmos :—

---

[1] John xx. 27.   [2] John xx. 19, 26.
[3] John xx. 17.   [4] Rom. i. 4 ; Acts xvii. 31.
[5] See 1 Cor. xv. 12-22.

'I am the First and the Last, and the Living One; and I became dead, and behold, I am alive for evermore; and I have the keys of Death and of Hades.'[1]

We now come to our Lord's post-Resurrection teaching. If we regard this from the Christian standpoint, we may fairly expect to find here the highest expression of His message. Often in His earthly ministry He had used a pregnant expression, not understood at the time, in order to stimulate the after-thoughts which He desired. And surely His parting words would be designed to guide aright the after-thoughts of all future generations.

Our earliest authorities for the post-Resurrection teaching of Jesus Christ are, our First and Third Gospels, and the opening verses of the Acts of the Apostles. We have had occasion more than once to comment upon the tendency of these two evangelists to expand and interpret the eschatology in St. Mark's Gospel, making it more definite and more eschatological. Hence if there had been any eschatological element in our Lord's last instructions, it is in the highest degree probable that St. Matthew and St. Luke would have recorded it, and laid considerable emphasis upon it.

But, as a matter of fact, in the post-Resurrection narratives, the eschatological element is noticeable only by reason of its absence. On the road to Emmaus, for instance, our Lord explains to the two disciples that their Messianic hopes had been in part erroneous, and that His own earthly life had indeed fulfilled the true ideal of Messiahship; but of the future nothing is said.[2] In His last charge to the disciples, He speaks as one who possesses the full authority of Messiahship;[3] He promises to the disciples His Messianic gift of the

---

[1] Rev. i. 18. [2] Luke xxiv. 25-27. [3] Matt. xxviii. 18.

ABSENCE OF ESCHATOLOGY

Spirit, but there is no hint that the end of this world or the Second Coming of the Messiah are to take place in the immediate future. On the contrary, the gift of the Spirit is to inspire a campaign of world-wide preaching, 'in Jerusalem, and in all Judaea and Samaria, and unto the uttermost part of the earth.'[1] This would need a long period to accomplish. Or think of the Lord's parting promise to His Church :—

> 'Lo, I am with you all the days, even unto the consummation of the age (πάσας τὰς ἡμέρας, ἕως τῆς συντελείας τοῦ αἰῶνος).'[2]

How much more naturally these words suggest a long vista of years than a brief interval before the 'consummation.' And when the disciples press for definite information as to the length of the waiting-time, He declines to give it them :—

> 'It is not for you to know times or seasons, which the Father hath set within his own authority.'[3]

Only after the Ascension is the angelic message recorded :—

> 'This Jesus, which was received up from you into heaven, shall so come in like manner as ye beheld him going into heaven.'[4]

And even this reveals no details of time.

Surely this absence of eschatology in our Lord's post-Resurrection teaching is exceedingly significant. It confirms our objections to the 'consistent eschatological' view of the life of Jesus. If the centre of gravity of our Lord's mission lay in His eschatological teaching, is it likely that in His last instructions He would have made no reference to it of sufficient importance to

---

[1] Luke xxiv. 49; Acts i. 8. [2] Matt. xxviii. 20. [3] Acts i. 7.
[4] Acts i. 11.

remain in the memory of the disciples? The 'consistent eschatologists' will no doubt tell us that the records of Christ's doings after the Resurrection are not to be regarded as literal history, but only as 'reflections' of early Church doctrine. Even if so, why is it that these records fail so conspicuously to reflect that early Christian expectation (*urchristliche Erwartung*) of the Second Coming which, as Schweitzer rightly points out, is of the very essence of primitive Christianity?

On the contrary, the post-Resurrection *logia* support our contention that there were higher spiritual truths lying behind our Lord's eschatological language;— above all, the call to a holy life, and to spiritual fellowship with a Heavenly Father. These, we may well believe, were 'the things concerning the Kingdom of God,' which the Lord taught His apostles during the forty days;[1] these constituted the purpose for which repentance and remission of sins were to be preached in Christ's name to all the nations. No part of the New Testament supplies a more convincing proof of the inadequacy of the 'Eschatological Theory' than the narratives of our Lord's post-Resurrection sayings.

[1] Acts i. 3.

CHAPTER XIX

THE ESCHATOLOGY OF OUR LORD IN THE FOURTH GOSPEL

HITHERTO we have considered the eschatology of Jesus Christ entirely from the standpoint of the Synoptic Gospels. The reasons for this course have been stated in the introductory chapter to this part of our subject.[1]

But before we conclude our study of Christ's eschatology, it is essential to examine the presentation of it in St. John's Gospel. However much allowance may be made for the tendency of the Fourth Evangelist to interpret instead of recording plain matters of fact, there still remains the strong evidence that the author had been an intimate companion of Jesus during His lifetime on earth.

> 'Whereas it is probable that not one ancient in a thousand, or one in ten thousand, would have written as the author of the Fourth Gospel has done, if he had not been an eye-witness; it would have been the only natural way for him to write, if he had been an eye-witness.'[2]

St. John's Gospel is certainly not a pure work of the imagination, but the explanation of that which the writer had seen and heard.

It does not fall within our present scope to discuss whether the Johannine record of the place and time

---

[1] See above, p. 118.   [2] Sanday, *Criticism of the Fourth Gospel*, p. 97.

of our Lord's ministry may be reconciled with the Synoptists. Rather we must devote our attention to the Johannine doctrines of Christ's Person and teaching.

The reader will remember, from our study of the Synoptic Gospels, how intimately Christ's eschatology is connected with His Messianic Consciousness. In the Fourth Gospel, the Christology is of even more fundamental importance for the student of eschatology, and a brief consideration of it seems desirable at this early stage of the chapter.

In order to understand St. John's doctrine of our Lord's Person and Messiahship, it is necessary first to inquire what meaning he attached to the terms 'Son of Man' and 'Son of God.' In the Synoptists we found that our Lord's use of the phrase 'the Son of Man' ("ὁ υἱὸς τοῦ ἀνθρώπου") showed a distinct development, from the ambiguous meaning of the earlier instances to the thoroughly eschatological and personal significance of those which occur after the 'Great Confession' of St. Peter. In St. John no such development is readily discernible; none of the occurrences of the phrase are parallel to those in the Synoptists, and in no case can there be any doubt that it refers to Jesus personally; while in most cases it clearly points to His eschatological Messiahship, conceived in a manner that reminds us much of the 'Similitudes' of Enoch. This is especially noticeable in the two earliest Johannine instances, St. John i. 51:—

'Ye shall see the heaven opened, and the angels of God ascending and descending upon the Son of Man';

and St. John iii. 13:—

'No man hath ascended into heaven, but he that descended out of heaven, even the Son of Man.'

A similar eschatological tone marks almost all the Johannine occurrences of the phrase 'Son of Man.'[1]

The term 'the Son of God' ("ὁ υἱὸς τοῦ Θεοῦ") was also, as we have seen, an occasional apocalyptic title for the Messiah; and in the very first occurrence of the phrase in the Fourth Gospel, the thought of Messiahship is clearly evident: 'Rabbi, thou art the Son of God; thou art King of Israel.'[2] Many similar passages might be cited; and they lead us to the conclusion that the two terms 'Son of Man' and 'Son of God' in St. John's Gospel are both of them Messianic titles of our Lord; indeed, it is not always easy to discover the difference between them.[3]

It is interesting, too, to notice that the third of the great Johannine titles of our Lord—'The Logos'—is also in harmony with the Enochic conception of the Messiah. For the 'Logos,' like Enoch's 'Son of Man,' is pre-existent with God before the world began, and is a mediator or agent through whom God speaks to the world. Only, 'the Logos' is primarily a philosophical conception, while 'the Son of Man' is a dramatic and active Person.

It will thus be seen that the use of these titles in St. John's Gospel is clearly associated with an idea of Messiahship, and that not of the political, but of the heavenly and eschatological kind.

Our investigation of the Synoptic narratives led us to the following conclusions concerning the method by which our Lord revealed His Messiahship to the world:

---

[1] In another passage which seems most distinctly reminiscent of Enoch, we get the form "υἱὸς ἀνθρώπου."—'He hath given him authority to execute judgment, because he is υἱὸς ἀνθρώπου' (v. 27). The phrase occurs nowhere else without the article. Perhaps here it 'concentrates attention upon the nature and not upon the personality of Christ' (Westcott's *Gospel of St. John*, notes *ad loc.*).

[2] John i. 49.

[3] In John ix. 35 the MSS. vary between 'Son of Man' and 'Son of God.' See also above, p. 161.

(i.) That He Himself was conscious of His Messiahship from the beginning of the ministry; (ii.) that in public He referred to it in a guarded manner, lest His own lofty ideal should be misunderstood and degraded by the hasty zeal of the populace; (iii.) that the disciples first grasped the great truth at Caesarea Philippi, when St. Peter confessed, 'Thou art the Christ'; (iv.) that the people as a whole remained in a state of uncertainty till the last; (v.) that the first explicit claim to Messiahship from our Lord's own lips was at the trial before the Crucifixion.

The general impression conveyed by the Fourth Gospel appears at first sight widely different. At the very outset of the ministry, Jesus is recognised as Messiah by John the Baptist, by Andrew, and by Nathanael.[1] He Himself proclaims His Messiahship to the Samaritan woman in the plainest terms,[2] and in the interview with Nicodemus He is described as 'the Son of Man' who has come down from heaven.[3] In the later ministry He plainly asserts His pre-existence: 'What then if ye should behold the Son of Man ascending where he was before?'[4]—'Before Abraham was, I am.'[5] There is no wavering, no uncertainty; from first to last Jesus proclaims that He is the Messianic and eschatological Son of Man and the Divine Son of God. Are we then to conclude that we misunderstood the Synoptists when we thought we discovered signs of a gradual unveiling of our Lord's Messiahship to the people? Or shall we say that the Synoptists and the Fourth Gospel are mutually contradictory, so that the one or the other must be a work of fiction? Or is there yet another alternative?

Before we attempt to answer, let us glance at the

---

[1] John i. 34, 41, 49; cf. iii. 30.　　[2] John iv. 25, 26.
[3] John iii. 13.　　[4] John vi. 62.
[5] John viii. 58.

AGREEMENT WITH THE SYNOPTISTS

Johannine account of the attitude of the people towards our Lord. This agrees in a striking manner with the Synoptic narratives. From them we saw that our Lord's Galilean preaching was intelligible only on the assumption that He was unwilling to accept the Messianic honours from the people until He had raised their ideals of Messiahship; and St. John shows us how dangerous was the popular Messianic Hope to our Lord, when he mentions that the people were once 'about to come and take him by force, to make him king.'[1] We can thus understand how needful it was that the claim to Messiahship should be veiled for the time being. But, as we have just seen, the Johannine account seems to affirm that this claim was not veiled in the Judaean ministry. Yet what, according to St. John, was the attitude of the populace at Jerusalem towards our Lord?

'If thou be the Messiah, tell us plainly.'[2]

Clearly *they* hold that no distinct claim to Messiahship has yet been made by Him. His answer implies that He had indeed told them already, but by works, not by words:—

'I told you, and ye believe not: the works that I do in my Father's name, these bear witness of me.'[3]

And this was (according to the Johannine chronology) during our Lord's fourth visit to Jerusalem; so that the people had often had the opportunity of hearing His claims. Somewhat earlier, on the occasion of Christ's third visit to the Holy City, we read of much difference of opinion among the people:—

'Some of the multitude ... said, This is of a truth the Prophet. Others said, This is the Christ. But some said,

[1] John vi. 15.   [2] John x. 24.   [3] John x. 25.

What, doth the Christ come out of Galilee? Hath not the Scripture said that the Christ cometh of the seed of David, and from Bethlehem, the village where David was? So there arose a division in the multitude because of him.'[1]

But no one appeals to any words of Jesus which were a *direct* claim to Messiahship. It seems then that St. John himself was quite aware that our Lord had never spoken of His Messiahship in terms which would be unmistakable to the people.

How then are we to explain the Johannine passages where our Lord is represented as speaking plainly of His Messianic authority? It will not do to say that the Fourth Gospel has no relation to history or to the Synoptists; for the attitude of the populace in St. John is in striking agreement, as we have seen, with the Synoptic narratives, and indeed is needed to explain their full significance. If the Fourth Gospel appears to be inconsistent with the Synoptists, it also appears to be inconsistent with itself.

The only explanation which satisfies the case is that the Fourth Gospel is a 'spiritual gospel.' The author sought to record the thoughts of Christ rather than His actual words. So the older *logia* are assimilated to the later ones, because the light of experience has shown that the Lord Himself never changed. The evangelist is sure that in many a 'dark saying' of the early ministry the Messianic Consciousness is not far below the surface, and so he interprets the saying so as to bring to light its full meaning. He fully recognises that the whole truth was not grasped at the time;[2] but for that very reason he feels it all the more necessary to explain it now.

---

[1] John vii. 40, 41.—'The Prophet' is probably the one foretold by Moses, Deut. xviii. 15.
[2] John xii. 16.

DOCTRINE OF MESSIAHSHIP

There is thus nothing in the Johannine presentation of our Lord's Messianic Consciousness to invalidate the general conclusions which we gathered from the Synoptic narratives. On the contrary, St. John helps us to understand much that was not clear from the Synoptists alone. He shows us, more clearly than they do, how it was that Jesus did not fulfil any of the current ideas of Messiahship. Some objected that our Lord's origin was not sufficiently mysterious for Him to be the Messiah :—

> 'We know this man, whence he is; but when the Christ cometh, no one is to know (γινώσκει) whence he is.'[1]

Such words exactly reflect the natural attitude of men familiar with Enoch's doctrine of a supernatural Messiah from heaven; while on the other hand those who looked for a Christ of David's line at once pointed to our Lord's Galilean parentage as a conclusive proof that He was not the Messiah.[2] And lest the indecision of the populace should incline more favourably towards the new Prophet, the aristocracy took every opportunity to let it be known that no educated person with any self-respect had paid the slightest heed to His teaching :—

> 'Hath any of the rulers believed on him, or of the Pharisees?'[3]

All this throws fresh light upon the course of events as recorded in the Synoptists, and explains why the Jewish people never brought themselves to recognise the Messiahship of Jesus.

The Johannine doctrine of our Lord's Messiahship also helps us to understand something of that higher conception of Messiahship which our Lord endeavoured to teach His followers and the world. Like Enoch's

---

[1] John vii. 27.   [2] John vii. 41, 42.   [3] John vii. 48.

'Son of Man,' the true Messiah is pre-existent 'in the beginning with God';[1] unlike Enoch's 'Son of Man,' He truly shares our human nature, for He 'became flesh, and dwelt among us.'[2] 'Because he is Son of Man,' He is to be the judge, not only at the Last Day, but also in the present world.[3] He possesses in Himself the life-giving spirit, so that He *is* 'the resurrection and the life.'[4]

It is unquestionable that this Johannine doctrine of Christ's Person appears to be more spiritual than that of the Synoptists. But does it follow that it could not have been part of the Lord's own teaching? On the contrary, we would suggest that the facts of the case are best explained by regarding the Johannine doctrine of our Lord's Messiahship as a reflection, not of early Christian speculation, but of that sacred intimacy which existed between the Master and the beloved disciple.

This brief outline of the Johannine Christology will now help us to a better understanding of the Johannine Doctrine of the Last Things. Much of St. John's eschatology is expressed by a series of paradoxes. We read that 'God sent not his Son into the world to judge the world,' and a few verses later: 'This is the judgment, that light is come into the world.'[5] Or again, we are told that the believer '*has* passed from death unto life,' and yet that the hour is coming when all the righteous *will* come forth from the grave for 'the resurrection of life.'[6] And other similar instances might be cited. What is the meaning of these apparent paradoxes? Some critics bring forward a theory of

---

[1] John i. 1; cf. iii. 13, vi. 62.   [2] John i. 14; cf. ii. 25, etc.
[3] John v. 25-28.—See Westcott's note on v. 25.
[4] John xi. 25; cf. vii. 39.   [5] John iii. 17, 19.
[6] John v. 24, 28.

interpolations; but this is purely arbitrary, and without warrant from textual criticism; and further, it does not by any means solve all the difficulties.

Our study of the Johannine doctrine of our Lord's Messiahship will suggest another answer: that the author wished to explain the spiritual meaning of current eschatology in a manner consistent with his doctrine of our Lord's Person. He nowhere denies the Jewish Doctrine of the Last Things; on the contrary, he shares the expectation of the Messianic Woes,[1] of a general resurrection,[2] and of the Last Day.[3] But his real interest does not lie in those matters, but in the spiritual life of the present. His mission is not to teach the 'dramatic eschatology' of the Last Things, but rather those moral principles of eschatology which were so prominent in the teaching of Jesus Christ. Viewed from the Johannine—may we not add, from the Christian—standpoint, the great principles of justice and love are the principles which guide the course of events, both now and through all the ages. He who has grasped these principles knows the inner meaning both of history and of eschatology; and although his expectation of the Last Things may change in form, it will remain unchanged in spirit. So when St. John compares the Jewish expectation of the Judgment with the actual advent of the Messiah that had lately come to pass, he sees that our Lord did not judge the world as the Jews expected; but that the coming of Christ was nevertheless a real judgment, because it tested men's spiritual life:—

> 'He that believeth not hath been judged already, because he hath not believed on the name of the only begotten Son of God.'[4]

[1] John xv. 20, xvi. 2, 33, etc.
[2] John v. 28.
[3] John vi. 39, 40, 54, xii. 48.
[4] John iii. 18.

It is the same with the 'Kingdom of God' in the Fourth Gospel. In the few places where the phrase occurs, it is regarded not merely as a future event, but rather as a condition of the soul.[1] Generally, the term 'eternal life' ($\zeta\omega\dot{\eta}$ $\alpha\dot{\iota}\dot{\omega}\nu\iota\sigma s$) takes the place which is occupied in the Synoptists by 'the Kingdom of God.' For example:—

> 'He that believeth on the Son hath eternal life; but he that obeyeth not the Son shall not see life, but the wrath of God abideth on him.'[2]

One might say that by 'eternal life' St. John denotes the highest ideal of the Kingdom of God in its relation to the individual.

It is the individual, again, who is generally uppermost in St. John's mind when he speaks of the resurrection, though he does not ignore the collective aspect. And so the all-important point is that the Spirit of life should be given to a man. If he possesses this, then he is already potentially a partaker of the future resurrection; otherwise the power of life is not in him.[3] Christ alone can give this Spirit of life; and so He is 'the Resurrection and the Life.'[4] The supreme bliss of the future will be 'to be with Christ';[5] and He has returned to the Father's presence in order to prepare a place for them that are His.[6]

These 'spiritual' thoughts seem almost independent of time and place. The mind of the evangelist towards those who sought for detailed revelations of the future, asking, When, or Where shall these things be? is expressed by the last words of Jesus which he has recorded:—

---

[1] John iii. 3, 5; cf. xviii. 36, where the two meanings might be both included.
[2] John iii. 36.
[3] John vi. 39-54, vii. 37, 38; cf. v. 21-24.   [4] John xi. 25.
[5] John xvii. 24.   [6] John xiv. 2, etc.

A SPIRITUAL ESCHATOLOGY

'If I will that he tarry till I come, what is that to thee? Follow thou me.'[1]

The value of St. John's Gospel for the student of Christ's eschatology is twofold. In the first place, it throws fresh light on the course of events which influenced the form of our Lord's ministry and teaching. Considering the marked contrast in 'tone' between the Fourth Gospel and the Synoptists, it is most remarkable to observe the number of incidental allusions in the former, which not only agree precisely with the general circumstances of the events recorded by the Synoptists, but even explain points which otherwise would be less clear, if we only possessed the earlier narratives. More than one instance of this has been noted in the preceding pages.

In the second place, St. John's Gospel fulfils an expectation suggested but not completely satisfied by the Synoptic evangelists. From them we inferred that our Lord was desirous to teach a more spiritual form of eschatology than was current among the Jews; but that it was impracticable, for reasons which we have already indicated, to proclaim this openly and fully. But while we concluded that this might fairly be inferred from the Synoptic narratives, it was only an inference; it is not directly stated by them in plain words. Now in the Fourth Gospel, we find that what the Synoptists led us to infer is clearly and fully stated; our Lord is represented as laying the chief emphasis on the spiritual truths which underlay the familiar eschatological phrases. Thus the Synoptists and St. John confirm each other's truth in this matter; not because of any outward or artificial resemblance—for that is notably absent—but because together they enable us to form a consistent idea of Christ's work,

[1] John xxi. 22.

which would be impossible from either, if isolated from the other.

Many scholars, it is true, hold that the Johannine eschatology was not derived from our Lord, but is a free creation of the evangelist's religious consciousness. We have tried, however, to show that on critical grounds this conclusion is not warranted. And, from quite another point of view, there is a consideration that deserves to be borne in mind.—All those who are brought into close contact with the moral and spiritual needs of men and women in actual life agree that St. John's Gospel fulfils those needs in a way that no other book is able to do; and if St. John's Gospel is not in accordance with the mind of Christ, we are driven to conclude that the thoughts of the disciple were greater than the thoughts of his Lord. Is it not more reasonable to hold that although the Johannine eschatology may be expressed in the words of the evangelist, yet the spirit is in very truth the Spirit of Christ?

CHAPTER XX

CHRIST'S ESCHATOLOGY—GENERAL CONCLUSIONS

THE study of the eschatology of Jesus Christ has led us into many detailed questions of criticism and interpretation, so that it has not always been easy to keep in mind the main outlines of the subject. In this concluding chapter we shall endeavour to gather up the main points of importance, and to indicate especially those features which distinguish our Lord's teaching from that of His predecessors and contemporaries. It will be convenient to deal first with His eschatology of the world, and secondly with His eschatology of the individual; and we shall also endeavour to estimate the extent to which the 'Eschatological Theory' of Schweitzer contributes to a true knowledge of our Lord's teaching.

The foremost feature of Christ's 'cosmic eschatology' is His unwavering faith in the final victory of God's will over the forces of evil. The phrase 'the Kingdom of God,' which, as we have seen, lay at the very heart of His teaching, is itself an expression of this faith; for only when the evil is finally conquered by the good, will the ideal of the Kingdom of God be truly realised. And in the story of our Lord's earthly life, we may trace the perfecting of this faith through the deepest sufferings possible for man. All through the bitter disappointment of the 'Great Refusal,' in the hour of agony at Gethsemane, and at the sharp anguish of the Cross, He keeps His eyes steadily fixed on the glory which shall be hereafter. A faith such as this had been a special feature of Jewish eschatology, though nowhere perfectly realised before the coming of our Lord. Even in the darkest days of trouble, the faithful Jew never contemplated the possibility that the dawn would never break; he never wavered in his confidence that somehow and somewhen God's purpose would be made plain, and His triumph would be revealed. To us this may seem almost a truism; yet it was far different in many of the ethnic beliefs of the future life. In Babylonia, Egypt, and Greece, for instance, while there was often a strong belief in the immortality of the soul, there was no sense of a unifying purpose running through history, nor of the

> 'One far-off Divine event,
> To which the whole creation moves.'

But how did our Lord conceive of the *process* by which this final victory of the good will come to pass? Did He share the views which have become generally prevalent in our day, that the world is steadily progressing, so that the evil will in time die a natural death, and the Perfect World be evolved from that which is imperfect? The general trend of His teaching gives little support to this idea. We have pointed out that the Jewish apocalypses, with very few exceptions,[1] inculcated a diametrically opposite view—namely, that the conflict between good and evil will grow more and more intense, till at length the victory of the former is effected by a miracle of Divine power. And our Lord, in the 'Eschatological Discourse' and other allied passages, not only adopts apocalyptic language, but

---

[1] See above, p. 75.

THE MANNER OF THE CONSUMMATION 217

also follows the general scheme of development which is customary in the apocalyptic books.[1]—Troubles and portents are to grow worse and worse, till suddenly the Son of Man shall appear descending from heaven. Now, after every allowance has been made for the symbolical and pictorial character of the language, and for the possibility that the apocalyptic 'tone' has been intensified by primitive Christian ideas, it still seems impossible to reconcile even the bare outlines of such teaching with the belief that all evil will gradually give place to goodness. The Parable of the Tares, too, clearly foretells that what is evil will continue to grow by natural law just as much as that which is good, until 'the harvest,' when the natural course of development will be modified by a Power from without.

On the other hand, the fact should not be ignored that certain of the earlier Galilean Parables, if they stood alone, would rather favour the idea that the future Kingdom of God is to be the outcome of an evolutionary process. The mustard-seed, which grows from small beginnings into a great tree;[2] the corn-seed, which brings forth 'first the blade, then the ear, then the full corn in the ear';[3] and, above all, the leaven, which permeates the meal 'till the whole is leavened';[4] —all these accord more naturally with the idea of a gradual development of the good than with the expectation of a catastrophic consummation.

But these parables form only a small part of our Lord's recorded teaching; the general impression conveyed by the Gospels is that He distinctly sanctioned the normal Jewish belief that the end of this World-Era and the final victory of the good will be brought about by a miraculous interposition of Divine power.

---

[1] See (e.g.) above, pp. 173, 174.
[2] Mark iv. 30 ff., etc.
[3] Mark iv. 26 ff.
[4] Matt. xiii. 33, etc.

Nevertheless, the aforementioned parables warn us not to exclude with too great rigidity the possibility that the alternative view may have had a place in our Lord's mind. The two views seem to our human faculties to be mutually exclusive; but the whole truth of so vast a theme as cosmic eschatology is doubtless 'broader than the measure of man's mind,' and may include elements which we fancy to be irreconcilable with one another.

It may also be well to recall that we noticed above, in connection with our Lord's 'preaching of the Kingdom,' that there was in it a *conditional* element,[1] due to the uncertainty which must always attach to human action, if human free-will be a reality and not a phantom. And even in the vast drama of cosmic eschatology, must not human free-will always be one of the factors determining its course? And if so, there must also (so far as we can see) be always a measure of uncertainty as to that course;—an uncertainty which cannot be eliminated without reducing human responsibility to an unreal illusion, and degrading man himself to the level of a machine. These considerations may perhaps throw some light upon any apparent inconsistency between various parts of our Lord's teaching concerning the eschatology of the world.

One other essential feature in our Lord's 'cosmic eschatology' must be noticed—a feature all the more significant because nothing like it had been found in the teaching of any other of the world's religious leaders. We refer to the way in which our Lord's Doctrine of the Last Things centres around His own Person. When He spake of Himself as the Judge at the Last Day, and taught that the final destinies of men would depend on their attitude to Him in this world, He was making a

[1] See above, pp. 141, 142.

THE CENTRALITY OF CHRIST 219

claim that was absolutely unique in the world's history. Other teachers (and, above all, the holiest among them) when speaking of the things belonging to eternal salvation, had tried to point their fellow-men away from themselves, to God, the Maker and Judge of all; but Christ, when dealing with the same solemn theme, endeavours to concentrate attention upon Himself, as not only the Guide to, but also the Giver of, eternal life :—

'I am the Way, and the Truth, and the Life.'[1]

'He that eateth my flesh and drinketh my blood hath eternal life; and I will raise him up at the last day.'[2]

'Whosoever shall be ashamed of me and of my words in this adulterous and sinful generation, of him shall the Son of Man also be ashamed, when he cometh in the glory of his Father with the holy angels.'[3]

In the chapter on the 'Eschatological Discourse,' we considered some of those perplexing sayings of Christ which suggest at first sight that He anticipated that His Second Coming was very near at hand.[4] We came to the conclusion, however, that this interpretation of the passages in question is by no means proved beyond doubt. Other sayings of our Lord distinctly suggest that His Second Coming is more or less remote;[5] and allowance should be made for the instinctive tendency of the evangelists (a tendency which can be traced more than once by comparing St. Mark with parallel passages in the later Gospels)[6] to interpret our Lord's words in accordance with Jewish eschatological ideas. Under the circumstances, the contention that our Lord's cosmic eschatology was erroneous in this important particular cannot be regarded as established.

Turning now to our Lord's eschatology of the in-

[1] John xiv. 6.   [2] John vi. 54.
[3] Mark viii. 38 (A.V.).   [4] See above, Chapter XVII.
[5] See above, pp. 186, 201, etc.   [6] See above, pp. 143 and 177.

dividual, there can be no shadow of doubt that He believed and taught that the human soul is immortal, by virtue of its spiritual relation to a God who is 'not the God of the dead, but of the living.' No word of Christ's ever gives the slightest countenance to the supposition that physical death marks the extinction of the whole life. On this fundamental question His verdict is clear and unmistakable.

Our Lord further affirms 'that the dead are *raised up*.' But when we seek in His recorded teaching for definite statements as to the time and manner of the resurrection, the evidence is found to be much less conclusive. With regard to the time of the resurrection, the general tenor of His answer to the Sadducees[1] would agree well with the idea that a spiritual 'resurrection life' begins at once after death. On the other hand, the importance assigned to 'the Day of Judgment' in our Lord's teaching would seem rather to support the normal Pharisaic belief that souls enter at once after death into an Intermediate State, and then are raised at the Last Day to be judged and to receive their final recompense. The Parable of Dives and Lazarus, too, suggests an intermediate state of departed souls; but the language is obviously metaphorical. The uncertainty which meets us here serves to illustrate what has been already said[2] with regard to the difficulty of applying the idea of *time* to the life beyond the grave.

The manner of the resurrection is similarly not defined in our Lord's teaching. Certainly there is nothing therein to justify the extremely materialistic conception of the resurrection which soon became prevalent in the Church.[3] But on the other hand the Christian world has always instinctively felt that the

---

[1] Mark xii. 24-27. See above, pp. 190 ff.
[2] See above, p. 188.   [3] See below, on Athenagoras, pp. 357 f.

THE RESURRECTION

idea of a purely bodiless existence after death stands condemned, not perhaps by any recorded words of our Lord, but by the fact that His own Resurrection was not a bodiless survival, but a 'resurrection of the body,' —although not of a body subject to the limitations of ordinary matter. A definition of the manner of the resurrection more precise than this cannot rightly claim the authority of Christ's teaching or example.

There is one other question which arises in connection with our Lord's doctrine of the resurrection.—Did He imply that a resurrection is the natural and inevitable destiny of all mankind, or that it is a privilege reserved for the righteous only ? The records of Christ's answer to the Sadducees in St. Mark and St. Matthew [1] on the whole suggest a 'general resurrection,' and this is explicitly affirmed in one Johannine passage.[2] Furthermore, we have seen reason to believe that the Lucan passages which suggest the other alternative owe their present form to the hand of the evangelist.[3] But there is a real element of truth in this view, which is emphasised also in parts of St. John's Gospel ; [4] for if our hope of the future life depends upon our spiritual kinship with God, because 'all live unto him,' then a man who is wholly bad can have in him no spark of the eternal life. But it has to be proved that such men exist, before we deny that the resurrection is the common lot of humanity. This whole subject is complicated, when we try to follow it out, by the insoluble problem of human free-will.

When we turn from these doubtful questions to our Lord's teaching concerning the Last Judgment, it is possible once more to speak with confidence ; for the main principle is affirmed with unwavering assurance.

---

[1] See (e.g.) Mark xii. 24-27 ; Matt. xxii. 29-33.
[2] John v. 28, 29.   [3] See above, p. 194.   [4] See above, p. 212.

Whatever elements of Christ's eschatology may be undefined, one dogma at least stands out clear and strong,—that each man's life—his thoughts, words, and deeds,—will be judged by God after death, and that a sentence will be pronounced in strict accordance with the law of justice.[1] No aspect of eschatology has so practical a bearing as this upon human conduct in the present world; and none is emphasised with such unreserved vigour in the words of Christ. And it came upon the world as a fresh revelation.—

> 'The Christian notion of the enormity of little sins, the belief that all the details of life will be scrutinised hereafter; ... was altogether unknown among the ancients, and, at a time when it possessed all the freshness of novelty, it was well fitted to transform the character.'[2]

The above words refer primarily to the Pagan world; but they apply with almost equal truth to Judaism in the time of our Lord. The Jewish apocalyptic literature was not, for the most part, inspired by pre-eminent zeal for a life of well-doing. The writers were more keen to set forward the aims of their party than to relieve the fatherless or care for the widow. But in the teaching of Jesus, the old prophetic enthusiasm for 'righteousness' revived, and more than revived. He Himself set the example of a life of self-sacrifice for the sake of His brethren; and He tells His disciples that only those who follow in His steps will be admitted at the Last Judgment Day into the Kingdom of God. Never before or since have eschatology and practical morality been so intimately connected as in the teaching of Jesus. On the one hand, the doctrine of the Last Judgment gives force and intensity to His call to

---

[1] The problems of atonement and forgiveness, and the relation of these to the law of strict justice, open up a vast subject upon which it is impossible here to enter.

[2] Lecky, *History of European Morals* (London, 9th ed., 1890), vol. ii. p. 3.

a holy life, and the doctrine of the future Kingdom of God shows the ultimate purpose of His zeal for righteousness; while conversely, the eschatology of our Lord derives its true value from His call to repentance and holiness. We cannot understand Christ's Doctrine of the Last Things apart from His moral teaching, nor His moral teaching apart from His Doctrine of the Last Things. And this could not be said of any contemporary system of eschatology.

If our Lord's emphatic proclamation of coming Judgment was intended to be, first and foremost, a call to practical morality, it is a question of secondary importance to determine whether the rewards and punishments are to be 'objective' or 'subjective,'— whether, that is, they are to consist of pleasure or pain coming upon us from without, or of mental and spiritual joy or sorrow, growing ever more and more intense under the influence of 'conscience' within.[1] The latter idea appears to be growing more prevalent in modern times, and we may safely maintain that it will be one element of retribution.—

> 'I sent my Soul through the Invisible,
>   Some letter of that After-life to spell;
>   And by and by my Soul returned to me,
>   And answered, "I Myself am Heaven and Hell":
>   Heaven but the Vision of fulfilled Desire,
>   And Hell the Shadow from a Soul on fire.'

Yes; a true element, and not the least effective, in all retribution; and our Lord's language may rightly be taken to include this. But the idea of an objective, external retribution was deeply rooted in the Jewish mind, and those who heard Christ's preaching of the Judgment and its sequel would certainly understand

---

[1] There is also the question, how far 'the Last Judgment' may be regarded as an event *in time*; for this, see above, pp. 188 f.

it in a realistic and dramatic sense; yet He never (so far as we know) condemned them in this respect. So that we may infer that the doctrine of external and objective retribution is in accord with the doctrine of Christ, or at least, not contrary to it. After all, it is rather a question of the different kinds of human temperament: a simple matter-of-fact mind will naturally conceive of retribution in a dramatic and objective form, while to a contemplative nature the thought of spiritual joy or anguish will be more real, and more beneficent in its results, than the former idea could ever be.

We have already referred at some length to our Lord's teaching concerning the final destinies of man, the possibility of repentance after death, and eternal punishment.[1] It is unnecessary to repeat the argument here, but we may briefly recall the conclusions. We noticed that Christ in many places describes both future bliss and future punishment as 'eternal,' but that in some cases this word obviously signified *intensity* rather than unending time. It is important in this connection to keep in mind the practical bearing of our Lord's teaching. The objections brought against the doctrine of eternal punishment, and the desire to believe in the possibility of repentance after death, often spring, it is true, from an amiable shrinking from excessive sternness; but there is not infrequently another motive—the desire to find some pretext for moral slackness. To those who love the broad and pleasant paths of easygoing selfishness, a stern doctrine of retribution is naturally distasteful; and any note of uncertainty, or any hint of the possibility of repentance after death, is readily seized upon as an excuse for ignoring the call to immediate repentance here and now. Perhaps this was one of the reasons why our Lord refrained from

[1] See above, pp. 187-189.

giving His authority to any theory which would soften the sternness of the sentence passed at the Great Judgment.—' He knew what was in man.'

If we would form a true estimate of our Lord's eschatology as a whole, we must take account, not only of His recorded words, but also of the general impression created by the story of His earthly life. For the sequence of events therein—Life, Death, Resurrection—co-operates with His spoken message in teaching the great principle of Christian eschatology, that the only road to eternal life is the road of self-sacrifice :—

> 'He that loveth his life loseth it; and he that hateth his life in this world shall keep it unto life eternal.'[1]

And further, the historical fact of Christ's Resurrection gives to His eschatology a certainty and an authority which no other can claim. It is, as it were, the seal of the Divine approval upon the life and teaching of One 'who was declared to be the Son of God with power, by the resurrection of the dead.'[2] Especially does the Resurrection of Christ confirm Christ's promise of resurrection to His followers; for His Resurrection is, as it were, the foretaste or the 'first-fruits of theirs.'[3]

We have so far been dealing with the positive features of our Lord's Doctrine of the Last Things; but if we would clearly appreciate its significance, we must compare it with current eschatological systems, in order to realise the *peculiar* characteristics of His message: what He omitted to teach, and what new features He added.

What features of current eschatology did our Lord omit to teach? To any one familiar with the Jewish

---

[1] John xii. 25.   [2] Rom. i. 4.   [3] 1 Cor. xv. 20.

Q

apocalypses, there is nothing in His eschatology (both of the world and of the individual) so striking as His unvarying restraint when speaking of the details of the world to come. There is a notable absence of anything to correspond with the apocalyptic visions of the detailed events of the Last Days; Christ's use of imagery is bold and simple, and at once turns our thoughts away to plain practical lessons.

We seek in vain for any dogmatic pronouncements from His mouth concerning the intermediate state of departed souls, or the exact nature and time of the resurrection. Where He refers to these matters, His language is symbolical or metaphorical. And further, He gives no countenance to the elaborate calculations of the time that is to elapse before the Last Things. 'It is not for you,' He said, 'to know times or seasons.'[1] All these were questions on which the Jewish apocalyptists were ready to pronounce the most definite opinions. But our Lord is silent, knowing that it is impossible for our finite minds to understand the conditions of life in a world which lies outside our present knowledge.

Nor do we find in our Lord's teaching any definite instructions concerning prayers for the dead, or the intercession of the saints on our behalf. He does indeed speak of the power of prayer: 'Whatsoever ye shall ask the Father in my name, he will give it you,'[2] and He also tells us that the souls of the departed are living, just as truly as we are living, in spiritual union with God, fellow-members with us of His great Family and Church, knit with us in the Communion of Saints. But He leaves it to us to apply these principles to the solution of our controverted questions.

Scarcely less noticeable than the absence of apo-

[1] Acts i. 7.   [2] John xvi. 23 (A.V.).

calyptic details in our Lord's teaching is the absence of national prejudice. Christ's vision of the future is not distorted by Jewish exclusiveness. It is true that His message is first delivered to the Jews alone;[1] but this is only for a time; and when once He bids His followers turn to the Gentiles, He implies that they are to be approached as the spiritual equals of the Jews, the divinely-appointed recipients of the privileges which the Chosen People had forfeited. In Jewish eschatology, the Gentiles are to be destroyed at the Last Crisis, or, if spared, it is only to become absorbed into the Hebrew religion. In Christ's eschatology, they are to be the rightful inheritors of the Covenant-Promises. He is content with nothing less than a world-wide Kingdom :—

> 'They shall come from the east and west, and from the north and south, and shall sit down in the Kingdom of God.'[2]

Closely allied with the absence of Jewish 'nationalism' is the absence of any political element in Christ's eschatology. In spite of the vigorous assertions of Schweitzer and the 'Eschatological School,' we find plenty of evidence that the political element was often prominent in contemporary Jewish eschatology. But in our Lord's teaching there is no trace of this.—

> 'Render unto Caesar the things that are Caesar's, and unto God the things that are God's.'[3]

A comparison of the Gospels with contemporary Jewish literature thus shows that Christ omitted three important elements in the current eschatological hopes. But if we were simply to remove from the Jewish apocalypses all the puerile details, all Pharisaic exclusiveness,

[1] See above, pp. 138, 139.   [2] Luke xiii. 29.   [3] Mark xii. 17.

and all political worldliness, the result would still be something very different from the eschatology of our Lord. In the latter there are additions as well as omissions. The chief of these additions have been already referred to, in dealing with the positive features of Christ's eschatology. The great prominence given to the call to practical morality was certainly not copied from the bulk of Jewish apocalyptic literature; while the manner in which Christ's Doctrine of the Last Things centres round the Figure of the speaker Himself is without a parallel in history. And the example of Christ's Life and Death and Resurrection was, of course, an entirely new factor to be reckoned with.

A few words ought perhaps to be added, concerning the relation of our Lord's eschatology to that of non-Jewish religions. But, in fact, there is little to say, beyond that all the distinctively non-Jewish features of these religions appear to have been deliberately omitted from His eschatology. The attempts to prove that He borrowed from them are for the most part singularly futile. The pantheism which underlies so much of the eschatology of the remoter East, is certainly not to be found in the canonical Gospels. One of the Oxyrhynchus 'Logia' does indeed suggest pantheistic ideas; but the authenticity of this is very doubtful.[1] The attempts to prove that Christ's teaching derived much of its inspiration from Buddhist sources appear (to the present writer, at any rate) to be examples of singularly inconclusive reasoning.[2] Nor is there any word of our Lord's which supports the

---

[1] Logion 30 in J. H. Ropes's article 'Agrapha' in Hastings' *Dictionary of the Bible*, extra vol. p. 347: 'Raise the stone, and there thou shalt find Me; cleave the wood, and there I am.'

[2] See (*e.g.*) Lillie, *Influence of Buddhism on Primitive Christianity*, London, 1893.

doctrine of the pre-existence of the soul, nor of the transmigration of souls.[1] Perhaps we hardly realise the importance of this, because these ideas are so foreign and unfamiliar to Western modes of thought. But, once accepted, they transform the whole meaning of this life, which is then seen as but a link in an endless chain of existences. Such a conception of life is sundered from our own by a gulf in comparison with which even the sharpest of our inter-Christian cleavages on eschatological controversies seems insignificant. And although Christ nowhere explicitly denies either pre-existence or transmigration, it is hard to suppose that so fundamental and far-reaching a belief would have been passed over in silence, had it seemed to Him to be in accordance with the truth.

We have had occasion so frequently to refer to the views of Schweitzer and the 'Consistent Eschatological School' of Continental critics, that it seems well to recall here our conclusions with regard to their main contentions.

Their theory that Christ simply accepted the Jewish idea of a transcendental and eschatological Kingdom, and proclaimed its immediate advent, without attempting to alter the ideals of the people, cannot be reconciled with the evidence of contemporary Jewish literature, nor with the narratives of any of our Gospels. For, on the one hand, contemporary Jewish literature shows that the expectation of 'the Kingdom of God' was rarely, if ever, purely transcendental in character, and often very much the reverse; while, on the other hand, many of our Lord's sayings recorded

[1] The evidence of St. John ix. 1-3 (the man born blind) is very slight; but if our Lord's words, 'Neither did this man sin, nor his parents,' have any bearing upon the idea of transmigration, they indicate an attitude of disapproval.

in the Gospels were clearly intended to correct and modify the current beliefs on this subject. It is equally inconsistent with the evidence at our disposal to hold that Christ never claimed to be Messiah in His earthly life, but only expected that one day He would be the eschatological Son of Man. On the contrary, the general 'plot' of the Gospel narratives becomes intelligible only on the assumption that our Lord from the beginning of His ministry believed Himself already to be (and not merely destined to be in the future) the Messiah.

But while we have thus disagreed with the fundamental points of the 'Consistent Eschatological Theory,' it would be ungrateful to ignore the service which its upholders have rendered to the study of the life of Christ. By attacking the 'subjective' tendencies of the dominant Liberal School, and by insisting that Christ's teaching must be studied in relation to the background of contemporary eschatological expectation, they have let in, as it were, a breath of fresh air from the hills of Judaea upon the somewhat conventional atmosphere which pervades a good deal of modern German criticism. They have thrown a flood of light upon many obscure problems, and have adduced many fresh proofs that at least our Second Gospel is instinct with the life and thought of the very earliest age of Christianity.

The great fault of the 'consistent eschatologists' is —their consistency. They have concentrated their attention upon one set of facts in the Gospels—facts which undoubtedly had not previously been appreciated at their full significance—and from these they have deduced, with relentless logic, and with magnificent indifference to all evidence which points in a contrary direction, the 'Consistent Eschatological Theory.' Not a few of the

"NOT TO DESTROY, BUT TO FULFIL" 231

most influential heresies of old time may be traced to the desire of their advocates to be at all costs consistent. With faultless arguments their tenets were deduced from data which were often true as far as they went, but were only a part of the whole truth. It may perhaps be pardonable to surmise that among the number of the above, future ages will reckon the 'Consistent Eschatological Theory' of Albert Schweitzer.

It seems best to defer for the present any consideration of the evidential value of Christ's eschatology. The conclusions outlined in this chapter have been, for the most part, along the lines of very familiar truths, and no attempt has been made to propound a startling or original theory. But truths are none the less true because they have been discovered by men of old time; nor, because a doctrine is simple, is it necessarily lacking in depth. And enough has been said in this and the preceding chapters to show that our Lord's Doctrine of the Last Things, though it may consist of but a few simple and familiar truths, is a doctrine of no ordinary dignity and comprehensiveness, and that it accords well with the tremendous claim of Christ, with which we commenced our study of His eschatology :—

"Οὐκ ἦλθον καταλῦσαι, ἀλλὰ πληρῶσαι."

PART IV

THE ESCHATOLOGY OF THE APOSTLES

CHAPTER XXI

THE MOST PRIMITIVE CHRISTIAN ESCHATOLOGY (THE ACTS OF THE APOSTLES)

THE 'appeal to the primitive Church' as the standard of true Christianity seems to be an instinct deeply rooted in the Christian consciousness throughout the Church's history. Nor is it in any way contrary to true scientific principles, nor inconsistent with absolute loyalty to the unique authority of Christ.

> 'The more powerful the personality which a man possesses, the less can the sum-total of what he is be known only by what he himself says and does. We must look at the reflection and the effects produced in those whose leader and master he became.'[1]

In other words, we cannot rightly appraise the Person of Jesus Christ merely from a study of the Gospels, while the rest of the New Testament is neglected. Some knowledge of the apostolic teaching is needful to complete our estimate, and to ensure that its proportions are true. The same knowledge is equally necessary if we would appreciate the later history of Christendom;

---

[1] Harnack, *What is Christianity?* (English translation, London, 1901), p. 10.

PRIMITIVE CHURCH TEACHING 233

for in every great controversy appeal is continually made back to the teaching of the first 'pillars' of the Church.

The sources for this branch of our study are practically coincident with the New Testament; chiefly, of course, the Acts, the Epistles, and the Apocalypse of St. John. The Gospels also help us to understand the attitude of the disciples in the first days after the Resurrection.

A comparison between the last recorded words of our Lord and the first recorded preaching of the apostles after the Ascension shows a remarkable contrast between the two. In St. Matthew xxviii., St. Luke xxiv., and Acts i., the eschatological element, as we have seen, is not prominent. The Lord's parting words, 'Lo, I am with you all the days, until the end of the world,'[1] show nothing in common with the restless desire to hasten the end of these present evil times, which is so characteristic of contemporary Jewish eschatology; on the contrary, they seem to teach contentment and quiet trustfulness amid the things of this life.

But in the past, the disciples had always been slow to relinquish their old ideas; and it was the same after the Resurrection. Surely the political element is not wholly absent from the lament of the two disciples: 'We hoped that it was he which should redeem Israel';[2] nor yet from the question with which the assembled Church met the risen Lord: 'Dost thou at this time restore the Kingdom to Israel?'[3] The answer of Jesus

---

[1] Matt. xxviii. 20. There seems to be a *special* stress on "πάσας τὰς ἡμέρας," for according to current apocalyptic ideas the Messiah's presence would not be recognised till the "συντέλεια τοῦ αἰῶνος" had begun to take place.

[2] Luke xxiv. 21.

[3] Acts i. 6. If, indeed, the Lord had been trying, without complete success, to lift the thoughts of His followers to a higher plane, then these words of theirs are full of human nature. But if (as Schweitzer maintains) the political element in Jewish eschatology never existed, then the question is unintelligible, either as a genuine record, or as a 'reflection' of early Christian ideas.

does not encourage the expectation of an immediate crisis: 'It is not for you to know times or seasons, which the Father hath set within his own authority.'[1] And yet, He can hardly have wished to repudiate *all* eschatological ideas; for He promises the outpouring of the Spirit to His followers within a few days, in order that they might be His witnesses throughout the world.[2] Now this promise had been associated in the prophets with the beginning of the Messianic Era,[3] and the disciples naturally regarded our Lord's words as a sign that the 'Last Days' had really come. Though in the past He had seemed at times to offer but little encouragement to their eschatological hopes, here (they would say),—here, in the renewal of Joel's prophetic promise— He surely was giving them His sanction. They would now feel free to preach the message nearest to their hearts, and to clothe their 'witness of Jesus' in the familiar apocalyptic language. And although the intense eschatological expectation of the primitive Church is strange and foreign to modern thought, it cannot be maintained that it is wholly without warrant from our Lord's parting commands; for the Old Testament words in which He foretold the Pentecostal outpouring of the Spirit on His Church were plainly calculated to suggest the thought of an impending crisis to the hearers. It may, indeed, be true that the early Christians laid excessive emphasis upon this thought; but at most they were exaggerating a real truth contained in Christ's teaching; they were not inventing an arbitrary doctrine, founded only upon their own fancies or desires.

Our knowledge of the first apostolic preaching is

---

[1] Acts i. 7.   [2] Luke xxiv. 49; Acts i. 5.
[3] Joel ii. 28; Isa. xxxii. 15, etc.

THE EARLIEST CHRISTIAN TEACHING 235

dependent mainly on the speeches recorded in the Book of Acts. Their genuineness has often been questioned, but the more radical attempts to discredit them have apparently failed to gain widespread acceptance.[1] A certain resemblance running through all the speeches suggests that their present literary form may be due in part to the author of Acts; but the peculiar Judaeo-Christian ideas which they contain are suitable only to the most primitive era of the Church's life.[2]

The primitive Christian eschatology depicted in Acts shows us the first effects produced by our Lord's teaching upon His followers. Compared with later dogmatic theology, we may find the ideas crude and incoherent; but they are the thoughts of men fresh from contact with the Master Himself. No one will deny that personal devotion to Jesus as the Christ or Messiah, was the mainspring of the apostolic preaching, and dominates it in every part.—

> 'Let all the house of Israel know assuredly, that God hath made this Jesus whom ye crucified to be both Lord and Messiah.'[3]

These words of St. Peter's are the very kernel of the earliest Christian preaching. All the rest of this speech of his, and all the other apostolic discourses in the early chapters of Acts, simply explain the logical result (from a Jewish point of view) of this belief in the Lordship and Messiahship of Jesus.

> 'The new religion did not spread, the new Kingdom was not founded, simply or chiefly through the fascination

---

[1] See (*e.g.*) Percy Gardner in *Cambridge Biblical Essays* (London, 1909), Essay XII., 'The Speeches of St. Paul in Acts.'

[2] There are also some significant points of contact between the language of the speeches in Acts and the Epistles by the same speakers; *e.g.*, cf. the Pauline use of δικαιόω in Acts xiii. 39 with that in Romans, etc.

[3] Acts ii. 36.

exerted by the moral beauty of the character and teaching of Jesus; but by virtue of the faith that "the Christ" was such an one, that as "the Christ" Jesus had said and done and endured what He did.'[1]

Moreover, the earliest Christians did not think that this Messiahship was only *about to be,* in the future; but they associated it also with the historical life of Jesus on earth. Schweitzer, as we have seen,[2] asserts that the idea of an earthly Messiah was inconceivable to a Jew. It was evidently not inconceivable to the primitive Jewish Christians. They believed that it was as Messiah that Jesus had lived; nay more, that none but an earthly and suffering Messiah could have fulfilled the Divine prophecies :—

'The things which God foreshowed by the mouth of all the prophets, that his Messiah ($X\rho\iota\sigma\tau\acute{o}s$) should suffer, he thus fulfilled.'[3]

Jesus the Messiah had come to His own people; and they had rejected Him. This was the historical fact proclaimed by the apostles; and from this historical fact they deduced, in true Jewish fashion, an eschatological hope. In the apostolic preaching these two features—the story of the recent past, and the hope of the immediate future—formed one consistent whole. Just as the tragic earthly career of the Messiah had been predestined, and foretold in prophecy, so His glorious future as the supernatural 'Son of Man' might be learnt from a study of the sacred writings of old time.[4] The Cross had formed the last scene and climax of the earthly tragedy; and now, the Resurrection of Jesus,

---

[1] V. H. Stanton, *The Jewish and Christian Messiah* (Edinburgh, 1886), p. 150.
[2] See above, p. 130 f.
[3] Acts iii. 18; cf. ii. 23, xiii. 23-25, 27.
[4] Acts ii. 25-36, iii. 21, xiii. 33-37, etc.

His Ascension as Messianic Son of Man to God's right hand, and the outpouring of the Spirit at Pentecost, were the first miracles of the New Era; not only signs that the end of this world had come nigh, even to the doors, but actually themselves *part of* the oft-foretold 'Last Things.'

Other great predestined events of the Last Crisis were yet to come, in accordance with the predictions of the prophets. These were, the descent of the 'Son of Man' (Jesus) on the clouds of heaven;[1] the general resurrection;[2] the judgment of all men by the Son of Man, when every one receives his reward or punishment for eternity;[3] and lastly, the inauguration of the Kingdom of God at Jerusalem.[4] All these were hourly expected at first by the primitive Christians; and it was this eschatological expectation which gave to their preaching its intense earnestness and urgency.

It would be a grave mistake, however, to suppose that the apostolic preaching merely consisted in a bare announcement of the impending Advent of the Christ. The call to repentance, which had been an essential part of the first preaching of our Lord, was also an important factor in the first preaching of His followers. When the Jews inquired of the apostles to learn the practical application of Christianity to this present life, the answer they received was the same which the Church has given ever since:—

> 'Repent ye, and be baptized every one of you in the name of Jesus Christ unto the remission of your sins; and ye shall receive the gift of the Holy Ghost.'[5]

This 'repentance' of the early Christians was no mere form of words, but a fundamental change of life

---

[1] Acts iii. 20, 21.   [2] Acts iv. 2, etc.
[3] Acts x. 42, xvii. 31, etc.   [4] Acts xv. 15-18.   [5] Acts ii. 38.

(μετάνοια), both outward and inward. 'They praised God, and had favour with all the people.'[1] St. Paul, writing some twenty years later, and enumerating some of the pagan vices then in fashion, adds: 'Such *were* some of you; but ye were washed, but ye were sanctified.'[2] This contrast between Christian and non-Christian was doubtless most noticeable among the Gentile peoples; but even among the Jews there can be little question that the righteousness of the primitive Christians did exceed—outwardly as well as inwardly—the righteousness of the scribes and Pharisees. This intensely practical side of Christian preaching has been a real strength to the Church in every age; and it formed a link which held firm while certain features of primitive Christian eschatology were giving way under the protracted delay of the Lord's Coming.

Since the preaching of the apostles produced these beneficent practical results, it may seem surprising that they should have come at once into conflict with the Jews. It should be noted, however, that the opposition, as recorded in Acts, came at first from the upper classes only. 'With the people,' we read, 'they had favour.'[3] It was the Sadducaic priests who first opposed the early Church; and the reason is not far to seek. The apostolic preaching tended to arouse among the common people a spirit of restlessness and excitement, which was dangerous to both political and religious peace and stability. The Christians were suspected of revolutionary tendencies, and of wishing to 'change the customs which Moses delivered.' And further, primitive Christianity was filled with a belief in the supernatural, and an expectation of miraculous interventions in the course of nature, which offended the rationalistic sobriety of the Sadducees. The latter show at first no personal

---

[1] Acts ii. 47.   [2] 1 Cor. vi. 11.   [3] Acts ii. 47.

animosity against the apostles; all they wish is to stop their preaching.¹ If the apostles had been content to preach Jesus simply as a moral teacher, the Sadducees would very likely have smiled approval. But the preaching of 'Jesus *and the resurrection*' was 'mischievous fanaticism,' and must at all costs be suppressed.² It was 'touching the hope and resurrection of the dead' that St. Paul was persecuted by the Jews as a seditious demagogue.³ The fear of excessive enthusiasm would more than counterbalance any admiration which might otherwise have been felt for the moral excellence of early Christianity.

It is well, too, in this connection, to remember that the moral teaching of the apostles, important though it was, derived its peculiar vigour and intensity from the eschatological expectation which pervaded their whole life and thought. Our very familiarity with the New Testament often leads us to overlook this; for we are accustomed to interpret it in accordance with modern ideas; but if we read the speeches in Acts in the light of contemporary Jewish apocalyptic, we shall realise how intimately the call to righteousness was dependent upon the belief that the end of all things was at hand. The primitive Church felt that the rejection of the Messiah by the Jews must bring upon their nation some dreadful doom, and this sense of impending catastrophe forms the background of primitive Christian eschatology, so that 'the Gospel' in the earliest preaching of the apostles is above all the Good Tidings of the possibility of escape from the wrath to come. For, although the rejection of Jesus has sealed the doom of this world, yet even now, at this eleventh hour, every one who recognises and believes in His Messiahship will be saved from the

---

¹ Acts iv. 18.   ² Acts iv. 2.
³ Acts xxiii. 6, xxiv..21.

coming destruction. One opportunity has indeed been refused, but another is now being offered.

'What must I do to be saved?'—'Believe on the Lord Jesus, and thou shalt be saved.'[1]

We are liable to miss this eschatological meaning of 'salvation'; for it has been merged in a wider significance in the course of time. But in Acts it is generally, if not always, connected with the thought of the impending crisis, when 'God will judge the world by the man whom he hath ordained.'[2] It was this eschatological background which gave such urgency to St. Peter's appeal, 'Save yourselves from this crooked generation,'[3] and such deep thankfulness when 'the Lord added to them daily such as were being saved.'[4]

Nor are the apostolic speeches in Acts vague in their description of the *manner* of salvation. This is conceived of in the typical Jewish fashion. Jesus is exalted as Messiah to God's right hand; and from heaven He is ready to grant to the repentant believer the remission of sins. As Messianic Judge, He is about to decide the penalties and rewards for each soul;[5] and as Messiah He is to pour forth the gift of the Spirit, which will 'seal' the recipient against the coming dangers. So the essentials for salvation were, first, Remission of Sins, and, secondly, the Gift of the Spirit; both were to be obtained from Jesus alone, and only by those who 'believed in Jesus.' 'Belief in Jesus' as Lord and Messiah was thus from the very first required as the primary condition of the profession of Christianity; and

[1] Acts xvi. 31; cf. Acts ii. 37-40, iii. 23-26.

[2] Acts xvii. 31. This 'eschatological' conception of 'salvation' may be regarded as the temporary application of an ancient word, of broad significance, to the peculiar circumstances of the moment; and this restricted meaning is in no way inconsistent with that wider usage which has since then become prevalent in the Christian Church.

[3] Acts ii. 40.   [4] Acts ii. 47.

[5] Acts x. 42, etc. See p. 148 above.

ESCHATOLOGY AND MORALITY

it is not a little significant to observe how this belief always brought with it the change of everyday life. The two were indissolubly connected in the primitive Church. 'Believe on the Lord Jesus,' and 'Repent and be baptized,' were simply the inward and outward parts of the same process.

This close union between eschatological belief and practical morality in the teaching of the apostles is a true reflection of the example of our Lord. Yet the proportions of the two elements in the teaching have been somewhat altered. We have seen reason to believe that our Lord used eschatological language partly because it emphasised an important aspect of the truth, and partly because by the use of this familiar imagery He was best able to bring home to His hearers the real significance of His message. The apostles, on the other hand, were keenly interested in eschatology for its own sake. There is no hint in Acts that, at the outset of the Church's history, they regarded eschatology as symbolical, or as other than a literal statement of facts.

We noticed that our Lord's eschatology was always dependent on the fulfilment of certain moral conditions;[1] and in the preaching of the apostles these are still present, though not to the same extent. They are noticeable in St. Peter's speech in Solomon's Porch:—

> 'Repent ye therefore, and turn again, that your sins may be blotted out, that so there may come seasons of refreshing from the presence of the Lord; and that he may send the Messiah who hath been appointed for you, Jesus: whom the heaven must receive until the times of restoration of all things.'[2]

[1] See p. 141 above.
[2] Acts iii. 19-21. The peculiar Jewish cast of thought is even more noticeable in the original Greek: "... ὅπως ἂν ἔλθωσιν καιροὶ ἀναψύξεως ἀπὸ προσώπου τοῦ κυρίου, καὶ ἀποστείλῃ τὸν προκεχειρισμένον ὑμῖν Χριστὸν Ἰησοῦν,
(Continued on next page.)

Here repentance is not only the condition of the remission of sins, but also of 'the seasons of refreshing' (that is, of release from the pains of the Messianic Woes), and of the sending of the Messiah. We feel at once that this teaching relieves the apostolic eschatology from the burden of an arbitrary predestination, and lifts it into harmony with the dignity of human responsibility. It is a true witness of the mind of our Lord; and it offered a suggestive line of explanation when the hopes of primitive Christianity remained apparently unfulfilled.

If we compare the eschatology of Acts with that of the Gospels on the one hand, or of the sub-apostolic age on the other, we shall see that it possesses several peculiar characteristics of its own.

1. It is the eschatology of an age when the whole Church was Judaeo-Christian, and as yet untouched by the influence of the Gentile world. In after times Judaeo-Christianity became, first an antiquated school of thought, and later still, a heresy. But in these first days of the Catholic Church, the whole groundwork of thought is Jewish to the core, and the outlook is for the moment limited to the Chosen People. It almost seems as if the commission to preach to all the nations had passed out of the mind of the Church, until the Master recalled it to her memory by the force of outward circumstances.

2. The eschatology is preached almost without explanation, as was the case with the bold proclamation of the doctrine of retribution by the early Hebrew prophets.[1] So here, in Acts, we find once more a

---

ὃν δεῖ οὐρανὸν μὲν δέξασθαι ἄχρι χρόνων ἀποκαταστάσεως πάντων." For "ἀποκατάστασις," denoting the condition of things in the Messianic Kingdom, cf. Mal. iv. 6 (LXX), Matt. xvii. 11.

[1] See above, Chapters III. and IV.

SUMMARY

great new doctrine—the Messiahship of Jesus—which is similarly affirmed with all the force and freshness of an absolute conviction; as yet the difficulties are not explained, nor even foreseen.

3. The eschatology of the apostles was not prompted at the outset by their own personal sufferings, but by the consciousness of Divine inspiration, and loyalty to the commission they had received from their Lord. Now almost every example of Jewish apocalyptic may be traced to a great national crisis, in which the writers themselves were in grave trouble and danger, and from which they naturally desired to be delivered. But the early followers of Christ began to preach their Doctrine of the Last Things before persecution had come upon them, and at a time when the opportunity presented itself of returning quietly to their former occupations. True, they were anticipating a great crisis in the immediate future; but that crisis had no terrors for them; it would be the welcome return of their Master and Friend. Their urgent call to repentance was prompted by no selfish motives; they threw themselves into their new life-work simply because it seemed to them to be a necessary consequence of their devotion to the Christ, and part of the message given to them by His Spirit. Each one of them would have said with St. Paul: 'Woe is me, if I preach not the Gospel!'

To sum up: We shall not be far wrong if we say that the most distinctive features of primitive Christianity—and of primitive Christian eschatology—are, its Judaism, its simplicity, its freedom from selfish motives, and its note of inspired conviction.

CHAPTER XXII

THE ESCHATOLOGY OF THE NON-PAULINE EPISTLES

A NEW doctrine boldly affirmed is certain to arouse opposition and questionings; and these in their turn elicit from the defenders of the doctrine efforts to explain the meaning more clearly. The Epistles of the New Testament are in part the expression of these efforts; they might be described as the earliest *explanations* of the doctrine of the Messiahship of our Lord, and of the eschatology connected with it.

The Epistles may conveniently be divided into two classes, Pauline and non-Pauline. The former are the writings of a man of striking intellectual power, who was trained in the strictest school of Pharisaic Judaism, but gradually freed himself from Jewish exclusiveness. Of the non-Pauline Epistles, those ascribed to St. John offer the same peculiar characteristics as the Fourth Gospel. They contain great thoughts which carry us far beyond the range of normal Jewish ideas; but the outlook is deep rather than wide; it is the result of communion with God rather than of contact with the world. The remainder of the non-Pauline Epistles are full of the peculiar thoughts of primitive Jewish Christianity. These in their turn fall into two groups: the first probably addressed to Jewish readers, and the second designed for converts from various nationalities.

The former of these two groups, consisting of the Epistle of St. James and the Epistle to the Hebrews, now claims our attention.

The first preaching of the Gospel was in many ways simpler when the hearers were Jews than when they were Gentiles. In the former case, the first principles of the new religion were known and accepted by the hearers, and could be used by the preachers as a basis for further instruction. In the case of a Gentile audience, the teachers had to begin at the very beginning. So the two letters which we are now considering, being addressed to converts from Judaism, have no occasion to deal at length with those doctrines which Judaism and Christianity held in common. The converts have believed in Jesus as their Messiah; and the purpose of the Epistles is to confirm that belief and to explain what may be deduced from it. In these epistles, Jewish methods of exegesis, and especially the practice of appealing to 'proof-texts' from the Old Testament, are used without hesitation.

The Epistle of St. James is generally assigned to a date before A.D. 50;[1] *the Epistle to the Hebrews*, shortly before A.D. 70. The former is a plain letter of practical advice; the latter is a thoughtful treatise on the relation between the Old Dispensation and the New, evidently addressed to men of intellectual ability. Yet there are important features common to the two epistles. Both of them contain little or no reference to the great problem of Gentile Christianity; and both of them take for granted the fundamental doctrines shared by Judaism and Christianity.[2]

---

[1] See Hastings' *Dictionary of the Bible*, article 'Epistle of James,' by Dr. J. B. Mayor, vol. ii. p. 545 f. Those who reject the traditional authorship (*e.g.* Harnack and Jülicher) place the Epistle well on in the second century.

[2] See especially Heb. v. 11-vi. 2.

Eschatology being one of the points where popular Judaism and primitive Christianity had much in common, we shall not expect to find in either of these epistles a detailed exposition of the Doctrine of the Last Things. But so far as we do meet with eschatology, it is of the same type as primitive Christian expectation in Acts.

First, as regards the Christology. Most of the references to our Lord in these two epistles do not add much to the information we derived from Acts. Thus St. James refers to the Saviour as 'our Lord Jesus Christ of glory,'[1] and 'the Righteous One,'[2] and expects His Second Coming in the near future:—

> 'The Judge is standing before the doors.'[3]

Similarly the writer to the Hebrews in his opening words speaks of our Lord in terms which, while in full accord with later Christian dogma, are yet characteristic of Jewish ideas of Messiahship:—

> 'God, having of old time spoken unto the fathers in the prophets by divers portions and in divers manners, hath at the end of these days spoken unto us by a Son (ἐν υἱῷ), whom he appointed heir of all things, through whom also he made the worlds; who being the effulgence of his glory, and the very image of his substance (χαρακτὴρ τῆς ὑποστάσεως αὐτοῦ), and upholding all things by the word of his power, when he had made purification of sins, sat down on the right hand of the Majesty on high.'[4]

There are many other indications of the current eschatological hopes, but for the most part they are but

---

[1] James ii. 1; cf. Acts vii. 56.
[2] James v. 6; cf. Acts vii. 52.   [3] James v. 9.
[4] Heb. i. 1-3.—The passage seems to be reminiscent of (1) the 'Son of Man' in Enoch, etc.; (2) the Logos doctrine; and (3) the idea of the Priesthood of Christ. See below, p. 247, note (3).

THE PRIESTHOOD OF CHRIST 247

incidental references to doctrines which we have already met with in Acts.¹ The author says plainly that a detailed treatment of eschatology does not lie within his present scope :—

> 'Let us cease to speak of the first principles of Christ, and press on unto perfection; not laying again a foundation of . . . resurrection of the dead, and of eternal judgment (κρῖμα αἰώνιον).'²

But one aspect of our Lord's Person and Work, which had attracted little or no attention in the first days of the apostolic preaching, is developed by the writer to the Hebrews in a suggestive manner. This is the doctrine of the High-Priesthood of our Lord, and His sacerdotal intercession on our behalf.³ In Acts, the remission of sins, and the salvation ensuing therefrom, is viewed chiefly as an act of Messianic omnipotence. But in Hebrews it is traced back to our Lord's sacerdotal ministry :—

> 'He is able to save to the uttermost them that draw near unto God through him, seeing he ever liveth to make intercession for them.'⁴

And this doctrine of our Lord's Priesthood gives a new colour to our conception of God and our expectation of the Second Advent. The awfulness of the Divine Presence becomes more tolerable as we think of 'Jesus the Mediator of a new covenant, and the blood of sprinkling that speaketh better things than that of Abel.'⁵

The doctrine of our Lord's Person as we find it in

---

¹ See Heb. i. 8, iv. 3, 9, x. 35-37, etc.
² Heb. vi. 1; cf. v. 11-14.
³ For the Priesthood of the Messiah, see Ps. cx. 4, and Test. XII. Patr. (above, p. 77) and cf. also the idea of the 'Suffering Servant' (Isa. liii. etc.) offering Himself as a sacrifice for the people.
⁴ Heb. vii. 25.   ⁵ Heb. xii. 24.

Hebrews, and the eschatology associated with it, represent the high-water-mark of Christian thought along distinctively Jewish lines. About a decade after the writing of the Epistle, the vital spirit of Judaism received a crushing blow through the capture of Jerusalem by Titus, and by the end of the century, Judaeo-Christianity was manifestly a decaying sect.[1] The Epistle to the Hebrews is the greatest literary product of that type of Christianity, while it was yet in living sympathy with the Catholic Church.

Besides the doctrine of Christ's Person, there are in these epistles two other points which are of special importance for our subject: one is, the problem of suffering; the other, the problem of Christian sinfulness. The presence of suffering in this world, often apparently undeserved, has exercised a constant influence upon Christian eschatology; for men have desired to be assured that the inequalities of this world will be remedied in the next. We noticed that the apostolic eschatology in Acts was at first independent of this motive; but as soon as persecution arose, it was inevitable that its effects should be seen in the Christian Doctrine of the Last Things. The problem of suffering must have been very trying to those early converts from Judaism. For their Lord's sake they had gone 'outside the camp' of orthodox Judaism, 'bearing his reproach.'[2] From St. James's Epistle we gather that they were an object not only of contempt, but also of definite ill-treatment by their prosperous countrymen.[3] This sense of oppression gives not only the sense of a sharp contrast between Church and World, but also a certain tone of bitterness and class-hatred to St. James's outlook on the future, which was absent

---

[1] The Didache is the chief example of later Judaeo-Christian literature. See below, pp. 309 ff. [2] Heb. xiii. 13. [3] James i. 2, ii. 5, 6.

THE PROBLEM OF SUFFERING 249

in the first apostolic preaching. There is surely a note of exultation in his words :—

' Go to, now, ye rich, weep and howl for your miseries that are coming upon you. . . . Ye have lived delicately on the earth, and taken your pleasure; ye have nourished your hearts in a day of slaughter. Ye have condemned, ye have killed the Righteous One; he doth not resist you.' [1]

In these and other similar words of St. James's we see perhaps the earliest signs of the hardening effect which persecution was destined to produce upon Christian eschatology. We cannot shut our eyes to the fact that some of the greatest Christian thinkers [2] have looked forward with delight to witnessing the sufferings of the lost in Hell. It is an attitude of mind which belongs to an age very different from ours; we can only say that we have not so learned Christ.

St. James points out to his hearers that trials manfully borne produce a patient disposition.[3] The writer to the Hebrews lifts this thought into a yet higher plane, and explains the sacredness of suffering, because it was part of the human experience of our Lord :—

' Let us run with patience the race that is set before us, looking unto Jesus the author and perfecter of faith, who for the joy that was set before him endured the cross, despising shame, and hath sat down at the right hand of the throne of God.' [4]

Nor is this all; the author of our salvation *was made perfect* through sufferings; [5] and since 'it behoved him in all things to be made like unto his brethren,' [6] we may fairly say that the writer to the Hebrews was

[1] James v. 1, 5, 6.
[2] *e.g.* Tertullian, *De Spectaculis* xxx.   [3] James i. 2, 3.
[4] Heb. xii. 1, 2; cf. 2 Cor. i. 7.   [5] Heb. ii. 10.   [6] Heb. ii. 17.

the first Christian thinker to set forth the great principle that suffering is generally necessary for the formation of human character. As a recent writer has expressed it : 'The conditions of difficulty, danger, pain, and fear, which make cowards of us, are precisely the only ones which could beget courage or heroism in us.'[1] This thought helps us to understand why our Lord tells us that those who are sad in this world will be glad hereafter.[2] It is because their sufferings here have strengthened their moral character. And so it would seem to be true that the balance of sorrow and happiness which we now see around us will be in part reversed in the Kingdom to come.

The remaining feature in these two epistles which requires special notice is their treatment of the problem of Christian sinfulness. The first preachers of the Gospel always assumed that Christian practice would be in strict accordance with Christian profession. The profession of faith was accepted without question as evidence that the convert was truly moved by the Holy Spirit.[3] Hence the primitive Christian eschatology of the individual is very simple, and strictly logical. Belief in Christ is to be followed as a matter of course by a change of life; and this will, equally naturally, lead to the inheritance of the Messianic Kingdom. St. Paul, however, soon foresaw that tares as well as wheat would spring up within the fold of the Church;[4] indeed the case of Ananias and Sapphira, or of Simon Magus, had already afforded only too clear proof of this. And among the Jewish Christians to whom St. James wrote, there were already conflicting doctrines,[5] and quarrellings among the brethren.[6]

---

[1] Du Bose, *Gospel in the Gospels*, New York, 1906 edition, p. 97.
[2] Luke vi. 20-26, etc.
[3] Cf. 1 Cor. xii. 3 : 'No man can say "Κύριος Ἰησοῦς," except in [the] Holy Spirit.'   [4] Acts xx. 30.   [5] James iii. 1.   [6] James iv. 1, 2.

St. James, though he utters a stern rebuke, does not suggest that those who have committed the sin have *ipso facto* forfeited their position as Christians; but the writer to the Hebrews takes up a more uncompromising position. He insists that the consistency of Christian doctrine and practice must be maintained at all costs :—

> 'As touching those who were once enlightened and tasted of the heavenly gift, and were made partakers of the Holy Ghost, and tasted the good word of God, and the powers of the age to come, and then fell away; it is impossible to renew them again unto repentance, seeing they crucify to themselves the Son of God afresh, and put him to an open shame.'[1]

In this stern attitude towards Christian sinfulness the writer to the Hebrews expresses a view which was possible only in the primitive days of Christianity. In later ages, the Church, by formulating a system of penance, has recognised that the gates of salvation may be opened more than once for the same individual. Doubtless she has thereby increased her catholicity and toleration; and yet she has been forced to acquiesce in a lower standard of Christian morality.

It is well that we should frankly recognise this difference between primitive and modern Christianity; for it helps us to understand one of the greatest difficulties which Christian eschatology presents to the modern mind. The difficulty is this :—we find that in practice we can draw no sharp distinction between the good and the bad, so that one half of mankind should go into bliss and the other half into punishment. But Christian eschatology speaks for the most part of only two abodes of the dead, Heaven and Hell, each being the antithesis of the other; which does not

[1] Heb. vi. 4-6.

suggest a scheme of rewards duly graded so as to be appropriate to the known varieties of human merit. But such an idea was thoroughly consistent, when viewed from the primitive Christian standpoint. To those early Christians, baptism was in literal reality a death to sin; the guilt of their former sins had been expiated by the death of their Lord; and by the sanctifying gift of the Spirit they were 'perfected for evermore'[1] even in this life. It was no violation of the strictest moral requirements for the primitive Church to speak of only two abodes of the dead—one for the Saints who had been perfected, and the other for those who had persisted in sin to the end.[2] And we must also remember that the doctrine of Christian Perfection did not seem so very unattainable to those who, like St. James and the writer to the Hebrews, were hourly expecting the return of their Lord and the end of their trials.[3]

We may now turn to the second group of non-Pauline epistles : *1 Peter*, *2 Peter*, and *Jude*—the letters of Jewish Christians to Churches mainly Gentile.

The genuine apostolic origin of 1 Peter is maintained by the majority of English scholars, and the date generally assigned is about A.D. 64, or a little earlier.[4]

In the case of 2 Peter and Jude there is more difference of opinion. Dr. Chase holds that Jude was written by the apostle of that name 'within a year or two of 1 Peter,' but that 2 Peter is a pseudonymous

---

[1] Heb. x. 14.
[2] The 'better resurrection' of the Old Testament Saints (Heb. xi. 35) need not imply that there are various kinds of 'resurrection unto life,' but is simply contrasted with 'the resurrection unto condemnation.'
[3] Heb. x. 25.
[4] See (*e.g.*) Dr. Chase in Hastings' *Dictionary of the Bible*, vol. iii. pp. 779 ff. (article '1 Peter'), and Dr. Bigg's introduction to 1 Peter in the *International Critical Commentary*. Ramsay prefers a date about A.D. 80 (*The Church in the Roman Empire*, London, 1893, pp. 279-288).

writing of the middle of the second century A.D.¹ Dr. Mayor's conclusions are substantially the same.² Dr. Bigg, on the other hand, holds that 2 Peter is earlier than Jude, and that both were written by the apostles whose name they bear, somewhat later than 1 Peter.³ The majority of German scholars, 'moderate' as well as 'advanced,' place both Jude and 2 Peter in the second century.⁴

All three epistles have this in common, that they are, on the whole, thoroughly Jewish in tone, and yet were probably destined to be read by Churches where the Gentile element predominated. In the following pages, we shall assume without hesitation that 1 Peter is genuine; but in the case of 2 Peter and Jude, we shall endeavour as far as possible to leave open the question of date.

The chief points to be noticed in connection with the eschatology of these three epistles are: (1) St. Peter's doctrine of predestination; (2) the two Petrine passages on 'the preaching to the dead'; (3) the use of Jewish apocalyptic in 2 Peter and Jude.

Taking these in the above order, we come first to the doctrine of predestination in 1 Peter.

When the Jew said that something was 'predestinated,' he thought of it as already existing in a higher sphere of life. So the writer to the Hebrews speaks of 'the copies of things in the heavens.'⁵ The world's history is thus predestined because it is already, in a sense, pre-existing and consequently fixed. This typically

---

[1] Hastings' *Dictionary of the Bible*, articles '2 Peter' (vol. iii. pp. 796 ff.), and 'Epistle of Jude' (vol. ii. pp. 799 ff.).

[2] J. B. Mayor, *Jude and 2 Peter* (London, 1907), Introduction, pp. cxxiv, cxlv ff.

[3] Introductions to 2 Peter and Jude in the *International Critical Commentary*.

[4] Zahn, however, accepts both epistles as genuine (*Introduction to New Testament*, Eng. trans., Edinburgh, 1909, vol. ii. pp. 263-268). [5] Heb. ix. 23.

Jewish conception of predestination may be distinguished from the Greek idea of pre-existence by the predominance of the thought of Divine purpose; and nowhere is this Jewish conception more prominent than in 1 Peter. The letter is addressed 'to the elect . . . according to the foreknowledge (πρόγνωσιν) of God the Father.'[1] The Doctrine of the Last Things throughout the epistle is full of the thought that all is predestinated. God, being Himself in the higher sphere where the 'heavenly copies' of the future are now existing, sees them all spread out before Him; and those who have the gift of His Spirit can also foresee it, although in a less perfect manner. So St. Peter tells us that the Spirit in the prophets had foreseen that salvation would come, but had not enabled them to determine the exact time of its coming.[2] Our Lord's earthly life in like manner 'was foreknown indeed before the foundation of the world, but was manifested at the end of the times for your sake.'[3] And so now, the future salvation of the saints, and the kingdom that they will inherit, are waiting in the higher sphere, 'ready to be revealed in the last time.'[4] The Second Coming is thus an 'apocalypse' or unveiling of that which is now existing, but hidden from our sight. We shall never understand the primitive Christian outlook on the future unless we recognise that the events so confidently expected were thought of not only as foreknown and predestined by God, but also as already in existence in the heavens.

Two famous passages in 1 Peter have been the occasion of much learned controversy :—the one describing Christ's preaching to the spirits in prison (iii. 18-20), and the other, the preaching of the Gospel to the dead (iv. 6).

---

[1] 1 Peter i. 1, 2.   [2] 1 Peter i. 10, 11.   [3] 1 Peter i. 20.
[4] 1 Peter i. iv. 5: ". . . εἰς κληρονομίαν . . . τετηρημένην ἐν οὐρανοῖς εἰς ὑμᾶς, τοὺς φρουρουμένους . . . εἰς σωτηρίαν ἑτοίμην ἀποκαλυφθῆναι ἐν καιρῷ ἐσχάτῳ."

THE SPIRITS IN PRISON

In the earlier passage, the writer has been describing the persecutions of the faithful, and continues thus:—

'Christ also suffered for sins once, the righteous for the unrighteous, that he might bring us to God; being put to death in the flesh, but revived to life in the spirit, in which also he journeyed to preach to the spirits in prison, which were once upon a time disobedient when God's long-suffering in the days of Noah waited while the ark was being built, by entering which a few—that is, eight souls, —were saved through water.'[1]

Now this reference to the 'spirits in prison' and 'the days of Noah' reminds us at once of the Book of Enoch. There we found it recorded that the men of the pre-Deluge period were put in dungeons to await the Last Judgment.[2] Of these primitive men only a very few —eight—had been saved by Noah's ark; but now Christ has journeyed to the dungeons, and offered to those imprisoned there—so we gather from the second passage, 1 Peter iv. 6—the salvation which they failed to obtain in the days gone by. And when did Christ make this offer of salvation? Not when He was in the flesh, but 'in the spirit'; that is, after His life of earthly suffering had been exchanged for the higher life of the spiritual world.[3]

In 1 Peter iv. 6, after reading of the loose living prevalent among the Gentiles, we are told:—

'But they shall render an account to him that is in readiness to judge living and dead; for, for this purpose

---

[1] 1 Peter iii. 18-20.—The following is the Greek text in full: "καὶ Χριστὸς ἅπαξ περὶ ἁμαρτιῶν ἔπαθε, δίκαιος ὑπὲρ ἀδίκων, ἵνα ἡμᾶς προσαγάγῃ τῷ Θεῷ, θανατωθεὶς μὲν σαρκί, ζωοποιηθεὶς δὲ πνεύματι, ἐν ᾧ καὶ τοῖς ἐν φυλακῇ πνεύμασι πορευθεὶς ἐκήρυξεν, ἀπειθήσασί ποτε, ὅτε ἀπεξεδέχετο ἡ τοῦ Θεοῦ μακροθυμία ἐν ἡμέραις Νῶε, κατασκευαζομένης κιβωτοῦ εἰς ἣν ὀλίγοι, τοῦτ' ἔστιν ὀκτὼ ψυχαί, διεσώθησαν δι' ὕδατος."

[2] Eth. En. x. 9-15.

[3] The words of v. 19: ". . . ζωοποιηθεὶς πνεύματι, ἐν ᾧ καὶ τοῖς πνεύμασιν . . . ἐκήρυξεν," further suggest that Preacher and hearers alike shared in a similar mode of existence (πνευματικός).

was the gospel preached also to dead men, that though they be judged according to men in the flesh, they should live according to God in the spirit.'[1]

'To be judged κατὰ ἀνθρώπους in the flesh' is probably, as Dr. Bigg suggests,[2] a synonym for 'being put to death in the flesh' (iii. 19). The general purport of the passage is clear; it explains how it will be possible for Christ to judge the dead as well as the living; it is because the good tidings of salvation have been preached even to the dead. Dead and living have had the same offer of salvation; and so both can be justly judged in the same manner. There is thus no reason to doubt that the article of the Creed, 'He descended into Hell,' as commonly interpreted to-day, is in substantial accord with the mind of the primitive Church.[3]

No argument can be based upon these passages concerning the possibility of repentance after death in the case of those who have heard the Gospel on earth, and rejected it. But it is clear that St. Peter did believe that those who had died *without* hearing the good tidings on earth, might in the other world come to the knowledge of the truth. It may well be that St. Peter knew that there was a feeling of anxiety abroad among the Churches.—How would the men of the Old Covenant be able to learn of the Messiahship of Jesus, and respond to His invitation to the Kingdom?[4] So the apostle points out that the 'preaching to the dead' would have

---

[1] 1 Pet. iv. 5, 6. "οἳ ἀποδώσουσι λόγον τῷ ἑτοίμως ἔχοντι κρῖναι ζῶντας καὶ νεκρούς· εἰς τοῦτο γὰρ καὶ νεκροῖς εὐηγγελίσθη, ἵνα κριθῶσι μὲν κατὰ ἀνθρώπους σαρκί, ζῶσι δὲ κατὰ θεὸν πνεύματι."

[2] *International Critical Commentary*, notes ad loc.

[3] Irenaeus apparently held that the purpose of Christ's descent was not so much to offer salvation, but rather to rescue the departed Saints from 'the land of sepulture' (*Adv. Haer.* v. 31, i.; but cf. iv. 27, ii.). For another early reference, see the *Gospel of Peter*, § 9 (ed. Swete, London, 1893).

[4] See above, p. 22, where it is suggested that a similar thought may have prompted the prophetic doctrine of the resurrection.

afforded them just the needed opportunity of learning and responding.

Most of the other eschatological references in 1 Peter only repeat the thoughts of the Petrine speeches in Acts. 'The end of all things is at hand,'[1] and the sufferings of the present will soon be replaced by the glory of the world to come.

> 'Insomuch as ye are partakers of Christ's sufferings, rejoice; that at the revelation (ἀποκάλυψις) of his glory also ye may rejoice with exceeding joy.'[2]

If we pass now to *Jude* and *2 Peter*, one feature of these two epistles at once strikes the reader who is acquainted with Jewish apocalyptic;—namely, the remarkable resemblance between the last-named literature and the general tone of the eschatology of these two epistles. It is not only that St. Jude directly cites the Book of Enoch,[3] and that there are incessant parallels between the language of both the epistles and the Jewish apocalypses; but the general outlook upon the world reminds us constantly of that literature, which we considered in Part II. of this essay.

The call to practical morality is still found in these two epistles,[4] but the primitive enthusiasm for righteousness seems to be less buoyant; the converts are exhorted to be holy because it is part of the Christian faith and a necessary condition to ensure salvation,[5] rather than because of the voice of the Spirit within them. The writers seem to be oppressed by the evils of their own times, but endeavour to find comfort in the recollection that the apostles had foreseen the course of events.[6] Since the first preaching sufficient time has elapsed to

---

[1] 1 Pet. iv. 7.   [2] 1 Pet. iv. 13.
[3] Jude 14, 15 = Eth. En. i. 9, with reminiscences of other Enochic phrases. See above, p. 76.   [4] 2 Pet. i. 5-7, iii. 11.
[5] 2 Pet. i. 10, 11; cf. Jude 3.   [6] Jude 17.

arouse doubts among the sceptical-minded: "Where is the promise of his coming?"[1] And the answer given by 2 Peter is but an adaptation of the arguments of the Jewish apocalyptists: 'One day with the Lord is as a thousand years, and a thousand years as one day.'[2] The details of the Last Catastrophe, when the world will be destroyed by fire, are painted in vivid colours;[3] and the doctrine of angels plays a far more important part than in any other of the New Testament epistles.[4]

While the leading authorities are, as we have seen, at variance with one another concerning the date of these two epistles, those of us who have not devoted any special study to the question cannot venture to come to any definite conclusion. The evidence to be weighed is complicated, and is derived from many sources. But so far as may be judged from a study of the eschatological features, there is a marked difference between these letters and those which undoubtedly belong to the first century. True, the language of Jude and 2 Peter is that of primitive Christian eschatology; but the Person of the Lord Jesus seems to have receded somewhat into the background. He is still a great figure in the drama of the Last Things; but the attention of the believer is now directed with almost equal emphasis to the angels, and fallen stars, and other accessories which will accompany the Last Crisis. It was different in the first days of the Church. Then the figure of Jesus the Messiah filled the whole of the eschatological horizon, and left no room for anything of less importance. For this reason the eschatology of these two epistles, and more especially of 2 Peter, does not seem to belong to the *most* primitive type of Christian eschatology.

The last group of non-Pauline Epistles which claims

[1] 2 Pet. iii. 4.   [2] 2 Pet. iii. 8. See above, p. 105, on 'Slavonic Enoch.'
[3] 2 Pet. iii. 10-12.   [4] Jude 6-10; 2 Pet. ii. 4, 11.

our attention comprises the *Epistles of St. John.* The reader who turns from the Second Epistle of St. Peter to the First Epistle of St. John finds that he has passed from the troubled atmosphere of Jewish apocalyptic into a region of refined and peaceful mysticism. Instead of the convulsions of the universe, he reads of the inner workings of the human heart.

Probably the Johannine Epistles are the latest examples of genuine apostolic writings, and were indited by St. John in extreme old age, about A.D. 100. There is little to be said about their eschatology which has not already been said in dealing with the Fourth Gospel. The Third Epistle of St. John contains no doctrine of the Last Things; so that we may confine our attention to the First and Second Epistles.

The eschatological terms are here used in a spiritual sense. Our Lord's mission was to manifest eternal life ($\zeta\omega\grave{\eta}$ $\alpha\grave{\iota}\acute{\omega}\nu\iota\sigma$),[1] and we share in that life here and now, in so far as we are partakers of His Spirit of love.[2] St. John holds the belief in a future coming of the Lord, and indeed thinks that he is living in 'the last hour' of the world's history.[3] Yet he does not dwell upon the outward form which the Second Coming will take, but only upon its personal and spiritual aspect; and even here he speaks with a reverent restraint :—

> 'Beloved, now are we children of God, and it is not yet made manifest what we shall be. We know that, if he shall be manifested, we shall be like him ($\ddot{o}\mu o\iota o\iota$ $\alpha\grave{\upsilon}\tau\hat{\wp}$); for we shall see him even as he is.'[4]

The Christian hope has never been expressed in more beautiful language than in these words of St. John.

The use of the word 'Anti-Christ' in the First and Second Epistles of St. John requires special notice. In

---

[1] 1 John i. 2.   [2] 1 John iii. 14.
[3] 1 John ii. 18.   [4] 1 John iii. 2.

Jewish history there are two aspects of the Anti-Messiah;—the human and the supernatural.[1] In 1 and 2 John the latter alone is present; but the phrase is not here used to designate any one person; "ὁ ἀντίχριστος" is rather the spirit of evil in its most dangerous form. When St. John wrote, the greatest danger to Christianity came from unworthy doctrines of the Person of our Lord :—

> 'This is the antichrist, even he that denieth the Father and the Son.'[2]
> 'Every spirit which confesseth that Jesus is come as Messiah in the flesh (Ἰησοῦν Χριστὸν ἐν σαρκὶ ἐληλυθότα) is of God; and every spirit which confesseth not Jesus is not of God; and this is the spirit of the antichrist.'[3]

It might seem as if there were little that is eschatological in such a conception of the Anti-Christ; but St. John deduces therefrom the expectation that the end is at hand :—

> 'It is the last hour: and as ye heard that antichrist cometh, even now have there arisen many antichrists; whereby we know that it is the last hour.'[4]

In the First Epistle of St. John, the primitive eschatology of Judaeo-Christianity receives its loftiest and most spiritual interpretation. We feel that in spite of the difference in expression between St. John and the other non-Pauline Epistles, there is a unity of fundamental ideas running through them all. It is possible—though very far from certain—that in St. John's teaching we may see traces of a refined Alexandrian Hellenism; but the change of outward form is not due only to the importation of features from Greek or other foreign religions; it is the result of the deep meditations of one whose life on earth was very near to God.

---

[1] See below, on 2 Thessalonians, pp. 266 ff. [2] 1 John ii. 22.
[3] 1 John iv. 2, 3 ; cf. 2 John 7. [4] 1 John ii. 18.

CHAPTER XXIII

THE ESCHATOLOGY OF ST. PAUL

THE eschatology of St. Paul offers a field of unique interest, because the long series of his letters, and the comparative certainty of their relative chronological order, give us not merely a series of isolated pictures, but a history of the development of thought in one of the world's greatest men. A large part of St. Paul's eschatology might be described as the explanation of our Lord's Messiahship in a manner adapted to the Gentiles. The sympathies of the apostle lay above all with the non-Jewish converts, and his letters consist in great measure of arguments for their especial benefit.

It will be convenient to consider the eschatology of the Pauline Epistles under the usual classification [1]:—

1. The Judaeo-Christian Epistles (1 and 2 Thessalonians).

2. The Epistles of the Third Missionary Journey (1 and 2 Corinthians, Galatians, Romans).

3. The Epistles of the Imprisonment (Colossians, Ephesians, Philippians).

4. The Pastoral Epistles (1 and 2 Timothy, Titus).

§ 1. *The Judaeo-Christian Epistles* (A.D. 53–54)

(*a*) 1 *Thessalonians.—The Nature of Christ's Second Coming.* The earliest records of St. Paul's eschatology

[1] For Zahn's classification, see detached note, below, p. 291.

show us that the apostle started from a standpoint completely Jewish. It is the eschatology of a man who 'after the strictest sect of the Jews' religion had lived a Pharisee.' In 1 Thessalonians, written probably about A.D. 53,[1] the outlook is identical with that depicted in Acts. The description of the Christian life in 1 Thessalonians i. 10, belongs clearly to the first few decades of the Church's history :—

> 'Ye turned unto God from idols, to serve a living and true God, and to wait for his Son from heaven, whom he raised from the dead; even Jesus, which delivereth us from the wrath to come.'

We have seen in the preceding chapter that the converts to whom St. Peter wrote were perplexed about the fate of the departed saints of the Old Testament, and how they could share in the privileges of the New Covenant. The Thessalonian Christians were similarly anxious about their brethren who had recently died; and the explanation which they receive from St. Paul is a typical exposition of Judaeo-Christian eschatology :—

> 'If we believe that Jesus died and rose again, even so them also that have been laid to sleep through Jesus ($κοιμηθέντας$ $διὰ$ $τοῦ$ $Ἰησοῦ$) will God bring with him. For this we say unto you by the word of the Lord, that we which are alive, which survive till ($περιλειπόμενοι$ $εἰς$) the coming ($παρουσία$) of the Lord, shall in no wise precede them that have been laid to sleep. For the Lord himself shall descend from heaven with a shout, with an archangel's cry, and with a trump of God; and the dead in Christ shall rise first; then we that are alive, that survive, shall together with them be caught up in the clouds, to meet the Lord in the air; and so shall we be ever with the Lord.'[2]

[1] Or, according to Harnack's chronology, circ. A.D. 49. See (*e.g.*) Lock, in Hastings' *Dictionary of the Bible*, art. '1 Thessalonians,' vol. iv. p. 743.
[2] 1 Thess. iv. 14-17. (The above rendering varies slightly from the R.V.)

THE MANNER OF THE 'PAROUSIA' 263

Now this language would seem perfectly natural in the mouth of a pious Jew who expected the Messianic advent as set forth in Daniel and Enoch. There is no hint that St. Paul when he wrote these words understood the descent from heaven and the 'meeting in the air' otherwise than in a perfectly literal sense. Yet let us not overlook the fact that the word 'Parousia,' by which St. Paul here denotes the coming of the Messiah, lent itself naturally to a spiritual interpretation, since it is capable of denoting 'presence' as well as 'coming.'[1] And besides, the apostle had accepted in its fulness the Messiahship and Lordship of Jesus; and that belief was destined in course of time to teach him many things undreamt of at first.

Although St. Paul clearly states in 1 Thessalonians that the exact date of the 'Parousia' is unknown,[2] he nevertheless expects it to come at least within the present generation; this is shown by the expression 'we which are alive at the Coming.' Hence the concluding prayer of St. Paul, 'May your spirit and soul and body be preserved entire, without blame at the Parousia of our Lord Jesus Christ,'[3] is addressed to men who believed they would witness the Second Advent in their present earthly life; it has no reference to any doctrine of the resurrection of the body, nor to the intermediate state of the faithful departed; but only to a deliverance from the intermediate Messianic Woes, which already seemed to be beginning on the earth, through the persecution of the Christians.

When we say that St. Paul's early eschatology is thoroughly Jewish, we are not overlooking the lofty character of the teaching in this epistle. Not only is the eschatology closely united with the call to a holy

---
[1] For the former meaning, see (*e.g.*) 2 Cor. x. 10; Phil. ii. 12.
[2] 1 Thess. v. 2, 3.   [3] 1 Thess. v. 23.

life,[1] but the final goal—'to be ever with the Lord'[2]—needs no re-statement for any age. In its practical application to the present life, and in this sublime ideal of the final consummation, St. Paul's eschatology never altered throughout his writings. But unless we frankly recognise that Jewish forms of expression are more prominent in St. Paul's early letters than in those which were written later on, we shall be liable to think that the essence of St. Paul's message changed; while the alteration really affected only the outer form.

In this, the earliest of St. Paul's extant epistles, we already find a reference to the great problem with which St. Paul's name will ever be associated,—the Problem of the Gentiles. In chapter ii. he refers to

'The Jews . . . who forbid us to speak to the Gentiles that they may be saved; to fill up their [the Jews'] sins alway; but the wrath is come upon them (ἔφθασεν ἐπ' αὐτοὺς) to the uttermost.'[3]

Thus we see that though St. Paul still thought and spake as a Jew in most matters, he had lost all trace of Jewish exclusiveness. St. Paul was one of the first men to be inspired with what has been called 'the Enthusiasm of Humanity.' Perhaps it was the peculiar circumstance which seemed to separate him from his countrymen, and also from his fellow-apostles, that helped to form this unique outlook of his;—but certain it is that the wider sympathies and larger hopes which were, so to speak, imposed upon the other disciples by force of circumstances and against their will, were welcomed by St. Paul as the inspiration of life. He alone reckoned it a privilege to be 'the Apostle to the Gentiles.'

(b) *2 Thessalonians.—The Delay of the Second*

---

[1] 1 Thess. iii. 13-iv. 8.   [2] 1 Thess. iv. 17.
[3] 1 Thess. ii. 14-16. See above, p. 134, note (2).

Coming. In the short interval which probably elapsed between the writing of 1 Thessalonians and 2 Thessalonians,[1] the eschatological expectation had grown in intensity till it had become unwholesome, and liable to lead to a dangerous reaction; and although St. Paul shares the common hope of an immediate consummation, he sees that some restraint is needed. The fear of excessive enthusiasm and consequent disappointment was much greater now that the Gospel was being spread among the Gentiles; for to them the eschatological hope was something quite new. Unlike the Jews, they had not learnt from experience to be patient in the face of delay; and if the hope remained long unfulfilled, they possessed no reverence for it as a tradition of their forefathers, and would without scruple reject both it and the religion with which it was associated.

With typical Pauline discretion, the apostle begins his second letter with a sympathetic reference to the persecutions suffered by the Thessalonians, and to the coming judgment. Having thus implied that they and he are at one in the essentials of eschatology, he proceeds to correct some errors in their expectation. They are not to think that the Day of the Lord must be absolutely imminent. Several things are to happen first [2]:—(i.) 'the falling away' (ἡ ἀποστασία); (ii.) the taking away of 'the Restrainer' (ὁ κατέχων or τὸ κατέχον); (iii.) the unveiling of the 'Man of Sin' or 'of Lawlessness' (ὁ ἄνθρωπος τῆς ἁμαρτίας, or τῆς ἀνομίας). All these phrases are foreign to our modern thoughts, and require explanation.

(i.) "Ἡ ἀποστασία."—A widespread apostasy of the faithful was a frequent part of the Messianic Woes in Jewish apocalyptic, and was one of the 'signs of the

---

[1] See (e.g.) Lock, in Hastings' *Dictionary of the Bible*, art. '2 Thessalonians,' vol. iv. p. 746.   [2] 2 Thess. ii. 3-12.

end.'[1] The same idea is contained in St. Paul's parting message to the elders of Ephesus : ' From among your own selves shall men arise, speaking perverse things, to draw away (ἀποσπᾶν) the disciples after them.'[2] St. Paul is simply accepting the current Jewish view when he says that ' the Apostasy ' must precede the End.

(ii.) *'The Man of Sin'* (or *'of Lawlessness,'* in some MSS.).—The second necessary preliminary to the End is thus described by St. Paul :—

> '[It will not be] . . . except the man of sin be revealed, the son of destruction, who is resisting and exalting himself against everything that is counted as God or as an object of worship, so that he goes into the Sanctuary of God, and seats himself, making a show that he is a god.'[3]

Various interpretations of 'the Man of Sin' have been suggested : he has been identified with the Caesar, or the spirit of Judaism, and so forth. But if so, why should he need to be revealed? Both the Caesar and the spirit of anti-Christian Judaism were at that time very much in evidence. The growth of Emperor-worship might justify (and may, in fact, have suggested) the language here used; but the Emperor-worship by itself could hardly be described as coming ' with every kind of power and miracle and lying portent.'[4]

The only solution which satisfies St. Paul's language is suggested by the Jewish apocalyptic idea of an arch-enemy of the Messiah.[5] This 'Anti-Christ' is sometimes represented as a man, sometimes as a supernatural

---

[1] See (*e.g.*) Jubilees xxiii.; Test. XII. Patr. (Levi x.; Dan. v.).
[2] Acts xx. 30.
[3] 2 Thess. ii. 3, 4 ". . . ἐὰν μὴ ἀποκαλυφθῇ ὁ ἄνθρωπος τῆς ἀνομίας, ὁ υἱὸς τῆς ἀπωλείας, ὁ ἀντικείμενος καὶ ὑπεραιρόμενος ἐπὶ πάντα λεγόμενον Θεὸν ἢ σέβασμα, ὥστε αὐτὸν εἰς τὸν ναὸν τοῦ Θεοῦ καθίσαι, ἀποδεικνύντα ἑαυτὸν ὅτι ἔστι Θεός."
[4] 2 Thess. ii. 8 "ἐν πάσῃ δυνάμει καὶ σημείοις καὶ τέρασιν ψεύδους."
[5] See M. R. James in Hastings' *Dictionary of the Bible*, art. 'Man of Sin,' vol. iii. pp. 222-228.

ANTI-CHRIST

being. These variations are probably to be traced to the various sources of the legend. Bousset has adduced evidence which indicates that the Babylonian Dragon is one of the ancestors of Anti-Christ.[1] Other supernatural features of Anti-Christ may be traced to the Zoroastrian 'Satan,' prince of the evil spirits, often called 'Beliar' in Jewish apocalyptic. Gog and Magog, the leaders of the last assault of the Gentiles upon the Holy City, probably contributed some of the human features to the Anti-Christ,[2] and the apocalyptic denunciations of the oppressors of the people suggested fresh details.[3] In literature contemporary with St. Paul, the idea of Anti-Christ as the last great *human* ruler is found in the Apocalypses of Baruch and Ezra;[4] while in the Testaments of the Twelve Patriarchs,[5] and in the Jewish 'Vision of Isaiah,'[6] the great opponent of the Messiah is the evil *spirit* called Beliar or Satan.

The material and supernatural features of Anti-Christ became strangely blended in later times, and suggested a comparison with the human and divine in the true Messiah. In St. Paul's 'Man of Sin,' the supernatural element predominates. He is already in heaven, and his appearance at the Last Crisis will be a revelation, or 'apocalypse,'[7] just as truly as the appearance of the Messiah. He will claim to be some great one—no doubt the Messiah—and will perform

---

[1] Bousset, *The Antichrist Legend* (English translation, London, 1896), pp. 144-145.

[2] Ezek. xxxviii. xxxix.

[3] Dan. xi. 36 : 'The king shall exalt himself, and magnify himself above every god . . . till the indignation be accomplished' ; Pss. Sol. ii. 33, etc.

[4] Ap. Bar. xxxix. ; 4 Ezra v. 6 ; cp. below, pp. 324-328, on *Sibylline Oracles*.

[5] Test. Judah xxv., Test. Dan. v.

[6] Asc. Isaiah ii. : 'The angel of lawlessness, who is the ruler of this world, is Beliar.' Charles assigns this section to a Jew of the first century A.D. For the name 'Beliar' as a title of Satan, cf. also 2 Cor. vi. 15 (Greek, and R.V. marg.).

[7] 2 Thess. ii. 3.

miracles, perverting many into belief in his own Messiahship.[1] The supreme act of blasphemy will be to take his seat in the Holy of Holies (ναός),[2] claiming to be Jehovah Himself. But then will come the 'apocalypse' of the true Messiah, who will slay the pretender 'with the breath of his mouth, and bring him to nought by the manifestation of his coming.'[3] The language exactly expresses the Jewish apocalyptic idea of Beliar, the last leader of the hosts of evil. At the same time, the phrase "ὁ ἄνθρωπος τῆς ἀνομίας" reminds us that Anti-Christ was expected to appear in human form and to partake of the character of a prince of this world.

(iii.) '*The Restrainer*' (ὁ κατέχων, τὸ κατέχον). This is perhaps the most difficult of the three phrases; for the parallels in Jewish apocalyptic are much less clear. But St. Paul knows that the phrase is familiar to the converts,[4] and it may well be that if the extant fragments of apocalyptic were more complete, further light on the phrase would be forthcoming. We do know, however, that there were to be necessary preliminaries before the Last Crisis—sometimes repentance; very often the completion of a fixed period of time, or an appointed series of dynasties. This last idea, which may be traced right back to the proto-apocalyptist himself,[5] may well have led St. Paul to connect 'the Restrainer' with Imperial Rome; and some of the apocalyptists had indicated that Rome would be the last great world-power.[6] And from another point of view, an acute observer could not fail to note that the order and stability of the Imperial Government were

---

[1] 2 Thess. ii. 9, 10 ; cf. Asc. Isa. iii.
[2] 2 Thess. ii. 4 ; for "ναός," cf. Mark xv. 38.
[3] 2 Thess. ii. 8.
[4] 2 Thess. ii. 6 (τὸ κατέχον οἴδατε).
[5] Dan. vii. 17-24.   [6] *e.g.* Ap. Bar. xxxix. etc.

ADAPTATION OF FAMILIAR PHRASES 269

the very antithesis of catastrophe and miracle. But when the Empire was broken up—who could say what might happen?

In discussing these difficult phrases of St. Paul's, the important point to remember is this:—that he is not propounding entirely new theories, but recalling familiar beliefs and applying them to the circumstances of the time. We shall thus be on our guard against attributing too much importance to these apocalyptic details; they were part of the Judaism handed down to him by tradition, not part of the distinctively Christian truth which he had learnt through his Christian experience since his conversion. And so when we come to the question of the particular reference of these expressions in St. Paul's letter to the Thessalonians, we shall remember that the phrases existed before they were associated by him with particular persons or institutions. If St. Paul thought that the Caesar was 'the Man of Sin,' or that the Empire was 'the Restrainer,' it is not necessary to suppose that these phrases *exactly* expressed his opinions of Imperial Rome. A single point of resemblance might have been sufficient to suggest the application of these familiar 'ready-made' terms to the events and personalities of the day.

§ 2. *The Epistles of the Third Missionary Journey* (A.D. 57-58)

During the five years or so which separated the letters to the Thessalonians from the next group of Pauline Epistles, the Jewish Christians had begun to take up an attitude of determined hostility to St. Paul's preaching to the Gentiles. The result of this opposition is manifest in the four Epistles of the Third

Missionary Journey (1 and 2 Corinthians, Galatians, and Romans). St. Paul is determined to hold by his former contention, that the Gentiles are to be admitted to the Church of Christ without submitting first to Jewish ordinances. Consequently he is forced to take up an anti-Judaising attitude, which influenced all his teaching, including his eschatology. When he had come to regard the Mosaic Law itself as a bondage from which the Christian has been set free,[1] he was not likely to feel bound to follow the teachings of Jewish apocalyptic, where these conflicted with the Spirit within him. So we find that the eschatology of the Epistles to the Corinthians, Galatians, and Romans, is less typically Jewish than in the case of the two earlier letters of St. Paul.

Another cause contributed to the same result. At Thessalonica the Church had been first planted among the Jewish residents, and probably through their influence Thessalonian Christianity retained a strong Jewish tone; at any rate, St. Paul's letters give no intimation that the Gentile element was of an intellectual or sceptical type. But at Rome, and above all at Corinth, it was different. In these centres of Roman and Greek civilisation, the axioms of Judaism and of Jewish eschatology would not be accepted without good reason given. It thus became necessary to present the Gospel in a form which would commend itself to Gentile reason and common-sense, apart from the authority of the Hebrew Scriptures.

We need not here enter upon the question of the relative dates of the four epistles now under our consideration.[2] For practical purposes, they are so nearly

[1] Gal. v. 1.
[2] See (*e.g.*) Lightfoot's *Biblical Essays*, or C. H. Turner in Hastings' *Dictionary of the Bible*, art. 'Chronology of New Testament,' vol i. p. 423.

ESCHATOLOGY LESS PROMINENT 271

of one date that they all represent the same stage in the history of St. Paul's eschatology.[1]

It is partly, no doubt, because the Jewish element in this second group of Pauline Epistles is distinctly less dominant than in the earlier epistles, that the Doctrine of the Last Things likewise occupies a less important place. This is also what might be expected from the historical circumstances under which these epistles were written, for the particular emergency which prompted the letters to the Thessalonians had now passed away. But it is easy to exaggerate the contrast between the two groups of letters. St. Paul could not divest himself at once of his heritage of Jewish thought, even though his sympathies no longer lay with the aims of his fellow-countrymen. The eschatology of the Epistles to the Corinthians and Romans retains the same Jewish outlines with which we are so familiar. 'The Day of the Lord,' 'the apocalypse of Jesus Christ,' 'the Kingdom of God,'—these and similar terms remind us that St. Paul has not broken with the past, but is only interpreting it afresh to meet new needs and to answer new difficulties.

Yet the Last Things have certainly receded somewhat into the background, and the Great Crisis seems less imminent. Also the interpretation of some of the eschatological doctrines shows unmistakable signs of non-Jewish influence. St. Paul himself in writing to the Corinthians frankly admits that his letter contains some doctrines which they had not heard from him when he first preached to them by word of mouth. Then, he had come 'to preach the Gospel, not in wisdom of words, lest the cross of Christ should be made void.'[2] But now, in face of an educated agnosticism, the 'wisdom of words' had become necessary. The 'strong meat' of

---

[1] But see detached note, below, p. 291.   [2] 1 Cor. i. 17.

intellectual argument must be added to the 'milk' of simple Gospel-preaching; but as yet only a little can be done, for the converts are still weak in their faith.[1] St. Paul thus implies there was a fuller meaning in the simple Gospel, which he himself knew, but did not yet think well to proclaim. It will be evident that this makes it difficult for us to determine whether the development of doctrine, which is so noticeable in his letters, is really a mirror of the progress of his own thought, or whether it only corresponds to the growth of the spiritual capabilities of those to whom the letters were written. The latter, however, will be indicated in any case; and for the student of the history of Christian eschatology as a whole this is the most important consideration. It is well to remember that while St. Paul admits the development of his doctrine, he maintains that there is no fundamental change. 'Other foundation can no man lay than Jesus Christ.'[2]

We may now turn to some of the new lines of thought which St. Paul, in these Epistles of the Third Missionary Journey, deals with in close connection with the problems of eschatology, and which help to elucidate these problems.

(a) *The position of the Gentiles in the Christian Church.* This is the main theme of the Epistle to the Galatians, which contains little that is directly eschatological. We have already referred to the effect which was produced upon St. Paul's eschatology by the hostility between himself and the Judaising party. The Apostle of the Gentiles came to regard Judaism as a type of 'the flesh,' in contrast to 'the Spirit' which inspired true Christianity.[3]

And yet St. Paul's heart yearns after his 'kinsmen according to the flesh'; and in the Epistle to the

[1] 1 Cor. iii. 1, 2.   [2] 1 Cor. iii. 11.   [3] Gal. iii. 3, iv. 29.

Romans he explains how he reconciles their present unbelief with the ultimate fulfilment of the Divine promises. Although he lays down the principle that 'there is no distinction between Jew and Greek,'[1] yet he recognises the peculiar dignity of the Chosen People. The Divine plan had been to bless the Gentiles through Israel; but Israel would have none of this, and so the Gentiles were blessed instead of Israel.[2] What then was to be the final fate of the Jews? 'Had God cast off His people?' St. Paul's answer is hopeful and confident:—

> 'A hardening in part hath befallen Israel, until the fulness of the Gentiles be come in; and so all Israel shall be saved.'[3]

We notice here how the apostle's outlook on the future is wide, indeed almost illimitable, in its hopefulness, and we can well understand how the same spirit of hopefulness refused to rest content with any vision short of that which he sets before the Corinthians as the final goal of history: 'that God may be all in all.'[4]

(b) *The Doctrine of the Resurrection.* One feature of the primitive Gospel which seemed to the Gentiles to conflict with natural law and reason was the doctrine of the Resurrection of our Lord and the general resurrection of mankind. The great apologetic chapters, 1 Corinthians xv. and 2 Corinthians iv. and v., endeavour to justify the doctrine of the resurrection to Gentile minds.

Let us consider first the closely-reasoned argument of 1 Corinthians xv. St. Paul begins with the Resurrection of Christ, and appeals to the unanimous witness of the Church:—

> 'Whether I or they, so we preach, and so ye believed.'[5]

---

[1] Rom. x. 12.   [2] Rom. xi. 1-24.   [3] Rom. xi. 25, 26.
[4] See below, pp. 280 *f.*   [5] 1 Cor. xv. 11.

This wide and unbroken consensus of opinion establishes Christ's Resurrection as a historical fact beyond reasonable doubt. But if Christ's Resurrection be a fact, then a resurrection from the dead is not contrary to experience.¹ And on the other hand, if there has been, and can be, no resurrection of the dead, then Christianity is a fraud, and can have no power to effect a moral reformation in the hearts of its adherents:—

> 'If Christ hath not been raised, your faith is vain; ye are yet in your sins.'²

But the Corinthian Christians knew as a fact of personal experience that they *had* been freed from their sins by Christ; they were *not* still 'in their sins.' And so the fact of Christ's Resurrection and the possibility of a general resurrection are proved by a *reductio ad absurdum*. St. Paul then proceeds to show that the connection between Christ's Resurrection and ours is not contrary to experience. As Adam's death had affected all men, so does Christ's Resurrection; for it is but the first example or 'first-fruits' of the working of a law which will apply to all those who are His.³ It may be said that this argument would not appeal to Gentile readers. But St. Paul is not here using the Old Testament as the only proof for his argument, but is pointing to the Old Testament to illustrate what he has just proved by the appeal to experience.⁴ Then, after reference to the final consummation,⁵ and the obscure custom of 'Baptism for the Dead,'⁶ the apostle meets the question,

---

¹ 1 Cor. xv. 12.   ² 1 Cor. xv. 17.
³ 1 Cor. xv. 21, 22; cf. 2 Cor. iv. 14.
⁴ Also the story of Adam and Eve would probably be familiar to most of his Gentile readers. See Hatch, *Influence of Greek Ideas on the Church* (London, 1890), pp. 73-74.   ⁵ See below, pp. 279-287.
⁶ See Plummer in Hastings' *Dictionary of the Bible*, art. 'Baptism for the Dead,' vol. i. p. 245. It is possible that phrase refers to vicarious baptism of the living instead of the dead (Tertullian, *De Resurrect.* 48, etc.), but the
(*Continued on next page.*)

THE RESURRECTION

'How are the dead raised up, and with what body do they come?' It was an old question of the Jewish apocalyptists, but no less natural for the Gentile; and the apostle's answer is cogent for both, though it specially refutes the objection that a resurrection is contrary to nature. The old analogy of the seed, which had brought comfort to the ancient Egyptians, confirms the resurrection-hope of the Christian.

> 'That which thou thyself sowest is not quickened, except it die; and that which thou sowest, thou sowest not the body that shall be, but a bare grain; it may chance of wheat, or of some other kind; but God giveth it a body even as it pleased him, and to each seed a body of its own: . . . So also is the resurrection of the dead; . . . there is sown a natural body; there is raised a spiritual body' (σπείρεται σῶμα ψυχικόν, ἐγείρεται σῶμα πνευματικόν [1]).

The processes of nature are a parable of the Mind of God; if He can revive the lower forms of nature after apparent death, why not also the higher?

In the Second Epistle to the Corinthians, St. Paul explains more fully his conception of the 'spiritual body' (σῶμα πνευματικόν).

> 'If our earthly dwelling-house (ἡ ἐπίγειος ἡμῶν οἰκία τοῦ σκήνους) be dissolved, we have a building from God, a house not made with hands, eternal, in the heavens. For verily in this we groan, longing to be clothed upon (ἐπενδύσασθαι) with our habitation which is from heaven: if so be that being clothed we shall not be found naked. For indeed we that are in this tabernacle do groan, being burdened; not for that we would be unclothed, but that we would be clothed upon; that what is mortal may be swallowed up of life.' [2]

In the Epistle to the Romans, St. Paul adduces

---

meaning is too doubtful to justify any application of this conclusion to apostolic eschatology.   [1] 1 Cor. xv. 36-38, 42, 44.   [2] 2 Cor. v. 1-4.

another reason for believing in the resurrection. He appeals again to the personal experience of his readers. He knew that they would readily admit that since their conversion they had most really possessed a new spiritual life.

> 'But if the Spirit of him that raised up Jesus from the dead dwelleth in you, he that raised up Christ Jesus from the dead shall quicken also your mortal bodies through his Spirit that dwelleth in you.'[1]

In so far as we share in the Spirit of Christ, we possess the same resurrection-power as He did.

The above are the most important passages dealing with the resurrection in the second group of Pauline Epistles. There are four important points to be noticed:—

(i.) *St. Paul recognises an upward movement in nature*: 'That is not first which is spiritual ($\pi\nu\epsilon\upsilon\mu\alpha\tau\iota\kappa\acute{o}\varsigma$) but that which is natural ($\psi\upsilon\chi\iota\kappa\acute{o}\varsigma$); then that which is spiritual.'[2] It follows that the resurrection-life will not be merely a replica of this life, but something higher, wider, greater. It is surely not fanciful to say that here St. Paul is very near to a theory of Evolution, and to the prevalent modern belief that History, viewed as a whole, is the record of progress, not of decadence.

(ii.) *St. Paul regards the body as a 'wrapping' of the real 'ego,'* so that a change of body need not involve change of identity. Our bodies vary with outward circumstances. For the New Life our present bodies would be unsuitable; the spiritual life will require a spiritual body, which will be the "$\epsilon\iota\kappa\acute{\omega}\nu$" or 'representation' of the sphere of life to which it belongs:—

> 'As we have borne the image of the earthy ($\tau\grave{\eta}\nu$ $\epsilon\iota\kappa\acute{o}\nu\alpha$ $\tau o\hat{\upsilon}$ $\chi o\ddot{\iota}\kappa o\hat{\upsilon}$), we shall also bear the image of the heavenly ($\tau\grave{\eta}\nu$ $\epsilon\iota\kappa\acute{o}\nu\alpha$ $\tau o\hat{\upsilon}$ $\epsilon\pi o\upsilon\rho\alpha\nu\acute{\iota}o\upsilon$).'[3]

---
[1] Rom. viii. 11.   [2] 1 Cor. xv. 46.   [3] 1 Cor. xv. 49.

THE RESURRECTION

This thought of the body as something external to our real selves is found again in 2 Corinthians, where there is an undoubted tendency to disparage the 'earthly dwelling-house':—

> 'Whilst we are at home in the body, we are absent from the Lord.'[1]

Hence the resurrection is viewed as a welcome 'dissolution' or release from the constraints of earthly life. In this we can hardly fail to see the result of St. Paul's classical education. Pure Judaism did indeed distinguish between the component elements of man's nature; but the thought of the body as a kind of garment, 'half concealing and half revealing' the true 'ego' beneath, and hindering the freedom of the spiritual life, is characteristic of Hellenic rather than of Hebrew thought. It is possible too that St. Paul's depression of mind, of which he speaks in 2 Corinthians,[2] may have co-operated with his knowledge of Greek eschatology to produce this distaste for the present life. On the other hand, St. Paul's resurrection-doctrine is very far from being purely Hellenic. The Greek longed to be freed from a body; St. Paul hopes 'to be clothed upon,' and receive a new body capable of performing higher functions. It is unlikely that either Judaism by itself or Hellenism by itself would have produced the thought of a 'spiritual body,' for the phrase combines valuable elements from both of these types of eschatology.

(iii.) *St. Paul affirms that 'flesh and blood ($\sigma \grave{\alpha} \rho \xi$ καὶ αἷμα) cannot inherit the Kingdom of God.'*[3] It has been contended that the apostle here refers to our lower (*i.e.* bad) nature, not to the material substances. And certainly "$\sigma \grave{\alpha} \rho \xi$" is used by St. Paul in an ethical sense.[4]

---

[1] 2 Cor. v. 6. [2] 2 Cor. ii. 4, iv. 17.
[3] 1 Cor. xv. 50.
[4] Rom. viii. 6, etc. See Iren. *Adv. Haer.* v. 9.

But in this passage, closely connected as it is with the analogy of the seed, it is more natural to take the words 'flesh and blood' as referring to material substances. These, being the "εἰκών" of this material world, are unfitted to continue in the spiritual world to come. The passage is a valuable protection against crude interpretations of the Christian doctrine of the resurrection of the body.

(iv.) *The transformation of the earthly into the spiritual will take place at the Last Day.* In later times, when the Last Day was thought to be far distant, men began to speculate as to the manner of existence during the 'waiting-time' before the resurrection. But while the Parousia was hourly expected, there was no need felt for any doctrine of the intermediate state, because the 'waiting-time' seemed so short; and we shall seek in vain for such in the apostolic writings. The faithful dead would sleep for a few days or weeks, and then

> 'We shall not all sleep, but we shall all be changed, in a moment, in the twinkling of an eye, at the last trump; for the trumpet shall sound, and the dead shall be raised incorruptible, and we shall be changed.'[1]

But although there is nothing in St. Paul's epistles to hint that between death and resurrection there is a period of change or purgation, there is one passage in 2 Corinthians which rather suggests the Johannine idea that the spiritual transformation takes place in the midst of this present life. After saying that Christ has taken away the veil which blinded the eyes of the men of the Old Dispensation, St. Paul continues thus:—

> 'But we all, with unveiled face reflecting [as a mirror] the glory of the Lord, are transformed (μεταμορφούμεθα)

---

[1] 1 Cor. xv. 51, 52.

THE RESURRECTION

into the same image from glory to glory, even as from the Lord the Spirit.'[1]

But, in truth, the present and future transformations are not mutually irreconcilable, but complementary; for a spiritual conversion here is an 'earnest' of the resurrection unto life hereafter.

These four points appear to be the most notable features of St. Paul's teaching on this great subject. Undoubtedly the doctrine of the resurrection in the system of the Christian Church owes its present form in great part to the master-mind of St. Paul. The 15th chapter of his letter to the Corinthians has exercised an unique influence on Christian eschatology. That we need for eternity, not a bodiless existence, but a higher form of body; not to be stripped, but to be clothed upon; that our hope depends, not on sentimental fancies, but on sure historical facts;—these are the essentials of St. Paul's Gospel of the Resurrection.

'It is sown in corruption; it is raised in incorruption:
It is sown in dishonour; it is raised in glory:
It is sown in weakness; it is raised in power:
It is sown a natural body; it is raised a spiritual body.'[2]

'Now we see in a mirror, in a riddle; but then face to face: now I know in part; but then shall I know fully, even as also I have been fully known.'[3]

(c) *The Last Consummation: its Date and Character.* In the course of St. Paul's exposition of the doctrine of the resurrection in 1 Corinthians xv., there is a reference to the Last Consummation which claims our notice.

'In Christ shall all be made alive. But each in his own order (τάγμα): Christ the first-fruits; then they that

---

[1] 2 Cor. iii. 18.   [2] 1 Cor. xv. 42-44.   [3] 1 Cor. xiii. 12.

are Christ's, at his Parousia (ἐν τῇ Παρουσίᾳ αὐτοῦ). Then [cometh] the end, when he shall deliver up the Kingdom to God, even the Father; when he shall have abolished all rule and all authority and power. For he must reign, till he hath put all his enemies under his feet. The last enemy that shall be abolished is death. . . . And when all things have been subjected unto him, then shall the Son also himself be subjected to him that did subject all things unto him, that God may be all in all' (ἵνα ᾖ ὁ Θεὸς πάντα ἐν πᾶσιν[1]).

One important point to notice here is that one of the events of the Last Things will take place when Christ hands over (ὅταν παραδιδοῖ) the Kingdom to God the Father (τῷ Θεῷ καὶ Πατρί). From this the inference seems clear, that this present World-Era, up till the Last Consummation, is regarded by St. Paul as 'the Kingdom of Christ.' We found the same idea in the explanation of the Parable of the Tares, where the period before the harvest is the 'Kingdom of the Son of Man,' which is distinguished from the eschatological 'Kingdom of the Father.'[2] So St. Paul's doctrine is no innovation. But in the earliest Judaeo-Christian eschatology, the thought of the present Kingdom of Christ on earth is not found; indeed, so long as the Final Consummation was thought to be absolutely imminent, there seemed little room left for it. St. Paul's language, however, in 1 Corinthians xv. opens up a long vista of the history of the world, during which Christ shall reign 'till he have put all enemies under his feet.' This vista was closed to the vision of most of the earliest Christians, by the expectation of an immediate Parousia. They believed that Jesus the Messiah was already reigning on high, but they expected this reign to be revealed on earth at any moment. The 'meanwhile' seemed so short and

---

[1] 1 Cor. xv. 22-28.
[2] Matt. xiii. 41-43. See above, p. 135.

insignificant that they never thought of describing it as a reign of Christ distinct from that which was to come. But in 1 Corinthians it is different; there St. Paul implicitly suggests that the end may not be so very near, and describes the 'interim' as the Kingdom of Christ. In so doing, he has abandoned the certainty of an immediate crisis, which is the distinctive feature of the most primitive Christian eschatology.

It is often said that the hope 'that God may be all in all' implies an 'universalistic' eschatology, and is inconsistent with the doctrine of eternal punishment. To our human minds, the two ideas do appear irreconcilable; yet neither of them can lightly be dispensed with.

> 'If we approach the subject from the side of man, we see that in themselves the consequences of actions appear to be for the doer like the deed, indelible; and also that the finite freedom of the individual appears to include the possibility of final resistance to God. And again if we approach it from the Divine side, it seems to be an inadmissible limitation of the infinite love of God that a human will should for ever refuse to yield itself to it in complete self-surrender when it is known as love.'[1]

These words of a great bishop utter a needful warning to us not to be hasty in rejecting one aspect of the truth because we do not see how it is to be reconciled with another. The whole truth remains beyond the conception of the human mind; but it is not necessarily the less true because partly incomprehensible.

(d) *The Eschatological Significance of the Pauline Doctrine of Justification.* To the casual reader, it may seem as if the Epistle to the Romans contains little

[1] Westcott, *The Historic Faith* (London, 1904 edition) p. 151. 'See also below, p. 386 *f.*

eschatology. As a matter of fact, the eschatological element is very near the centre of the general argument, which is to prove the impossibility of 'justification' under the Old Dispensation, and the possibility of it under the new.

Now 'justification' (δικαίωσις) in Romans is, as has often been pointed out, a forensic term; but it is also, in its primary signification, eschatological, for it is used with reference to the Last Judgment. This is clear, for instance, in Romans ii. 13-16 :—

> 'Not the hearers of a law are just before God, but the doers of a law *shall be justified*; . . . *in the day when God shall judge the secrets of men.*'

'Justification' here evidently means, God's verdict of 'Not Guilty' at the Last Judgment. But although the term is thus primarily eschatological, it soon began to acquire a more present significance, as we can see even in the Epistle to the Romans. For St. Paul teaches that the Divine verdict will not take account of our outward actions, but of our underlying motives and our general attitude towards God and His Son Jesus, which must be an attitude of faith. By faith the Christian becomes spiritually one with Christ; and God pronounces him 'Not Guilty' here and now, in anticipation of the final verdict.

> 'Being therefore justified (δικαιωθέντες) by faith, we have peace with God through our Lord Jesus Christ; through whom also we have had (ἐσχήκαμεν) our access by faith into this grace wherein we stand.'[1]

Or again :—

> 'There is therefore *now* no condemnation to them that are in Christ Jesus.'[2]

So the time of justification is shifted from the end of

[1] Rom. v. 1.   [2] Rom. viii. 1.

the world to the conversion of the believer; and the distance between the two events became greater as the eschatological hope of the Church became less intense. We shall see the further effects of this doctrine of justification in the next group of St. Paul's Epistles.

§ 3. *The Epistles of the Imprisonment*

The four letters, to the Ephesians, Philippians, Colossians, and to Philemon, which constitute the third group of St. Paul's Epistles, were apparently written from Rome, *circa* A.D. 62.[1]

The letter to Philemon contains nothing eschatological; hence we have only to deal with Colossians, Ephesians, and Philippians. Broadly speaking, the eschatology shows a further development of the principles laid down in the Second Group of Epistles, particularly along the lines referred to above in connection with the Epistle to the Romans,—namely, that salvation and justification are gifts granted to us now as well as promised hereafter.

As long as the primitive Church was expecting the end of the world at once, the events of the Last Crisis seemed so imminent that they might naturally be described in terms either of the future or of the present. The early Christians when speaking of their deliverance from the wrath to come, could say that they 'were being saved' or even 'had been saved,' because their 'salvation' (in its objective aspect), though not yet actually accomplished, was expected every hour. But there is nothing in Acts, nor in the *earliest* New Testament Epistles, to suggest that salvation actually takes place before the Last Crisis.[2]

---

[1] "The theory that they were written from Caesarea is now universally abandoned." (H. St. J. Thackeray, in *Journal of Theological Studies*, October, 1911.)

[2] In the Fourth Gospel, though the thought of obtaining 'life' through
(*Continued on next page.*)

Now in the Epistle to the Romans, St. Paul, as we have seen, taught that the final justification was anticipated in the case of the believer in whom dwelt the Spirit of Christ. In the epistles of the imprisonment, this same 'anticipation' is extended to other eschatological doctrines. Salvation, resurrection, and heavenly life were all primarily connected with the Last Crisis; but in these epistles St. Paul implies that salvation and resurrection are already *past*, and that the heavenly life is a *present* possession of the believer.

> '[God] delivered us out of the power of darkness, and translated us into the Kingdom of the Son of his love.'[1]
>
> 'God quickened us together with Christ (by grace have ye been saved), and raised us up with him, and made us sit together with him in the heavenly places ($\dot{\epsilon}\nu$ $\tau o \hat{\imath}\varsigma$ $\dot{\epsilon}\pi o\nu\rho a\nu\acute{\iota}o\iota\varsigma$) in Christ Jesus.'[2]
>
> 'Our citizenship is ($\dot{\upsilon}\pi\acute{a}\rho\chi\epsilon\iota$) in heaven, from whence also we are waiting for ($\dot{a}\pi o\delta\epsilon\chi\acute{o}\mu\epsilon\theta a$) a Saviour, the Lord Jesus.'[3]

In these and many similar passages St. Paul uses the old eschatological terms to denote the spiritual life of the Christian in this present world. The believer is conscious that he is sealed by the Spirit; and this is a pledge to him that the victory over death is already potentially gained, and that his salvation from sin and resurrection to holiness in this life are in very truth a type of that which shall be hereafter. For although St. Paul speaks of salvation and resurrection as past, he still holds firmly to the eschatological hope, and awaits the apocalypse of Jesus Christ and the full inheritance of the Kingdom of God. The spiritual life of the

---

Christ is often applicable to this present time, the terms 'salvation' or 'redemption' are rarely so used. See, however, John x. 9. But in any case it would be a mistake to suppose that St. John's 'timeless' conception of 'eternal life' represents the norm of primitive Christian thought.

[1] Col. i. 13.   [2] Eph. ii. 6.   [3] Phil. iii. 20.

Christian on earth needs to be perfected in the last times.

> 'Not that I have already obtained, or am already made perfect; but ... I press on toward the goal, unto the prize of the high calling of God in Christ Jesus.'[1]

Although the Christian has already been 'translated into the Kingdom of God's Son,' he must press on toward the perfect Kingdom of the Father.

In thus recognising the real value of our present spiritual experiences, imperfect though they be, the apostle gives us a true echo of the teaching of the Master,[2] and the Christian community as a whole came in time to adopt the same doctrinal position. A salvation both past and future; a resurrection already experienced and yet still awaited; a heavenly life actually lived in this world and yet the goal of our highest effort;— these paradoxes of Pauline teaching have become part of the doctrine of the Catholic Church.

Another thought which underlies much of the teaching in this group of epistles is that it is the goal of humanity to become more and more like Jesus Christ. In a famous passage of the Epistle to the Ephesians, St. Paul thus describes his conception of the final aim which every Christian should keep before his eyes :—

> '[God gave some] ... unto the building up of the body of Christ; till we all attain unto the unity of the faith, and of the knowledge of the Son of God, unto a full-grown man, unto the measure of the stature of the fulness of Christ.'[3]

This conception of Christ as the 'goal of humanity' is one of the doctrines in which St. Paul stands out as a

---

[1] Phil. iii. 12, 14.   [2] See above, pp. 139 f.
[3] Eph. iv. 12, 13 "... εἰς ἄνδρα τέλειον, εἰς μέτρον ἡλικίας τοῦ πληρώματος τοῦ Χριστοῦ." A very similar thought inspires the resurrection-doctrine of Phil. iii. 20: 'Christ shall fashion anew the body of our humiliation, that it may be conformed to the body of his glory.'

great forerunner of modern thought. For many centuries the Church has dwelt with special emphasis on the perfect Godhead of our Lord, so that the gulf between Him and ordinary men has seemed at times to be so impassable as to produce a feeling almost of estrangement. Christ has been rather an object for distant reverence than for definite imitation. But now, in the last few years, there seems to be a growing tendency to lay stress upon the perfect Manhood of Jesus: He is presented to men as the example of what they ought to be, and of what they *may* be;—in other words, as the goal of humanity. Perhaps sometimes we are inclined to pride ourselves upon our firm grasp of this doctrine of Christ's true Humanity, as if it were almost a new discovery of our age. If so, it may be well to remember that the great Apostle of the Gentiles realised the Humanity of our Lord so thoroughly, that he would set before himself no other aim for his own life's work, whether in this world or the next, than 'to attain unto the measure of the stature of the fulness of Christ.' When each Christian shall have attained to this greatest of all human ideals, then and thereby will another of St. Paul's visions be fully realised, and the Church will be in very truth, and not in name alone, 'the Body of Christ.'

§ 4. *The Pastoral Epistles*

If the last group of Pauline Epistles are genuine letters of the apostle, they must have been written after his release from Rome, *circa* A.D. 63-65. We shall here assume their genuineness as a working hypothesis.[1]

The primary purpose of these letters to Timothy and Titus is to offer practical advice; and we shall not expect

---

[1] A concise statement of the reasons for and against Pauline authorship will be found in Bennett and Adeney's *Biblical Introduction* (London, 1904), pp. 406-414.

PRAYERS FOR THE DEAD

to find in them a detailed exposition of eschatological doctrine. There are, however, one or two matters of considerable interest for our present study.

An interesting question in the Pastoral Epistles is raised by *the Prayer for Onesiphorus* :—

> 'The Lord grant unto him to find mercy of the Lord in that day.'[1]

It is probable, though not absolutely certain, that Onesiphorus was dead at the time when St. Paul wrote thus; and hence the passage has been hotly disputed by the opponents and defenders of the practice of praying for the departed. In many cases the opinions of commentators have obviously been fixed beforehand on the subject, and their only desire is to adapt St. Paul's language to their own views. The most natural impression conveyed by the manner in which Onesiphorus is mentioned certainly implies that he was either dead, or at least that St. Paul was unable to communicate with him. The former alternative seems the more probable. On the other hand, the practice of praying for the dead can hardly have been a recognised custom in the primitive Church, otherwise we should read of it somewhere in the New Testament; and where our sources of information are so extensive, this *argumentum e silentio* is of much weight.[2] Indeed, so long as the return of the Lord was expected immediately, there seemed no need for the custom; for the dead were but sleeping for a little while till Christ should bring them back again at His Parousia. St. Paul's prayer in this passage is the natural expression of love for one who had gone before ;—a prayer not based upon any reasoned doctrine, but springing instinctively from a faith which had learnt the power of prayer, and which stretched out across the

---

[1] 2 Tim. i. 18. See (*e.g.*) Milligan in Hastings' *Dictionary of the Bible*, art. 'Onesiphorus,' vol. iii. p. 622.   [2] See below, p. 373, note (2).

barrier of physical death into that spiritual world where the Communion of Saints is still a reality, and where human love remains an ever-abiding power. Our Lord, so far as we know, gave no explicit instructions either commanding or forbidding the practice of praying for the dead; and the Church of England has followed His example. It is left to the discretion of Christ's followers on earth to decide whether they shall plead for those who have passed beyond the veil, or leave the matter in the hands of God. But neither this nor any other passage in the New Testament gives the slightest support to the doctrine of an intermediate state of prolonged purgatorial suffering through which all the faithful must pass, but which may be lightened by the intercessions of the living. Such a conception is wholly foreign to the faith of the early Church; it is entirely different from St. Paul's prayer for Onesiphorus, which is concentrated, not on any intermediate state, but on the crisis of 'that Day,' *i.e.* the Last Judgment.

It is in the Pastoral Epistles that we find the first reference to eschatological heresies :—

> 'Hymenaeus and Philetus . . . have erred, saying that the resurrection is past already.'[1]

Now we saw that St. Paul himself in his letter to the Ephesians used language which may have given rise to this error :—'God *hath* raised us up with Christ.'[2] But St. Paul was able to believe in a spiritual resurrection in this life without giving up his hope of the resurrection at the Last Day. Men of shallower minds thought that the two ideas were irreconcilable; and if they held the first, they rejected the second. There is little doubt that this was the error of Hymenaeus and Philetus; they said that the resurrection was altogether past and done

---

[1] 2 Tim. ii. 17, 18. Another reading is 'a resurrection.'
[2] Eph. ii. 6.

with, and thereby they overthrew the Christian faith in the resurrection to come. Because they could not understand the fulness of St. Paul's doctrine of the resurrection, they selected one aspect of it alone, and maintained that this constituted the whole truth. In so doing they manifested the typical spirit of heresy.

One other feature of the Pastoral Epistles deserves our notice. The thought that 'the times are waxing late' seems here restored to greater prominence than in the two previous groups of St. Paul's letters.; and the reason is not far to seek. Times of trouble and disappointment are generally times when the eschatological hope shines brightest; and when St. Paul wrote the Pastoral Epistles, there was not only the prospect of impending war between the Church and the World, but also a special outburst of unwholesome doctrine within the Church herself. So St. Paul reminds his readers that these disquieting signs are themselves the forerunners of coming deliverance.

> 'The Spirit saith expressly, that in later times some shall fall away from the faith.' [1]
>
> 'Know this, that in the last days grievous times shall come. For men shall be lovers of self, lovers of money ... holding a form of godliness, but having denied the power thereof.' [2]

This is a line of argument which, although characteristic of early Christianity, is yet somewhat different from the spirit of the most primitive apostolic eschatology, which sprang from enthusiasm rather than from despondency.[3]

In concluding this chapter, it remains for us to endeavour to estimate the value of St. Paul's eschatology. It would be hard to name any man in the history of the Christian Church who has done so much as St. Paul to

[1] 1 Tim. iv. 1.   [2] 2 Tim. iii. 1-5.   [3] See above, p. 243.

influence the development of the Christian Doctrine of the Last Things. He was the first to realise that the fundamental ideas of primitive Judaeo-Christian eschatology were of permanent value apart from the intense and immediate expectation of the Lord's return. And he was also the first to translate the ancient Jewish phrases into language which was more intelligible to the Gentile mind. So it has come to pass that wherever the Gospel of Jesus Christ has been preached throughout the whole world, there also the doctrines of the great Apostle of the Gentiles have been welcomed as an inspired interpretation of his Master's teaching.

We gain nothing in true reverence for St. Paul by refusing to recognise the great change which passed over his doctrines as the years rolled by. If the Lord Himself 'increased in wisdom,' how much more must the disciple have needs done the same! But on the other hand, the doctrinal development which we observe in St. Paul's epistles is a true evolution, and not a revolution. The vision which he saw on the road to Damascus remained before his eyes all the days, until his earthly race was run; and for the foundation of his Christian teaching, from the first to the last, he preached Jesus Christ, and Him crucified. But as St. Paul meditated on his belief in the Messiahship of Jesus, and on the new visions of the future which it revealed, fresh truths one by one flashed upon his mind; and he saw that the Christian Faith did not destroy but rather fulfilled the noblest aspirations, not only of the Hebrews, but also of the Gentile world. And so he shows how the Christian doctrine of a resurrection-body not only provides an answer to those longings of the human heart which had prompted the Greek idea of a bodiless immortality of the soul, but is indeed more truly satisfying to our reason. He teaches that the New Life must begin in this world if it is to be fully realised hereafter; and thus he emphasises the real value of the present. Yet he points onward to the final consummation of all things in God, when all the 'broken lights' of earth shall be seen in their fulness and glory. Although St. Paul destroyed some of the outward forms of primitive Christian eschatology by adapting it to Gentile thought, yet by that very process he helped to unveil its inner meaning. He disturbed the outward simplicity and symmetry of the earliest apostolic doctrine of the Last Things; but he showed that the foundations rested on a bed-rock of truth, which has never yet been shaken.

[NOTE.—In Zahn's *Introduction to the New Testament* (Eng. trans., Edinburgh, 1909—published since the above chapter was written), it is contended that the Epistle to the Galatians was the earliest of all St. Paul's letters, written in A.D. 53, "not very long before the writing of 1 Thessalonians" (vol. i. p. 199). If this conclusion were accepted, the argument of pp. 270-272 above, with regard to the growth of St. Paul's opposition to Judaism in the interval between Thessalonians and Galatians, would require to be modified.]

CHAPTER XXIV

THE APOCALYPSE OF ST. JOHN

THE Revelation of St. John deals more directly and more fully with the Doctrine of the Last Things than any other book in the Canonical Scriptures. Yet the very fulness of the treatment, with its wealth of traditional imagery and symbolism, makes it all the more difficult to grasp those features which are the most essential. The Johannine Apocalypse clearly shares the peculiar form of the apocalyptic literature in general; and a true interpretation of the book must take due account of this fact.

The difficult question of authorship is not one upon which we need enter. If the book belongs to the apostolic age, its value as an illustration of primitive Christian eschatology is assured, whether it be from the pen of St. John or no. The balance of English scholarship is divided between a date in the times of Nero (*circa* A.D. 65) and a date towards the close of Domitian's reign (*circa* A.D. 95).[1] The book was certainly written while the memory of persecution was fresh in the mind of the author, and when Imperial Rome was the greatest enemy to the spread of the Christian religion. The later date is preferred by Dr. Swete, and is strongly supported by

---

[1] See Swete's *Commentary*, Introduction, pp. xcix-cvi. In Dr. Hort's posthumous work on the Apocalypse (ed. 1908), he favours the beginning of Vespasian's reign (A.D. 69 or 70).

external testimony. On the other hand, there are certain sections which seem to agree best with the reign of Nero; and it may be that the book contains elements of various dates.

The most convenient method of studying the eschatology of the Johannine Apocalypse will be to glance briefly at the general plan of the book, and then to discuss in greater detail one or two of the most important points. The main divisions are as follows :—

(a) Prologue (i. 1-8).
(b) Christ and the Seven Churches (i. 9-iii. 22).
(c) The Vision of the Opening of the Sealed Book (iv. 1-xi. 19).
(d) The Vision of the Fall of Rome (xii. 1-xviii. 24).
(e) The Vision of the Last Judgment (xix. 1-xx. 15).
(f) The Vision of the City of God (xxi. 1.-xxii. 21).

(a) In the Prologue there is little that calls for our special notice. The writer's reference to the coming of Christ 'with the clouds' is obviously a reminiscence of Daniel; and so is the vision of our Lord in glory, which immediately follows. It is significant that Daniel's description of the 'Ancient of Days' should here be applied without hesitation to Jesus of Nazareth.

It should also be noticed that the book claims to deal with 'the things which shall *shortly* ($\dot{\varepsilon}\nu$ $\tau\acute{\alpha}\chi\varepsilon\iota$) come to pass' (i. 1),—surely a warning against rash attempts to discover the fulfilment of the apocalyptic details of the book in events of modern history.

(b) The next section (i. 9-iii. 22) consists of the Letters to the Seven Churches of Asia. The chief eschatological references in these letters occur in the promises to 'him that overcometh.' The interpretation of some of these is obscure, but in most cases they refer to current, eschatological beliefs,[1] or else they are explained in the later part of the book.[2]

(c) *The Vision of the Opening of the Sealed Book* (iv. 1-xi. 19)

The writer describes a vision of Heaven, where the Most High is seen sitting upon a throne, surrounded with seated elders and four living creatures;[3]

> 'And in the midst of the throne and of the four living creatures, and in the midst of the elders, a Lamb standing, as though it had been slain.'[4]

The sealed Book of Destiny is seen in the hand of the Most High, and He delivers it to the Lamb, who begins to open the seals one by one (iv. 1-v. 14). As the Lamb breaks each of the first four seals, four horsemen come forth one by one, symbolising in turn Victory, War, Famine, and Death. Then, after the fifth seal is broken, the author hears the cry of God's martyred saints, praying that the times may soon be fulfilled (vi. 1-11).

Up to this point, the vision corresponds with the historical circumstances of the Christian Church at the close of the first century A.D. Rome had forced her way to prosperity, heedless of the sufferings thereby entailed upon the world; her victory had brought war, and famine, and death in its train. Her hand was

---

[1] *e.g.* 'the tree of life in the Paradise of God' (ii. 7), or 'the book of life' (iii. 5), etc. See Swete's notes *ad loc.* for reference to Jewish apocalypses.

[2] *e.g.* 'the second death' (ii. 11; cf. xx. 14), or the 'white garments' (iii. 5 ; cf. vii. 9).

[3] Cf. Ezek. i. 5 ff.

[4] Rev. v. 6. The phrase "ἀρνίον ... ὡς ἐσφαγμένον" may well be adapted from Isa. liii. 7 (LXX) "ὡς πρόβατον ἐπὶ σφαγὴν ἤχθη." But in the Jewish apocalypses human persons are often symbolised by sheep or lambs (*e.g.* Eth. En. xc.). The dramatic change by which our Lord is first described as 'the Lion of the tribe of Judah' (v. 5), and then as 'the Lamb' (v. 6), is no doubt designed to emphasise two aspects of His Person.

THE OPENING OF THE SEALED BOOK 295

now beginning to press heavily upon the followers of Jesus Christ; and the cry of those whom she had murdered was pleading before God that He would soon redeem His promises. There can be little doubt that the author of the Apocalypse is here describing the events of his own day; and we can further gather that he himself was living in the times of the breaking of the fifth seal, for when we come to the opening of the sixth and seventh seals, we find the whole atmosphere is changed. After the sixth seal is broken, the universe is shaken with convulsions; the sun and moon become black, and the stars fall upon the earth; 'the heaven is removed as a scroll when it is rolled up, and every mountain and island are moved out of their places.'[1] We feel that we have passed from an apocalyptic retrospect of history to an apocalyptic prediction of the Messianic Woes. It follows that the events described in the remainder of this 'Vision of the Seals' had not taken place when the apocalyptist wrote, but are 'revelations' of the future. After the cosmic portents comes a temporary respite, while the servants of God are sealed to protect them from the coming troubles; and we are shown a noble vision of the white-robed multitude of the elect, gathered before the throne (vii. 1-17).

Next the seventh and last seal is broken; and in the midst of prolonged silence, seven angels with trumpets prepare to proclaim the coming of the Seven Last Woes. The description of these Woes, which follows in chapters viii. and ix., reminds us very much of the Jewish apocalyptists. There will be hail and fire, a third part of the sea and of the rivers will be polluted, a third part of the sun, moon, and stars will be darkened, the men who are not sealed will be

[1] Rev. vi. 14.

tormented by scorpions and plagues, and a third part of mankind will be killed. But these punishments do not lead to amendment on the part of the survivors.

'The rest of mankind, which were not killed with these plagues, repented not of the works of their hands, that they should not worship devils, and the idols; . . . and they repented not of their murders, nor of their sorceries, nor of their fornication, nor of their thefts.'[1]

Next a fiery angel descends from heaven, and swears that 'there shall be time no longer;'[2] and he gives to the seer a fresh commission to prophesy, under Ezekiel's figure of a little book, bitter to the belly, but sweet to the mouth.[3]

At this point we come to chapter xi., which is one of the most puzzling in the whole book. The seer is instructed to measure the Temple, and is told that the Holy City, and even the outer Court of the Temple itself, is to be delivered for three and a half years[4] to the Gentiles. If the Apocalypse belongs to the time of Domitian, after the Fall of Jerusalem, then 'the Temple' and 'the Holy City' must here be symbolical expressions.[5] On the other hand, if this section had been written *circa* A.D. 65, the terms might be interpreted literally and naturally to refer to the writer's expectation of the impending fate of Jerusalem. In xi. 3 we read of the two prophetic 'witnesses,' who will prophesy during the three and a half years, and will then be slain by a beast coming up from the abyss. But after three and a half days they will be raised up, and will ascend to heaven. Who are the 'two

---

[1] Rev. ix. 20, 21.   [2] Rev. x. 6.
[3] Rev. x. 8-11 ; cf. Ezek. iii. 1-3.
[4] Rev. xi. 2. No doubt an 'interpretation' of Dan. vii. 25 : 'He [the little horn] shall think to change the times and the law ; and they shall be delivered into his hand until a *time and times and half a time.*'
[5] So Dr. Swete (p. 132, notes on xi. 1) takes 'the Temple' to denote the Church, and 'the outer court' to signify the Synagogue.

witnesses'.? In verse 4, they are expressly identified with the 'two olive-trees and the two candlesticks' described in Zechariah iv., and there interpreted to be 'the two sons of oil (*i.e.* "anointed ones") that stand by the Lord of the whole earth.' It is generally supposed that Zechariah was referring under this symbol, either to Joshua and Zerubbabel, or else to angelic attendants on the Deity, commissioned to minister to Israel. But while the Christian Apocalypse adopts the ancient symbol, it is unlikely that the ancient significance of it was strictly retained. Many patristic interpretations of the 'two witnesses' are cited by Dr. Swete; such as Moses and Elijah, the Law and the Gospel. Dr. Swete himself considers that the witness of the Church is intended, the language being partly borrowed from Zechariah iv., and influenced by Malachi's picture of the forerunner and by the appearance of Moses and Elijah at the Transfiguration of our Lord.[1] But whatever may have been the spiritual meaning present to the writer of the Apocalypse, there can be little doubt that the readers of the book would understand the 'two witnesses' to be individual prophetic forerunners of the Last Crisis, who testify against the evils of the Last Times. Whether they would identify them with Moses and Elijah, as the Transfiguration might suggest, or with Elijah and Enoch, as the reference to their assumption might seem to imply, is a question which we have not sufficient evidence to answer. In either case the beast who slays them is a type of the last great outburst of evil; perhaps Anti-Christ himself.[2]

After the death of the two witnesses comes a great earthquake, and then the New Era is inaugurated. 'The Kingdom of the world becomes the Kingdom

[1] Swete, p. 134, notes on xi. 3.
[2] See Bousset, *The Antichrist Legend*, chap. xiv.

of our Lord and of his Christ,'[1] and the heavenly temple is opened to be the scene of the perfected worship of God.[2]

(d) *The Vision of the Fall of Rome*

The vision of the opening of the seals ends with chapter xi.; the next chapter begins a series of visions which depict the Fall of Rome. First we read of the birth of our Lord, 'the man child who is to rule all nations with a rod of iron' (xii. 5), and of the hostility of Satan, 'the dragon,' towards the man child and the rest of His mother's children (*i.e.* the Christians) (xii. 3-6, 13-17). Then in chapter xiii. comes a description of the Roman power, under the form of a seven-headed and ten-horned beast, coming up out of the sea, and inspired by Satanic power, who claims the worship of the world and makes war upon the Saints of God (xiii. 1-9). Then there comes from the earth another beast, who promotes the worship of the first beast by false miracles, and sets a mark on the foreheads and right hands of all who are subjected to him (xiii. 11-17). The number of the beast is six hundred and sixty-six (xiii. 18).

The first beast clearly symbolises the Roman Empire, with special reference to the prevalence of Caesar-worship. The interpretation of the second beast is doubtful. Dr. Swete thinks that it signifies the popular superstitions which, for their own advantages, supported the cult of the Emperor. But the language seems equally consistent with the theory that here we have a blending of the Jewish idea of a supernatural anti-Messiah with the expectation of the resurrection of Nero and his return as a great conqueror.[3] The

---

[1] Rev. xi. 15.   [2] Rev. xi. 19.
[3] A list of passages, both in classical authors and in the Sibylline Oracles,
(*Continued on next page.*)

interpretations of the number six hundred and sixty-six are various, though it is evidently a cryptic reference to Rome, in some aspect or another.¹

In chapter xiv. the scene is again laid in heaven, where the hundred and forty-four thousand, bearing on their foreheads, not the mark of the Beast, but the Name of the Lamb, are gathered before the throne. A succession of angelic messengers is seen, proclaiming the Fall of Rome and the impending Great Judgment. The Son of Man appears seated on the clouds, and sends forth His angels to gather in the harvest of the world.

Next, after a vision in chapter xv. of the victorious martyrs standing by the heavenly sea, we come in chapter xvi. to another account of the Woes, symbolised this time by the outpouring of the bowls of God's wrath upon the earth. These Woes are very similar to those described in the vision of the opening of the seals (chapters viii.-xi.). Men are plagued with sores and burns; the sea and the rivers are polluted; the earth is filled with the spirits of devils, and rent with fearful convulsions. Chapter xvii. describes the vision of Rome, the Scarlet Woman, sitting on seven hills, and 'reigning over the Kings of the earth.' The symbolic description of the political situation at the time, under the familiar figures of beasts and horns, need not detain us here. Dr. Swete² considers that the reign of Vespasian is the date indicated; so that

---

where this popular belief is referred to, will be found in Hastings' *Dictionary of the Bible*, vol. iii. p. 517, art. 'Nero.' See also below, pp. 324-328.

¹ See Swete, pp. 175-176; cf. Introduction, p. cxxxviii. The most probable explanation is that it is the numerical value of the Hebrew letters נרון קסר (Nero Caesar), or else of the Greek "ΛΑΤΕΙΝΟΣ." If the former be correct, it is an argument for a date in Domitian's reign, after the figure of Nero had become invested with supernatural and legendary attributes. For early Christian conjectures, see Iren. *Adv. Haer.* v. 30.

² Swete, pp. 220-221, notes on xvii. 10, 11.

either this vision is of earlier date than other parts of the Apocalypse, or else the writer has deliberately written from an earlier standpoint.

Chapter xviii. describes the Fall of Rome. In surging language, which rises at times into a triumph-song of terrible ferocity, and anon falls into a mournful dirge, a word-picture is painted without parallel in the New Testament. Nothing could illustrate in more striking manner the change which had come over the Church's outlook since the days — at most half a century, and perhaps only two decades earlier—when St. Paul, writing to the Thessalonians, looked to Rome as the bulwark of religious liberty. Now, all is changed :—

> 'Come forth, my people, out of her, that ye have no fellowship with her sins, and that ye receive not of her plagues; for her sins have reached even unto heaven, and God hath remembered her iniquities. Render unto her even as she rendered, and double unto her the double according to her works. . . . Woe, woe, the great city, Babylon, the strong city! for in one hour is thy judgment come! . . . Rejoice over her, thou heaven, and ye saints, and ye apostles, and ye prophets; for God hath judged your judgment on her. And a strong angel took up a stone, as it were a great millstone, and cast it into the sea, saying, Thus with a mighty fall shall Babylon, the great city, be cast down, and shall be found no more at all.'[1]

(e) *The Vision of the Last Judgment*

In chapter xix. the subject of the vision again changes, and we are introduced to the preparations for the 'marriage-supper of the Lamb.' The Old Testament figure, of Israel the bride of Jahveh,[2] is here transferred to the Church, the bride of her Lord, who in the last

---

[1] Rev. xviii. 4-6, 10, 20, 21.   [2] Hosea ii. 19, etc.

days will become truly one with Him. The Divine Bridegroom appears riding on a white horse; 'His name is called The Word of God, . . . and he hath on his garment and on his thigh a name written, "King of Kings, and Lord of Lords."'[1]

Then (vv. 17, 18) follows an invitation—strange and harsh to our Western minds—to the scavenger-birds to come and devour the carcases of the slain enemies of God (xix. 17-18). Parallels from the Jewish apocalypses are not wanting.[2]

After this, the Beast and the false prophet are slain (xix. 19-21), and Satan is shut into the abyss for a thousand years (xx. 1-3). Then a judgment is held, and the faithful dead who have remained loyal to their Faith are revived to life at the 'first resurrection,' and reign with Christ a thousand years (xx. 4-6). At the close of the thousand years, Satan is released for a time, and goes forth to gather the hosts of evil, with Gog and Magog, for the final struggle. He is vanquished, and then finally consigned to unending torments (xx. 7-10). A second and universal resurrection then takes place, and a second and universal judgment of mankind is held; and those who are condemned by it are consigned 'to the lake of fire, which is the second death.'[3]

The idea of a 'millennium' had occurred before St. John's time, in some of the Jewish apocalypses.[4] In the New Testament Apocalypse, the doctrine is not presented in a materialistic form; but even so, it is exceedingly difficult to attach to it any meaning which

---

[1] Rev. xix. 11-16.
[2] Ap. Bar. xxix. 3-8; Eth. En. lx. 7, 8; 4 Ezra vi. 49-52; cf. Ps. lxxiv. 14. Dr. Oesterley (*Doctrine of the Last Things*, pp. 122-123, etc.) associates this idea with that of the banquet prepared by God for His Saints in the Kingdom, Eth. En. lxii. 14. But surely there is a wide difference between the two.
[3] Rev. xx. 14.
[4] *e.g.* Slav. En. See above, p. 105.

seems likely to possess a permanent value; nor can we claim for it any authority in the teaching of our Lord.[1]

(f) *The Vision of the City of God*

The last two chapters of St. John's Apocalypse afford us a picture of the ideal City of God, which in many respects is unsurpassed in the whole of the New Testament for the nobility of its conception.

> 'I heard a great voice out of the throne, saying, "Behold, the tabernacle of God is with men, and he shall dwell with them, and they shall be his peoples, and God himself shall be with them, and be their God; and he shall wipe away every tear from their eyes; and death shall be no more; neither shall there be mourning, nor crying, nor pain, any more; the first things are passed away." . . . And I saw no temple [in the city]; for the Lord God, the Almighty, and the Lamb, are the temple thereof. And the city hath no need of the sun, neither of the moon, to shine upon it; for the glory of God did lighten it, and the lamp thereof is the Lamb. And the nations shall walk amidst the light thereof; and the kings of the earth do bring their glory into it. And the gates thereof shall in no wise be shut by day; for there shall be no night there. And they shall bring the glory and the honour of the nations into it. And there shall in no wise enter into it anything unclean, or he that maketh an abomination and a lie; but only they which are written in the Lamb's book of life.'[2]

This vision of the final consummation, in the concluding chapters of the Apocalypse, shows us how deep was the spiritual insight of the writer. And so the book

---

[1] The supposition that such sayings as Matt. xix. 28, 'Ye shall sit on twelve thrones . . . etc.,' or Luke xix. 17, 'Be thou ruler over ten cities,' were intended by our Lord to refer to future events upon this earth, scarcely needs serious refutation.

[2] Rev. xxi. 3, 4, 22-27.

is valuable in the first place as a warning that it is unwise to assume that the apocalyptic imagery of the early Christians is to be understood quite literally. In the Johannine Apocalypse, if anywhere, this imagery occupies a pre-eminent place, and it might seem that the writer intended to offer a series of detailed predictions of future events. Yet ever and anon we meet with a few words of explanation which show that underneath the eschatological language, which sounds so strange to our ears, there is a spiritual teaching not less noble than that of St. Paul or of the Fourth Gospel. In reading the Apocalypse, the central thought to be borne in mind is the age-long conflict between good and evil, between the Church and the World, culminating in the triumph of the righteous by the help of God's almighty power.

The Apocalypse is also of special value as an illustration of a type of thought prevalent in the primitive Church. Many incidental sayings in the Epistles and Gospels become filled with new life when we compare them with the pictures in the Apocalypse; and abstract doctrines are seen clothed with a living reality which would bring them home to the hearts of the people. For instance, while the meaning of St. Paul's eschatology in Ephesians would scarcely be understood save by men of some intellectual training, the dramatic pictures of salvation and judgment in the Apocalypse would convey a clear meaning even to the simplest mind.

One other point deserves to be noticed. Of all the apocalypses, Jewish and Christian, which have come down to us, the Apocalypse of John is the only one which is not presented under an assumed name. In this respect, the book is a prophecy rather than an apocalypse; for the writer knows he has received a message from God Himself, and is not ashamed to proclaim it to the world in his own name as the messenger of the Almighty. Herein we see the real strength of primitive Christian eschatology; it was no mere repetition of past traditions, but an outburst of intense conviction. The language belonged to Jewish apocalyptic, but the spirit was of Christ.

We have now concluded our study of apostolic eschatology as illustrated by the books of the New Testament. But it is not possible to define any one moment of time at which the apostolic teaching ceased and the sub-apostolic teaching began. The successors of the apostles lived and taught for a time by the side of the first pillars of the Church, and the progress of doctrine went forward without interruption. Hence we shall be better able to estimate the true significance of apostolic eschatology when we have studied the writings of the age which followed; and at this point it will be sufficient briefly to recall the main conclusions reached in the foregoing section of our study.

We saw that the most primitive Christian eschatology followed the outlines of current Jewish expectation, but added a new doctrine,—the Messiahship of Jesus, and His immediate return on the clouds of heaven. It was a simple and consistent teaching, based on the most disinterested motives, and inspired by the courage of absolute conviction.

Next we traced the development of this primitive creed along Jewish lines in the Epistles of St. James, St. Peter, St. Jude, and in the Epistle to the Hebrews; and we saw that St. John, by profound meditation, sought out the eternal truths which lay behind the dramatic imagery. In all these epistles the Doctrine of the Last Things is considered from the standpoint of men trained in Jewish modes of thought, and familiar with the axioms of Jewish eschatology. But in some of the later epistles, the peculiar primitive features are less prominent; apocalyptic details become more plentiful, the depreciation of this world more marked, and the expectation of the Messiah's return less intense.

In the earliest letters of St. Paul we found that the eschatology was no less Jewish than in the non-Pauline Epistles. But later on, the apostle set himself to explain the meaning of the primitive Christian eschatology to his Gentile converts, and interpreted the Judaeo-Christian doctrines in the light of Greek ideas. Besides this, St. Paul, like his fellow-apostle at Ephesus, had evidently been pondering much upon the inner meaning of the eschatological doctrines.

Lastly, in the New Testament Apocalypse, we found a store-house of eschatological symbolism, which explains many hard sayings in the apostolic teaching, and abundantly illustrates the thoughts and hopes of the primitive Christians.

In the concluding part of this essay we shall trace the further course of primitive Christian eschatology, and endeavour to follow the process by which it became gradually assimilated to the normal type of eschatology which has prevailed throughout the later ages of the Church.

PART V

ESCHATOLOGY IN THE SUB-APOSTOLIC CHURCH

CHAPTER XXV

THE DECLINE OF PRIMITIVE JUDAEO-CHRISTIAN ESCHATOLOGY

IN the first century of the Christian Era, the eyes of all the nations were fixed upon Rome, the centre of the world's government, and the mistress whom none dared to disobey. The spread of the Roman Empire and the growing consolidation of its various parts had done much to break down the barriers between race and race, and to facilitate intercourse between one country and another. 'The world,' says Dr. Bigg, 'woke up to find itself one family.'[1] One result of this new sense of unity among the peoples of the earth was an interchange of ideas upon all subjects, including religious beliefs and customs. Even in earlier times there had been close and frequent intercourse between Rome and Greece, and Rome was continually influenced by the keen intellectual ability of her less prosperous neighbour; but the lore of the mysterious East was as yet scarcely known to the Western world. But in

---

[1] Bigg, *The Church's Task under the Roman Empire* (Oxford, 1905), p. 37.

the first and second centuries of our Era, Oriental cults and creeds gradually spread westward, were welcomed there as the latest novelty in religious matters, and were admitted to terms of equality with the worship of the ancient gods of Greece and Rome.

The readiness with which foreign beliefs were accepted in the West during the early years of the Church's history adds to the difficulties of studying the literature of this period. For it is unsafe to rely exclusively on internal evidence to determine when and where the various books were written, since the doctrines formerly associated with one particular religion were now spread over a great part of the world.

To an impartial observer living at the end of the first century, Christianity would have seemed to be one of the most insignificant of the Eastern superstitions which were making their way into Western civilisation. Compared with its more imposing rivals, such as, for instance, the revived worship of Isis and Osiris,[1] its chances of obtaining a prominent place among the recognised forms of religion must have appeared small indeed. But, in fact, Christianity demanded even more than a prominent place. For whilst the other cults only asked to be admitted to share in the Pantheon, the religion of Christ boldly claimed to be the only worship of the one true God. The verdict of history has justified that claim, absurd though it must have seemed at the time; and therein we see one of the most striking proofs of the unique power of Christianity. But although the Church came forth victorious from her long struggle for supremacy, she bears to this day the marks of the conflict. Hellenism, Montanism, Gnosticism have ceased to be living powers in the world, and are now but names

---

[1] See (*e.g.*) Bigg, *op. cit.* pp. 40-46.

of the past; yet some features from each have become permanently impressed upon the doctrines of Christianity. The reader who turns straight from the perusal of the New Testament to the writings, say, of Origen, will realise how immense has been the influence of Gentile—and especially of Greek—ideas upon the Christian Church.

In this Part of the present essay it will be our aim to trace the history of the Christian Doctrine of the Last Things during the period when it became more and more associated with Greek ideas in Western Christendom, and to note at the same time the more conservative character of the eschatology which prevailed in certain branches of the Church.

It will be convenient to divide our study of this period into three parts. (i.) The decline of primitive Judaeo-Christian eschatology. (ii.) The apocalyptic literature of early Christianity. (iii.) The influence of Greek thought upon primitive Christian eschatology. Such divisions are not wholly satisfactory; for we have just pointed out that there was a widespread interchange of ideas all over the Western world at this time; and we shall find that many of the early Christian books might be placed under any or all of the above headings. But some classification is desirable in order to guide our thoughts, and to remind us of the general tendencies of Christian belief during the first two centuries of the Church's life. The remainder of the present chapter will be occupied with the first of the above-mentioned divisions—'*the decline of primitive Judaeo-Christian eschatology.*'

The primitive type of Jewish Christianity which produced the Epistle of St. James and the Epistle to the Hebrews naturally looked to Jerusalem as the centre of its worship. But after the fall of the Holy

City, it spread to some extent outside the limits of Palestine. In the cities of Syria and of Asia Minor the Jewish element in the Christian teaching appears to have been prominent and persistent. Syria was a natural place of refuge for the Christians of Judaea in the times of Roman invasions, and they would influence the local character of the Christianity in that region. Also, the long residence of St. John at Ephesus, followed by the sacred memory of his teaching after his death, would make the Christians of Asia peculiarly unwilling to alter the primitive and Jewish form of the apostolic teaching. Thus the Churches of Palestine, Syria, and Asia Minor represent the Jewish and conservative type of sub-apostolic Christianity, in which the influence of Greek thought is not quickly evident. These were the Churches that produced the sub-apostolic literature which we are now about to consider,— a literature which is in many respects a true successor of the primitive Judaeo-Christian epistles of the New Testament. The chief extant examples of this type of writing are, the Didache, the Epistle of Polycarp to the Philippians, and the Fragments of Papias.

1. *The Didache, or 'Teaching of the Twelve Apostles'*[1]

The theology of this book is of a strongly Jewish cast, and confirms the other indications of a Palestinian or Ephesine origin.[2] The general line of thought reminds us of the primitive Christian teaching in Acts and in the earlier non-Pauline Epistles, although the non-canonical book displays an undoubted deterioration.

---

[1] The quotations are from Lightfoot's translation, except in some cases where the Greek is also given.
[2] Taylor, *Teaching of the Twelve Apostles* (Cambridge, 1886), pp. 112-118.

The primitive tone of the Didache agrees well with a date in the first century A.D.[1]

The eschatology of the Didache is found chiefly in the concluding section.—

'Be watchful for your life; let your lamps not be quenched, and your loins not ungirded, but be ye ready; for ye know not the hour in which our Lord cometh. . . . For in the last days the false prophets and corrupters shall be multiplied, and the sheep shall be turned into wolves, and love shall be turned into hate. . . . And then shall the deceiver of the world appear, as Son of God (τότε φανήσεται ὁ κοσμοπλανὴς ὡς υἱὸς Θεοῦ); and he shall work signs and wonders, and the earth shall be delivered into his hands; and he shall do unholy things, which have never been since the world began. Then all created mankind shall come into the fire of testing, and many shall be offended and perish; but they that endure in their faith shall be saved by the very curse (ὑπ' αὐτοῦ τοῦ καταθέματος). And then shall appear the signs of the truth; first, a sign spread out (σημεῖον ἐκπετάσεως) in heaven; next, a sign of a trumpet's voice; and the third, a resurrection of dead men (ἀνάστασις νεκρῶν), yet not of all, but as it was said, "The Lord shall come and all the saints with him." Then shall the world see the Lord coming upon the clouds of heaven.'[2]

The eschatology of this passage is typically Judaeo-Christian, and bears no sign of the influence of Greek thought. Yet compared with the earliest Christian preaching, we notice a few points of difference. In the first place, the expectation of the Second Coming is confirmed by an appeal to the evils of the time. We commented on this same feature in the later Epistles of St. Paul,[3] and in the Epistles of St. John.[4] It is a sign

[1] So Taylor, *op. cit.*; and Vernon Bartlett in Hastings' *Dictionary of the Bible*, extra vol. pp. 448-449. Stanton (Hastings' *Dictionary of the Bible*, vol. iii. p. 533) suggests 125-150 A.D.; Harnack places it still later.
[2] Didache 16.   [3] 1 Tim. iv. 1; 2 Tim. iii. 1.   [4] 1 John ii. 18.

of an age of persecution and trouble; and it was absent, as we saw, from the *most* primitive Christian eschatology.¹

Again, the idea that the Anti-Messiah will be, as it were, an image of the true Messiah, is in the above passage more clearly expressed than in earlier literature. In 1 Thessalonians, St. Paul had described the miracles which 'the Man of Sin' would work;² here we are told that he will 'appear as Son of God,' and will rule over the earth.³ This expectation of the rule of Anti-Christ intervening before the Last Consummation tends also to throw the Return of the Lord somewhat further into the background. There was no room for any such intervening period in the earliest teaching of the apostles; for then they believed that the 'Last Days' had already begun. It is significant that in Thessalonians the idea of Anti-Christ was used by St. Paul to explain the delay of the Parousia.

The meaning of the "$\dot{\epsilon}\kappa\pi\dot{\epsilon}\tau\alpha\sigma\iota\varsigma$" in heaven is somewhat doubtful. Probably it is intended to explain the 'sign of the Son of Man' in St. Matthew xxiv. 30; and Dr. Taylor's suggestion that it refers to the sign of the cross seems likely enough. The very occurrence of such an interpretation of our Lord's words indicates that we are here passing from the most primitive period, when the meaning of the eschatological language was familiar to all, into a later age when it needed explanation. Lightfoot, however, renders it simply as 'a rift in heaven.'

The 'first resurrection' in this passage is to comprise the Saints only, who are to be raised in order to take part in the glorious Coming of the Son of Man. Nothing is said of a general resurrection; for the extant narrative

¹ See above, p. 243. ² See above, p. 266.
³ For a fuller exposition of this idea, see Hippolytus, *Christ and Anti-Christ*, § 20 (Ante-Nicene Christian Library, vol. ix. p. 110).

ends with the Advent of the Lord upon the clouds of heaven. The preliminary rule of Anti-Christ, and the 'first resurrection' of the saints alone, are features common to the Didache and the Apocalypse of St. John, and in them may be seen the beginnings of later Chiliasm.

At times the language of the Didache with reference to immortality and eternal life reminds us of the Johannine Books.—

> 'We give thee thanks, Holy Father, . . . for the knowledge and faith and immortality which thou hast made known unto us by thy Son ($\pi\alpha\hat{\iota}\varsigma$) Jesus. . . . Thou didst bestow upon us spiritual food and drink and life eternal, through thy Son.'[1]

In spite of the Judaeo-Christian tone in the Didache, there is nothing which suggests that it is the controversial manifesto of an aggrieved minority in the Church. This confirms the impression that we are here dealing with a work of the first century, before the bodies of Jewish Christians had degenerated into schismatic sects. The Didache thus exhibits a type of eschatology which was fully recognised within the Catholic Church.

2. *The Epistle of Polycarp to the Philippians*

Polycarp, Bishop of Smyrna, was one of the last survivors of those who had enjoyed personal intercourse with the apostles. His letter to the Philippians is not remarkable for great thoughts on any subject; but the very simplicity of his words may well be a genuine echo of the oral teaching of the apostles. The absence of any sign of Gentile influence in St. Polycarp's epistle leads us to place it among those books which retain most

[1] Didache 10.

completely the characteristics of the earliest Judaeo-Christian teaching.

The name of Polycarp is specially associated with the school of St. John; but there are not many echoes of the great apostle's teaching in the extant letter of the Bishop of Smyrna. He does indeed quote the Johannine description of Anti-Christ;[1] but the great thoughts of St. John are echoed but faintly in this letter as a whole.

Altogether, there are very few references to eschatology throughout the epistle; and those that occur do not enter into any details. 'Jesus Christ,' we read, 'is coming to judge the living and the dead';[2] but whether soon or late is not stated. The writer looks forward to a 'future world' and a 'reign with Christ' as the reward of the faithful,[3] and vigorously maintains the fundamentals of Christian eschatology.—

'Whosoever shall say that there is neither resurrection nor judgment, that man is the first-born of Satan.'[4]

In short, the zeal and simplicity of this epistle remind us of the most primitive type of Christian eschatology. At the same time, the eschatological hope has unquestionably receded into the background, and no longer occupies a dominant position. And we also note the writer's tendency to become a *laudator temporis acti*: 'Neither am I, nor is any other like me, able to follow the wisdom of the blessed and glorious Paul.' Such words are in marked contrast to the inspired conviction of the New Testament writers; and this decline of personal inspiration in the sub-apostolic age is of deep significance in the history of Christian doctrine.

[1] Polyc. *ad Phil.* 7 : 'Whosoever shall not confess that Jesus Christ is come in the flesh, is Antichrist' (=1 John iv. 3).
[2] Polyc. *ad Phil.* 2.
[3] Polyc. *ad Phil.* 5 (cf. *Martyrdom of Polycarp*, 14).
[4] Polyc. *ad Phil.* 7.

3. *Papias*

Papias, Bishop of Hierapolis, was, like his brother of Smyrna, a disciple of the school of St. John. He was probably born about the time of the Fall of Jerusalem, and died towards the close of the first half of the second century. In the chief fragment of his writings which deals with eschatology we find the simplicity of Polycarp exaggerated into a grotesque credulity. It is unnecessary here to repeat at length the description of the joys of the millennial kingdom of God on earth—a description which Papias asserts to be derived from our Lord Himself, through the oral tradition of St. John and 'the elders.'

> 'The days will come, in which vines shall grow, each having ten thousand shoots, and on each shoot ten thousand branches, and on each branch again ten thousand twigs, and on each twig ten thousand clusters, and on each cluster ten thousand grapes, . . . '; and so forth.[1]

'These things,' concludes the good bishop, 'are credible to them that believe.' Surely Eusebius was not too severe when he described Papias as a man 'very limited in his comprehension,' who misunderstood the apostolic records.[2] It is interesting, however, to note that Papias's conception was not an original one, being borrowed in large part from the Apocalypse of Baruch.[3] The other Fragments of Papias have little bearing on eschatology. One, however, refers to the history of the angels;[4] and Anastasius of Sinai states that Papias 'interpreted the sayings about Paradise spiritually.'[5] The extract taken

---
[1] Iren. *Adv. Haer.* v. 33, 3f. (Fragment iv. in the Ante-Nicene Christian Library, vol. i. p. 443.)
[2] Euseb. *H.E.* iii. 39.
[3] Ap. Bar. xxix. 5. See above, p. 97, note (1).
[4] Fragment vii. in the Ante-Nicene Christian Library, vol. i. p. 444 (from Andreas of Caesarea).
[5] Anastasius, *Contempl. Anagog. in Hexaem.* vii.

from Papias by Irenaeus, and given above, will modify our regret that further details of these 'spiritual interpretations' have not been recorded. We are also told by Eusebius that Papias stated that there will be a period of about a thousand years (χιλιάδα τινα ἐτῶν ἔσεσθαι) after the resurrection of the dead, and that the Kingdom of Christ will be set up in material form on this very earth.[1] It would thus seem that Papias was one of the first to teach Christian 'Millenarianism' in a clear and developed form.

The above brief review of three writers representing the Jewish type of sub-apostolic Christianity may suggest some of the reasons why the peculiar features of the earliest apostolic preaching have become changed in the history of the Church. In the first place, the expectation of an immediate and visible return of the Lord became less and less vivid as the time passed by without bringing its fulfilment. Even in the Didache it does not seem to be absolutely imminent, although undoubtedly expected shortly. This expectation had been the main inspiration of the primitive apostolic eschatology; but in the Judaeo-Christian writings of the sub-apostolic age it is fading away; and nothing takes its place. And further, these writers of the conservative school show remarkably little intellectual power or spiritual insight. The eschatological beliefs of Polycarp and Papias were not such as would commend themselves to the reason of the civilised world without some explanation; and there is nothing in their writings which suggests that they had any explanation to offer which would satisfy the more intelligent of their Gentile contemporaries. They give us at best but a feeble echo

[1] Euseb. *H.E.* iii. 39. Cf. the quotation from 'the elders' in Iren. *Adv. Haer.* v. 36, where the conception of the future life is strongly materialistic.

of the deep thoughts of St. John, and no trace of the wide outlook of St. Paul. The simplicity of Papias, which could measure the glory of the Kingdom of God by the quantity of its agricultural produce, was scarcely likely by itself to command attention and respect. It was not enough, in the face of criticism, merely to repeat the formulas of the primitive apostolic eschatology; there was need also for explanation and interpretation; and these were not forthcoming from the successors of St. James and St. John. And so it came to pass that the peculiar simplicity of the earliest Christian Doctrine of the Last Things scarcely extended beyond those who had associated in person with the apostles.

We might have expected that the primitive type of Christian eschatology would have survived with little change among the Ebionites and other Judaeo-Christian sects. But there is no evidence that this was the case,[1] perhaps because the tendency of these sects was towards a contemplative mysticism, which was out of sympathy with the dramatic eschatology of the primitive Church.

In those quarters where the early Christian Doctrine of the Last Things was elaborated by the addition of apocalyptic details, it remained in favour, as we shall see in the next chapter, with the less educated adherents of Christianity; and in those branches of the Church where it was interpreted in accordance with Greek thought, its real value was recognised by the greatest minds. But when proclaimed without addition or interpretation, it gradually lost its influence in the Church; its vivid local colouring ceased to harmonise with the altered circumstances of Palestinian Christianity; and so it either expired, or else became trans-

---

[1] See (*e.g.*) Cruttwell, *A Literary History of Early Christianity* (London, 1893), vol. i. pp. 131 ff.

formed, together with the primitive type of Jewish Christianity from which it had sprung.[1]

[1] Since this essay was first written, a valuable addition to the earliest Christian literature has become accessible to the English reader, in Rendel Harris's *Odes and Psalms of Solomon* (Cambridge, 1909). The Odes, here translated from the Syriac for the first time, are among the most beautiful of the non-canonical Christian writings of their age, which (according to Dr. Rendel Harris) is first century A.D. Harnack, it is true, takes a different view of the Odes, regarding the groundwork as Jewish, dating from before the Fall of Jerusalem, with Christian interpolations, *circa* A.D. 100 (*Texte und Untersuchungen*, xxxv. 4). But English scholarship up to the present seems decidedly in favour of a Christian authorship for the Odes as a whole, although disposed to put the date later than Rendel Harris's. So Dr. Bernard, in the *Journal of Theological Studies*, October 1910: 'The evidence here gathered is hardly consistent with the earliest age.' And Dr. Headlam, in the *Church Quarterly Review*, January 1911: 'There is not a word in the whole collection which could not have been written by a Christian, and in the second century.'

Of 'dramatic' eschatology there is scarcely a trace, though Ode xxiii., describing the descent of a sealed message from heaven, is rather apocalyptic in tone, and in Ode xlii. there appears to be a reference to the Descent into Hades.

'Eternal life' and 'Immortality' are often referred to, and are conceived of after the Johannine manner, as a gift already received, through spiritual union with the Life Himself.

'He that is joined to Him that is immortal will also himself become immortal' (Ode iii.).

'The Lord renewed me in His raiment, and possessed me by His light; . . . He carried me to His Paradise, where is the abundance of the pleasure of the Lord, and I worshipped the Lord on account of His glory' (Ode xi.).

'Death hath been destroyed before my face, and Sheol hath been abolished by my word; and there hath gone up deathless life in the Lord's land, and it hath been made known to His faithful ones, and hath been given without stint to all those that trust Him' (Ode xv.).

The discovery of the Odes is of no little value, for if the Christian authorship be accepted, it shows us—what hitherto had been supported by very little extant evidence—that an intensely devotional spirit among the early Christians was not always dominated by the expectation of an immediate return of Christ. We see in these Odes the expression of a distinctly non-eschatological type of primitive Christianity, earnest and enthusiastic, yet exhibiting no tendency to drift into the extravagant expressions which the non-eschatological mystics in the various Gnostic sects affected in the second century. Our appreciation of primitive Christianity is substantially enhanced by the discovery of the Odes of Solomon.

CHAPTER XXVI

THE APOCALYPTIC LITERATURE OF EARLY CHRISTIANITY

In Part IV. of this essay we endeavoured to show that in spite of the general similarity between primitive Christian eschatology and the doctrines of Jewish apocalyptic, there were yet not a few points in which the superiority of the former was manifest. The suppression of superfluous apocalyptic details, the intimate association of eschatology with morality, the lofty and disinterested motives which inspired the apostolic preaching,—these were some of the features of the most primitive Christian eschatology which claimed our admiration; and in every case they were derived from the teaching of the Lord Himself. So again in the New Testament Apocalypse, we found that although some things were hard to be understood and appreciated, the book was marked throughout by a lofty spiritual tone, and was a noble witness to the mind of Christ.

When we turn from the New Testament to the early Christian apocalypses, written by men who had not known Christ after the flesh, a great change is noticeable. Not only is there a much closer resemblance to Jewish apocalyptic, but numerous features are borrowed from the eschatology of Greece, Persia, and Egypt, not to mention the possibility of occasional fragments from the wisdom of the far East.

A large proportion of the Christian apocalypses

were probably written in Egypt or at Alexandria. The latter city possessed the most cosmopolitan population to be found in the Empire, and every religious system of the Western world was represented there. The atmosphere appears to have been favourable to the growth of apocalyptic literature, both before and after the beginning of the Christian Era.

The early Christian apocalypses are valuable for our present study because they illustrate the way in which the primitive eschatological teaching was understood by the less educated classes in the Christian Church. From one point of view they may be regarded as an attempt to adapt the apostolic doctrines to changed circumstances, not by seeking for an inner meaning of permanent value, but by adding interesting details which appealed to the popular imagination. From another point of view they might be described as the successors of the Jewish apocalypses, partially transformed by an infusion of Christian ideas.

The Epistle of Barnabas

Before considering the Christian apocalypses themselves, it may be well to refer to one of the earliest—perhaps the very earliest—of the Christian books which sprang from the Alexandrian Church. The Epistle of Barnabas, though not itself an apocalypse, helps us to understand the religious atmosphere of that branch of the Church in which the Christian 'revelations' became specially popular. It is variously assigned to the reigns of Vespasian, Nerva, and Hadrian; Lightfoot chooses the first-named, and places it between A.D. 70 and 79.[1] The writer is aggressively anti-Jewish, and complains that they have misunderstood the Old Testament; but

[1] *Apostolic Fathers* (1898 edition), pp. 240-241, where the alternative dates are discussed.

his own interpretations scarcely commend themselves to modern taste, for they are fantastic and puerile.

The writer believes that he is living in the Last Days, when Anti-Christ, here called 'the Black One' (ὁ μέλας) is about to come;[1] and he warns his readers to 'remember the Day of Judgment night and day,'[2] and to labour to save souls from the impending catastrophe. He also gives us a typical Alexandrian exegesis of the Creation-narratives in Genesis :—

> '" Give heed, children, what this meaneth : ' He ended [the Creation] in six days.'—He meaneth this, that in six thousand years the Lord shall bring all things to an end; for the 'day' with Him signifieth 'a thousand years.' Therefore, children, in six days,—that is, in six thousand years,—everything shall come to an end. And, 'He rested on the seventh day.'—This He meaneth : when His Son shall come, . . . then shall He truly rest on the seventh day. . . . Finally, He saith to them, 'Your new moons and your sabbaths I cannot away with.' Ye see what is His meaning : 'It is not your present sabbaths that are acceptable, but the sabbath which I have made, in the which, when I have set all things at rest, I will make the beginning of the eighth day, which is the beginning of another world.'"'

In other words, the writer interprets the 'days' to be periods of a thousand years, so that the close of this Era will be six thousand years after the Creation; then will come the millennium, or Seventh Day of a thousand years, inaugurated by 'the coming of God's Son'; and finally 'the Eighth Day, which is the beginning of another world.'[3] All this is very primitive, and agrees well with the early date preferred by Lightfoot; one cannot, however, say that it is inspiring. The value of Barnabas is that it helps us to understand the popularity of the

---

[1] Ep. Barn. 4.   [2] Ep. Barn. 19.
[3] Ep. Barn. 15 ; cf. Slav. En. ; see above, p. 105.

Alexandrian apocalypses. Those Christians who delighted to discover a hidden meaning in every sentence of Scripture would find no difficulty in believing that the details revealed by the apocalyptists were truly parts of the Divine revelation, which had hitherto been concealed under the carnal and apparent meaning of the written word of God.

We may now turn to the Christian apocalyptic books, properly so called.

1. *The Ascension of Isaiah*

This is one of the earliest Christian apocalypses; but it appears to be a composite work of various dates. Dr. Charles considers that chapters iii.-v. ('The Testament of Hezekiah') are a Christian work written between A.D. 88 and 100; and that the remaining chapters vi.-xi. ('The Vision of Isaiah') are also Christian, 'at the close of the first century A.D.'[1] On the other hand, Dr. Armitage Robinson[2] holds that chapters i.-vi. are based upon a Jewish book, which was altered and edited by a Christian, who also added the 'Vision of Isaiah,' some time before the middle of the second century. Under the circumstances, it is necessary to use the evidence of the book with some caution.

The 'Testament of Hezekiah' deals mainly with the legend of Anti-Christ (here called 'Beliar'),[3] associated with the expectation of Nero's revival to life as the leader of the hosts of evil.[4] In iii. 13 ff. we read of the times of the Incarnation, described as 'the going forth from the seventh heaven' of our Lord and of the Angel of the Christian Church, both of whom had been pre-

---

[1] Charles's Introduction to *Ascension of Isaiah* (London, 1900).
[2] Hastings' *Dictionary of the Bible*, vol. ii. p. 500b.
[3] See above, on 2 Thess. pp. 267 f.
[4] See above, p. 298 note (3).

existent in the heavens. Then will come times of apostasy, when prophecy will cease, and after this the coming of Anti-Christ :—

> 'Beliar will descend from his firmament[1] in the likeness of a man, the slayer of his mother. . . . He will do and speak like the Beloved, and say, I am God; . . . and they will sacrifice to him, saying, This is God, and beside him there is none other. And the greater number of those who shall have been associated together, in order to receive the Beloved, he will turn aside after him. And there will be the power of his miracles in every city and region, and he will set up his image before him in every city.'

At length, after Beliar has reigned for the thirteen hundred and thirty-five days foretold by Daniel,[2] the true Messiah will descend and cast him and his armies into Gehenna.[3] There can be little doubt that here we have the Jewish expectation of a supernatural Anti-Messiah blended with the legend of 'Nero Redivivus.' The Apocalypse of St. John affords some obvious parallels to the narrative in the 'Ascension'; and the date suggested by Dr. Charles (88-100 A.D.) seems best to satisfy the features of the latter. We shall again find this legend of Nero's return very prominent in those sections of the Sibylline Oracles which appear to be a product of Alexandrian Christianity of about the same date, namely, towards the close of the first century.

Two other points in this section of the 'Ascension' deserve to be noticed. The first is the doctrine of a spiritual resurrection apart from the body, which is apparently to take place after the Second Coming :—

> 'The saints will come with the Lord, with the garments which are stored up on high in the seventh heaven; . . .

---

[1] The 'firmament' in this book is the space below the seven heavens, in which the evil spirits dwell.
[2] Dan. xii. 12.   [3] Asc. Isa. iii. 3-iv. 14.

they will descend and be present in the world. . . . And afterwards they will turn themselves upward (or "return above") in their garments, and their body will be left in this world.'[1]

If the 'Ascension was written in Egypt or Alexandria, it may be that this doctrine of a bodiless resurrection was influenced by the Philonic doctrine that matter is essentially evil. This possibility is also suggested by the language of iii. 13, where the Beloved is said to be transformed 'into *the likeness* of a man'; for a true *incarnation* would be inconceivable to a disciple of Philo, who would naturally tend to select a phrase such as the above, which, while essentially Christian in sound, is ambiguous in meaning.

Another point to be noticed is the final destiny of the wicked.—

'Fire will go forth from him [the Beloved], and it will consume all the godless, and they will be as though they had never been.'[2]

We have pointed out previously that 'destruction' in Jewish language need not mean annihilation; but here the writer seems expressly to convey the latter idea, and to exclude the possibility of unending punishment. In modern language, we should say that he held the doctrine of 'conditional immortality.'

The 'Testament of Hezekiah' concludes with an account of the descent of Christ into Sheol; but Dr. Charles considers this to be an 'editorial addition' of the second century A.D.

In the last chapter of the 'Ascension,' we read a vivid description of Isaiah's vision of the descent of the Messiah, from the seventh heaven through the other heavens down to earth. The prominence of the seven

---

[1] Asc. Isa. iv. 14, 15. [2] Asc. Isa. iv. 15.

heavens reminds us of the Slavonic Book of Enoch, a Jewish Alexandrian work of the first century A.D.[1] This 'Vision of Isaiah' is full of the thought of the pre-existence of all things in the heavens. The intermediate state of the righteous after death is a foretaste of their final reward; they are clad in splendid garments; but their crowns and thrones of glory are kept back from them till after the coming of the Messiah.[2] In other passages the 'garments' too are a part of the final reward.

The theology and christology of the 'Ascension' are peculiar; for the Son and Spirit are objects of worship, but they in their turn worship God.[3] As the Messiah descends to earth through the heavens, He divests Himself in each heaven of some part of His Divine glory, till He reaches the earth 'in the form of a man.' It is a somewhat fantastic conception of the Incarnation, and one which tends to Docetism.

Whatever be the exact date of the Ascension of Isaiah, it is a good example of the early Christian apocalyptic literature of the Alexandrian type. As a contribution to Christian thought it has little value; but it shows how the simple outlines of Judaeo-Christian eschatology were decked in a crude but vivid imagery which appealed to the popular mind.

2. *The Sibylline Oracles* [4]

We have already had occasion to refer to those portions of the Sibylline Books which were apparently written by an Alexandrian Jew in the second century B.C.[5] This type of literature was evidently very acceptable to the people of Alexandria; for our present collection of

---
[1] See above, pp. 104, 105.   [2] Asc. Isa. ix.   [3] Asc. Isa. ix. 27-41.
[4] Greek quotations from Alexandre, *Oracula Sibyllina* (Paris, 1869).
[5] See above, pp. 103 f.

the Oracles contains elements of various dates, ranging over several centuries, but nearly all bearing indications of Egyptian or Alexandrian origin.[1] Nor were the Oracles current only among the Jewish element in the population; the primitive Christians of Alexandria also presented their predictions of the future under the mysterious authority of the Gentile prophetess.

The eschatology of the Christian portions of the Sibylline Oracles is dominated by the legend of the return of Nero as Anti-Christ. The figure of the Emperor assumes Satanic proportions, and was evidently a spectre which continually haunted the imagination of the Christians of North East Africa. In particular, the assassination of his mother in A.D. 59 seems to have startled the public opinion of those times.[2]

In the fourth Book we read of the flight of the accursed matricidal king to the regions beyond the Euphrates;[3] and then after the period of Messianic Woes, he will return into Europe :—

'Then to the West shall come martial Victory aroused,
And he that fled from Rome, brandishing a great spear,
Crossing Euphrates together with countless hosts.'[4]

This will be a sign of impending judgment; and if men do not then repent, the whole world will be consumed

[1] See the Introduction in Alexandre, *op. cit.* Of the later portions, Alexandre considers that Book IV. was written by a semi-Judaising Christian of Alexandria, *circa* A.D. 80; the Prooemium and Book viii. 217-429 about the close of the first century; while Books iii. 295-488, v., and viii. 1-217 were composed in Egypt about the middle of the second century. A convenient summary of the dates assigned by Alexandre, and also by Ewald, is given in Hastings' *Dictionary of the Bible*, extra vol. p. 68. Book V. seems to be purely Jewish.
[2] See (*e.g.*) Bury, *Student's Roman Empire* (London, 1900), p. 279.
[3] Sib. Or. iv. 117-122.
[4] Sib. Or. iv. 137-139 :
"Εἰς δὲ δύσιν τότε νεῖκος ἐγειρόμενον πολέμοιο
Ἥξει, καὶ Ῥώμης ὁ φυγάς, μέγα ἔγχος ἀείρων,
Εὐφρήτην διαβὰς πολλαῖς ἅμα μυριάδεσσιν."

by fire. At the Last Times all men will be raised in the flesh :—

'Human bones and dust shall God once more form again,
And again set up mortal men, as they used formerly to be.'[1]

Men will then receive their due recompense; the wicked will go to Tartarus and Gehenna, and the righteous will partake of the Divine Spirit of immortality. This doctrine of the resurrection seems to combine Jewish and Greek ideas, and is much more refined than in most of the non-canonical books; indeed, it almost reminds us of St. Paul's hope of being 'clothed upon, that the mortal may be swallowed up in life.'

In the central portion of Book VIII., dating probably from the beginning of the second century A.D., there is little that calls for comment, except perhaps the concluding description of the future life, which rises somewhat above the commonplace :—

'Henceforward shall no one any longer say with grief, "The morrow is coming,"
Nor, "Yesterday is past," . . .
No sunset nor sunrise shall there be; for I will create one long Day.'[2]

In Book V. it is possible to determine the date with more certainty. It opens with a 'prophecy' of Roman history, which ceases to correspond with the facts after the times of Marcus Aurelius; so there can be little doubt that it was composed during his reign, 161-180 A.D. Here the expectation of Nero's return has become yet more terrifying. His coming will be accompanied by

---

[1] Sib. Or. iv. 180-181 :
"'Οστέα καὶ σποδιὴν αὐτὸς θεὸς ἔμπαλιν ἀνδρῶν
Μορφώσει, στήσει δὲ βροτοὺς πάλιν, ὡς πάρος ἦσαν."

[2] Sib. Or. viii. 424-427 :
"Οὐκέτι λοιπὸν ἐρεῖ λυπούμενος, Αὔριον ἔσται;
Οὐκ, 'Εχθὲς γέγονεν· οὐκ ἤματα μακρὰ μερίμνης;
Οὐ δύσις, ἀντολίη· ποιήσω γὰρ μακρὸν ἦμαρ."

convulsions of nature, and he himself is described in words which contain scarcely a trace of either Jewish or Christian feeling :—

> 'A mighty King of mighty Rome; a godlike man;
> Born, so they say, of Zeus and august Hera;
> Many shall he destroy, together with his unhappy mother.'[1]

In this same section we find the typically Jewish expectation that at the close of Nero's reign the true Messiah will descend from heaven.[2] Although there is nothing in this section to suggest a Christian origin, yet the legend of Nero was doubtless generally current among the populace of Alexandria and Egypt, including the adherents of Christianity; and we see here how it became more and more associated with supernatural accessories.

The remaining section of the Oracles which belongs to the period of the second century is Book viii. 1-216, probably written by an Egyptian Christian. We find the legend of Nero as prominent as ever, and associated this time with a dragon-myth.[3] But at the last the Messiah will come as a holy king (ἅγνος ἄναξ) and establish a kingdom of joy and gladness.[4]

The Christian portions of the Sibylline Oracles are interesting because they show us how the primitive Christian expectation of the return of the Lord was adapted to fit in with popular legends. There are, as we have seen, occasional passages of some intrinsic merit, but, on the whole, the Oracles have played no part in the development of the doctrine of the Church. Incidentally, it is a striking proof of the non-critical

---

[1] Sib. Or. v. 138-141 :
"Τῆς μεγάλης 'Ρώμης βασιλεὺς μέγας, ἰσόθεος φώς,
Ὃν, φασίν, αὐτὸς Ζεὺς τέκεν [ἠδ' ἡ] πότνια Ἥρη·
. . . ἀπολεῖ πολλοὺς σὺν μητρὶ ταλαίνῃ."

[2] Sib. Or. v. 413-432. [3] Sib. Or. viii. 88-90.
[4] Sib. Or. viii. 169-213.

spirit of early Christianity that these writings should have been accepted as genuine prophecies of the Sibyl by many of the leaders of the early Church.[1]

3. *The Apocalypse of Peter*

The date of this apocalypse is assigned by Robinson and James [2] to the second century A.D., though there are not many indications of the exact date. It was received in Egypt, and Palestine, and partly at Rome.[3]

We find at the beginning the usual warnings against false prophets, and a prediction that God will come to judge the wicked; but nothing suggests that the Last Days are immediately at hand. The most notable feature is the elaborate account of the abodes of the righteous and of the wicked. The blessed dwell in 'a very great space, outside this world ($\mu\acute{\epsilon}\gamma\iota\sigma\tau os$ $\chi\hat{\omega}\rho os$ $\dot{\epsilon}\kappa\tau\grave{o}s$ $\tau o\acute{v}\tau o\upsilon$ $\tau o\hat{\upsilon}$ $\kappa\acute{o}\sigma\mu o\upsilon$),' bright and beautiful with flowers and white angels.[4] Opposite to this is the abode of the wicked, who are immersed in a lake of flaming mire, hung up by their tongues or hair, eaten alive by noisome reptiles, or flung down again and again from the summits of towering crags.[5] We cannot fail here to see reminiscences of the Greek Tartarus, coloured perhaps by the peculiar ferocity for which the populace of Alexandria, and of Egypt generally, was notorious. The morbid taste which is here so prominent has been only too persistent in the popular Christianity of later ages; but its occurrence at this early date [6] throws into yet stronger relief the dignity and restraint

---

[1] *e.g.* Justin, Clement of Alexandria, Tertullian. See J. Rendel Harris, in Hastings' *Dictionary of the Bible*, extra vol. p. 67 (art. 'Sibylline Oracles').

[2] Robinson and James, *Gospel and Apocalypse of Peter* (London, 1892).

[3] Robinson and James, *op. cit.* p. 46.

[4] Apoc. Petr. 3-5.   [5] Apoc. Petr. 6-20.

[6] A great many of the early Christian apocalypses contain a number of later interpolations; and some of the details of the Petrine apocalypse may not be so very early.

of the primitive Christian eschatology of the New Testament.

4. *The Testament of Abraham*

This apocalypse was probably composed in the second century A.D., and re-edited some eight centuries later.[1] The Egyptian features are quite unmistakable; the weighing and testing of souls occupies a prominent place,[2] and the monstrous many-headed figure of Death is no doubt derived from late Egyptian mythology and zoolatry.[3]

The theme of the book is as follows:—Abraham receives a visit from the archangel Michael, who tells him that his body will remain on the earth for seven thousand aeons ($\dot{\epsilon}\pi\tau\alpha\kappa\iota\sigma\chi\acute{\iota}\lambda\iota o\iota$ $a\grave{\iota}\hat{\omega}\nu\epsilon\varsigma$); and then will come the resurrection. This shows that by the time of the composition of this apocalypse, the Last Consummation had receded into the distant future of expectation. Abraham is then taken by an angel to visit the sights of heaven. He inspects the broad gate that leads to destruction and eternal punishment, and the narrow gate that leads to life. Only one soul in seven thousand, he is told, will pass through the latter. Indeed the patriarch himself feels some personal anxiety when he compares the straitened dimensions of the narrow gate with his own portly figure; but he is reassured by his angelic attendant.

> 'Abraham said unto Michael: "Woe is me! What am I to do? for I am a man of ample presence ($\epsilon\grave{\upsilon}\rho\grave{\upsilon}\varsigma$ $\tau\hat{\omega}$ $\sigma\acute{\omega}\mu\alpha\tau\iota$); and how can I enter in at the narrow gate, into which a child of fifteen years cannot pass?" And

---

[1] M. R. James, 'Testament of Abraham,' p. 55 (*Texts and Studies*, ii. 2). The quotations are from this edition.
[2] Test. Abr. 12 (Recension A), etc.
[3] Test. Abr. 17 (Recension A).

Michael answered and said unto Abraham: "Fear not thou, Father, nor be anxious; for without difficulty thou shalt pass through it,—yea, and all that are like unto thee."'[1]

Next, Abraham sees a vision of Judgment, which is to be threefold. In the first place, men are judged in this present world by Abel. The angel says to the patriarch :—

'Seest thou, all-holy Abraham, the terrible man that sitteth on the throne?—This is the Son of Adam the first-formed (ὁ πρωτόπλαστος), who is called Abel, whom Cain the wicked one slew; and he sitteth to judge all creation, and to convict (ἐλέγχων) righteous and sinners. Therefore God has said, "I will not judge you; but every man shall be judged by a man"; for this reason He hath entrusted judgment to him [Abel], to judge the world until His great and glorious Coming (παρουσία).'[2]

The idea that Abel will be judge is very peculiar. May it not be a reminiscence of the Egyptian myth of Osiris, the judge of all men? For Osiris and Abel were both righteous men who were murdered by an evil brother; and it was a characteristic of Alexandrian Christianity to adopt the features of foreign religion under the guise of traditional names. The second judgment will take place "ἐν τῇ δευτέρᾳ παρουσίᾳ," when the judges will be the twelve tribes of Israel. After this will be a third judgment, by God Himself (ὁ δεσπότης Θεός).[3] These two last judgments seem to be an artificial attempt to interpret literally the various pictures of the judgment in the New Testament.

In one passage, we read how Abraham's prayer, united with the intercession of Michael, delivered a soul from the judgment. Abraham sees a soul held by an

---

[1] Test. Abr. 9 (Recension B); James, *op. cit.* p. 113.
[2] Test. Abr. 13 (found in Recension A only). James, *op. cit.* p. 92.
[3] Test. Abr. 13. (James, *op. cit.* p. 92.)

angel in the midst of the Judgment-Hall, and asks why it is detained there. He is told it is because the soul's sins weigh exactly the same as its good deeds.

> 'Then Abraham said, "Come, O Michael, the chief captain (ἀρχιστράτηγος), let us make prayer for this soul." . . . And they made supplication and prayer for the soul; and God heard them. . . . And Abraham said [to the angel that had held the soul], "Where is the soul that thou wast holding in the midst?" And the angel said, "It has been saved by thy righteous prayer." And lo, a bright angel took the soul, and led it to Paradise.'[1]

In another passage, the prayer of Abraham avails to restore the dead to life.[2] It seems possible, indeed, that these incidents are recorded as special illustrations of the patriarch's miraculous powers, rather than as the 'reflection' of a prevalent custom of praying for the dead; but the latter explanation seems the more natural.

This apocalypse throws much light upon the popular eschatology prevalent among the Christians of the second century. The details are often interesting, and sometimes entertaining, adopted as they are from many sources without much discrimination. But we seek in vain for any really helpful ideas, or for any suggestive exposition of the fundamentals of Christian eschatology.

5. *The Testament of Isaac*[3]

Another short apocalypse, closely allied to that we have just been studying,[4] is the Testament of Isaac. Here again we find details of the torments of the lost.[5]

[1] Test. Abr. 14. (James, *op. cit.* p. 94.)   [2] Test. Abr. 18.
[3] See W. E. Barnes's 'Extracts from the Testament of Isaac,' appended to James's 'Testament of Abraham' (*Texts and Studies*, vol. ii. 2, pp. 140-151).
[4] See James, 'Testament of Abraham,' p. 157 :—'The writer, whether identical or not with the author of the Testament of Abraham, was acquainted with that book.'
[5] Barnes, *op. cit.* pp. 147-148.

332   THE CHRISTIAN APOCALYPSES

The value of the observances of ritual is here seen rising into new importance : admission to the Kingdom of God may be gained by offerings of incense, or the observance of vigils, or the repetition of prayers with the correct prostrations.[1] The writer also looks for a millennium, when 'Christ will be present with [the saints] in the first hour of the feast of the thousand years, that they may keep festival in everlasting light in the kingdom of our Lord and our God and our King and our Saviour Jesus the Christ.'[2]

6. *The Vision of Paul*

Another early Christian apocalypse edited by Dr. M. R. James is the 'Visio Pauli.'[3] Here the general tone is thoroughly Zoroastrian, and the angels form the centre of interest. All souls are met by their guardian angels after death, and led off to judgment.[4] There are traces of sun-worship,[5] an expectation of the millennial reign of Christ on earth,[6] a doctrine of the *resurrectio carnis*,[7] and an elementary idea of purgatory. The last-named is described thus :—

> 'If any one is a fornicator and ungodly, and has turned and repented and brought forth fruits worthy of repentance, then as soon as he has departed from the body, he is brought to worship God; and then at the Lord's command he is given to Michael the angel, and he baptizes him in the terrible (*aceriosus*) lake. Then he brings him into the City (*civitas*) of Christ together with those who have not sinned.'[8]

Even this brief extract will suffice to show how

---
[1] Barnes, *op. cit.* p. 149. [2] Barnes, *op. cit.* p. 151.
[3] *Texts and Studies*, ii. 3.
[4] Vis. Paul, 9-18 (James's edition); cf. below, on the *Shepherd of Hermas*, p. 348.
[5] Vis. Paul, 7.   [6] Vis. Paul, 21.   [7] Vis. Paul, 14.
[8] Vis. Paul, 22. We read that penitent sinners will be immersed 'in aceriosum locum,' and then admitted to the Divine Presence.

marked is the Zoroastrian influence in this interesting apocalypse.

In James's 'Apocrypha Anecdota' (*Texts and Studies*, vols. ii. and v.), the reader who is interested in this phase of early Christian thought will find a number of other Christian apocalypses, containing a vast store of little-known material for the student.[1]

The few examples which we have been considering will be sufficient to show that this literature has departed very far from the earliest type of primitive Christian eschatology. The Second Coming of the Lord is no longer the keynote; the freshness and conviction of the apostolic teaching is replaced by an elaborate artificiality; and the ancient Jewish outlines are obscured by a mass of details from foreign sources, heaped together with an irresponsible prodigality which is already manifesting a tendency to the most extravagant superstition.

Neither Jewish nor Christian 'apocalyptic' found favour with the religious leaders of its time. It was always a type of literature which displayed little culture and little intellectual ability; but it was admirably suited to the tastes of the common people. Indeed, through the persistency of oral tradition, both Jewish and early Christian apocalyptic notions are still influencing the popular interpretation of the Church's Doctrine of the Last Things.

Before concluding this chapter, a few words may be added with regard to *the eschatology of the Gnostic sects*. In many ways this was diametrically opposed to the ideas of the apocalypses; for it was contemptuously hostile towards the naïve and popular notions

[1] *e.g.* The Testament of Jacob (vol. ii. 2), the Testament of Job (vol. v. i), and the Acts of John, of Thomas, and of Andrew (vol. v. 1), and others of even less importance.

which formed the kernel of apocalyptic teaching. But Gnosticism rivalled or even surpassed the apocalypses in the unrestrained profusion of its puerile speculations as to the unseen world and the unknown future.[1] The Gnostic idea of immortality was thoroughly Hellenic;[2] the soul of man is pre-existent, and the supreme desire of the good soul is for purification from the uncleanness of material things. The Gnostic 'Hymn of the Soul,' edited by Bevan,[3] will serve to illustrate this. The awakening of consciousness is thus described:—

> 'I remembered that I was a son of kings, and my free soul longed for its natural state.'

The material body is 'an Egyptian garb,' and the resurrection is a casting-off of material shackles:—

> [At the resurrection] 'I stripped off their filthy and unclean garb, and left it in their [the 'Egyptian,' *i.e.* material] country.'

At length the purification is accomplished:—

> 'I did homage to the Majesty of my Father, ...
> For He rejoiced in me and received me,
> And I was with Him in His Kingdom.'[4]

On the whole, Gnosticism probably had little effect upon primitive Christian eschatology. The hostility between the Gnostics and the Catholics would render mutual approximation improbable; although the Alexandrian Fathers adopted some Gnostic ideas, and styled themselves 'true Gnostics.' But 'the [Gnostic] scheme itself was not Christian, nor properly even theistic; and to include the facts of the Christian creed in such a scheme was to transform their native character.'[5]

---

[1] See Iren. *Adv. Haer.* Books I. and II.
[2] See above, pp. 101-103.
[3] A. A. Bevan, in *Texts and Studies*, vol. v. No. 3. The date of this hymn is probably late second century (*op. cit.* pp. 1-7).
[4] Bevan, *op. cit.* p. 5.   [5] Robertson, *Regnum Dei* (London, 1901), p. 152.

CHAPTER XXVII

THE INFLUENCE OF GREEK THOUGHT UPON PRIMITIVE CHRISTIAN ESCHATOLOGY

So far we have traced the course of early Christian eschatology along two lines of development. On the one hand we saw that in those Christian communities of the East which clung most closely to the traditions from which they had sprung, the form of the primitive doctrine was retained, but without the old intensity of interest or the profound spirituality which characterised so many of the first disciples of our Lord. The spirit of rigid 'literalism,' which in later years came to be specially associated with the School of Antioch, was already at work in the minds of men such as Papias. They clung tenaciously to the letter of the primitive teaching, but they missed its essential meaning, and lacked its spirit and its power.

From the decaying eschatology of Jewish Christianity we turned to the Christian apocalyptic literature of Egypt and Alexandria. Here we found a doctrine of the Last Things vigorously expounded and widely appreciated by the people; but withal lacking in refinement, and powerless to meet the scepticism of the intellectual world of its day. If primitive Christian eschatology had developed along no other lines beside these two, the history of Christian doctrine during the sub-apostolic age would have offered but little promise for the future.

But so far we have left the Church in Europe out of our consideration. Most of the European branches of the Christian Church sprang up in the midst of Greek life and thought. There the Christian apologists had to meet with some of the keenest intellects which the world has produced; and there, if anywhere, we shall expect to find the true worth of primitive Christian eschatology revealed by the fire of criticism. We have already referred to some of the characteristics of Greek eschatology;[1] but it may be convenient here to recall some of the chief points of contrast between it and the Hebrew methods of thought in which Christianity was cradled. It is well to remember, though, when we speak of 'Greek eschatology,' that among the Greeks there was no central doctrinal authority, exercising a unifying influence such as that of the Old Testament among the Jews; so that the term really covers a number of heterogeneous ideas and speculations with regard to the future. There are, however, several broad differences between the Greek and Jewish outlook on the future, which may thus be summarised :—

1. The Hebrew always *started* from the belief in God and the Divine Covenant, and deduced his doctrines therefrom. If they satisfied the longings of his heart, so much the better; but it was absolutely essential that they should be consistent with that which Jahveh had revealed about Himself. The Greek, on the other hand, sought first for an idea which would fulfil his soul's highest aspirations; and his doctrine of the future life could generally be stated without mentioning the name of God.

2. In Hebrew eschatology, the centre of interest

[1] See above, pp. 101-103.

was the Doctrine of the Last Things, when God's Purpose for the world and for Israel will be revealed; though with this Doctrine of the Last Things there was interwoven (at least in later Judaism) a doctrine of individual resurrection and immortality. But in Greek eschatology there is little thought of the ultimate end of the world as a whole; attention is concentrated on the immortality of the individual soul. Some of the Stoics, it is true, looked for a great conflagration at the end of this World-Era; but this was not connected with the idea of a Last Judgment, or a resurrection, or any aspect of individual eschatology; it is simply an event in the physical world, the occurrence of which was deduced from astronomical observations, which were thought to prove that all things took place in periodic 'cycles.' The present cycle of events would end in a conflagration, and another would then recommence; but there is little or no idea of a Divine purpose running through the process.[1]

3. The Hebrews regarded the material body as an integral part of the man; they saw no fundamental antithesis between matter and spirit, and they could conceive that our earthly bodies might be transformed into "σώματα πνευματικά." But the Greeks contrasted the real 'ego' with the material 'prison-house' which impedes its true life.[2]

We must now return to the literature of the early Christian Church, and consider those writings which were either produced amid Greek influences, or were intended to be read by those familiar with Greek thoughts.

[1] But see Mayor, Fowler, and Conway, *Virgil's Messianic Eclogue* (London, 1907), pp. 107-111, where it is contended that Virgil expressed an idea of a future 'Golden Age' which is truly akin to the Hebrew 'Kingdom of God.'

[2] See F. C. Porter on 'Pre-existence of the Soul in Wisdom and the Rabbinic Writings,' in the *American Journal of Theology*, vol. xii. No. 1 (January 1908); and see also p. 102 above.

1. The Epistle of Clement of Rome to the Corinthians

The strength of orthodox Latin Christianity has ever lain in sober and disciplined common-sense, rather than in depth of mystical contemplation or lofty flights of enraptured prophecy. The letter of Clement, probably the earliest extant example of the literature of Gentile Christianity,[1] is in many ways typical of the Western Church. It is full of sound practical advice, but does not attempt to throw fresh light upon the Christian doctrines, which are accepted without misgiving or perplexity. It was written at the close of Domitian's persecution, *circa* A.D. 95.

The eschatology of St. Clement's letter is simple and earnest, and distinctly of the 'primitive Christian' type. Yet the influence of the writer's Gentile surroundings is unmistakable; he tends to replace the technical Jewish terms by others more intelligible to Gentile readers. For instance, when he speaks of the expected return of the Lord, he uses the prosaic term "ἔλευσις"[2] instead of the more Jewish expressions "παρουσία" or "ἀποκάλυψις," which were capable of a more elastic interpretation.

The thought of a spiritual salvation from sin and resurrection to eternal life in this world, which is found in the later Pauline Epistles, and especially in the Johannine writings, does not seem to have been prominent in the mind of St. Clement. Salvation is for him an object of hope, rather than a fact of experience; it is the final reward of Christian virtue, rather than the initial blessing of the Christian life;[3] similarly, the

---

[1] St. Clement himself was probably a Jew, if we may judge from his profuse references to the Old Testament; but his letter naturally reflects the Gentile surroundings in which it was written.   [2] See (*e.g.*) Clem. *ad Cor.* 17.

[3] See (*e.g.*) Clem. *ad Cor.* 58: "'Ο ποιήσας . . . τὰ ὑπὸ τοῦ Θεοῦ δεδομένα δικαιώματα καὶ προστάγματα, οὗτος ἐντεταγμένος καὶ ἐλλόγιμος ἔσται εἰς τὸν ἀριθμὸν τῶν σωζομένων."

resurrection is 'that which shall be hereafter'; and neither salvation nor resurrection will be accomplished till the Lord has come again.

In Clement, too, the doctrine of the resurrection is more nearly that of a material 'resurrection of the flesh' than anywhere in the New Testament. St. Paul had indeed likened our resurrection to Christ's; but he firmly maintained that 'flesh and blood cannot inherit the Kingdom of God.' The great apostle believed that we shall be raised by the same spiritual power that raised up Jesus; but he did not attempt to define the resemblance between the 'spiritual body' which will be ours and the Resurrection-body of our Lord. With St. Clement it is different. He first tells his readers that Christ was the first-fruits of the resurrection, and reminds them briefly of the analogies of day and night, seed-time and harvest. Then he proceeds to refer to the legend of the phoenix, 'the marvellous sign which is seen in the regions of the East.' This bird dies once in five hundred years;

> 'But as the flesh rotteth, a certain worm is engendered, which is nurtured from the moisture of the dead creature, and putteth forth wings. Then, when it is grown lusty, it taketh up the coffin where are the bones of its parent, and carrying them journeyeth from the country of Arabia even unto Egypt, to the place called the City of the Sun; and in the day-time in the sight of all, flying to the altar of the Sun, it layeth them thereupon, and this done, it setteth forth to return. . . . Do we then think it to be a great and marvellous thing if the creator ($\delta\eta\mu\iota\upsilon\rho\gamma\acute{o}\varsigma$) of the universe shall bring about the resurrection of them that have served Him with holiness in the assurance of good faith, seeing that He showeth us even by a bird the magnificence of His promise?'[1]

Surely it is evident that this conception of the

[1] Clem. *ad Cor.* 25, 26.

resurrection falls very far below that of the New Testament writers. The legend of the phoenix does not teach a resurrection to higher life, but simply a restoration to material life. The man who could appeal to this legend to support the resurrection-hope of the Christian was indeed far from the noble doctrine of St. Paul.

Side by side with this somewhat crude conception of the resurrection, St. Clement holds the belief that the saints become at the moment of death partakers of the joys of heaven. 'Paul,' he tells us, 'departed from the world and went to the holy place.' Peter 'went to his appointed (ὀφειλόμενον) place of glory.'[1] It is not easy to see how this belief leaves much need for a doctrine of a future resurrection in their case. If the saints are now in glory, what lack they yet? It is characteristic of St. Clement that the difficulty does not seem to have struck him. His use of the phoenix legend suggests that he may have expected that the saints would be restored to a life on this earth; but this is not expressly stated.

The Epistle of St. Clement might be described as 'a partial translation without a commentary.' The old Jewish phraseology is partly translated into language which is more intelligible to the Gentile world; but no explanation is added, and the apparent inconsistencies are allowed to pass without remark. Greek thought had barely exercised any influence upon the eschatology of St. Clement of Rome.

2. *The Epistles of Ignatius*

The letters of Ignatius, Bishop of Antioch, display a type of early Christianity which differs considerably from that of Clement of Rome. Accepting (as a

---

[1] Clem. ad Cor. 5.

working hypothesis) Lightfoot's conclusion that the Seven Epistles mentioned by Eusebius are genuine, we have in these letters much valuable information as to the eschatology of a great leader of the Church about the beginning of the second century. Antioch stood midway between Palestine and Asia; and it is interesting to notice in the Ignatian letters a combination of typical Jewish phraseology and thought, with the love of spiritual interpretations which we associate specially with the Ephesine School of St. John.

The language of Ignatius is undoubtedly Jewish; a striking example of this is in the greeting to the Ephesian Church, ' her which hath been foreordained ($προωρισμένη$) before the ages to be for ever unto abiding and unchangeable glory.' So too we frequently meet the old familiar terms of the Jewish eschatology, such as ' the Parousia,' ' the Resurrection,' ' the Kingdom of God.'

And yet the outlook of Ignatius is widely different from that of the primitive Judaeo-Christian Doctrine of the Last Things; for although much of his language is inherited from Judaism, his interpretation is distinctively non-Jewish. For instance, when he speaks of the 'Parousia,' he places it *before* the historical facts of our Lord's life and death :—

> 'The Gospel hath a singular pre-eminence in the advent ($παρουσία$) of the Saviour, even our Lord Jesus Christ, and His passion and resurrection.'[1]

Here the order of the phrases makes it clear that by the "$παρουσία$" Ignatius means the first coming of our Lord at His Nativity, and that there is no reference to a future Coming.

Or again; when Ignatius speaks of 'the resurrection,' he seems to be referring to the 'perfecting of the Saints' which takes place at once after death :—

[1] Ign. *ad Phil.* 9.

'Even though I am in bonds for the Name's sake, I am not yet perfected in Jesus Christ.'[1]

'If I shall suffer, then am I a freed-man of Jesus Christ, and I shall rise free in Him.'[2]

'It were expedient for them to have love, that they may rise again.'[3]

This is 'a resurrection *unto life*,' and only those who have the Spirit of Christ will share in it. Such expressions seem to imply that a resurrection is not the common lot of all men; and further, they more naturally suggest the idea of a spiritual revival of each faithful soul after death, than the idea of a future resurrection-day when all will be raised simultaneously, and for which the departed are now waiting.

Further, Ignatius is quite certain that all will be judged individually for their deeds, both men and angels and heavenly powers;[4] he speaks of the unquenchable fire for the wicked,[5] and of the deposits of good works which the righteous man is storing up in order that he may receive his assets in the next world.[6] But the Ignatian Epistles contain no reference to the Jewish and primitive Judaeo-Christian expectation of the Last Judgment, when all mankind shall be gathered simultaneously before the Throne of God.

There is indeed little in the eschatology of Ignatius which separates it from that of the Church of later ages. The intense expectation of an immediate return of the Master, and the simple acceptance of the ruling ideas of Jewish eschatology, which were so characteristic of the earliest days of the Church, have vanished in

[1] Ign. *ad Eph.* 3; cf. *ad Phil.* 5, and *ad Rom.* 4, 5, 9.
[2] Ign. *ad Rom.* 4; cf. *ad Eph.* 11: 'my bonds, my spiritual pearls in which I would fain rise again.'
[3] Ign. *ad Smyrn.* 7.   [4] Ign. *ad Smyrn.* 6.
[5] Ign. *ad Eph.* 16, etc.
[6] Ign. *ad Polyc.* 6: "τὰ δεπόσιτα ὑμῶν τὰ ἔργα ὑμῶν, ἵνα τὰ ἄσκεπτα ὑμῶν ἄξια κομίσησθε."

IGNATIUS 343

the Ignatian letters. The writer, following the steps of St. Paul and St. John, has penetrated below the surface, and has endeavoured to discover the fundamental principles of eschatology. And the result has been the discarding of many of the peculiar features of the most primitive Christian teaching on this subject.

In some ways this was inevitable and even beneficial; but in the Ignatian Epistles we can see the beginnings of one tendency which has not always been a power for good in the history of the Church of Christ. This was the growing disposition on the part of the leaders of the Church to insist upon the performance of external actions rather than purity of heart as the essential condition without which no man can inherit eternal life. In the Ignatian Epistles we read :—

> 'As many as are of God and Jesus Christ, they are with the bishop, and as many as shall repent and enter into the unity of the Church, these also shall be of God, that they may be living after Jesus Christ. Be not deceived, my brethren; if any man followeth one that maketh a schism, he doth not inherit the Kingdom of God.'[1]

And again, the Eucharist is described as 'the medicine of immortality, and the antidote that we should not die, but live for ever.'[2] There is no reason to suppose that Ignatius himself thought of the reception of the Sacrament apart from the act of faith which normally accompanies it, or that he denounced the act of schism apart from the spirit which prompted it. Yet surely these passages do indicate the beginnings of that tendency which culminated in the mediaeval Church, when the performance of rites and ceremonies was no

[1] Ign. *ad Phil.* 3.
[2] Ign. *ad Eph.* 20; cf. Iren. *Adv. Haer.* iv. 8 : 'Our bodies, when they receive the Eucharist, are no longer corruptible, having the hope of resurrection to eternity.'

less necessary for salvation than justice, truth, and love.

Closely allied with this is the value which Ignatius sets on submission of the will and thought to episcopal authority. This is of considerable significance for our present study. Hitherto Christian eschatology, as we have seen, has been exuberant rather than systematic, and no attempt has been made to formulate a consistent theory to include the divergent views held in various quarters. But now Ignatius urges uniformity of doctrine: 'Do nothing apart from the bishop and the presbyters, neither test the reasonableness of anything on the strength of your own judgment.'[1] Now if the people are thus taught to appeal to their ecclesiastical superiors for an official statement of the Church's doctrine, it becomes at once desirable that all branches of that doctrine should be carefully formulated and defined. And so, although Ignatius himself has very little to say about the Last Things, his teaching on the need of submission to authority helped fundamentally to change the 'tone' of Christian eschatology, transforming the prophetic, and perhaps somewhat unreflecting, vigour of the primitive apostolic message into an orderly dogmatic system.

Do the Ignatian Epistles show signs of Greek influence? On the whole, we may say that the general tone suggests rather that the writer was familiar with the teaching of St. John; and so far as Greek influence is found in Ignatius, it probably reached him mainly through the Johannine theology. But at least one saying in Ignatius is distinctively non-Jewish, and without parallel in the New Testament: 'Nothing visible is good'[2] (οὐδὲν φαινόμενον καλόν). And besides

[1] Ign. *ad Magn.* 7 : "ἄνευ τοῦ ἐπισκόπου καὶ τῶν πρεσβυτέρων μηδὲν πράσσετε· μηδὲ πειράσητε εὔλογόν τι φαίνεσθαι ἰδίᾳ ὑμῖν." [2] Ign. *ad Rom.* 3.

this, the non-Jewish, indeed anti-Jewish, tone of the Ignatian letters opened the way, as in the case of St. Paul, for a more friendly attitude towards the beliefs of the Gentile world.

3. *The Second Epistle of Clement*

In the Ignatian Epistles, the peculiar features of primitive Christian eschatology seemed to have died out, till only the Johannine doctrine—and not the whole of that—remained. But in the ancient homily, commonly called 'The Second Epistle of Clement,' and probably written at Corinth some twenty years after the martyrdom of St. Ignatius, we find an interesting combination of the primitive Jewish ideas with some unmistakably Greek features.

The writer looks for a future resurrection of the flesh,[1] and for 'the day of the manifestation' (ἡμέρα τῆς ἐπιφανείας) of our Lord.[2] His conception of the future life is closely connected with a doctrine of the pre-existence of the Church.

> 'If we do the will of God our Father, we shall be of the first Church, which is spiritual (πνευματική), which was created before sun and moon. ... The Books and the Apostles plainly declare that the Church existeth not now for the first time, but hath been from the beginning (τὴν ἐκκλησίαν οὐ νῦν εἶναι, ἀλλὰ ἄνωθεν); for she was spiritual, as was our Jesus also, but He was manifested in the last days that He might save us. Now the Church, being spiritual, was manifested in the flesh of Christ, thereby showing us that, if any of us guard her in the flesh and defile her not, he shall receive her again in the Holy Spirit; for this flesh is the copy (ἀντίτυπος) of the spirit. No man therefore, when he hath defiled the copy, shall receive the original (τὸ αὐθεντικόν). This

---

[1] 2 Clem. 9 : "ὃν τρόπον γὰρ ἐν τῇ σαρκὶ ἐκλήθητε, καὶ ἐν τῇ σαρκὶ ἐλεύσεσθε."
[2] 2 Clem. 17.

therefore is what He meaneth, brethren: Guard ye the flesh, that ye may partake of the Spirit. But if we say that the flesh is the Church, and the spirit is Christ, then he that hath dealt wantonly with the flesh hath dealt wantonly with the Church. Such an one therefore shall not partake of the spirit, which is Christ. So excellent is the life and immortality which this flesh can receive, if the Holy Spirit be joined to it.'[1]

In connection with this passage, we notice first that there is very little mention of the Divine purpose or predestination as the *raison d'être* of pre-existence. It seems probable, then, that the writer's idea was derived from Greek rather than Jewish sources, though this conclusion can hardly be regarded as beyond question. And then, what does he mean here by 'the Church' (ἡ ἐκκλησία)? His description of the Church is explicitly founded on the Pauline metaphor of the Church as 'the Body of Christ.' From this he apparently passes to the idea of a pre-existent spiritual counterpart (ἡ ἐκκλησία ἡ πρώτη ἡ πνευματική), which he seems to conceive of as a kind of spiritual essence—as it were an 'elixir of life,'—which was manifested in the flesh of Christ at the Incarnation, and will be given to His true followers as their great reward. And just as the sum-total of the bodies of the faithful constitutes the visible Church on earth, so the sum of the gifts of this 'spiritual essence' which they will receive constitute the 'spiritual Church.'—Such, in crude language, appears to be the writer's idea. And further, since the flesh is the 'copy' of the spirit, we honour the spirit by honouring the flesh. The moral of this teaching is thus to keep the body pure. If this is done, then our bodies will be raised at the last day, and the true spiritual essence, which constitutes 'life and

[1] 2 Clem. 14.

immortality,' will be added to them. The writer of 2 Clement thus combines the 'resurrection of the flesh' with the hope of spiritual immortality, in a way that reminds us of St. Paul. He does not share the Greek contempt for 'the fleshly prison-house of the soul,' but tells us that our bodies are capable of receiving a higher spiritual life. He also follows the later epistles of St. Paul when he speaks of salvation as a spiritual change of life which has already taken place.[1] In other passages, however, he does seem to disparage this earthly life as something mean ($\mu\iota\kappa\rho\acute{o}s$) and of short duration.[2]

In one matter 2 Clement marks a distinct departure from the earliest Christian ideal. We may recall how the writer of the Epistle to the Hebrews would make no allowance for failure on the part of Christians to live up to their profession. For those who fell away after they had been once called, there was no hope.[3] But the writer of 2 Clement is more lenient; he does not require that every Christian man shall live up to the highest standard. 'If we cannot all be crowned, at least let us come near the crown.'[4] We can see here how the lofty ideal of Christian life which was held by the first followers of our Lord was being abandoned in the face of experience. And thereby, as we have already pointed out,[5] later Christian eschatology has suffered from an apparent inconsistency.

Viewing this epistle as a whole, we may say that although it is not a striking example of profound thinking, it affords us a very interesting example of the mutual influence of Greek thought and Christian beliefs upon each other.

[1] 2 Clem. 2 and 3.   [2] 2 Clem. 5.
[3] Heb. vi. 6.
[4] 2 Clem. vii. Cf. Clem. Alex. *Paed.* i. 2, 'Let us try to sin as little as possible.'
[5] See above, pp. 251 ff.

4. *The Shepherd of Hermas*

This book belongs in many respects to the apocalyptic literature;[1] but internal evidence shows that unlike most of the 'revelations,' it was written from Rome, probably in the second quarter of the second century A.D.[2] It differs in some ways from the apocalypses of the Alexandrian and Egyptian Churches; for most of the visions are designed to enforce precepts for the present life, rather than to unveil the events of the future.

The writer's doctrine of penance is important for the history of later eschatology. Hermas, like the author of 2 Clement, recognises Christian sinfulness as a normal fact of experience. He sees a vision of the building of a tower, which is symbolical of the Church, and notices that some stones are rejected and thrown away.

> 'These,' he is told, 'have sinned, and desire to repent, therefore were they not cast far away from the tower, because they will be useful for the building, if they repent. . . . They will be strong in the faith, if they repent now, while the tower is building. But if the building shall be finished, they have no more any place, but shall be castaways.'[3]

It seems clear from this that the writer limited the possibility of repentance to this world, while the Church is being built. Later on, Hermas asks whether there is repentance for *all* the rejected stones.

> 'They can repent,' comes the answer, 'but they cannot be fitted into this tower. Yet they shall be fitted into another place much more humble, but not until they

---

[1] *e.g.* the Vision of the great Whale-monster (Vision iv.) is thoroughly after the manner of Jewish apocalyptic.
[2] For various views of date see (*e.g.*) Dr. G. Salmon in Smith's *Dictionary of Christian Biography*, vol. ii. pp. 912-920.
[3] *Past. Herm.* Vision iii. 5.

have undergone torments, and have fulfilled the days of their sins.'[1]

The important point to be noticed is this :—This figurative language if it stood alone, might apply either to penance in this world or to purgatory in the next. But since Hermas limits the opportunities of repentance to this life, there is no doubt that he himself was here referring to penance. Nevertheless we feel that we are here standing on the threshold of a doctrine of purgatory.

The angelology of Hermas seems to be derived from Zoroastrian sources. Each man has two 'guardian angels,' one righteous, and one wicked.[2] The Romans had come into contact with Persian ideas during the Parthian wars,[3] and this may explain the origin of these features.

The 'Shepherd' is an anomalous book, but it shows that in the West, as well as in the East, there was an early tendency in the Church to ponder over the details of Christian doctrine till the atmosphere of thought became strained and artificial. This was not confined to the Church. 'The world,' says Dr. Hatch, speaking of this era, 'had created an artificial type of life, and was too artificial to be able to recognise its own artificiality.'[4] The lack of that fresh simplicity which had been so characteristic of the apostolic preaching, is painfully noticeable in the 'Shepherd' of Hermas.

The letters of Clement and Ignatius, and the 'Shepherd' of Hermas, are examples of early writings which were intended for circulation *within* the Church. Shortly before the middle of the second century, a new

---

[1] *Past. Herm.* Vision iii. 7, and Similitude 6 (Lightfoot's chapter-headings).
[2] See especially Commandment vi. 2 ; and cf. the ' Visio Pauli,' above, p. 332.
[3] See Bury, *Student's Roman Empire*, pp. 117-124.
[4] Hatch, *Influence of Greek Ideas upon the Church* (London, 1890), p. 49.

type of Christian literature came into being. The
'Apologies' were written by Christians, but designed to
be read by the outside world. There are two diverging
tendencies in the apologetic literature. Some of the
writers are conciliatory, and anxious to point out that
Christianity is the fulfilment of the old order; others
take up an uncompromising attitude and teach that all
non-Christian religions are works of the devil. Of these
two, the former class were naturally the more favourably
disposed to assimilate Hellenic ideas. But all the
apologists, consciously or unconsciously, adopt something of the methods of Greek dialectic, and something
of the precision of Greek thought. Before the age of
the apologists, the eschatology of the Church had lost
most of its distinctively primitive peculiarities; and in
the following pages we shall see how, under the accurate
reasoning of the defenders of the faith, those peculiarities
completely disappeared. Let us now turn to a few
typical examples of this type of literature.

1. *The Apology of Aristides* [1]

This work was written in the reign of Antoninus
Pius, probably about A.D. 140, and is thus one of the
earliest apologies. The references to eschatology are
for the most part simple, and afford little matter for
comment. The most notable of them are in chapter 16.
There we read that the Christians 'labour to become
righteous, as those that expect to see their Messiah
(Χριστός) and receive from Him the promises made to
them, with great glory.' The language might seem to
imply that the writer expected to see the Second Coming
within his own generation; but this is not explicitly
stated. There is no evidence from contemporary

[1] The Syriac text is translated by M. R. James, in *Texts and Studies*, vol. i. 1.

writings that this primitive belief had survived so far into the second century; so the passage may refer to the resurrection of the faithful dead, who will then behold the Christ. On the other hand, the general tone of Aristides is distinctly primitive, and there is little sign of Greek influence. He tells us that the final consummation is being delayed by the prayers of the Christians.[1] This being so, it is possible that he did expect that the Second Coming was very near at hand.

2. *The Epistle to Diognetus*

Another Apology, nearly contemporary, so far as we can judge, with that of Aristides,[2] is the Epistle to Diognetus. In this the signs of Greek influence are unmistakable. The author speaks as a Greek to Greeks, and endeavours to justify Christianity from that standpoint. There are not many references to eschatology, but those that do occur disparage things material and look forward to a freer existence hereafter.—

> 'The soul hath its abode in the body, and yet is not of the body (ἐκ τοῦ σώματος). . . . The soul, though itself immortal, dwelleth in a mortal tabernacle (σκήνωμα); so Christians sojourn amidst perishable things, while they look for the imperishability (ἀφθαρσία) which is in the heavens. . . .'[3]

There is no reference to the resurrection of the flesh; but the writer looks for a Last Judgment, followed by an eternity of weal or woe.[4]

3. *Justin Martyr*

Justin, perhaps the most famous of all the apologists, was a Greek by descent, born in Flavia Neapolis, one

[1] *Apol. Arist.* 16.
[2] See (*e.g.*) Lightfoot, *Apostolic Fathers* (1898 ed.), pp. 487-489. The last two chapters (11 and 12) are generally regarded as of later date.
[3] *Ep. ad Diogn.* 6.   [4] *Ep. ad Diogn.* 7, 10.

of the cities of Samaria. He was well acquainted with the various systems of Greek philosophy, but found that Christianity alone satisfied the needs of his soul. His two Apologies and the Dialogue with Trypho were probably written *circa* 150 A.D. The other works attributed to Justin, including the fragment 'On the Resurrection,' are considered by many critics to be by another writer, and their evidence must be used with caution.

We should naturally expect that Justin, who to the last retained the cloak of a Greek philosopher, would afford a notable example of the influence of Greek thought upon the Church. But, as a matter of fact, there are very few ideas in Justin's works which show signs of this influence. The dialectical methods of the apologist are Hellenic; but the substance of his teaching is purely Christian, sometimes of a Jewish type.

Justin is silent concerning an immediate return of our Lord, and he explains that the Second Coming is being delayed in order that the number of the elect may be fulfilled, and that the hosts of evil may be subdued. Prophecy, he says, has foretold

> 'That God the Father would bring Christ to heaven after He had raised Him from the dead, and would keep [1] Him there till He has subdued His enemies the devils, and till the number of those foreknown by Him is complete, on whose account He has still delayed the consummation.' [2]

Elsewhere he maintains that the destruction of the world is delayed 'because of the seed of the Christians, who know that they are the cause of the preservation of nature.' [3] Thus Justin does not attempt to set any

---

[1] The Greek, κατέχειν, reminds us of 'The Restrainer' of 2 Thess. ii. 6, 7.
[2] *1st Apol.* 45.
[3] *2nd Apol.* 7; the last clause is obscure: "διὰ τὸ σπέρμα τῶν Χριστιανῶν, ὃ γινώσκει ἐν τῇ φύσει ὅτι αἴτιόν ἐστιν." Cf. *Apol. Aristidis* 16.

limit to the delay of the Second Coming; and he has quite ceased to repeat the watchword of primitive Christian eschatology : ' The Lord is at hand.'

When once the Church came to believe that the Second Coming of the Lord had been indefinitely postponed, a new feeling of interest sprang up concerning the intermediate state of departed souls. The 'waiting-time' of the faithful dead now seemed so much longer than before, that the conditions of life there became a matter of much greater importance. Justin is, so far as we know, the first Christian writer outside the field of apocalyptic who makes a definite statement on this subject.—

> 'The souls of the pious remain in a better place, while the unjust are in a worse, waiting for the time of judgment.' [1]

It will be seen that Justin's view is practically identical with that of Enoch and many of the Jewish apocalypses. But Justin goes so far as to say that a belief in the intermediate state is one of the *essentials* of the Christian Faith.—

> 'If,' he says to Trypho, 'you have met with some who are *called* Christians, who say that there is no resurrection of the dead, *and that their souls as soon as they die* (ἅμα τῷ ἀποθνήσκειν) *are to be taken to heaven* ; do not imagine that they *are* Christians.' [2]

The doctrine of the Anti-Christ appears in the Dialogue with Trypho. Justin appeals to the authority of Daniel vii. 25, where the last of the kings is to rule 'a time and times and half a time'; but he rejects the Jewish exegesis that "a time" denotes a century

---
[1] *Tryph.* 5.
[2] *Tryph.* 80 ; cf. Iren. *Adv. Haer.* v. 31 : 'The heretics affirm that immediately upon their death they shall pass above the heavens.'—Irenaeus confutes this by an appeal to the example of Christ.

2 A

(in which case Anti-Christ would reign three hundred and fifty years), and he warns his readers that this Anti-Christ, 'the man of apostasy,' 'is even already at the door, about to speak blasphemous things against the Most High,' and to 'do unlawful deeds on the earth against the Christians.'[1] This expectation that Anti-Christ is at the door approaches nearer than any other passage in Justin to the primitive hope of an immediate crisis; but probably Justin thought that the coming of Anti-Christ might take place some time before the second Advent of Christ. 'The times are running on to their consummation';[2] more than this Justin does not venture to say.

The expectation of a millennium was held by Justin. He is asked by Trypho :—

'Do you expect that Jerusalem shall be rebuilt, . . . and your people gathered together and made joyful with Christ and the patriarchs and prophets, both men of our nation, and proselytes?'

He replies :—

'I and many others are of this opinion; . . . but many, who belong to the pure and pious faith, and are true Christians (ὄντων Χριστιανῶν) think otherwise. . . . But I and others are assured that there will be a resurrection of the dead, and a thousand years in Jerusalem, which will then be built.'[3]

We noticed that in the Ignatian letters, the word 'Parousia,' which in the New Testament had been a technical term for the return of our Lord, was used of the Nativity.[4] Justin goes a step farther, and formally distinguishes between 'the First Parousia' (*i.e.* the Incarnation) and 'the Second Parousia' (*i.e.* the Return from Heaven in glory).[5] This again marks

[1] *Tryph.* 32 and 110. [2] *Tryph.* 32. [3] *Tryph.* 80.
[5] See above, p. 341. [4] *Tryph.* 32; cf. 110-111.

JUSTIN MARTYR

another stage of the departure from the most primitive Christian eschatology. The apostles had regarded the Life of Christ in the flesh and His future return in glory as parts of one and the same Coming of the Messiah, in which the Ascension to God's throne was but a short interlude. But in the times of Justin, the return of the Messiah on the clouds of heaven had receded so far into the future that it could no longer be regarded as part of the great Messianic drama of the Life and Death and Resurrection of Jesus. The two seemed widely separate from each other; so in Justin for the first time we find them described as 'the First Advent' and 'the Second Advent'; and the distinction, both in language and in thought, has become permanent in the Christian Church.[1]

It is not certain whether Justin's conception of the resurrection was of a material or spiritual kind.

> 'We expect,' he says, 'to receive again our own bodies, though they be dead and cast into the earth.'[2]

This might suggest a material resurrection; but we read in another place that Christ at His Second Coming 'shall clothe the bodies of the worthy with immortality.' This suggests a more spiritual idea; and we may compare a quotation from Methodius *On the Resurrection* :—

> 'Justin of Neapolis . . . says that that which is natural is inherited, but that which is immortal inherits; and that the flesh indeed dies, but the Kingdom of Heaven lives.'[3]

If this be a genuine saying of Justin's, then his doctrine of the resurrection was certainly not limited to a mere restoration of our present material bodies. If, on

---

[1] We find the idea (*e.g.*) in Irenaeus (*Adv. Haer.* iv. 11), also in Hippolytus (*circ.* A.D. 220), 'Christ and Anti-Christ,' § 21.
[2] *1st Apol.* 18.
[3] See the Ante-Nicene Christian Library, vol. ii. p. 356.

the other hand, we could appeal to the treatise *De Resurrectione* as a genuine work of Justin's, we should be obliged to conclude that Justin taught a literal 'Resurrection of the flesh.'

> 'Shall not God be able to collect again the decomposed members of the flesh, and make the same body as was formerly produced by Him?'[1]

And in this same treatise we find one, at least, of the reasons for this material conception of the resurrection: it is because our resurrection will be like our Lord's. Now it seems that the writer of the *De Resurrectione* held that Christ's resurrection-body was simply His pre-resurrection-body restored again to life, and composed of flesh and blood without change from its former conditions.[2] In that case it would follow naturally enough that our resurrection-bodies will be composed of the same matter as those we now possess. Bodily infirmities will be healed,[3] but there is nothing to suggest a 'spiritual body.'

Justin insists very strongly that the doom which men receive after the resurrection can never come to an end nor be altered.

> 'Each man goes to everlasting punishment or salvation (ἐπ' αἰωνίαν κόλασιν ἢ σωτηρίαν) according to the value of his actions.'[4]

He argues, in opposition to Greek philosophy, that if punishment in the next world is to serve any useful purpose, the soul must retain some consciousness of the sins committed in this world.[5]

---

[1] Justin, *De Resurrect.* 6.   [2] *De Resurrect.* 2.   [3] *De Resurrect.* 4.

[4] *1st Apol.* 12; cf. 52, and *Oratio ad Graec.* 35: 'Your fathers are now lamenting in Hades, and repenting with a too late repentance; and if it were possible for them to show you thence what had befallen them after the termination of this life, ye would know from what fearful ills they desired to deliver you.'

[5] *Tryph.* 1 and 4; *1st Apol.* 18.

The eschatology of the genuine writings of Justin thus displays many characteristics which distinguish it from the earliest Christian preaching. But, on the whole, the particular form of his teaching seems to be due to his own meditations, or to the need of adaptation to changed circumstances, rather than to any conscious reproduction of Greek ideas.

4. *The Apology of Athenagoras*

About A.D. 177, Athenagoras, a converted Athenian philosopher, wrote an Apology,[1] which has come down to us, and which is of interest as showing the outcome of the materialistic type of resurrection-doctrine which we have noticed in some earlier writers, when pushed to its extreme logical conclusions. Athenagoras looks for a literal gathering together of material particles, and discusses the problems that arise when we remember that the same particles which form our bodies pass after our death into other substances—such as the bodies of animals which feed upon human corpses. He finds an answer to such difficulties in the thought of the omnipotence of God:—

> '[God is able] to separate that which has been broken up and distributed among a multitude of animals of all kinds which are wont to have recourse to such bodies, . . . and unite it again with the proper members and parts of members, whether it has passed into some one of these animals, or into many, or thence into others, or after having been dissolved along with these, has been carried back again to the original elements.'[2]

It would be hard to find a more literal conception of the *resurrectio carnis* than is expressed in this passage.

---

[1] See Mansel in Smith's *Dictionary of Christian Biography*, vol. i. pp. 204-207 (art. 'Athenagoras').

[2] *De Resurrect.* 3, and cf. the whole treatise (Eng. trans. in Ante-Nicene Christian Library).

It is an illustration of careful deductive reasoning which leads us on with relentless logic to a conclusion from which our instinct shrinks. The practical bearing of Athenagoras's teaching, however, is unexceptionable : he points out that it is a complete refutation of the charge of cannibalism which was often brought against the Christians, and also that it is an incentive to a clean and moral bodily life.

It is worthy of note that Athenagoras teaches that young children, while sharing in the resurrection, will not undergo judgment, because they have committed neither good nor evil.[1] He does not refer in this connection to the question of their baptism ; from which it seems probable that in his day the belief in the absolute necessity of sacramental grace was not always held so rigidly as in later times, when St. Augustine (for instance) believed in the damnation of all unbaptized infants.

5. *Irenaeus*

Dr. Sanday has said that Irenaeus 'represents the best type of orthodoxy'; and there is much truth in this. For in the writings of Irenaeus, the appeal to authority, and to the written Rule of faith, is the argument by which every objection is met; and as a consequence, there is a notable absence of those idiosyncrasies and strongly-marked peculiarities of place and date which, in the case of more independent writers, tend to disturb the proportions of the orthodox creed. Associated as Irenaeus had been with the three important Churches of Asia, Rome, and Gaul,[2] his influence upon the doctrine of the Church has been very considerable, and his authority regarded with no little deference.

[1] *De Resurrect.* 14.
[2] He was a native of Asia, visited Rome at least once on ecclesiastical business, and became Bishop of Lyons shortly afterwards.

His great work *Adversus Haereses* was probably written circa 180-185 A.D. In it we find an extensive treatment of eschatological doctrine which may be fairly said to represent, with a few exceptions, the normal doctrine of the Church in later ages. The various features of New Testament eschatology are here gathered into a compact body of doctrine, and if any passages seem to mar the consistency of the whole, it is maintained that the contradiction is apparent and not real.[1] From the very fact of the constant appeal to Scripture—not only to the Old Testament, but also to the apostolic writings—a continuity with primitive Christian eschatology is guaranteed in the matter of language; but the meaning is not altogether the same, and the relative importance of the various elements of the teaching has somewhat changed.

The observations of Irenaeus upon the Parable of Dives and Lazarus afford a typical instance of his method of carefully 'weighing' the Scriptures, sentence by sentence, and then deducing therefrom a number of clear-cut doctrines :—

> 'By these things [recorded in the Parable] it is plainly declared, that souls continue to exist; that they do not pass from body to body; that they possess the form (*figura*) of a man, so that they may be recognised, and retain the memory of things in this world; . . . and that each class of souls receives a habitation such as it has deserved, even before the judgment.'[2]

Irenaeus teaches that immortality is conditional only, being a reward for the righteous, while 'those who, in this brief temporal life, have shown themselves ungrateful to Him that bestowed it, shall justly not receive from Him length of days for ever.'[3] Yet the wicked

---
[1] See (*e.g.*) *Adv. Haer.* v. 6, 9, 11.
[2] *Adv. Haer.* ii. 34. i.   [3] *Adv. Haer.* ii. 34. iii.

will not be merely non-existent, but will be 'sent into eternal fire.'[1]

The doctrine of the resurrection tends with Irenaeus to become somewhat materialistic, and he contends for a very literal 'raising again of the flesh.'[2] The Pauline passages which appear unfavourable to this view are dealt with at length, with a view to reconciling them with the teaching of the writer. Thus, a 'spiritual body' is explained to be a material body animated by the Spirit;[3] the terms 'carnal' and 'spiritual' are to be understood *morally*, not physically;[4] and the saying 'flesh and blood cannot inherit the Kingdom of God' refers only to flesh and blood *apart from the Spirit*.[5] In all this, Irenaeus has been the forerunner of many a later commentator, who, holding the same doctrinal presuppositions, has been compelled to adopt the same somewhat 'forced' exegesis.

In the writings of Irenaeus, we feel that we have completely passed out of the peculiar atmosphere of primitive Christian eschatology. In the place of enthusiastic spontaneity, we meet with precise and reasoned dogmatic statements, each one fortified by an appeal to a proof-text of Scripture. Indeed, on the whole, the eschatology of Irenaeus bears a closer resemblance to that of modern Christianity, more than seventeen centuries later, than to that of primitive Christianity, less than two centuries before.

There are, it is true, a few points in Irenaeus's teaching which have not been generally accepted by later generations, and which at first sight remind us of primitive Christianity. Such are, his doctrine of Anti-Christ, and his expectation of the millennium. The

---

[1] *Adv. Haer.* iv. 27. iv.
[2] *Adv. Haer.* v. 3-15, and 31-35.
[3] *Adv. Haer.* v. 7. ii.
[4] *Adv. Haer.* v. 11.
[5] *Adv. Haer.* v. 9.

language in which Anti-Christ is described [1] does certainly remind us more of primitive Christianity than of later ages; but if we compare it with the language of writers some seventy or eighty years earlier, whose imaginations were continually haunted by the spectre of 'Nero Redivivus,' [2] we shall see that this surviving remnant of Judaeo-Christian and Eastern eschatology is undoubtedly declining in importance. The figure of Anti-Christ accorded well, however, with the expectation of a millennial reign of Christ on earth, which figures largely in the outlook of Irenaeus.

> 'In the times of the resurrection the righteous shall reign on the earth. . . .' [Quotations follow from Isaiah lxv. 21, 'They shall build houses, and inhabit them . . . etc.,' and other Old Testament passages.] '. . . These things cannot be understood in reference to super-celestial matters. . . . Nothing is capable of being allegorised, but all things are steadfast and true and substantial (*firma et vera et substantiam habentia*).' [3]

But this expectation, while not generally characteristic of later orthodoxy, is also not characteristic of the earliest apostolic eschatology, where in fact it very rarely occurs. In the sub-apostolic age, traces of it may be often found; as in Papias, the Epistle of Barnabas, the Shepherd of Hermas, 2 Clement, and especially in Justin; but the highly developed 'Chiliasm' of Irenaeus springs from an exaggerated emphasis upon a few texts of Scripture, and may fairly be described as an artificial addition to the earliest Christian teaching. It never obtained universal acceptance in the Church; it was rejected by the Alexandrian Fathers, and by 'central' Churchmen of the type of Eusebius of Caesarea, but lingered

---

[1] *Adv. Haer.* v. 25-30.
[2] *e.g.* Sib. Or. (see above, pp. 324-328).
[3] *Adv. Haer.* v. 34, 35.

on in the West, and also in Montanist circles, until the fourth century.¹

In spite of his 'Chiliasm' and a few other peculiarities, Irenaeus remains, on the whole, notable for the sobriety and 'balance' of his doctrine. We may not always be able to follow his line of argument; we may wish at times, as we read, that a burst of prophetic enthusiasm would now and again break through the careful orthodoxy of the priest; but if we would appreciate the teaching of Irenaeus at its true value, we need only turn to the fragments of heretical eschatology which are contained in his writings.² There we shall find such a maze of extravagant speculation and purposeless elaboration of theories, that we shall be thankful to turn back to the sane reasonableness of an orthodoxy based upon the Scriptures, and maintaining on the whole the ancient proportions of apostolic Christianity. For although we have spoken of Irenaeus as though in his writings the peculiar features of primitive Christianity had ceased, it need not be inferred that any essential points had been lost. On the contrary, the appeal to Scripture, which is so prominent a feature in Irenaeus, secures the retention of vital doctrines, even though the primitive forms, and in a measure also the primitive spirit, undergoes a change in the course of the centuries.

How far was the eschatology of Irenaeus influenced by Greek thought? Probably the extent of this influence is greater than appears at first sight, but affects the methods rather than the substance of Irenaeus's teaching.³ The precision of thought, which is so notable a feature of his works, and indeed accounts in great

¹ See Bethune-Baker, *Early Christian Doctrine* (London, 1903), pp. 68-71; also Robertson, *Regnum Dei*, pp. 124-159.
² *Adv. Haer.* Books I. and II.
³ There are a few instances of distinctive Greek ideas; *e.g. Adv. Haer.* ii. 33. iv.: 'Anima, participans suo corpori, modicum quidem impeditur.'

measure for his 'orthodoxy,' is far more Greek than Jewish. It has been said of the Greeks of the second and third centuries A.D., that they 'laid more stress upon the expression of ideas than upon the ideas themselves.'[1] And one might say that Irenaeus seems to value the form in which the resurrection-doctrine is expressed almost more than the resurrection-hope itself.[2] The primitive 'eschatology of the spirit' is giving way to the mediaeval 'eschatology of authority.'

The writings of Irenaeus may thus be fitly taken to mark the close of the distinctively primitive age of Christian eschatology; and any attempt to discuss in detail the eschatology of later writers would lead us on into another age of Church history, in which the methods and ideals are widely different from those of the period on which our interest has been concentrated in the above pages.

But before we conclude, our attention is claimed by a great school of Christian thought which, while differing fundamentally from the 'literalism' of Irenaeus, yet, like Irenaeus, played an important part in bringing to an end the primitive features of Christian eschatology.

6. *The School of Alexandria*

From the times of Philo onwards, Alexandria had been the home of an eclectic learning and an elaborate system of Biblical exegesis. In our study of the Christian apocalypses, we saw that among the less educated classes of that city, Christian eschatology came to be mingled with details of Jewish apocalyptic and other foreign elements, till its primitive features were at length obscured and lost to sight. In the writings of the Alexandrian Fathers, we find the same cosmo-

---

[1] Hatch, *Influence of Greek Ideas*, p. 49.
[2] See especially *Adv. Haer.* Book V.

politan spirit, always ready to adopt new ideas from foreign sources; only in their case the adoption is far more discriminating and refined. From one point of view, they were the first typically 'Liberal' Churchmen; for as Dr. Bigg has pointed out, 'their great Platonic maxim, "That nothing is to be believed which is unworthy of God," makes Reason the judge of Revelation.'[1] This appeal to the supremacy of Reason and Conscience, though not without justification from the teaching of the New Testament,[2] is in marked contrast, not only to the docile orthodoxy of Irenaeus, but also to the somewhat unreflecting simplicity of most of the primitive Christian writers whose works we have considered. Christian doctrine, under the new methods of the Alexandrian School, becomes permeated by a new spirit; and nowhere is the change more noticeable than in the Doctrine of the Last Things.

The first great teacher of the School was Clement, whose Headship extended from A.D. 190 to 203. He shares with Irenaeus—and indeed with all the early Christian teachers—a deep reverence for the authority of the Scriptures. But nevertheless we are conscious of a fundamental change in the *manner* of his appeal to Scripture. Others had *started* from the authority of Scripture as their fundamental axiom of belief, and from this had deduced a system of doctrine with more or less logical precision. But Clement's fundamental axiom, from which his teaching starts in the first place, seems to be rather the authority of his own Reason and Conscience, and his general theory of History. True, he is most anxious to prove that this is supported by Scriptural authority; but when the two do not appear to coincide, it is Scripture, not his own convictions,

---

[1] Bigg, *Christian Platonists of Alexandria* (Oxford, 1886), p. 51.
[2] *e.g.* 1 Thess. v. 21.

which suffers violence in the effort to enforce agreement. His convictions were partly independent of Scripture in their origin, and therefore independent also in their authority.

It will be readily seen that such methods would foster the allegorising tendency, which is very marked in Clement, and was carried to still greater extremes by his successors. There were texts in Scripture of which the obvious meaning did not agree with Clement's convictions. But since Scripture is Divine, and Reason and Conscience also Divine, the true meaning of Scripture *must* agree with Reason and Conscience. Therefore the obvious meaning of Scripture is not in such cases the true meaning. And so an allegorical significance has to be discovered.

Clement's methods, when applied to eschatology, affected its development in two ways. In the first place, his tendency to allegorise often led him to eliminate just the very features which were most characteristic of primitive Christianity, because these same features were frequently the most alien to the broad and cultured outlook of the Alexandrian scholar. And in the second place, Clement's strong personal convictions, which seem generally to spring simply from his own Reason and Conscience, independently of any Scriptural authority, lead him at times to propound ideas concerning the Last Things which are distinctly new in Christian history, and outside (though not necessarily contrary to) the plain teaching of Scripture. Thus, partly by the elimination of ancient features, and partly by the addition of new ones, Christian eschatology under the Alexandrian School loses almost all its peculiarly primitive features. An extract from the *Exhortation to the Greeks* (probably Clement's earliest work) will illustrate this :—

'Great is the grace of His promise, "If to-day we hear His voice." And that "to-day" is lengthened out day by day, while it is called "to-day." And to the end the "to-day" and the instruction continue; and then the true "to-day," the never-ending "day" of God, extends over eternity.'[1]

In this passage, we notice in the first place, how the original dramatic urgency of the psalmist's call to repent 'to-day' has died away under the softening influence of allegorism. The day of opportunity, according to Clement, is to continue 'to the end';[2] and in the last clause of the above quotation there is at least a suggestion of the idea which Clement hints at again elsewhere,[3] that in the eternal life there will still be opportunities for development, for choice, and for repentance. Such an idea could hardly have been suggested to him simply by the teaching of Scripture; its origin must be sought rather in Clement's own temperament and outlook; but when once the conviction had been formed in his mind, his methods of Scriptural exegesis enabled him to find support for it in Scripture, even if in somewhat unlikely texts.

Clement's general outlook on the future is that of a gentle and refined nature, unwilling to dwell upon the harsh and painful side of life. This tendency of his evidently influences his eschatological teaching. He seems to shrink, as men of his type have always shrunk, from the thought that man's eternal fate is irrevocably sealed at the grave; and hence his belief (to which we

---

[1] *Exhort. ad Gentes*, 9: "μεγάλη γὰρ τῆς ἀπαγγελίας αὐτοῦ ἡ χάρις, Ἐὰν σήμερον τῆς φωνῆς αὐτοῦ ἀκούσωμεν· τὸ δὲ σήμερον καθ' ἑκάστην αὐτοῦ αὔξεται τὴν ἡμέραν, ἔστ' ἂν ἡ σήμερον ὀνομάζηται· μέχρι δὲ συντελείας καὶ ἡ σήμερον καὶ ἡ μάθησις διαμένει· καὶ τότε ἡ ὄντως σήμερον ἡ ἀνελλιπὴς τοῦ Θεοῦ ἡμέρα τοῖς αἰῶσι συνεκτείνεται."

[2] Cf. *Paed.* i. 6: 'In this world, which is what He means by the Last Day. . . .'

[3] *e.g. Strom.* vi. 14, vii. 2. See also Hort and Mayor, *Clement of Alexandria, Miscellanies, Book VII.* (London, 1902), Introduction, p. xli.

have already referred) that opportunities for repentance will continue in the life to come. Like other Liberal Churchmen, he lays less emphasis on the heinousness of sin than did most of the early Christians; he dwells but lightly on the penal aspect of retribution,[1] and turns rather to the hope of purgation in the future world.—

> 'The believer, through great discipline, divesting himself of the passions, passes . . . to the greatest torment. . . . For God's righteousness is good, and His goodness is righteous. And the punishments cease in the course of the completion of the expiation and purification of each one.'[2]

But Clement's doctrine of Purgatory, while a distinct addition to the teaching of the New Testament, is but a simple and natural outcome of the longing for continued progress in the spiritual life;[3] and it differs widely from the hard and artificial doctrine of Purgatory in the Mediaeval Church.

Further, the whole trend of Clement's thought led him to an evolutionary view of the world's history.

> 'The Gospel in his view is not a fresh departure, but the meeting-point of two converging lines of progress, of Hellenism and Judaism. To him all history is one, because all truth is one.'[4]

For one who held this view, it was by no means easy to fit the primitive Christian eschatology, with its expectation of impending catastrophe and its Judaeo-centric outlook, into his existing circle of ideas. In fact, it was not done without a great transformation of the early teaching.

[1] Hort and Mayor, *op. cit.* Introduction, p. xliv.
[2] *Strom.* vi. 14; cf. vii. 16.
[3] Cf. Martensen's *Christian Dogmatics* (English translation, Edinburgh, 1866), p. 457.
[4] Bigg, *op. cit.* p. 48.

368 INFLUENCE OF GREEK THOUGHT

Clement's broad sympathies and interests extended to all foreign religions and philosophies; and at times the influence of these upon his teaching is clearly to be seen. His exaltation of the 'passionless' life as the highest ideal at once suggests the Eastern philosophies to which he refers elsewhere.[1] The following is a characteristic passage :—

'Our Instructor (παιδαγωγός) is like His Father, God, whose Son He is, sinless, blameless, with a soul devoid of passion (ἀπαθὴς τὴν ψυχήν). . . . He is wholly free from human passions; wherefore also He alone is judge, because He alone is sinless. As far, however, as we can, let us try to sin as little as possible. For nothing is so urgent in the first place as deliverance from passions and disorders (παθῶν καὶ νοσημάτων).'[2]

This ideal naturally colours Clement's eschatology. The path to salvation in his teaching lies along the lines of quiet contemplation and self-renunciation, rather than of strenuous conflict and active energy. It also accorded well with the subjective conception of the Kingdom of God as a state of mind within us, rather than with the more normal Judaeo-Christian expectation of inheriting an objective kingdom as the reward for faithful service.[3]

Clement also borrows many phrases and ideas from the Greek Mysteries. The resemblance between Christianity and the Mysteries is hinted at in the New Testament,[4] but under Clement the comparison is worked out in a way that led to new ideas of the Christian scheme of salvation. The Sacraments, when compared to the initiatory rites of the Mysteries, became

[1] See especially *Strom.* i. 15 ; and cf. Hort and Mayor, *op. cit.* Introduction, p. xxxv.
[2] *Paed.* i. 2.
[3] See Bigg, *op. cit.* p. 26.
[4] See (*e.g.*) the use of " μυστήρια " in 1 Cor. xiii. 2, xiv. 2, and of " φωτίζω " in Heb. vi. 4, and especially Eph. iii. 9.

invested with an ever-growing importance as the magic portal of admission to eternal life.[1]

The eschatology of Clement is a large subject, of which we have only touched the fringe. Perhaps enough has been said to show that it does not properly fall within the study of Primitive Christian Eschatology, except in so far as it illustrates some of the causes which brought about the decline of the primitive type of doctrine. The tendencies which we have noticed in Clement are seen in a far more advanced form in his great successor Origen; but though the eschatology of Origen is a fascinating theme, it is still further removed from the scope of our present inquiry. With Origen, the love of allegory runs to wild excess; but the greatness and beauty of some of his thoughts make us ready to pardon much. His theories of the pre-existence of souls and of universal restoration have not commanded general acceptance in the Church; but Christendom will not readily forget his great conception of history: 'The beginning and the end are God; poised, as it were, between these two divine Eternities are the worlds of which we are a part.'

The theology of the Alexandrian School was brilliant rather than orthodox; it fell into some grave errors, but it brought to light much new truth. It lacked just those features which had been the strength of primitive Christian teaching—the simple directness, the positive decision, and the intense restless energy of the first disciples; but it is full of helpful and suggestive thoughts, and is tolerant, charitable, and courteous. And 'love covereth a multitude of sins.'

[1] See Hort and Mayor, *op. cit.* Introduction, p. lv.

CHAPTER XXVIII

THE CHARACTERISTICS OF SUB-APOSTOLIC ESCHATOLOGY

It now remains for us to gather together a few general conclusions from our review of the eschatology of the sub-apostolic Church, down to the times of Irenaeus and Clement of Alexandria. Reviewing the period as a whole, the first feature that strikes us is the slow but steady decline of the eager expectation of an immediate return of the Lord. The beginning of this movement is seen even in the New Testament,[1] and thenceforward with every fresh decade the primitive hope silently retires more and more into the background. It has never entirely disappeared, and has always remained ready to revive in times of special anxiety or trouble; but generally speaking, it has ceased to be a living power in Christendom.[2]

As the keen attention which was at first concentrated on the Second Coming began to be relaxed, the interests of the Christians began to be more diffused. So another notable feature in the sub-apostolic age is the revival of speculations with regard to what we may call the 'accessories' of eschatology, which had been for a time thrown into the shade by the splendour of Christ's Person and by the insistence of His call to repentance. These speculations, dealing with such

---
[1] *e.g.* 2 Peter iii. 4-10.
[2] See Lecky, *History of European Morals*, vol. ii. p. 203, note (1).

matters as the intermediate state and the rewards and punishments of the departed, are seen in their most unbridled extravagance in the early Christian apocalypses; but even in the more sober and systematic writers the same tendency is manifest.

Another change in eschatological teaching, which is visible especially among the more orthodox writers, may be traced to their method of deducing the doctrine of the Last Things, not (as in the apostolic teaching) mainly from the Person and work of our Lord, but rather from isolated texts gathered from all parts of the Scriptures. In Irenaeus, especially, the results of this method are very apparent.

A widely different method (but one which also modified the form of Christian eschatology) was that of the Alexandrian Fathers, for whom the final test of value was their own Reason and Conscience. It thus became a pre-eminent requisite of all doctrines that they should be 'worthy of God,' and those elements of the primitive Doctrine of the Last Things which failed (in the judgment of the Alexandrian Fathers) to satisfy this requirement, though not rejected, were allegorised without mercy until brought into conformity with the ideal set up.

The influence of foreign beliefs upon sub-apostolic eschatology is very noticeable; and it is also very natural. For the influx of Greek ideas into the East, which had followed the conquests of Alexander and his successors, had given place to a tide in the opposite direction. It was now the turn of the East to influence the West; and a movement spreading with rapidity at such a time would be specially liable to absorb foreign elements. In the apocalypses we observed unmistakable Egyptian and Zoroastrian features; but these were mainly confined to this type of literature. Far more important was the influence of Greek thought upon the recognised leaders of Christian teaching. It is true that the somewhat irregular occurrences of Greek features which we have noticed in the above pages have not lent themselves to any very clear-cut theory of a steady growth of Hellenic influence in the Church. Sometimes they have been absent where we should most have expected to find them, as in the writings of Justin Martyr. Undoubtedly, the changes in the form of eschatological teaching between A.D. 50 and A.D. 150 are not slight; but to a great extent they are simply due to the logical working out of principles involved in the earliest doctrine, or else to the innate (though not always commendable) tendencies of the human mind. Greek influence undoubtedly helped to determine the form of some of these changes; but there is no reason to suppose that without that influence no changes would have taken place. On the whole, the most far-reaching effect of Greek thought upon Christian eschatology was (as we have pointed out above) indirect rather than immediate. Partly by force of example, and partly by the assaults of hostile criticism, the Greek induced the Christian to formulate his beliefs in new and carefully-chosen language, which would have sounded strange in the ears of the first generation of Christians, but which has become part of the heritage of Catholic Christendom.

But the Christian eschatology of the first two centuries, even where most influenced by Greek thought, retains throughout this period some features which, in so far as they have not permanently survived to later ages, may fairly be called 'primitive.' Amongst these, in addition to the waning anticipation of an immediate Second Coming, there is the belief in the Millennial Reign of Christ on earth, which was very widespread

GENERAL CHARACTERISTICS 373

in many parts of Christendom. Proof-texts for this belief were found in the 20th chapter of Revelation, and it accorded well with the current legends of the coming of Anti-Christ on earth, which seem to have acquired immense popularity in many parts of the world at this time. The idea of the 'Millennium' appealed strongly to the popular mind, and indeed to all whose ideas were of a strongly realistic cast; while those who opposed it (such as Origen and some of the Gnostics) generally favoured a 'subjective' type of religion, together with a liberal use of allegory. The story of the decline of this millennial expectation or 'Chiliasm' does not fall within the period which has come under our notice. The Alexandrian Theology on the one hand, and on the other hand the Augustinian conception of the Church as the Kingdom of God on earth, alike contributed to render it less acceptable to the Christian mind.[1]

It is interesting to observe in the literature of the first two centuries how the writers were unconsciously or half-consciously preparing the way for doctrines which were not clearly formulated for a long time afterwards. The idea of Purgatory, for instance, and the closely allied practice of praying for the departed, are nowhere set forth as recognised elements of primitive Christian faith and practice.[2] Yet the thoughts of the writers are moving along lines which (humanly speaking) were sure to lead them on to more definite opinions on these matters. So in several of the apocalypses, and in Clement of Alexandria, we find an elementary but unmistakable doctrine of purgation after death, while in the Testament of Abraham the efficacy of prayer for the

[1] Robertson, *Regnum Dei*, chap. iv.
[2] See H. B. Swete on 'Prayer for the Departed,' in the *Journal of Theological Studies*, vol. viii. 'The lack of evidence,' says Dr. Swete, 'continues until past the middle of the second century' (p. 501).

dead appears to be implied. These are but the beginnings of a vast edifice of eschatological doctrine reared in later ages by the Catholic Church.

The significance of these early 'germs of doctrine,' in view of modern controversies with regard to Purgatory and Prayers for the Dead, is capable of diverse interpretations. Some will see in them the beginnings of a development of doctrine which was guided by the Divine Spirit and ratified by the voice of the Church. Others, holding that Holy Scripture contains all things necessary to salvation, and remembering the significant silence of Scripture (and of our Lord) with regard to the intermediate state and all that appertains to it, will view this 'development of doctrine' as (at best) the expression of a pious conjecture, which has no authoritative claim upon the allegiance of Christian people.

Another question which evokes much interest in our day is the possibility of repentance after death. The majority of primitive Christian writers were opposed to the idea, though there were some notable exceptions. We must remember that as long as the return of the Saviour was expected to be imminent, there was no logical place for any doctrine of the intermediate state; and until the idea of an intermediate state had become a recognised part of Christian belief, no question would arise as to the possibility of repentance while in that state. Hence the 'argument from silence' must here be used with caution.

We have had occasion to lay stress upon the changes which passed over the Christian Doctrine of the Last Things during the 'primitive' period of the Church's history. But there is another side to the picture. All through this period of growth and change, the essential features of Christian eschatology were preserved by the Church. The doctrines of a future life, a future retribu-

GENERAL CHARACTERISTICS 375

tion, a future Presence of the Lord, were still joined with the Christian summons to repentance and holiness; and where these are found, there we have the essentials of Christian eschatology. And the very influence of Gentile ideas, while changing the form of Christian teaching, also helped to make it more intelligible to the Gentile mind. In the process, not a few evil elements were introduced into the primitive Gospel; but some measure of transformation was necessary, if the Church of Christ was to fulfil her mission to 'make disciples of all the nations.' The Judaeo-Christian mould in which the apostles embodied the eschatology which they had learnt from the Lord was not suited for every age nor for every race. 'Primitive Christianity had to disappear in order that Christianity might remain.'[1]

[1] Harnack, *What is Christianity?* p. 14.

PART VI

THE EVIDENTIAL VALUE OF PRIMITIVE CHRISTIAN ESCHATOLOGY

CHAPTER XXIX

GENERAL CONCLUSIONS

Now that we have completed our survey of primitive Christian eschatology, the question arises : Are the facts, as we have interpreted them, in agreement with the historic faith of the Church ? Do they 'evince the truth and excellence of the Christian religion' ? Before we can answer this question, it is needful to define our conception of the vital truth of Christianity. If it were essential, for the maintenance of the Church's position, to prove that her doctrines have continued without change all through the centuries, or if the truth of the Christian Religion depended upon the inerrancy of every passage in Holy Scripture, then the estimate of primitive Christian eschatology which we have formed in the preceding pages would fail to support the claims of Christianity. But to-day there seems to be an ever-growing tendency to hold that 'Christianity is in essence adherence to the Person of Jesus Christ,'[1] and that here alone is the citadel the defence of which is absolutely vital for the maintenance of the Christian

[1] Foakes Jackson, in *Cambridge Theological Essays* (Cambridge, 1905), Essay xii. p. 474.

position. It is from this standpoint that the evidential value of primitive Christian eschatology will be discussed in the following pages. And if the one essential truth of Christianity lies in the Catholic doctrine of the Person of Jesus Christ, as Perfect God and Perfect Man, we would submit that the study of primitive Christian eschatology, while undoubtedly bringing to light some difficult problems, does not present any insuperable obstacles, and indeed in many respects may well strengthen our loyalty to the Church's Faith.

It will follow from what has just been said that the crucial question before us is, whether the eschatology of our Lord, as depicted in the documents at our disposal, is consistent with the belief that He who taught thus was the Incarnate Son of God.

It may be convenient at the outset to recall, in the form of a brief tabular summary, the conclusions arrived at as the result of our study of Christ's eschatology :—

A. *Our Lord's eschatology of the world.*
 1. A perfect faith in the final victory of good over evil.
 2. A general tendency (with a few notable exceptions) to support the belief that this final victory of the good will be brought about by a miracle of Divine Power, rather than by a process of natural evolution.
 3. The Person of Jesus Christ is the central Figure in the Drama of the Last Things.
 4. The contention that Christ erroneously expected and foretold that the end of the world and His own Second Coming were to take place immediately is a contention which has not been proved.

B. *Our Lord's eschatology of the individual.*
 1. The soul of man is immortal.
 2. There will be a 'resurrection of the dead.' (But the time, manner, and scope of the resurrection are not defined with precision.)

3. Every man's life will be judged by God after death, and will meet with reward or punishment according to its deserts.
4. Both the rewards and punishments are described as 'eternal.'

C. *The bearing of the history of Christ's earthly life upon His eschatology, emphasising—*
   (a) The principle 'through death to life.'
   (b) The authoritativeness of Christ's teaching, on which God set His seal of approval by the Resurrection of Christ.
   (c) The certainty of our resurrection, of which Christ's Resurrection is the first-fruits.

D. *The contrast between Christ's eschatology and that of the Jews.*
   1. Omissions :— (a) apocalyptic details; (b) national prejudices; (c) politics.
   2. Additions :—(a) the emphasis on practical morality; (b) the pre-eminent importance of the Person of Jesus Christ.

E. *Christ's eschatology and that of non-Jewish religions.*
   There is no sign that Christ adapted any non-Jewish features from ethnic beliefs.

Now it will be generally admitted that if the essential features of the eschatology of Jesus are such as we have indicated above, their superiority over all earlier systems of eschatology is unquestionable. The question yet remains whether the time has come, or is ever likely to come, when they are inadequate for the highest aspirations of humanity. Do they represent only a transient stage of human thought,—the highest yet reached, but destined one day to be superseded; or can we discern in them, beneath the limitations of human (and even Jewish) language, a spirit which is Divine, and shall never pass away? Clearly the latter alternative, and the latter only, is in accord with the Christian Doctrine of the Incarnation. It is evident that this is no easy question to answer. The utmost that we shall attempt is to indicate a few very simple reflections.

Modern objections to Christ's eschatology come from two very different quarters. On the one hand it is contended that certain features of His teaching are inconsistent with modern science; and on the other hand, that the main doctrines, such as those enumerated above, are so obvious that they are no evidence of any special wisdom or knowledge on the part of their Author. Bearing in mind this double line of argument, let us now consider briefly the evidential value of the chief points in the above summary. We come first to Christ's eschatology of the world.

The doctrine of a future 'Kingdom of God' in which all that is evil will finally give way before the good, is inevitably bound up with faith in an almighty and beneficent God. This is 'a hope which, when moralised, must necessarily be the goal of every vigorous movement in human life, and forms an inalienable element in the religious view of history.'[1] The world is not likely to grow too old to believe in the future Kingdom of God, so long as it retains any religious instinct at all.

And yet Christ's faith in the final victory of the good is not a mere truism which needs no emphasis. Many professedly religious people have no sense of the Divine purpose guiding the world, and no real confidence in the future. As they look out upon human history, they would echo the words of Shelley:—

> 'Unfathomable Sea! whose waves are years,
>   Ocean of Time, whose waters of deep woe
> Are brackish with the salt of human tears!
>   Thou shoreless flood, which in thy ebb and flow
> Claspest the limits of mortality!

[1] Harnack, *What is Christianity?* pp. 141-142.

> And sick of prey, yet howling on for more,
> Vomitest thy wrecks on its inhospitable shore;
> Treacherous in calm, and terrible in storm,
> Who shall put forth on thee,
> Unfathomable Sea?'

Such a pessimism as this, though not without a weird attractiveness, and certainly not without a consistency of its own, is in sharpest antithesis to the sublime optimism which lies at the foundation of Christ's eschatology. Place these wild and tossing words of the poet side by side with the quiet assurance manifested by our Lord on the eve of His Passion,

> 'In the world ye shall have tribulation: but be of good cheer; I have overcome the world,'

and what man of reverent mind does not feel that in the latter there is a true evidential value, not perhaps of a purely intellectual kind, but consisting rather in an appeal to our moral and spiritual faculties? And we shall do well to remember that it was by virtue of this appeal to the conscience and the heart, rather than to the intellect, that Christianity won its first and greatest victories. So long as human nature remains as we know it, Christ's doctrine of the final triumph of the good—in other words, of the future 'Kingdom of God,' or (to use Professor Burkitt's phrase) 'the good time coming'—will always be a foundation-truth of self-evident value to the human conscience.

We turn now to the second point: that the general trend of Christ's teaching implies that the final victory of the good will be brought about by a miracle of Divine Power; although there are certain of the Parables which point rather to a *gradual* conquest of the evil by the good.

The doctrine of a catastrophic consummation to the

A CATASTROPHIC CONSUMMATION 381

history of the world is undoubtedly a hard thought for many men to-day. Each year increases our knowledge of the spheres of life in which natural law is unbroken and supreme, and it becomes more and more difficult for us to conceive of a definite termination to the present order of the world. And yet—the alternative seems even more unthinkable. We cannot conceive how that which is imperfect can ever develop by a gradual evolution into that which is absolutely perfect, any more than we can obtain infinity by adding to that which is finite. Nor does Science really support a theory of perpetual upward progress. In the sphere of physical life, the astronomer tells us that he sees no reason to suppose that our own planet will always continue to exist under conditions which will allow of 'life' under any form known to us. And in the moral sphere, the theory of a gradual upward evolution does not meet with universal approbation from the leaders of Science. Listen to Professor Huxley :—

> 'I hear much of the ethics of evolution. I apprehend that in the broadest sense of the term "evolution," there neither is, nor can be, any such thing. . . . The fittest which survives in the struggle for existence may be, and often is, the ethically worst.'[1]

In face of such evidence as this, it is unreasonable to condemn our Lord's eschatology as unscientific because it does not on the whole support the idea that the Kingdom of God will be gradually evolved from the present state of things. Those who reject the doctrine of a catastrophic consummation may fairly be asked whether the facts of life will not then lead them on logically to doubt whether the Kingdom of God will ever come. On the other hand, it need cause us no

[1] *Life of Huxley*, by his son, vol. ii. p. 303.

surprise that the fact of the development of that which is good *is* clearly emphasised in parts of our Lord's teaching, even to the extent of suggesting in places that this process will eventually lead to the complete victory of the good. The factors which will determine the future of the world are so vast that our minds cannot comprehend them in one consistent whole. Even the events of the present life appear to us to be irreconcilable with one another in any single theory; and how much more the events of the unknown future! So, while recognising frankly the difficulties in our Lord's teaching on this point, we would ask whether it is possible to conceive of any doctrine of the final end of this world which would be more true to the facts of life as we know them, and at the same time maintain so steadfast a faith in the ultimate victory of the good-will of God. Failing such an alternative, we can surely maintain that the Gospel records of our Lord's teaching on this point confirm our faith in Him as the Son of God.

Of the centrality of the Person of Christ in His own teaching concerning the end of the world it is needless to say much. Its evidential value consists in this: that it drives us to one of two alternatives.—Either our Lord's estimate of Himself was true, in which case this feature of His eschatology agrees completely with the Catholic doctrine of His Person; or else He was guilty of the most amazing and unwarranted presumption;—a conclusion which ill accords with the general impression of His humility and restrained dignity. We have already discussed the objection that our Lord expected that His return in glory would take place at once, and we concluded that this objection is not warranted by the evidence at our disposal.[1]

---

[1] See above, pp. 177-182, 186.

We can now pass on to consider the evidential value of our Lord's eschatology of the individual. In this, the fundamental doctrine is that of the immortality of the human soul. This is a great doctrine which is inseparable from the belief in a God of justice —to say nothing of a Heavenly Father. For it is only too evident that within the span of this life each man does not receive his due share of rewards or punishments. The ungodly flourishes to the end of his days like a green bay-tree, and the righteous man goes down to the grave in sorrow and suffering. For most of us it would be impossible to retain faith in God apart from a belief in the immortality of the human soul and a life beyond the grave, when God 'shall reward every man according to his deeds.'

The Christian doctrine of the resurrection of the dead has often been the object of much hostile criticism, and it must frankly be confessed that this criticism has been at times almost justified, owing to the gross and materialistic form in which the doctrine has been presented by Christian apologists. But if we follow the example of the New Testament, affirming the fact of the resurrection without hesitation, but refraining from idle speculations upon the manner of its occurrence, the greater part of current objections will be seen to be groundless. The essence of the doctrine of the resurrection is to maintain that the future life will be more than a bodiless, phantom-like existence; and surely (as we tried to point out in connection with St. Paul's eschatology) the idea of being 'clothed upon with immortality' is far nobler than that of being merely stripped of our present material 'prison-house of the soul.' Except where men hold the Gnostic theory that matter is inherently evil, the human mind will always find in the doctrine of the resurrection of the dead a response to and an agreement with its own highest aspirations for the future.

The doctrine of the Last Judgment is a feature of eschatology which is generally accepted in our day by all who believe in a God. 'The instinct of mankind is in conformity with the teaching of Holy Scripture, that we shall be judged for the things done in the body, whether good or bad.'[1] As long as the sense of sin remains in the human heart, so long will there be the expectation of the Last Judgment, and of retribution in the world to come. And certainly there is no other eschatological belief which exercises so real and practical an influence upon human conduct in this life, restraining from wrongdoing, and impelling to active beneficence. It is true that this influence derives its power from feelings which may be described as selfish—the fear of punishment and the desire for reward in the future life; and hence it is sometimes urged that it is not wholly to be commended.[2] Now it is true that if the Christian Doctrine of the Last Judgment simply focussed each man's attention on himself and his own destiny, it would indeed become a purely selfish motive, and deleterious to the character of the believer. But, in fact, the doctrine has its social as well as its individual aspect: it impels men to take a keen interest in the future destiny of others, as well as of themselves. Never has the belief in the Last Judgment been more intense than in the primitive Church; but were the primitive Christians selfish men? Their contemporaries, at least, did not think so. The influence which a doctrine of retribution exercises *need* not necessarily be a selfish one; whether it actually is so or not in any particular case will depend upon the spirit

---

[1] Pusey, *What is of Faith as to Everlasting Punishment* (Oxford, 1880), p. 17.
[2] Readers of Lecky's *History of European Morals* will remember how incessantly this is brought forward as proof of an unworthy element in primitive Christian teaching.

THE DOCTRINE OF RETRIBUTION 385

in which it is preached and received. The naturally self-centred man instinctively applies the thoughts suggested by it first and foremost to himself; and to him it is a selfish motive. But if preached and received in the spirit of true Christian love, the thought of coming Judgment will inspire the most disinterested self-sacrifice, which will strive at all costs to save the souls of others from the wrath to come, and to guide them into the strait and narrow path that leadeth to eternal life. Not that the prospect of personal weal or woe in the future will be forgotten, or cease to be a powerful motive; but it will no longer be exaggerated into undue importance, or interfere with the sympathy and love which each man owes to his fellow-men. And it is only in the latter case that the desire for personal happiness becomes 'selfishness' in an evil sense. The commandment, 'Thou shalt love thy neighbour *as thyself*,' surely indicates that there is a right kind of self-love which is not to be eradicated, but only restrained from gaining an inordinate prominence. And there is no reason to stigmatise the doctrine of future retribution as pandering to selfish motives because it includes (but does not necessarily emphasise) the appeal to each man's desire for his own future welfare. So long as it is taught in accordance with the general spirit of Christ's Gospel, this great Christian doctrine of retribution or of the Judgment is seen, both in its results, and also in the method of its appeal to human nature, to be a motive of genuine unselfishness; and worthy of a religion which claims to be of final and Divine authority.

We pass naturally from the doctrine of retribution to the problem of eternal punishment, which has probably aroused more antagonism than any other feature of Christian eschatology. We have already had

2 c

occasion to refer to some of the objections, and have suggested that the alternatives generally raise greater difficulties than those they were designed to obviate.[1] From the point of view of the Christian apologist, this is the utmost that can be expected in dealing with so vast a theme. We do not deny the difficulties of the Christian view; but if all other alternatives appear to be beset with equal or greater difficulties, there is no ground here for rejecting Christ's teaching as unworthy of His Divinity.

It may be well here to add one or two considerations to those already put forward in the earlier sections of this essay with regard to this difficult question.

1. If the word "αἰώνιος" denotes intensity rather than unending duration of time, then the doctrine of 'eternal punishment' and 'eternal life' introduces no new idea different in essence from the doctrine of retribution beyond the grave. It is then seen to be simply an affirmation of the intensity of that retribution —whether it take the form of punishment or reward.

2. It is often said that it would be unjust to punish a finite sin by an infinite punishment. But is it not somewhat rash to assume that all sins *are* finite? May not the "ἁμάρτημα αἰώνιον," of which our Lord speaks in St. Mark iii. 28, be truly deserving of the "κόλασις αἰώνιος"? Sin is always primarily an act of the will; and in the human will there is always a mysterious, if not an 'infinite' significance.

3. The problem of the final destiny of man is inextricably bound up with the relation between the human will and the Divine purpose, which in our present state of knowledge is an insoluble difficulty. So we find that our logic leads us to different conclusions according to the different premises from which we start.

[1] Pp. 187-189 and 224.

On the one hand, we cannot conceive of the life beyond the grave without some measure of human free-will; for a life without free-will would cease to be a *human* life. But where there is free-will, there is the possibility of continuance in sin. And where there is continuance in sin, the law of justice demands that there shall be also a continuance of the punishment. Hence it seems that eternal punishment must be an eternal possibility; and we have no right to deny that it may be an eternal fact. On the other hand, we may take our stand, as it were, upon the fact of God's Almighty Love, and deduce from this the certainty of the complete victory of Love in the end; so that with St. Paul we look forward to the goal of Time when 'God shall be all in all.'[1]

We conclude then that our Lord's doctrine of the final destiny of man, while (from the nature of the case) not demonstrable by human reason alone, is certainly not to be disproved by any method of argument except such as would equally disprove all other conceivable alternatives. And on the practical side, Christ's teaching on this point is, as we have already noticed, singularly well adapted to inculcate the deep significance of character and conduct in this world, and effectually to dispose of all those pretexts which the ingenuity of human nature loves to invent in order to evade the call to repentance.

The evidential value of Christ's eschatology is never so clearly seen as when we compare it with contemporary Jewish teaching. It is obvious that the absence of national prejudices and temporary political schemes in our Lord's doctrine is entirely favourable to the claim that that doctrine is suited for all time. And the same may be said of our Lord's restraint in the matter of

[1] See the quotation from Westcott's *Historic Faith*, above, p. 281.

detailed revelations of the future. This undoubtedly causes some disappointment to the curious, and the modern controversialist has to be content with a very scanty armoury of proof-texts. For the controversies which generally rouse the most vehement feelings, concerning prayers for the dead, the intermediate state, the manner of the resurrection, or the date of the Second Coming, are not to be conclusively settled by an appeal to the recorded words of Christ; for they seem to lie outside the scope of His teaching. Yet is not this very restraint with reference to details, and the consequent concentration upon fundamental principles, a striking proof of Christ's unique wisdom—a wisdom which both knows what is vital, and also knows the limitations of the human mind, which cannot altogether comprehend the things of the invisible world?

We spoke of Christ's 'concentration upon fundamental principles.' Most of these have been already referred to; but one is so essential, and at the same time so sharply opposed to a good deal of modern thought, that it seems well to emphasise it again, in concluding this estimate of the evidential value of Christ's eschatology. This is, the clear recognition of the reality of human free-will, especially in the moral sphere, which is implied in His doctrine of retribution. Man's choice of right or wrong here will be a factor modifying the course of events in the world to come. In this, Christ stands in irreconcilable opposition to the fatalism which sees in the past, present, and future nothing but the march of relentless Fate :—

> 'The Moving Finger writes; and, having writ,
> Moves on: nor all your Piety nor Wit
>   Shall lure it back to cancel half a Line,
>   Nor all your Tears wash out a Word of it.

> With Earth's first Clay They did the Last Man knead,
> And there of the Last Harvest sow'd the Seed:
> And the first Morning of Creation wrote
> What the last Dawn of Reckoning shall read.'

Were this true, moral effort would be powerless to influence the future; indeed, the sense of having any power to choose would be a phantom and a delusion. But Christ's teaching assumes throughout that we have a real power of choice, and that in the moral sphere the results of our choice will be seen, not only in Time, but also in Eternity. Place this conception of human life alongside of that of the Determinist, and can we doubt which is the more worthy to be the Religion of the Future?

The thoughts which have been briefly outlined above are very inadequate for so great a theme; but they may suffice to indicate some of the ways in which the study of Christ's eschatology serves to confirm our faith in Him as the Incarnate Son of God. True, we meet with difficulties, neither few nor small; but that is only what we must expect when we are dealing with things beyond the veil.

> 'It is not yet made manifest what we shall be.'

But we can understand enough of His teaching to gain from it help and encouragement. In no respect does it come short of our highest ideals; nay rather, it satisfies the deepest longings of our humanity. In it we find a blending of grandeur and simplicity that is without parallel in history, and which would be indeed inexplicable if it had sprung from one who was only a Galilean peasant; but it is in complete accord with the belief that Jesus of Nazareth was One 'Who for us men, and for our salvation, came down from heaven, and was made man.'

Before we finally leave this question of the evidential value of Christ's eschatology, a few words must be added with regard to the bearing of the 'Eschatological Theory' upon the truth of Christianity. It has been abundantly clear that Schweitzer has raised many problems of fascinating interest to the student of history and literature. But the issues at stake are not merely interesting, but of grave practical importance.

If the 'consistent Eschatological Theory' could be substantiated, it would seriously undermine the foundations of historic Christianity. A Christ whose whole sympathies are in the other world and who cares nothing even for the morality of this life, is hardly likely to save mankind from their sins. A Christ who saw nothing in Jewish eschatology that needed to be ennobled or purified does not command even the unqualified respect of thoughtful men; far less could He claim the worship of the world as the perfect image of the Father. Indeed, Schweitzer himself recognises this when he says that the discovery of the true character of Jesus would be a hindrance to true Religion.[1] It is not only that the Eschatological Christ is a 'Stranger' (*Fremdling*) to modern ideas—for even in the traditional conception of the Person of Christ there is no lack of that which is strange and extraordinary; but the strangeness of Schweitzer's Christ is not a strangeness which impresses us as something majestic and mysterious; rather does it perplex us as something alien from our sympathies, because lacking in many of those qualities—especially the moral qualities—which are nearest to our hearts. Above all, the gravity of the Eschatological Theory lies in the tacit assumption, which pervades all Schweitzer's arguments, that all the

[1] Schweitzer, *Von Reimarus zu Wrede*, p. 399: 'Die historische Erkenntniss des Wesens und des Lebens Jesu der Welt nicht eine Förderung, sondern vielleicht ein Ärgernis zur Religion sein wird.'

THE ESCHATOLOGICAL THEORY 391

unique and non-Jewish elements in the teaching of Jesus are to be discarded as not genuine. If Jesus was simply a Jew and nothing more, it is inconceivable that He should be the permanent Centre of the Absolute Religion for all mankind.

But if the conclusions reached in the above pages are true, then, while accepting in part the positive elements of the Eschatological Theory, as a valuable help towards understanding the historical background of our Lord's Life, we are justified in rejecting absolutely the negative aspect of the Theory, and we may unreservedly accept the teaching of Jesus of Nazareth as the very Word of God.[1]

[1] Since this essay was first written, another practical aspect of the 'Eschatological Controversy' has been brought before the English public in Tyrell's *Christianity at the Cross-Roads.* Tyrell, writing as one who is in sympathy with the 'Consistent Eschatologists,' points out that if the 'Kingdom of God' as preached by Jesus was so 'other worldly' that even moral distinctions have no place there, then 'the morality of Jesus was not the substance of His revelation' (p. 189). Now the bearing of such a conclusion upon the theological controversies of our day is exceedingly significant, as Tyrell with characteristic insight has perceived; and it seems likely to mark a line of cleavage between two essentially different conceptions of Christianity, the eschatological and non-eschatological, or (to use Tyrell's terms) the Liberal Catholic and the Liberal Protestant. The former, feeling free to let the moral element in Christianity slip into the background, is ready to accept a theory of the Church, her ministry, and sacraments, in which there is only a secondary emphasis on the *moral* conditions of salvation,—a theory which his opponents will denounce as 'magical' and 'superstitious' (see Tyrell, *op. cit.* pp. 72, 88), but which he will maintain to be truly according to the mind of Christ, as revealed by eschatological criticism of the New Testament. On the other hand, the type of Christianity of which Liberal Protestantism is the clearest modern expression, holding that our Lord's moral teaching is of the very essence of His Gospel, refuses to recognise any religious value in doctrines or ceremonies in which no moral element is apparent.—

> 'A religion without morality,' says a well-known English exponent of this type of thought, 'soon becomes an immoral religion; the religious emotions and sanctions, deprived of ethical quality and control, become the most debased and pernicious forces that can act upon the spirit of man' (Fairbairn, *Studies in Religion and Theology,* p. 38).

It is evident that the cleavage between these two types of thought is a very deep one; and if Tyrell's analysis of the 'Problem of Eschatology' be correct, no controversy of modern times is fraught with greater significance for the future of the Christian Church.

We have spent some time in trying to show that our Lord's Doctrine of the Last Things not only is consistent with, but also lends real support to, the Christian Doctrine of His Person; and if once this conclusion is established, other questions are of secondary and less vital importance, for they cannot touch the Citadel of our Faith. But it may perhaps be said that, even granting that no flaw can be found in our Lord's own teaching, at least the study of primitive Christian eschatology lends no support to any belief in the Divine mission of the Church. We may be told that the earliest apostolic teaching was crude and unsound; that its essential doctrines have been disproved by experience, and that its form has been preserved only through the accidental infusion of a foreign element into the Church.

Now it may be readily admitted that the primitive period of the Church's life was not the golden age which we sometimes fondly imagine :—

> '. . . The past will always win
> A glory from its being far;
> And orb into the perfect star
> We saw not, when we moved therein.'

But after the halo of unreal glory round the primitive Church has been dispersed, there remains much which confirms our estimate of the uniqueness of Christ. The eschatological expectation produced by His teaching was peculiarly intense, and it helped to form a moral standard among the early Christians which has rarely, if ever, been equalled before or since. But the expectation of an impending crisis does not always spur men on to active well-doing; for instance, it is a well-known fact that in the closing years of the tenth century of our era, a similar expectation paralysed all healthy effort. If we would rightly estimate the value of primitive Christian eschatology, we must take account of its effect upon primitive Christian life and conduct. For it was not our Lord's purpose to endue His followers with abnormal intellectual powers, but to reveal to them the Father's will. It is no serious disparagement of the eschatology of the early Christians to say that not one of them—not even St. Paul or St. John—fully understood their Lord's teaching; while it is a very strong proof of the value of their beliefs concerning the future to find that they were inspired thereby to walk in the footsteps of the Master. Nor need our estimate of the value of primitive Christian eschatology be disturbed by the consideration that it was soon influenced, and in part transformed, by the influx of Gentile ideas. If Christ came, 'not to destroy but to fulfil,' His followers need not be ashamed to acknowledge their indebtedness to whatever is good in the religions of the world.

In the history of Christian eschatology during the period which has come under our notice, there have been two processes visibly at work—rightful development and interpretation on the one hand, and, on the other hand, degeneration and corruption. Those who would fain believe that the Church has always been the infallible Teacher of Truth will naturally tend to minimise the latter feature; while those who regard pre-Reformation Church History as one long record of apostasy will be inclined to dispute the lawfulness of any development of doctrine.

Most persons, however, will admit that in the sphere of eschatology the apostolic writers, at any rate, contributed to Christian thought not a few ideas of real and permanent value. St. Paul's masterly vindication of the doctrine of the resurrection; St. John's lofty conception of 'salvation' and 'eternal life,' and the noble Christology of the Epistle to the Hebrews—to name but three instances—all represent a genuine development of doctrine in accordance with the principles of Christ's own teaching. In face of these and other instances, it needs no argument to prove that primitive Christian eschatology, as represented in the New Testament, possesses a real value of its own, and affords eloquent witness to the guidance of the Holy Spirit in the early Church.

When we pass beyond the New Testament, it must be admitted that valuable contributions to eschatological thought become very rare. With the possible exception of certain ideas characteristic of the Alexandrian Fathers (such as Clement's conception of a Divine purpose working itself out through the world's history), it would be hard to find any sub-apostolic writer who really throws fresh light upon the fundamental ideas of the Christian Doctrine of the Last Things. New features there are, it is true; but for the most part these now possess only an antiquarian interest; they do not mark any real advance in the history of human thought. Yet the very fact that the sub-apostolic age is so comparatively commonplace is itself a striking witness to the uniqueness of Jesus Christ. For this stands out no whit less strongly when compared with His followers than when compared with the generations of old time. At each new crisis in the Church's history, men have been raised up to interpret Christ's doctrine anew; but the good features which they have added were contained in the great principles of life and conduct laid down by our Lord Himself.

Mediocrity, however, is not the greatest failing in the eschatology of the primitive Church. Our study has shown us that in almost every quarter there was a marked degeneration in progress. The supremacy of righteousness as the essential condition of admittance to the Kingdom of Heaven was being tacitly challenged by the growing belief that the correct performance of rites and ceremonies were at least an acceptable substitute, if not actually of predominant importance. The bold outlines of Christ's teaching were being obscured in some quarters by the revival of Jewish methods and detailed 'revelations' of the future, so that men's interests were diverted from the call to repentance away to profitless speculations and unhealthy fancies. In other quarters, a precise scholarship was seeking to formulate an accurate system of eschatological dogma by means of catenae of proof-texts, oblivious of the fact that such methods often disregarded and sometimes violated the spirit and the principles which animated the words quoted, when viewed in their original contexts. It is all rather disheartening; and yet did not Christ foretell that His Kingdom on earth would contain tares as well as wheat, and that its net would gather in of all kinds, bad as well as good? And while we do not scruple to point out the bad and condemn it, let not this blind our eyes to the many signs, even in the eschatology of sub-apostolic times, that the Spirit of Christ was still working in the hearts of His servants.[1]

And surely we may trace the signs of Divine guidance too in the method by which the outward form of primitive Christian eschatology was transformed by the infusion of Gentile methods of thought.—

'The intuitions of Revelation, to be presented to the universal consciousness, must needs be recast in the form of thought which nearest approaches universality. And the world has yet to devise an instrument better fitted

[1] See above, p. 317, note on the *Odes of Solomon*.

to achieve this lofty task than the language of Greek philosophy.'[1]

Viewed in this light, a process which has been sometimes denounced as a corruption of the primitive Gospel is seen rather to be a signal instance of God's Providence for His Church.

Thus in the eschatology of the primitive Church we find nothing to cause us to abandon our former estimate of the eschatology of our Lord. The mingled elements of good and evil in the Church were foreshadowed in His own parables. The good is a true echo of His Spirit; the evil serves to throw into stronger relief His unsullied perfection. And as we look back upon the period as a whole, we can trace here and there signs of the Divine plan by which the peculiar beliefs of a few Galilean fishermen became the accredited creed of the civilised world.

It may not be out of place to conclude with two thoughts which are brought prominently before the mind of any one who studies primitive Christian eschatology, and which have a practical bearing upon the preaching of the Doctrine of the Last Things to the present generation.

The first is this: that a doctrine need not be any the less pure or noble because it is proclaimed under the form of some simple picture or image. Our Lord set us the example of presenting His eschatological teaching in the form of vivid and intelligible pictures; and the earliest apostles followed in His steps. To-day we are sometimes tempted to seek out the abstract doctrine underlying the imagery, and to isolate the former as if it were the one thing needful. That was

[1] Cruttwell, *A Literary History of Early Christianity* (London, 1893), Introduction, p. ix.

not the method of Christ; He knew that abstract doctrines can appeal only to the few; and His mission was to the many. It is for us to beware lest in our zeal to discover the inner meaning of the Doctrine of the Last Things, we should undermine the foundations of another's faith.

> ' O thou that after toil and storm
>   Mayst seem to have reach'd a purer air,
>   Whose faith has centre everywhere,
> Nor cares to fix itself to form,
>
> ' Leave thou thy sister when she prays,
>   Her early Heaven, her happy views;
>   Nor thou with shadow'd hint confuse
> A life that leads melodious days.
>
> ' Her faith thro' form is pure as thine,
>   Her hands are quicker unto good:
>   Oh, sacred be the flesh and blood
> To which she links a truth divine!'

The warning is not needless. It may be true that Christian eschatology does not now play the part it ought to play in the Christian life. If so, we shall not find the remedy by stripping off the traditional form of teaching till the abstract doctrine lies bare before us; but rather, by interpreting the old parables of the Last Things with new freshness and inspiration to meet the needs of our own age.

The other lesson which is impressed upon all who study primitive Christian eschatology is this: that the Doctrine of the Last Things must never be severed from the call to a holy life in this present world. In the earliest days of the Church, the two were indissolubly joined together; but this union has not always been maintained. A recent writer[1] has said that when Oriental mysticism spread westward, 'the

---
[1] Frazer, *Adonis, Attis, and Osiris*, p. 252.

centre of gravity, so to say, was shifted from the present to a future life; and however much the other world may have gained, there can be little doubt that this one lost heavily by the change.' The sarcasm is not altogether unmerited; nor does our own age stand beyond all criticism in this matter. The profession of belief in a future life seems often to be entirely disconnected from any corresponding moral conduct in this world, while a dilettante craving to know more about the conditions of the life beyond the grave is widely prevalent, and is often commended as the sign of a lively interest in matters religious. But this aimless curiosity is the very antithesis of the spirit of Christ's eschatology. Again and again, when He finds such thoughts in the minds of His disciples, He tries to recall them to the practical bearing of the subject. To the question, 'Are they few that be saved?' He replies: 'Strive ye to enter in by the narrow door.' And when the disciples, startled at His predictions of coming troubles, are insistent with the request, 'Tell us, when shall these things be?' He does not promptly gratify their curiosity, but sums up a long and enigmatic answer in the clear practical command: 'What I say unto you, I say unto all; Watch.'

We cannot doubt that He would speak according to the same tenor to His disciples in these latter days. If we would be loyal to His teaching, we shall not allow the bright prospect of His Second Coming to blind our eyes to the reality of His presence with us all the days; nor shall we strain our ears so eagerly to catch the sound of the archangel's trump, that we fail to hear the call which comes to us day by day on earth: 'Follow thou Me.'

THE END

APPENDICES

ON THE ESCHATOLOGY OF THE RELIGIONS OF BABYLONIA, EGYPT, AND PERSIA

APPENDIX A

BABYLONIAN ESCHATOLOGY

AUTHORITIES

1. Jeremias, *Babylonian Conception of Heaven and Hell* (Ancient East Series, English translation, London, 1902).
2. Maspero, *Dawn of Civilisation* (English translation, S.P.C.K., 4th edition, London, 1901).
3. The chapters on Babylonian religion in Charles's *Critical History of the Doctrine of a Future Life in Judaism*, and in Salmond's *Christian Doctrine of Immortality*; and Jastrow's article on 'Babylonian Religion,' in Hastings' *Dictionary of the Bible*, extra vol. pp. 531 ff.

THE official priestly religion of Babylonia was concerned mainly with the present, not with the future; so that Babylonian eschatology was largely the product of popular fancy. Throughout the beliefs of the Babylonians, which were cheerless in the extreme, there is a strong under-current of animistic ideas. They were afraid of the spirits of the dead, and endeavoured to propitiate them by means of necromancy.[1] Death was an inevitable and gloomy fate, bringing to an end all human happiness. The dead descended into the pit of Arâlu,[2] and lived on there in unending shadow and gloom. In the 'Epic Poem' describing the descent of Gilgamesh into the under-world, the hero asks:—

'"Tell me, O my friend, what the under-world is like."—" If I should tell thee," comes the answer, "thou wouldst sit down and weep. ... That wherein the heart on earth has rejoiced, that below is turned to dust."'[3]

---

[1] Maspero, *op. cit.* p. 684.
[2] Sometimes called 'Shualu'; whence the Hebrew 'Sheol.' See Charles, *op. cit.* p. 33.
[3] Jeremias, *op. cit.* p. 21.

And in the same poem Arâlu is thus described:—

> 'The house whence those who enter return not,
> The path which leads forth, but not back again,
> The house, wherein he who enters is deprived of light,
> The place where dust is their food, and clay their nourishment;
> Where they are clad in garments of wings as birds,
> Dust lies thick on door and bolt.'[1]

The abode of the dead was under the rule of separate gods, who were ill-disposed towards mankind, but might be pacified by magical charms.[2] We do indeed find references to 'the Isles of the Blessed,'[3] but these were the abode only of a select few, such as heroic warriors and the special favourites of the gods. 'The mass of humanity,' says Maspero,[4] 'had no pretensions to mount so high.'

It is evident that these fundamental ideas of Babylonian religion were similar to those of the Hebrews in pre-prophetic times, so far as the scanty evidence enables us to judge. But while the religion of the mother-people slowly decayed, because it was never closely united with moral teaching, the beliefs of Israel were purified and ennobled under the inspiration of the Spirit of God. The influence of Babylonian mythology was doubtless far-reaching and persistent; and it is quite likely that some of the features of later Jewish and Christian eschatology may have been handed down from the religion of Babylon through the folk-lore of the common people. Bousset considers that the Anti-Christ legend may be traced back in this way to the Dragon-myth of the Babylonians.[5] But if so, it is the *form* alone which has come down to us: the *ideas* of Babylonian eschatology had ceased to be a living power long before the Christian Era.

[1] Jeremias, *op. cit.* p. 18.
[2] Jeremias, pp. 23 ff.
[3] Jeremias, p. 39.
[4] Maspero, *op. cit.* p. 700A.
[5] Bousset, *The Antichrist Legend* (English translation, London, 1896), p. 144, etc.

APPENDIX B

EGYPTIAN ESCHATOLOGY

AUTHORITIES

1. Erman, *Handbook of Egyptian Religion* (English translation, London, 1907).
2. Wiedemann, *Realms of the Egyptian Dead* (Ancient East Series, English translation, London, 1902).
3. The chapters on Osiris in Frazer's *Adonis, Attis, and Osiris* (London, 1907 edition).

THE religion of the Egyptians presents exceptional difficulties to the student, because it contains so many different elements, and no attempt was made to reconcile these various elements with one another.

'A strange curse,' says Erman,[1] 'lay on the Egyptians; they could not forget. . . . Every fresh epoch of their long existence brought them new ideas, but the old ideas did not disappear in consequence. . . . In this way, the confusion of ideas, national and local, increased with every successive period.'

The old ideas of animism and ancestor-worship may frequently be discovered, although partly concealed by the elaborate structure of later mythology.[2] The earliest Egyptian gods were personifications of the powers of nature, and as early as the Old Kingdom (fourth and third millenniums B.C.) various nature-myths were current, of which the most important was the myth of Osiris.[3] Whether this was originally connected with the cult of the sun-god or of the corn-god is

---

[1] Erman, *op. cit.* p. 3.
[2] For various views of dates in Egyptian history, see Hastings' *Dictionary of the Bible*, art. 'Egyptian Religion,' extra vol. p. 196.
[3] Erman, *op. cit.* pp. 6-21, 35.

a matter of dispute.¹ The theme in either case would be the same :—life, death, and resurrection. The resurrection of Osiris from death was regarded as a pledge of the resurrection of all the faithful dead who are spiritually united with him :—

> 'Even as Osiris lives, he will live;
> Even as Osiris is not dead, he also will not die;
> Even as Osiris is not destroyed, he also will not be destroyed.'²

The moral element was supplied in later times by a judgment-scene, 'inserted bodily to fill up a mental hiatus,'³ where Osiris decides on the fate of each soul, in accordance with its life here on earth.⁴

Generally, the bodily life on this earth is regarded as the ideal one: the happiest lot which the blessed dead can desire is to 'do everything they did on earth.'⁵ Herodotus's account of the Egyptian doctrine of transmigration may perhaps be traced to the desire of the Egyptians that their spirits after death might be privileged to return to this earth, even in the bodies of animals.⁶ The next world was to be but a miserable half-life; and some of the Egyptians frankly avowed the principle of hedonism: 'Let us eat and drink, for to-morrow we die.'⁷

Another group of doctrines dealt with the nature of man, which was regarded as highly composite. Of special interest is the idea of the 'Ka' or 'second self,' which may have influenced the late Hebrew doctrine of 'guardian angels.'⁸ Probably the 'Ka' was originally associated with the 'Life' which leaves a man at death. Besides the 'Ka,' the Egyptians distinguished the 'Bâ' (soul), the 'Name,' and the 'Khou' of a man.⁹

The influence of the Egyptians upon Hebrew eschatology during the sojourn in Egypt before the Exodus appears, as

---

¹ See Frazer, *op. cit.* pp. 32-38, and p. 345; cf. Wiedemann, *op. cit.* pp. 34-37.
² Erman, *op. cit.* p. 95.
³ Wiedemann, *op. cit.* p. 27.
⁴ Maspero, *Dawn of Civilisation* (London, 1901), pp. 187 ff.
⁵ Erman, *op. cit.* p. 106.
⁶ See Erman, *op. cit.* pp. 86, 191.
⁷ See Wiedemann, *op. cit.* p. 28.
⁸ But see also Appendix C for Zoroastrian parallels with this doctrine.
⁹ See Wiedemann, *op. cit.* pp. 56 ff.

we have seen,¹ to have been remarkably slight. Traces of Egyptian cults in Palestine, dating probably from the twelfth century B.C., have been found here and there, but there is no sign that Egyptian influence during the Jewish monarchy was at all widespread. During this period, Egyptian religion was corrupt and lifeless; but in the eighth century B.C. there was a great revival of the old forms of worship, which were performed with even exaggerated zeal. Still, even this revival left little or no traces of its existence upon the religion of Israel. But later on, under Alexander and the Ptolemies, the Greeks did begin to assimilate the forms, if not the ideas, of Egyptian religion; and the Jews of the Dispersion were continually subject to the influence of a mingled Egyptian and Greek religion.² For instance, in the later Jewish apocalyptic descriptions of the Judgment, we find several features which seem to be distinctively Egyptian, such as the weighing of souls in the balances of truth, and the presence of recording angels.³

Even after the Christian Era, Egyptian influence continued. The Alexandrian Church was especially liable to be affected, owing to its spirit of tolerance and eclecticism. Egyptian gods are found mingled with images of the 'Good Shepherd,' and Christian phraseology occurs on the coffins of the mummies. Nor was the Alexandrian Church entirely free from the practice of Egyptian magic.⁴

But the Egyptian religion after the Christian Era had degenerated into a foolish zoolatry and practice of enchantments; and it gradually died away. 'It was among quacks and thieves that the ancient gods of Egypt found a final place of refuge.⁵

¹ See above, pp. 13, 14.
² Erman, *op. cit.* pp. 196-217.
³ See Eth. En. xli. 1, and above, pp. 329-331, on *Testament of Abraham.*
⁴ Erman, *op cit.* pp. 220-234.
⁵ Erman, *op. cit.* p. 238.

APPENDIX C

ZOROASTRIAN ESCHATOLOGY

AUTHORITIES

1. Darmesteter, *Le Zend-Avesta* (Paris, 1892).
2. Maspero, *Passing of the Empires* (English translation, S.P.C.K., 1900).
3. Mme. Ragozin, *Media* (London, 1889).
4. Cheyne, *Origin of the Psalter* (London, 1891).
5. Moulton, in Hastings' *Dictionary of the Bible*, art. 'Zoroastrianism (vol. iv. pp. 988 ff.).

THREE leading characteristics of Zoroastrianism are, its dualism, its morality, and its spirituality. It is not easy to determine how far Zoroastrian doctrines had developed when the Jews first came into contact with the Persian Empire. The books known as the 'Gathas' seem to be regarded on all hands as pre-Exilic, and probably the later writings contain much that existed previously in the form of tradition.

The idea of the perpetual conflict between good and evil is perhaps the best-known feature of Zoroastrianism. It is tempting to see the influence of this dualism in Ezekiel's picture of the last great struggle of Gog and Magog against Israel and Israel's God,[1] and in the apocalyptic visions of the Messianic Woes.

The moral character of Zoroastrian religion is nowhere more marked than in its eschatology. Even in the early books,[2] the world beyond the grave is a world of rewards and punishments on a moral basis, in sharp contrast to the colourless pit of Babylonian and early Hebrew eschatology. The earliest Mazdean teaching also looked forward to the final perfection

---

[1] Ezek. 38, 39.
[2] *e.g.* Yasna 33 ; see Ragozin, *op. cit.* p. 102.

ZOROASTRIAN ESCHATOLOGY 407

of the faithful,[1] and to a future kingdom of Ahura-Mazda;[2] this at once suggests the doctrines of the Hebrew prophets.

The Persians also laid much stress on the intermediate state, between death and judgment. For three days the soul hovers near the corpse, and then crosses the bridge Cinvat to be judged. After this judgment, the wicked go north to their own place, and the blessed ascend to Paradise. The good soul is conducted on its wanderings by a good spirit in the form of a beautiful maiden; the souls of the wicked are driven along by evil demons.[3] There is a striking parallel to this in the Jewish 'Testaments of the Twelve Patriarchs' (Asher 6), quoted above, p. 76. In Persian eschatology, the souls do not attain to their final destiny until the resurrection of the body;[4] but from the moment of death, the law of retribution begins to work.

The spiritualising tendencies of Zoroastrianism are visible in the elaborate doctrines of angels and spirits. In later times, the doctrine of 'Fravashis' or spiritual counterparts of men, came very much to the fore, and a similar doctrine of the 'guardian angels' of nations and churches, and even of gods. Though the 'Fravashis' are not mentioned in the 'Gathas,' it would seem as if they must be descended from ancestor-worship.

Yet another group of Zoroastrian doctrines gathered round the idea of 'Saoshyant.' In the Gathas, 'Saoshyant' is practically equivalent to the faithful people; but later on the term is used for an individual Messiah,[5] the prophet of Ahura-Mazda, who overthrows Ahriman, raises the dead, renews the earth, and prepares for a new Kingdom of righteousness. The parallels with Jewish Messianic doctrine and the renewal of the whole earth are here very striking. In the late books of the Bundehish, we find mention of the millennial reigns of the prophets who are to precede Saoshyant.[6]

If Zoroastrianism influenced Christian eschatology to an

---

[1] Ragozin, *op. cit.* p. 103.
[2] Cheyne, *op. cit.* p. 398 (quoted from Yasna 41).
[3] Darmesteter, *op. cit.* pp. 269 ff., 651 ff.
[4] Maspero, *op. cit.* p. 589.
[5] Cf. especially the history of the phrase 'Son of Man,' Chapters VIII. and XV. above.   [6] Cheyne, *op. cit.* pp. 438-439.

appreciable extent, it was mainly through the medium of Judaism. But some traces of Persian ideas may well have reached the Christian Church through the School of Alexandria, which was ever ready to adopt the good features of foreign religions.

Perhaps it is hardly safe for those who are not experts to go beyond the exceedingly cautious statement of Dr. Moulton: 'We shall probably do well to allow Persian influence in eschatology only some weight in stimulating what was none the less a native growth in Judaism.'[1]

[1] Hastings' *Dictionary of the Bible*, vol. iv. p. 993.

END OF APPENDICES

INDEX

Abel, to be Judge at the Last Day, 330
'Abomination of Desolation,' 59, 173
Abraham, eschatology of, 12
Abraham, Testament of, 329 f.
'Abraham's Bosom,' 184
Absence of eschatology :—
   in the Mosaic Code, 14
   in Christ's post-Resurrection teaching, 200 ff., 233
Acts, eschatology in the Book of, 233-243
Advents of Christ, 'the First' and 'the Second,' 354 f. ; 341
Alexandria, School of, 363-369 ; 100, 107, 334, 394
Allegorical exegesis in the early Church, 320, 365 f., 369
Amos, 27-30, 33, 36-38
Ancestor-worship, 8-12, 14 f., 403
Angels :—
   doctrine of, 43, 79, 92 f., 332, 349, 407
   guardian, 79, 349, 407
   souls in heaven compared to, 92, 193 f.
Animism, 8-12, 14 f., 401, 403
Annihilation after death, 15, 78, 323
Anti-Christ, doctrine of :—
   Origin, 30, 402
   in the Jewish apocalypses, 78
   in the Johannine Epistles, 259, f.
   in 2 Thessalonians, 266 f.
   in the writings of the early Church, 311, 313, 320, 321 f., 325 ff., 353 f., 360 f.
Apocalypse of St. John, 292-304
   date, 292-295
   plan, 293
   permanent value, 302 f.
Apocalyptic Books, the non-canonical Christian :—
   eschatology, 318-333, 348
   permanent influence, 333
Apocalyptic Books, Jewish :—
   characteristics of, 51-56, 108 f.

Apocalyptic Books, Jewish :—
   comparison with New Testament, 95, 98, 216 f., 225-228
   eschatology of, 68-79, 83-94, 96-99, 103-109
   list of, 50 *n.*
Apologists, the Christian, 350-363
   Aristides, 350
   Athenagoras, 357
   Irenaeus, 358
   Justin Martyr, 351
   the writer to Diognetus, 351
Apostolic eschatology, 232-305
   characteristics of the earliest type of, 242 f.
   summary of, 304 f.
Appeal to Scripture :—
   by the scribes, 41 f.
   by the Jewish apocalyptists, 52
   by our Lord, 114
   by Irenaeus, 359, 362
   by the Alexandrian School, 364 f.
Aristides, Apology of, 350 f.
Arnold, Dr., on the characteristics of apocalyptic, 55 *n.*
Ascension of Christ :—
   its bearing on the nature of the Resurrection, 198
   regarded by the apostles as part of the Last Things, 236
Ascension of Isaiah, 321-324
Assumption of Moses :—
   date, 83
   eschatology, 91 f.
Athenagoras, Apology of, 357 f.
Babylonian eschatology, 401 f. ; 12-15
Baptism, necessity of, for salvation, 358, 368
Baptism of Christ, 126 f.
Baptism for the Dead, 274
Barnabas, Epistle of, 319 ff.
Baruch, Apocalypse of, 95-99
Beliar, 78, 267 f., 321
Buddhism, influence of, on Christianity, 228, 368

INDEX

Catastrophic end to this world :—
  a characteristic of Hebrew thought, 48, 337
  in the teaching of our Lord, 216 ff.
  a difficulty to modern thought, 2, 380 ff.
Centrality of Christ's Person in His eschatology, 218 f., 228, 382 f.
Character, individual, after death :—
  development of, 185 f.
  permanence of, 184
  (*See also* 'Repentance in the future life')
Charles, R. H., his editions of the Jewish apocalypses, 50 *n*., Part III. *passim*.
Chasidim, 58 ff.
Chiliasm. *See* 'Millennium'
Christology :—
  in the Fourth Gospel, 204-208
  in St. James, 246
  in Hebrews, 246
  in St. John's Apocalypse, 293
Christ's eschatology, 110-231
  compared with other systems, 225 ff., 387 f.
  summary of, 215-231, 377 f.
Church, the :—
  as the Kingdom of God on earth, 140
  doctrine of, in 2 Clement, 345 f.
  ideal of, 286
City of God, 33, 302
Clement of Alexandria, 365-369
Clement of Rome, 338 ff.
Clement, 'Second Epistle of,' 345 ff.
Colossians, St. Paul's Epistle to the, 283 f.
Compensation in the future life, 183 f., 248 f.
Conditional element in eschatological prediction, due to human free-will, 141 f., 172, 218, 386 f.
Conscience, the appeal to, 364 f., 380-389
Conversion, reality of, in the early Church, and its bearing upon eschatology, 238, 274
Corinthians, St. Paul's Epistles to the, 269-283
Corn-seed, Parable of the, 217
Corruption of doctrine in the early Church, 394 f.
Cosmic eschatology :—
  absence in primitive times, 7-8, 15
  in the doctrine of the prophets, 26-38
  in Christ's teaching, 215-219, 379-382
  (*See also* 'Catastrophic end to this world,' 'Evolution in History')
Covenant, fulfilment of the, 18-19, 26, 31

Crucifixion of Christ :—
  eschatological significance of, 168-171, 197, 225, 249 f.
  regarded as forming part of the Last Things, 236 f.
Cycles of events in history, 337

Dalman, on the Messiahship of our Lord, 148, 153 f., 156
Daniel, Book of :—
  date, 62 ff.
  eschatology, 71-74, 86, 293
'Day of Jahveh,' 27-31
Decline of primitive Judaeo-Christian eschatology, 308-317, 360 f., 367 ff., 374 f.
Delay of Christ's Return :—
  indicated in the Gospels, 186, 219
  in 2 Peter, 258
  in St. Paul's Epistles, 264-269, 280
  in the early Church writings, 311, 315, 328 f., 333, 342 f., 352 f.
Descent into Hell, 256, 323
Details of eschatology :—
  in the Jewish apocalypses, 52 f.
  omitted by Christ, 114, 226, 388
  in St. John's Apocalypse, 303
  revival of interest in, by the early Church, 258, 333, 349, 370 f.
Deuteronomy, 11
Development of Doctrine, 374, 393 f.
Didache, 309-312
Diognetus, Epistle to, 351
Dispersion, eschatology of the Jews of the, 100-108
Dives and Lazarus, Parable of, 183 f., 359
Docetism, 324

Eastern cults, popularity of, in the West, 307, 368, 371 f.
Ebionites, 316
Ecclesiastes, 47 f.
Egyptian eschatology, 403 ff. ; 13
  influence of, on the Jews, 12 ff. ; 43 f., 93, 404 f.
  influence of, on the Christian Church, 325, 329 f., 405
Elephantiné, discoveries at, 44
Elijah, the forerunner of the Messiah, 43, 190 f.
Enoch, Ethiopic Book of :—
  composition, 61 *n*.
  date, 64 ff., 82
  eschatology, 69, 79, 83-93
  quoted by Jude, 76
Enoch, Slavonic Book of, 104 f.
Ephesians, St. Paul's Epistle to the, 283-286
Episcopal authority, growth of, and influence on eschatology, 344

INDEX 411

Epistles of the New Testament, eschatology of, 244-291
(*See also* under the titles of the several Epistles)
'Eschatological Discourse,' 173-183
 simplicity of its plan, 173-177
 apparently predicts an immediate return of Christ, 175, 181 f.
 suggestions towards solution of the difficulty, 177-181
 its positive teaching, 182 f.
Eschatological School of criticism :—
 leading idea of their Theory, 2, 111 f.
 history of their Theory, 111 *n*.
 and the Kingdom of God, 130-138
 and the Messianic consciousness of our Lord, 147 ff., 163
 and the Triumphal Entry, 190
 and the Feeding of the Five Thousand, and the Last Supper, 194 f.
 and the post-Resurrection sayings of our Lord, 201 f.
 truth and falsehood of the Theory, 229 ff., 233
 its bearing on Christian faith and morals, 390 f.
Esdras II. *See* 'Ezra, Apocalypse of'
Essenes, 123
Eternal punishment:—
 . in the Old Testament, 22
 in the Jewish Apocalypses, 78
 in the teaching of Christ, 184, 187 ff., 224
 in the early Church writings, 356, 360
 difficulties and significance of the doctrine, 385 ff. ; 187 ff., 224
Ethnic religions, relation of Christ's teaching to, 288 f., 393
Eucharist, 'the medicine of immortality,' 343
Evidential value of Primitive Christian Eschatology, 376-396
Evolutionary process in History :—
 in modern thought, 2, 381 f.
 in the Jewish apocalypses, 75
 in our Lord's teaching, 216 ff., 381 f.
 in St. Paul's teaching, 276
 in the Alexandrian Fathers, 367
Ezekiel, 20-23, 30, 33, 154
Ezra, Apocalypse of (*or* Fourth Book of), 95-99 ; 35

Faith in the victory of God's purpose, a fundamental of eschatology :—
 in the teaching of the prophets, 26, 34, 48
 in the Jewish apocalypses, 51 f., 99
 in Christ's teaching, 215 f., 379 f.
Fall of Jerusalem, apocalypses contemporary with, 95-99

Fatalism, opposed to Christ's teaching, 388 f.
Final destinies :—
 in the Jewish apocalypses, 78 f., 91 f.
 (*See also* 'Eternal punishment,' 'Repentance,' etc.)
Finality of Christ's teaching, 378-391
Forgiveness of sins, a function of the Messiah, 148, 240
Fourth Gospel :—
 character of, 117 f., 203, 208, 213 f.
 Christology of, 204-210
 eschatology of, 210-213
 relation to the Synoptists, 204-210, 213
Free-will, Christ recognises reality of, 386-389 ; 136, 218

Galatians, St. Paul's Epistle to the, 269-273
Genesis, absence of eschatology in, 12
Gentile phraseology, growth of, in the early Church, 338
Gentiles, future destiny of :—
 in Jewish eschatology, 29, 33, 36 ff., 78
 in Christ's eschatology, 139, 168, 227
 in St. Paul's eschatology, 264, 270, 272 f.
Gentiles, unfamiliar with Jewish eschatology, 245, 265, 270
Gnostic eschatology, 333 f.
'Great Confession' of St. Peter, the, 151 f., 160
'Great Refusal,' the, 164-172, 182, 196 f.
Greek eschatology, 101 ff., 336 f.
Greek influence :—
 on the Jews, 71, 101, 103-107
 on St. Paul, 270, 277
 on the early Church, 335-375, 395 f.
 on the Gnostics, 334

Harnack, A. :—
 on the eschatological hope, 30, 379
 on the Messiahship of our Lord, 150
 on the significance of primitive Christianity, 232, 375
Heaven, ideas of time and space with regard to, 188 f.
Heaven and Hell, popular ideas of, 251 f., 338
Hebrews, Epistle to the, 245-252
Hell, the Descent into, 256, 323
Hermas, Shepherd of, 348 f.
Herodians, the, 122 f.
Hippolytus, 355 *n*.
Hosea, 17, 23, 30
Humanity of Christ, 116, 286
Huxley, on Evolution, 381
Hymn of the Soul (Gnostic), 334

Ignatius, Epistles of, 340-345
Immediate return of Christ :—
  apparently foretold in the Gospels, 142, 175 f.
  not necessarily intended by Christ, 181 f., 186, 201
  dependent on fulfilment of certain conditions, 142, 180, 218
  the hope of :—
    a mainspring of apostolic eschatology in Acts, 234, 237, 240
    in the non-Pauline Epistles, 246, 257, 259
    in St. Paul's Epistles, 262 ff., 271, 278, 280 f., 289
    in the *Didache*, 310
    in Epistle of Barnabas, 320
    in Aristides, 350
    its practical effects, 392, f.
  decline of the hope :—
    in St. Paul's Epistles, 271, 280, 290
    in the Judaeo-Christian writings, 315
    in the Christian apocalypses, 328 f.
    in the Ignatian epistles, 342
    in Justin Martyr, 352 ff.
    in the Alexandrian Fathers, 366
    summary, 370
Immediateness of the Last Things, the instinctive hope of those in trouble, 30, 370
Immortality of the soul :—
  origin of belief in, 7 ff.
  absence of the belief among the early Hebrews, 15
  influence of the prophets, 19-25
  influence of the Psalms, 46 f.
  in the Jewish apocalypses, 71, 106
  in Christ's teaching, 193 f., 220, 383
  in the early Church writings, 312, 337
  (*See also* 'Resurrection')
Immortality, conditional, 323, 346 f., 359
  (*See also* 'Resurrection as a privilege')
Individual eschatology :—
  absent in early Hebrew religion, 15
  in the teaching of the prophets, 19-25
  in Christ's teaching, 219-225
  (*See also* 'Resurrection,' 'Intermediate state,' 'Eternal punishment,' 'Heaven')
Individualism, 20 f.
Intermediate state :—
  in the Jewish apocalypses, 69 f., 83
  in Christ's teaching, 185, 226
  in apostolic teaching, 278, 288
  in early Church writings, 324, 328, 353, 371, 374
  in Zoroastrian eschatology, 407
Invocation of the saints, 226
  (*See also* 'Ancestor-worship,' and 'Prayers for the Dead')
Irenaeus, 358-363

Isaiah, 17, 22, 29, 31 f., 34 f., 37
Isaiah, Ascension of, 321-324
Isaiah, Vision of, 321

James, Epistle of St., 245-252
James, M. R., on the Christian apocalypses, 328-333
Jeremiah, 20 f., 30, 34 f.
Jerusalem, to be the site of the Messianic Kingdom, 33, 237
Jewish people in the time of our Lord, 119-124
Job, 20, 44 ff.
Joel, 28 ff., 33 ff., 234
John the Baptist :—
  message of, 125 f.
  Christ's answer to, 157
John the Evangelist, St. :—
  Apocalypse of. *See* 'Apocalypse of St. John'
  Epistles of, 258 ff.
  Gospel of. *See* 'Fourth Gospel'
Jubilees, Book of :—
  date, 66 f.
  eschatology, 69, 79
Judaeo-Christian eschatology :—
  in Acts, 235-243
  in the New Testament Epistles, 245-252, 260-263, 271, 290
  decline of, in the early Church, 308-317, 360 f., 367 ff., 374 f.
Jude, Epistle of St., 257 f.
Judge, Christ as the Messianic, 147 f., 187, 210, 218 f., 237
Judgment, the Last :—
  in the teaching of the prophets, 26-31
  in the Jewish apocalypses, 72-77
  in Christ's teaching, 148, 187, 221-224
  in the Fourth Gospel, 210 f.
  in the earliest apostolic preaching, 237
  in St. Paul's Epistles, 282, 288
  in the early Church writings, 342, 351
  subjective or objective? 223 f.
  permanent value of the idea, 384 f.
Judgments, succession of, in the Last Days, 84 f., 330
Justification, eschatological significance of, 281 ff.
Justin Martyr, 351-357

Kenosis, Problem of the, 112 f., 175 f.
Kingdom of God :—
  in the Old Testament, 32
  political element in the Jewish idea of, 131 f., 233 f.
  in Christ's teaching, 128-146, 215
  its advent dependent on moral conditions, 133-138, 141 f.
  the Christian ideal of, 133, 138 ff. 145 f.

INDEX   413

Kingdom of God :—
  partially realised in this world, 138 ff., 250 f.
  the antithesis of the World, 166 f., 171 f.
  subjective or objective ? 143 ff., 212, 368
  permanent value of the idea, 379 f.
Kirkpatrick, on the eschatology of the Psalter, 46

Lagrange, M. J., on the 'Eschatological Discourse,' 176 f.
Last Judgment. *See* 'Judgment'
Last Supper, eschatological significance of, 194 ff.
Leaven, Parable of the, 217
Life of Christ :—
  its influence on Christian eschatology, 225
  regarded by the apostles as part of the 'Last Things,' 236 f.
'Little Apocalypse' in the Gospels, theory of the, 176
Logos, as a title of Christ, 205
Luke, Gospel of St., 116 f., 233, and Part III. *passim*

Maccabean Revolt, 58 ff., 60 *n.*
Maccabees :—
  Apocalypses of the, 58-79
  First Book of the, 58 f.
  Second Book of the, 58 f., 70, 72
Malachi, 43
'Man of Sin' in 2 Thessalonians, 266 ff.
Mark, Gospel of St., 116 f., and Part III. *passim*
Marriage of the King's Son, Parable of, 185
Matter, regarded as essentially evil :—
  in Greek thought, 102, 337
  by Philo, 107
  in St. Paul's Epistles, 277
  in the early Church writings, 323, 344
  by the Gnostics, 334
  influence on doctrine of the resurrection, 277, 383
Matthew, Gospel of St., 116 f., and Part III. *passim*
Memory, retention of, in the future life, 184, 356, 359
Messiah, the :—
  in the Old Testament, 31 ff.
  in the Jewish apocalypses, 77 f., 85-91, 96 f.
  political and eschatological conceptions of, 90 f., 154, 162 f., 205
  sufferings of, 168 ff.
  in Zoroastrian religion, 407

Messiahship of our Lord :—
  its reference not only to the future, but to the present, 147 ff., 236
  His earliest consciousness of, 127, 149 f.
  gradually revealed to the disciples, 151-163
  indicated by the phrase 'Son of Man,' 153-163
  indicated by the Triumphal Entry, 190 ff.
  in the Fourth Gospel, 203-210
  the centre of the most primitive Christian eschatology, 235 f., 240 ff., 263
Micah, 18, 30, 37
Millennium, the :—
  in the Jewish apocalypses, 97, 105
  in St. John's Apocalypse, 301 f.
  in the early Church writings, 312-315, 320, 332, 354, 361 f., 372 f.
  decline of, 373
Miraculous element, of the essence of primitive Christianity, 238
  (*See also* 'Catastrophic consummation')
Moral element in eschatology :—
  in the teaching of the prophets, 17
  in the Jewish apocalypses, 94
  in Zoroastrian religion, 408
  in Christ's teaching, 135-138, 141, 187, 222 ff., 397 f.
  in the earliest Christian preaching, 239, 241 ff.
  decline of, 257, 343 f.
  evidential value of, 384 f., 391, 397 f.
Mosaic Code, absence of eschatology in, 14
Moses, Assumption of. *See* '*Assumption of Moses*'
Mustard Seed, Parable of the, 217
Mysteries, the, influence of, on eschatology, 368
'Mystery of the Kingdom,' 132 f.
Mysticism, and communion with God :—
  in Job, 45
  in the Psalms, 46 f.
  in Christ's teaching, 193
  in the Johannine writings, 212, 259
  in the *Odes of Solomon*, 317 *n.*

Nationalism, Jewish, 14 f., 35, 227
Nature-worship, 10, 12
Nero Redivivus, legend of, 298, 321 f., 325 ff.
New Covenant, the, 34 f.
New Jerusalem, the, 33, 237, 302
Northern Ministry of Christ, 166
Number of the Beast (666), 299 *n.*
Nunc Dimittis, 124

Objections to Christ's teaching, modern, 379

INDEX

Odes of Solomon, 317 n.
Old Testament eschatology, 11-49
   summary of, 48 f.
Onesiphorus, the prayer for, 286 f.
Optimism, of the essence of Christian eschatology, 215 f., 379 f.
Oriental thought, influence of, in Europe, 307, 368, 371 f., 397
Origen, 369
Origin of eschatology, 7-10
'Otherworldliness' of Christ, 171 f.
Oxyrhynchus Logia, 143 n., 228

Palm Sunday, events of, 190 ff.
Pantheism, absence of, in Christ's teaching, 228
Papias, 314 f.
Parables, value of teaching by, 396 f.
Paradise, 196 f.
Parousia, 263, 338, 341
Passion, the, foreseen by Christ, 164 f., 168 f.
Passionless life, ideal of, 368
Passion-week, events of, 190-197
Pastoral Epistles of St. Paul, 286-289
Paul, St. :—
   Epistles of. *See* titles of the several Epistles
   eschatology of, 261-291
   summary, 289 ff.
Paul, Vision of, 332
Penance, 348
Permanence of the main principles of eschatology, 333, 374 f.
Permanent value of Christ's eschatology, 377-391
Permanent value of primitive Christian eschatology, 392-396
Persian Religion. *See* 'Zoroastrianism'
Person of Christ :—
   Jewish element in, 113, 390 f.
   standpoint of the essay with regard to, 115 f.
   supreme significance of, 112 f., 376 f., 382
Peter, St. :—
   Apocalypse of, 328 ff.
   First Epistle of, 252-257
   Second Epistle of, 257 f.
Pharisees :—
   origin of, 60
   apocalypses of the, 80-94
   twofold division of, 81, 119 ff.
   in the time of our Lord, 119 ff., 165 f.
   denunciation of, by our Lord, 167 f., 183
Philippians, St. Paul's Epistle to the, 283 ff.
Philo, 106 f.
Phoenix-legend, 339 f.

Politics :—
   absence of, in Christ's teaching, 163, 227
   element of, in the eschatology of the apostles, 132, 233 f.
Polycarp, Epistle of, to the Philippians, 312 f.
Popular legends, adopted by the Church, 327
Post-exilic Jews, eschatology of, 40-48
Post-resurrection teaching of Christ, absence of eschatology in, 200 ff.
Pounds, Parable of the, 186
Practical bearing of Christ's eschatology, 384 f., 398
Prayers for the Dead, 70, 226, 287 f., 330 f., 373 f.
'Preaching to the Dead,' Christ's, 254 ff.
Predestination, 41 f., 253 f.
Pre-existence :—
   of all things, in the heavens, 253 f., 324, 345 f.
   of the soul, 101 f., 105 f., 229, 369
Priesthood of the Messiah, 77, 247
Primitive Church, the appeal to the, 232 f.
Primitive Man, beliefs of, 7-10
Prophetic character of Christ's teaching, 114 f.
Prophets, eschatology of the Hebrew, 16-39
Prophecy :—
   indirect influence of, on eschatology, 16 ff.
   cessation of, 41
Psalms, the, 46 f. ; 33, 42, 154
Psalms of Solomon :—
   date of, 82
   Messianic Hope in, 89 ff., 131
Purgatory, doctrine of :—
   absent in New Testament, 226, 288
   beginnings of, seen in early Church writings, 332, 349, 367, 373
Purification after death, 334

'Q' document, 116 n.
Quest of the Historical Jesus (Schweitzer), 111 n.
   (*See also* 'Eschatological School')

Recognition in the future life, 97
Remnant, doctrine of the, 34
Repentance in the future life, possibility of :—
   in Christ's teaching, 184 f., 224
   in 1 Peter, 256
   in the early Church writings, 348, 356, 366 f., 374
Repentance, the call to, intimately associated with eschatology, 28, 126, 128, 141, 237 f., 397 f.
Restoration of Israel, 31 ff.

INDEX

'Restrainer,' the, in 2 Thessalonians, 268 f.
Resurrection of Christ :—
   influence on Christian eschatology, 197 ff., 225, 239, 273 f., 339, 356
   nature of, 198 ff., 356
   teaching of Christ subsequent to, 200 ff.
Resurrection of the Body :—
   in Christ's teaching, 193, 220 f., 383
   materialistic idea of, 339 f., 356, 357, 360
   the Pauline conception of 'a spiritual body,' 273-279, 326, 347, 383
Resurrection of the Dead :—
   in the Old Testament, 21-25, 45
   in the Jewish apocalypses, 70 ff., 84, 97 f.
   in Christ's teaching, 192 ff., 220 f.
   in the Fourth Gospel, 210, 212
   in St. Paul's Epistles, 262, 273-279, 284, 288, 290
   in the non-Pauline writings of the New Testament, 239, 247, 301
   in the sub-apostolic writers and Apologists, 310, 313, 339 f., 341 f., 347, 355 f., 357, 360
   in the Christian apocalypses, 322 f., 326
   in Egyptian eschatology, 404
   in Gnostic eschatology, 334
   in Zoroastrian eschatology, 407
   regarded as a privilege for the righteous, 193 f., 221, 342
   guaranteed by spiritual union with God, 193 f., 221, 276, 404
   permanent value of the doctrine, 383 f.
   (*See also* 'Transformation, spiritual')
Retribution, Doctrine of :—
   in the prophets, 16 ff.
   in Greek religion, 102 f.
   in Christ's teaching, 183 f., 187 f., 221-224
   in the Alexandrian School, 367
   permanent value of, 384 f.
'Righteousness' :—
   in the teaching of the prophets, 17 -
   in the Jewish apocalypses, 94
   in the teaching of our Lord, 141, 187, 222
Ritual, observance of, as a condition of admission to the Kingdom of God, 17, 187, 332, 343
Roman Empire, its influence on eschatology, 268 f., 298 ff., 306
Roman government in Palestine, 80 f., 123
Romans, St. Paul's Epistle to the, 269-273, 281 ff.

Sacraments, necessity of, for salvation, 358, 368 f.

Sadducees :—
   origin of, 60, 80
   in the time of our Lord, 121 f.
   Christ's answer to, concerning the Resurrection, 192 ff.
   their opposition to the early Church, 238 f.
Salvation, eschatological significance of, 239 f., 283 ff., 338 f.
Salvation by works, 98, 342
Schweitzer, A. *See* 'Eschatological School'
Scribes, teaching of the, 40 ff.
Scripture, authority of. *See* 'Appeal to Scripture'
Secret, Christ's Messianic, 132 f.
'Secrets of Enoch.' *See* 'Enoch, Slavonic Book of'
Selfishness, Christian eschatology charged with, 384 f.
Seven Churches of Asia, Letters to, 293 f.
Seven Heavens, the, 104, 321 f.
Sheol, 15, 22, 45, 83
Shepherd of Hermas, 348 f.
Sibylline Oracles, 103 f., 324-328
Sinfulness, the problem of Christian, 250 ff., 347 f.
Slavonic Enoch. *See* 'Enoch'
'Son of God' as a Messianic title :—
   in the Old Testament, 33
   in the Jewish apocalypses, 88 f., 97
   in the Gospels, 126 f., 149 f., 161, 205
'Son of Man' as a Messianic title :—
   in the Old Testament, 154
   in the Jewish apocalypses, 72 ff., 86-91, 154
   in the Synoptic Gospels, 153-162
   in the Fourth Gospel, 204 f.
   Aramaic original of the phrase, 153 f.
Spirit, gift of the, one of the 'Last Things,' 200 f., 234, 237, 240
Standpoint of the essay with regard to—
   the Person of Christ, 115 f.
   the Synoptic Problem, 116 f.
   the Fourth Gospel, 117 f.
   the Resurrection of Christ, 199 f.
Stoics, eschatology of, 337
Suffering Servant of Jahveh, 32 f., 170
Suffering, the problem of, 168-171, 248 ff., 383
   (*See also* 'Crucifixion of Christ')
Summaries :—
   the eschatology of the prophets, 38 f.
   the eschatology of the Old Testament, 48 f.
   the eschatology of the Jewish apocalypses, 108 f.
   'the Kingdom of God,' 145 f.
   'the Son of Man,' 161 f.
   Christ's eschatology, 215-231, 377 f.
   apostolic eschatology, 242 f., 304 f.
   sub-apostolic eschatology, 370-375

Synoptic Problem, 116 f.

Talents, Parable of the, 185 f.
Tares, Parable of the, 135, 140, 159, 217
Tartarus, Greek idea of, influence on Christian eschatology, 328
Temptation of Christ, 127
Ten Virgins, Parable of the, 184 f.
'Tendencies' in the Gospels, 142 f., 155 *n.*, 178 f., 219
Testament of Abraham, 329 f.
Testament of Hezekiah, 321 ff.
Testament of Isaac, 331 f.
Testaments of the Twelve Patriarchs :—
    date and composition, 67, 82
    eschatology, 71-79, 84 f., 407
Thessalonians, St. Paul's First Epistle to the, 261-264 ; 134
Thessalonians, St. Paul's Second Epistle to the, 264-269
Thief on the Cross, our Lord's promise to, 196 f.
Time, idea of, in the future life, 188 f., 223 *n.*, 224
Timothy, St. Paul's Epistles to, 286-289
Titus, St. Paul's Epistle to, 286
Torments of the wicked in hell, 92, 249, 328, 331 f.
Traditional orthodoxy, reverence for :—
    in the teaching of the scribes, 41
    in the Jewish apocalypses, 52
    in the early Church, 313, 358 f.
Transcendence of God, effect on eschatology, 42 f.
Transformation, spiritual, in this life, 212, 278, 284 f., 347
Transmigration of souls, 229, 404
'Transvaluation of values' in the Kingdom of God, 167-172
Triumphal Entry into Jerusalem, Christ's, 190 ff.
Troubles a sign of the Last Things, 30 f., 53, 173 ff., 289, 310
Twelve Patriarchs, Testaments of the. See 'Testaments'

Twofold division of the future world in popular thought, 251 f.
Two Witnesses, the, in St. John's Apocalypse, 290 f.
Two Worlds, doctrine of the, 35 f.
Tyrell, on the Eschatological Theory, 111 *n.*, 391 *n.*

Unchangeableness of the future state. *See* 'Repentance, possibility of'
Universalism :—
    the religious equality of all nations (in Amos), 36 ff.
    the ultimate salvation of all souls :—
        in the Gospels, 184, 189
        in St. Paul, 273, 281
        in Origen, 369

Victory of the Good, final, 26, 34, 215 f., 379 f.
Vision of Isaiah, 321
Vision of Paul, 332
Von Dobschütz, *The Eschatology of the Gospels*, 111 *n.*, 129 *n.*, 145 *n.*

Watchfulness, Christ's call to, 177, 185
Weighing of souls, 329 ff.
Weiss, Johannes, 111 *n.*, 130 f.
    (*See also* 'Eschatological School')
Westcott, B. F., on Final Destinies, 281
'Wisdom of Solomon,' 105 f. ; 11
Woes, the Messianic, 30, 96, 173 f., 217, 265 f., 295 f.
    (*See also* 'Catastrophic end to this world')

Zahn, on dates of St. Paul's Epistles, 305 *n.*
Zechariah, 30, 192
Zephaniah, 27, 30, 34
Zoroastrianism :—
    eschatology, 406 ff.
    influence on the Jews, 43, 76, 79, 93, 407 f.
    influence on the Christian Church, 332, 349, 407 f.

THE END

www.ingramcontent.com/pod-product-compliance
Lightning Source LLC
Chambersburg PA
CBHW071435300426
44114CB00013B/1441